Shared Devotion, Shared Food

Equality and the Bhakti-Caste Question in Western India

JON KEUNE

OXFORD
UNIVERSITY PRESS

OXFORD
UNIVERSITY PRESS

Oxford University Press is a department of the University of Oxford. It furthers the University's objective of excellence in research, scholarship, and education by publishing worldwide. Oxford is a registered trade mark of Oxford University Press in the UK and certain other countries.

Published in the United States of America by Oxford University Press
198 Madison Avenue, New York, NY 10016, United States of America.

Library of Congress Control Number: 2021933132
ISBN 978–0–19–757483–6

DOI: 10.1093/oso/9780197574836.001.0001

1 3 5 7 9 8 6 4 2

Printed by Integrated Books International, United States of America

Contents

PART II

Acknowledgments

Although this book originated in my dissertation research, its present shape is the result of much gestation and growth after the dissertation was finished. During the initial research and in the years since then, I have benefited from the help, guidance, and inspiration of more people than I can count. This is a good argument for writing a book more quickly—to finish it before the author can forget any of his debts.

I cannot overstate my gratitude to Jack Hawley, who guided me through my doctoral studies and has been a supportive and provocative conversation partner ever since. His steady encouragement and feedback on ideas created a stable ground on which I found my scholarly footing. The trouble with drawing inspiration from such a prolific scholar as Jack, however, is that it becomes difficult to recognize when I may be repeating something that he already wrote or said somewhere. I am sure that a systematic reading of all Jack's publications would reveal similarities to my own arguments beyond the ones that I have explicitly recognized. I hope this will be viewed sympathetically, as a sign of the deep intellectual impression that a teacher leaves on a student.

Many others have helped along the way, especially Rachel McDermott, Chun-fang Yü, Anupama Rao, Udi Halperin, Patton Burchett, Anand Venkatkrishnan, Joel Bordeaux, Katherine Kasdorf, Joel Lee, Christian Novetzke, and Anna Seastrand, all of whom I had the privilege of learning from, since we first met at Columbia University. Anne Feldhaus has provided inspiration and wise counsel, both in India and the United States. The Centre for Modern Indian Studies at the University of Göttingen was an inspiring place to spend two years, especially due to the friendship and intellectual vibrancy of Michaela Dimmers, Sebastian Schwecke, Stefan Tetzlaff, Rupa Viswanath, and Nathaniel Roberts, among others. At the University of Houston, Lois Zamora, Anjali Khanojia, and Keith McNeal were excellent conversation partners. I am grateful to Martin Fuchs for our conversations and for his very thought-provoking conferences in Erfurt over the years. In India, I have benefitted immensely from the expertise of more people than I can possibly thank here. These include especially V. L. Manjul, Sujata

Mahajan, Sucheta Paranjpe, Satish Badwe, Meera Kosambi, Shantanu Kher, Y. M. Pathan, Vidyut Bhagwat, and Narsimha Kadam. Yogiraj Maharaj Gosavi and his family in Paiṭhaṇ were very generous with their time and patience, allowing me to accompany them on pilgrimage and learn about their famous ancestor Eknāth and his legacy. R. S. Inamdar and B. S. Inamdar kindly introduced me to their family heritage and the background of a lesser-known text about Eknāth. Shashikala and Rajani Shirgopikar generously shared their fascinating experiences in the traveling theater troupe that is described in Chapter 6. The staffs at the Eknāth Saṃśodhan Mandir in Aurangabad and the Bhandarkar Oriental Research Institute in Pune provided much support in using their respective archives. Many others allowed me into their lives and made me feel at home in India, especially Wasim Maner and Tahir Maner and their respective families, as well as Maxine Berntsen, Michihiro Ogawa, Samrat Shirvalkar and Kalyani Jha, Smita Pendharkar, and Subhash and Sumitra Shah. Two of my guiding lights when I started learning about India in college, Eleanor Zelliot and Anantanand Rambachan, profoundly shaped my perspectives on and especially my relationships to Hinduism and India in ways that have endured and are even evident in this book.

My colleagues in the Religious Studies Department and the Asian Studies Center have made my time at Michigan State University (MSU) very collegial and fulfilling. Arthur Versluis and Siddharth Chandra have been especially supportive over these years, intellectually and administratively. I have treasured feedback from students, especially Anneli Schlacht, who spotted many ways to make the book more readable. Mahesh and Trupti Wasnik, members of the Ambedkar Association of North America, as well as Salil Sapre at MSU, have been very helpful and inspiring conversation partners. Enduring friendships and invigorating scholarly collaborations have been a source of endless inspiration, especially with Gil Ben-Herut and the Regional Bhakti Scholars Network, and with Max Rondolino and the Comparative Hagiology group.

My research and travel have been generously supported by grants from the American Institute of Indian Studies, the Dolores Zohrab Liebmann Fund, and the Fulbright-DDRA program, as well as from Columbia University, the University of Göttingen, the University of Houston, and MSU. This book would not have been possible without them and their sources of funding, including American and German taxpayers. I also appreciate the Schoff Publication Fund at the University Seminars at Columbia University for their help in publication. Material in this work was presented to the University Seminar: South Asia.

Oxford University Press has been very helpful in bringing this book to print, especially through the strange and difficult logistics brought about by the COVID-19 pandemic. Two anonymous reviewers gave tremendously valuable feedback on an earlier draft. Cynthia Read, Drew Anderla, and Zara Cannon-Mohammed have been a pleasure to work. Sarah C. Smith of Arbuckle Editorial and Do Mi Stauber provided crucial support in proofreading and indexing.

My families in Wisconsin and Taiwan have provided unwavering support and understanding through all the stages of this book. I am especially thankful to Tzulun for her patience and encouragement along the way. Although our intercontinental navigations added some challenges to the writing, these pale in comparison to all the joy, love, and wonder that have grown out of our journeying together.

From early on, my parents showed me the community-building power of a table that was always open and welcoming to anyone. It was not until writing this book that I realized how much of an impact that had on me and so many others who joined us for meals over the years. My mother has been a constant source of support and sagely advice about life (and cooking!). Words cannot express my gratitude. I especially want to remember my father, who passed away shortly before this book was finished. He offered crucial assistance in, among so many other things, building the treadmill writing desk at which I spent countless hours and miles. It stands—quite sturdily—as an example of how material objects move and sustain us, even in intellectual work. I dedicate this book to his memory and hope that it would have made him proud.

Abbreviations

Marathi

BhV	*Bhaktavijay*
EC	*Eknāthcaritra*
PC	*Pratiṣṭhāncaritra*
ŚKĀ	*Śrīkhaṇḍyākhyān*
SSG	*Sakalasantagāthā*

Sanskrit

BhG	*Bhagavad Gītā*
BhL	*Bhaktalīlāmṛt*
BhP	*Bhāgavata Purāṇa*
BU	*Bṛhadāraṇyaka Upaniṣad*
ChU	*Chāndogya Upaniṣad*
MBh	*Mahābhārata*
TU	*Taittirīya Upaniṣad*

Notes on Transliteration and References

My protocol for rendering Indic languages into English mostly follows the Library of Congress (LC) standard for transliterating scripts. I follow that scheme completely for Sanskrit. For Marathi, I vary from the LC standard by transliterating final anusvaras with *ṁ* rather than a tilde above the final vowel. I also render Marathi words more freely to reflect the spoken language, which drops some vowels between consonants and at the end of words. When discussing a Sanskrit text, I will write *prasāda*, but when referring to this term's appearance in a Marathi text, I write *prasād*. When there is variation in the spelling of a word in Marathi sources (such as *cāṇḍāla*, *caṇḍāla*, or *caṇḍāḷa*) or how a word is pronounced in a dialect, I reproduce what appears in the source.

Indic words and place names that are now common in English I render without diacritics, although I retain them in Marathi bibliographic references. For Indian people who frequently wrote their names in English (such as K. S. Thackeray instead of Ṭhākre), I follow their conventional spellings in the narrative of the book but follow transliteration standards for Marathi references. In cases of Indic figures who did not have widely known English spellings, I retain diacritics.

I capitalize "Dalit" and names of *jāti*s but not the four *varṇa*s: brahman, kṣatriya, vaiśya, and śūdra. My rationale is that *varṇa*s act as common nouns or general social categories, and thus need not be capitalized. Specific *jāti* names function on a more local level, like proper nouns. The term "Dalit" is similar to the term "Black" in the United States, referring to a diverse and diffuse community who are united in their experience of oppression and marginalization. Just as Americans debate the significance of capitalizing words that relate to race, there is no universal orthographic standard for doing so with "Dalit" and caste/*varṇa* names.

In most chapters, I cite references in the notes, as is common in the humanities. In cases where I cite the primary works extensively, such as in Chapters 3 through 5, I place chapter and verse numbers text in-line within parentheses. My goal is to be as precise as possible with information that some readers will find relevant without being too visually disruptive.

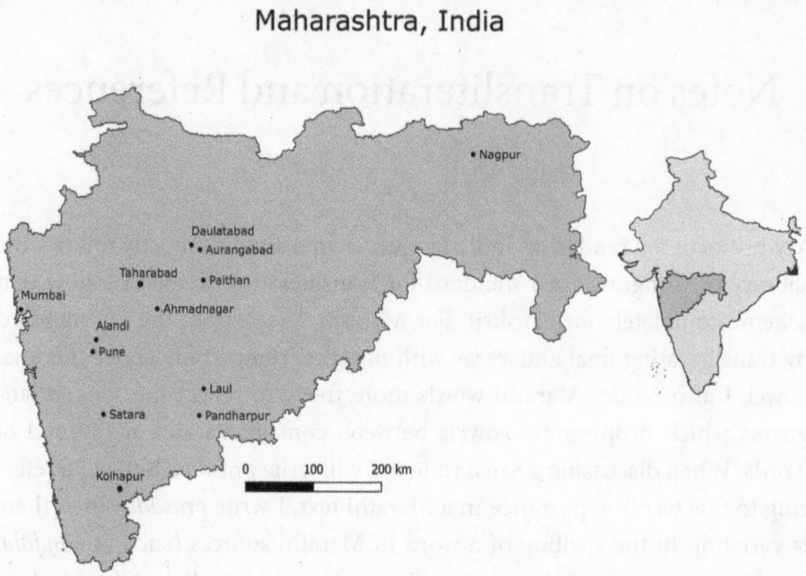

Western India (contemporary border of Maharashtra state), with places that are mentioned in the book.

Source: Created by the author, using public domain shapefiles from www.divagis.org.

Introduction

This book centers on a question: can the idea that people are equal before God inspire them to treat each other as equals? Can theological egalitarianism lead to social equality? Looking around the world today and in the past, there are many reasons to be skeptical or to say that what might be possible in theory has been realized rarely, if ever, in practice. Nonetheless, the appeal of equality does not go away. To the contrary, equality as an ideal has become almost a universal, objective standard by which cultures and religions should be measured, in many people's minds.[1] A religious leader who announces that their tradition teaches inequality among its adherents based on gender, race, ethnicity, or other factors would seem out of sync with the times. Such a tradition would be regarded as anti-modern, even threatening to the functioning of liberal democracies. Taking for granted this benchmark of modernity, as if it were the obvious developmental goal of societies, historians have sought to uncover how equality developed in the past. They have often identified religious doctrines and practices as being seeds of social equality.

On a recent trip to Japan, I joined some local colleagues for dinner at the Kofukuji Buddhist temple in Nagasaki's Chinatown. The chef for this meal was the temple's head priest, who said that he was following recipes that a Chinese monk in his lineage had carried to Japan several centuries ago.[2] The priest welcomed us into his home, seated us on *tatami* mats around a low table, and served us tea. Then, he placed in our hands a sheet of paper with information about the meal to come. Part of the description read, "The Fucha style of cuisine means to have tea and a meal together at a round table without recognizing social statuses of gathering guests so as to create a friendly atmosphere." Along with fond memories of the dinner and the camaraderie around the table, this sentence about ignoring social distinctions while eating stayed with me.

As someone who is used to studying South Asia, I hesitate to comment on what prompted this statement in a Japanese temple, whether five hundred years ago or when someone sat at their computer more recently, typing up that information sheet in English. But what is most interesting about this

Shared Devotion, Shared Food. Jon Keune, Oxford University Press. © Oxford University Press 2021.
DOI: 10.1093/oso/9780197574836.003.0001

claim is not its historicity but the sheer fact that it appeared at all, especially in a land whose society was notoriously rigid in medieval times. Experiencing this Buddhist meal in Nagasaki reinforced two hunches that had prompted me to write this book: modern people often try to identify seeds of social equality in premodern religious traditions, and food is often central in demonstrating that equality in practice.

In this book, I focus on a case of apparent egalitarianism, food sharing, and religion in India. At the core is a deceptively simple question about India's regional Hindu devotional or bhakti traditions, which have included in their ranks people who were routinely marginalized from most other Hindu traditions—women, low-caste people, and Dalits (so-called "Untouchables"). The question is this: did bhakti traditions promote social equality? Or more elaborately, when bhakti poets taught that God welcomes all people's devotion, did this inspire followers to combat social inequalities based on caste? This question hovers around many stories about bhakti saints, such as the following one.

> On the *śrāddha* day [a ritual to commemorate the ancestors] Eknāth behaved without distinction to everyone. Whoever thinks this way likewise satisfies others. He announced a meal to the community of brahmans. The food preparations began. Before the brahmans arrived, Dalits (*cāṇḍālas*) brought and set down bundles of wood for the kitchen.... Excellent raw rice, uncooked rice, and cooked rice were strained in the kitchen. At that time, a strong fragrance spread. All the Dalits experienced it. . . . Eknāth saw them directly, and he prostrated himself before them. The Dalit men and women remained standing with hands joined respectfully. Doing prostration from afar, they said "Please give us food. We Dalits are low and miserable. What savory food that is! If spice is available, then there is no salt—such is our food [i.e., something is always lacking]. Only in our dreams could we even hear of such savory food. We do not know it first-hand, Eknāth. This desire has come to us; please fulfill it. . . . If you think to trick us, then remember your oath to your guru Janārdana." Eknāth said, "Janārdana is in all beings. The Enjoyer is one. To imagine division is foolish." Eknath then fed the Dalits in his house. After they had eaten, he made a request: "The brahmans should not hear of this." He begged all the people to hold the secret in their bellies. Family and good friends everywhere agreed and kept the news hidden. They did not let it be known. Meanwhile, at the river, the brahmans did their bath, *sandhyā*, ritual offerings, and god-worship. Then

> a Dalit woman (*mātangīṇī*) came to the Gangā [Godāvarī] riverbank, carrying food with her. The Dalit woman sat near the brahmans. She had received the food from Eknāth. The brahmans reviled her, calling out "Hey, *cāṇḍāḷiṇī*!" and demanding that she leave. She said to the brahmans, "Ekobā [Eknāth] served us. Becoming the ancestors, we went to his house. He made us all satisfied. You should go for food. The cooking is finished. I will eat my food peacefully, here on the bank of the Gangā. Today we are Eknāth's ancestors. Why are you intimidating me? I just thought to have food on the bank of the Gangā, so I came." Hearing her words, the brahmans were shocked. "Eknāth, such a sage, has acted completely against prescribed behavior. To hell with his knowledge. No rice-balls [essential to the ritual] should be offered by us. There was no feeding of brahmans. He fed Dalit people." . . . One said, "There should be punishment." Another said, "His head should be shaved. Cut and throw away his sacred thread." One said, "Catch and beat him. A complete punishment must be given." One said, "Beating isn't necessary. Pull out his topknot and put it in his hands." One said, "Make him do purification rituals. Otherwise, his preparations will be destroyed. Nothing should be done in vain." . . . [Eknāth dispatched his servant, himself a brahman, to invite the brahmans to the *śrāddha*. Incensed at Eknāth's effrontery, the brahmans gave Eknāth's servant a beating. Later, the brahmans approached Eknāth's house and found, to their amazement, that after they had refused to partake of Eknāth's meal, the deceased ancestors were seated inside, eating.] They stood for a moment and watched the marvel. Whoever came to the meal recognized their own ancestors. The brahmans were stunned. They tried to speak, but no words came to them. The ancestors' meal concluded. . . . Eknāth put out the plates of leftovers at the end of it all, saying, "Our ancestors came here and certainly ate joyfully." Eknāth himself rolled in the leftover plates. The arrogance of the brahmans was destroyed. They stood there silently. Coming outside, Eknāth prostrated himself before the brahmans. "Svāmīs, have mercy here, you should certainly come to eat." Looking them in the face, Eknāth embraced all the brahmans. They replied, "The ancestors were obviously fed. Your deeds are incomprehensible. Blessed are your deeds. Blessed, blessed is your sincerity. Blessed is your path of devotion. Blessed are you, the one guru-bhakta."[3]

Was Eknāth challenging the primacy of caste when he defied ritual precedent and served food to the Dalits instead of brahmans? Why did Eknāth feed the Dalits without hesitation if he was so worried about how the brahmans would respond? Did the experience inspire the Dalit woman to perceive herself differently and become more assertive with the brahmans at the river? Setting aside questions about the story's historicity, why did hagiographers in later centuries find it valuable to repeat versions of this story? What exactly does it say about bhakti and caste?

Ambiguous stories about bhakti and caste are hardly limited to brahmans. One vivid example is about the 14th-century Dalit saint Cokhāmeḷā. Cokhāmeḷā, an unwavering devotee of the god Viṭṭhal, regularly worshiped him from outside his temple since Dalits were not allowed to enter it. One night, Viṭṭhal honors Cokhāmeḷā by inviting him inside for a conversation. A group of brahmans angrily assemble and ban Cokhāmeḷā from the town. While in exile, Cokhāmeḷā is visited by Viṭṭhal again, who sits down and joins the Dalit saint for a meal. A passing brahman hears Cokhāmeḷā talking to the god, but the brahman cannot see Viṭṭhal. The brahman thinks that Cokhāmeḷā is putting on an insolent theatrical display, so he slaps him across the face. That evening, when the brahman enters Viṭṭhal's temple, he sees that the god's stone image has a swollen cheek, exactly where he had slapped Cokhāmeḷā. Realizing his mistake, the brahman apologizes to Cokhāmeḷā and, taking his hand, brings him into the temple to be near Viṭṭhal again. What does this story, with the chastised brahman and vindicated Dalit saint, signify about caste? Did wholehearted devotion to God reshape the way followers treated people, or did such tales remain just entertaining tales, without inspiring listeners to change? Could bhakti have helped people to conceive of something like social equality, in a context when people assumed that caste differences were simply part of the natural order?

Since the late 19th century, some liberal Hindu reformers have asserted that bhakti did indeed have socially transformative power. On a popular level still today, many people are inclined to agree, considering the vast corpus of bhakti literatures across languages and regions that depict saints crossing caste boundaries and condemning arrogant brahmans. As many saintly figures around the world do, bhakti saints often exemplify virtues like courage, selflessness, and patience.[4] That Indian school textbooks and children's literature regularly highlight saints' ethical behavior to young learners should come as no surprise. It is easy to see why the image of bhakti saints promoting equality continues to resonate.

But dissenters abound as well. One of the most pointed and influential examples was the learned Dalit leader, Bhimrao B. R. Ambedkar, who offered a very clear assessment of the matter:

> The saints have never, according to my study, carried on a campaign against Caste and Untouchability. They were not concerned with the struggle between men. They were concerned with the relation between man and God. They did not preach that all men were equal. They preached that all men were equal in the eyes of God—a very different and a very innocuous proposition, which nobody can find difficult to preach or dangerous to believe in.[5]

Ambedkar wrote this in 1936, in the aftermath of a speech that was deemed too radical to be delivered in person. Organizers of the Jāt-Pat-Toḍak Maṇḍal (Society for Breaking Caste) had invited Ambedkar to deliver a lecture. But when they read an advance copy and realized just how forcefully Ambedkar planned to argue his case, they withdrew the invitation out of fear of violent reprisals. Undeterred, Ambedkar went ahead and published it himself—*Annihilation of Caste*. The publication quickly caught the attention of M. K. (Mahatma) Gandhi, who mostly agreed with Ambedkar's critique of untouchability but thought to address the problem in a very different way. In response, Gandhi penned "The Vindication of Caste," in which he argued that the abusive caste system is a corruption of an earlier, reasonable division of labor. He chided Ambedkar for focusing on negative examples of injustice while ignoring the many bhakti saints and reformers who represented Hinduism in a much better light.[6] Ambedkar emphatically denied that he had overlooked this and wrote the passage just excerpted: the saints' endorsement of spiritual equality did not extend to changing society. In 1935, Ambedkar famously had announced that he would not die a Hindu. Two decades later, after countless more speeches and agitations and after literally writing equality into Articles 14 and 16 of the Indian Constitution, Ambedkar converted to Buddhism and led some 400,000 Dalits with him—a very public rejection of Hindu norms.

Ambedkar's frank assessment of the bhakti saints is important for this book in many ways. His reference to two separate realms—spiritual and social—is exceptionally clear and effective in laying out the modern configuration of the problem. It issues a major challenge for scholars and proponents of bhakti, to assess soberly how bhakti has changed or not changed people's social behavior in practice. On the other hand, for many people, taking Ambedkar's critique of caste and untouchability seriously has meant completely turning away from popular religious traditions like bhakti, to envision a strictly rational and in some sense secular future. Figures like Jñāndev,

Kabīr, and Gandhi also cast shadows on modern understandings, but they do not leave bhakti in the dark in quite the way that Ambedkar's does. Reckoning Ambedkar's thought and legacy with bhakti traditions as historical entities and living communities today is a massive undertaking that extends far beyond this book.

Ambedkar's assessment of bhakti was unambiguously negative, but it is important to keep his context in mind. Ambedkar formulated the bhakti-caste question around social equality and then answered the question as he deemed it necessary, based on his experiences of Indian society and his goals for changing it. However, the question's directness belies a deeper complexity. As he rebutted Gandhi's criticism, Ambedkar responded to a particular man in a specific context. Ambedkar had other goals than to address all the historiographical nuances of how bhakti related to caste, if he considered them at all. He was not impelled to account for the forces that converged to make the question seem natural to ask in the first place. In the chapters ahead, I unpack assumptions that lie behind modern formulations of the bhakti-caste question and recover premodern ways of construing it that are less apparent to us now. But how can we become acquainted with these other ways of thinking and their possible impact on people's social behavior? I think it is helpful to pay attention to a substance that vitally connects theory and practice.

Food, as Ambedkar recognized in his writings and experienced often painfully in his life, was a basic tool for regulating caste. Social scientists have long observed food's essential roles in building and ordering communities around the world. It makes good sense to approach the bhakti-caste question through food and commensality. For it is in matters involving food that we see most clearly and mundanely the clashing values of bhakti's inclusivity and caste's hierarchy. Investigating shared food or "critical commensality" is a crucial yet under-studied site where we can see the theory of bhakti meeting the challenge of practice, just as it can help understand other cultures and time periods.[7]

How should we approach the question, "Did bhakti promote social equality?" A logical start is to analyze the two key terms—*bhakti* and *equality*—and trace what they meant to people who invoked them in the past. I carry out this spadework in Part I. Ultimately, however, only part of my interest is in modern people's use of the bhakti-caste question to interpret, appropriate, glorify, or denounce the past. How did people understand the relationship of bhakti and caste *before* modernity?

As we will see, framing the bhakti-caste question as one of social equality entails using modern concepts to imagine the premodern world. Whenever admirers of bhakti have suggested that it endorsed equality, critical voices quickly pointed out counterexamples in which caste continued to play major roles in bhakti traditions. Indeed, there are many historical examples of authors and traditions preaching devotion to God yet maintaining the social status quo. Even today, some bhakti traditions are explicit about observing caste, especially among their leaders.

The bhakti-caste question has troubled scholars, devotees, and the Indian populace alike, not only because of what it reveals about the past but because of what one's answer to the question implies for the world today. If bhakti did or at least could overcome caste to realize social equality, then there is a prospect of constructively inheriting something from bhakti traditions to work for social change now. In this perspective, living bhakti traditions have the potential to be agents of social change. But if bhakti did not and cannot promote social equality, this would suggest that bhakti traditions should be abandoned or, at least, that their messages should be relegated to the realm of personal piety or historical curiosity. Viewed in this way, living bhakti traditions would appear weighed down by obsolete and inadequate ideas, making it impossible for even devotees who sincerely desire social change to overcome caste. How we answer the question bears not only on understanding the past but on human relations in the present. This is especially the case for Ambedkar's followers and lower-caste adherents to bhakti traditions, who often find themselves now competing for limited resources. It is not only an academic issue.

I argue that three factors complicate the question of whether bhakti promoted social equality in premodern times. First, most people who address the bhakti-caste question in modern times pay little heed to processes that formulated the question as it now seems familiar to us. This includes a reliance on modern terms to analyze past societies, unnuanced readings of hagiographic sources, and the casual slippage of equality language from one realm of meaning to another. The very nature of the bhakti-caste question requires a multi-disciplinary approach—involving the study of history, hagiography, anthropology, and media—to reckon with the tangle of issues that converged to make the question appear meaningful now. We will distinguish these disciplinary differences clearly, especially in Part I.

Second, we have the problem that the term "equality" in modern usage occludes what I believe was an important practical logic that guided premodern authors in their handling of bhakti and caste. Because bhakti traditions thrived more on a popular level than an elite one, that logic often was grounded less in the search of intellectual clarity than in pragmatic concerns.[8] The legacy of western liberal discourse about democracy and individual rights—a very strong legacy in modern India—obscures the significance of the premodern terms that we find bhakti authors used. This especially happens when translators now resort to the word "equality" to render those key Indic terms into English. I show that the social impact of these Indic terms and the narratives associated with them related more to inclusion than equality. This practical logic appears with special clarity when we observe how stories about food and commensality transformed as they were retold over centuries—the focus of Part II.

Third, the bhakti-caste question defies a simple answer because in precolonial times, the issue was conceived not so much as a question but as a riddle. Arriving at one unambiguous conclusion was less important than holding the tension in mind, working it over and debating different positions, in the way that so many religious people do when dealing with core enigmatic doctrines. The practical logic employed by bhakti traditions when they repeated stories about bhakti and caste is subtle and has outcomes that are not only or even primarily intellectual. One major feature of this practical logic is authors' strategic use of ambiguity when they discuss bhakti, caste, and food. Stories about food and transgressive commensality allow us to witness that strategy in action.

I expect that some readers may object at this point and cite stories about saints who took staunch positions that are not at all riddle-like or ambiguous. As I discuss in the final chapter, some individual stories and poems may truly represent such radical stances. However, my argument is more about patterns that developed over time and within broader traditions than it is about specific instances. As I make clear in Chapter 1, historians make a crucial decision whether their narratives will focus on long-term trends or short-term exceptions. Within traditions themselves, the process of narration and performance gradually homogenized individual utterances, reshaping how they were retold and applied. When we observe a single telling of a bhakti narrative, it is not immediately evident how that story came into the form that we encounter. As I discuss in Chapters 5 and 6, precisely these details are essential to know to appreciate just what an individual utterance or story was *doing* and not only *saying*. After all, it was to this effect—of a tradition that coalesced over time—that Ambedkar was responding.

Despite Ambedkar's stark judgment of bhakti, it is by no means the case that his view of the bhakti-caste question reached or convinced everyone. Discussions of bhakti and equality did not subside after Ambedkar. One still finds the trope of egalitarian bhakti appearing in newspaper articles, overviews of Indian history, and in the work of scholars who briefly comment on bhakti before focusing their attention on some other historical or cultural feature. Advocates for social change, whether they belong to a bhakti tradition or not, occasionally still hearken to elements of bhakti traditions in efforts to mobilize people, especially in rural areas.[9] As we will see in Chapters 3 and 7, the idea that bhakti traditions possess something that, if activated properly, still could spark social change is certainly not dead. A similar sentiment appears among liberal religious advocates around the world, who argue that the spirits of their traditions support the struggle for human rights and social equality. The idea of human rights itself is entangled with religion in many ways.[10] Yet it is obvious, at the end of the second decade of the 21st century, that the success of these liberal religious efforts has been spotty at best. So what might that tell us about religion and equality? I think the bhakti-caste question and its relation to food offers a window through which we can perceive some possibilities.

Plan of this book

As I have mentioned, this book proceeds in two parts. In Part I, I trace how the bhakti-caste question in relation to social equality developed in western and Marathi scholarship over the last two centuries. The application of the word "equality" to society and religion is peculiarly modern, and when it took hold in Marathi discourse in the late 19th century, equality was mapped onto several premodern concepts in bhakti literature. In Part II, I recover some of those concepts and show how they functioned before they were displaced by "equality." In doing so, I consider how one tradition, the Vārkarī *sampradāy*, followed a practical logic to promote a socially inclusive message. This practical logic is most apparent if we zoom in on examples that span premodern and modern times. Stories of food and transgressive commensality, especially stories about the brahman saint-poet Eknāth interacting with Dalits, do just that. Food's capacity to symbolize many things makes it an ideal site for debating bhakti's implications about caste differences. As I trace the changes that food stories underwent in repetitions across various media from 1700 onward, I highlight how the bhakti-caste relationship went from being a strategically ambiguous riddle to a question that expected—and received—answers.

Although this book centers on the bhakti-caste question in Maharashtra, it deals with modern perspectives on religion that reach far beyond India. Chapter 1 examines these broader issues, especially the common modern narrative that religious traditions routinely failed to bring about social equality. I focus on social historians, whose interest in non-elite people grew out of Marxist sensitivities that, in the course of explanation, predisposed them to view religion as a symptom of distress or instrument of social control but not as a force for social change. I then trace equality's emergence as an important term in western political and social writing and how modern nation-state rhetoric from the late 18th century onward made it normative. It becomes clear that modern democracies too have often failed to bring about social equality. This enables me to offer a critical take on scholarship about equality in historical religions around the world, and thereby to frame the historiographical issues that occupy the rest of the book.

In Chapter 2, I discuss the regional variations of bhakti traditions and the ways in which this diversity complicates theorizing about bhakti in general. Attempts at providing a general overview take one or another (usually North Indian) regional tradition for granted as representative, thereby magnifying the importance of issues and problems which that tradition held as important. As a result, scholarship on bhakti has tended to overemphasize aspects of some traditions while neglecting others. I make clear that my perspective is based in the Marathi-speaking territory of western India (roughly speaking, Maharashtra) where issues of caste and untouchability featured prominently in the region's traditions. It is probably no coincidence that Maharashtra was home to some of India's most organized and vocal movements of Dalit assertion in the 20th century. Chapter 2 thus offers an unconventional overview of bhakti scholarship as perceived from western India, where bhakti's social contribution in terms of democracy, inclusion, and equality was of special interest.

Chapter 3 charts the establishment of equality language in colonial and postcolonial Marathi publications about Vārkarī literature and traditions, and it recovers earlier Vārkarī ways of envisioning the relationship between bhakti and caste. Liberal and some nationalist authors between roughly 1854 and 1930 mined sectarian literatures and stories to construct a non-sectarian sense of regional identity. This held special importance because of how vital Marathi literary history has been for imagining the region's social history. More critical views were voiced by low-caste authors and secular rationalists in the late 19th century, and later by Marxist historians. Food featured prominently in pivotal events in many of these proponents' and critics' lives. Having described the formation of modern discourse around bhakti and equality, I then begin to recover the precolonial devotional and nondualist Marathi terms that equality language later displaced.

Whereas Part I explores the modern formulation of the bhakti-caste question, Part II examines premodern views as they appear and changed in various renditions of stories about transgressive commensality. In Chapter 4, I show why food features so often in Marathi stories to illustrate problems of social cohesion and division: food functions this way in many cultures and time periods. I highlight interdisciplinary insights from anthropologists and historians about food, especially R. S. Khare and his work on food's semantic density. I then survey food references in various genres of Hindu literature before homing in on meanings of food in bhakti hagiographies—especially *ucchiṣṭa* or polluted leftover food.

Chapters 5 and 6 drill down even further, focusing on two food stories whose retellings changed across various media in the precolonial, colonial, and postcolonial periods. At the center of both stories are the brahman saint Eknāth and Dalits with whom he interacts. In the *śrāddha* story that we encountered earlier, Eknāth serves to Dalits a ritual meal that was intended for brahmans, and his unorthodox action is vindicated miraculously in the face of outraged brahmans. In the double vision story, antagonistic brahmans witness Eknāth in two places at once: simultaneously eating a meal at a Dalit couple's home and sitting in his own home. Chapter 5 traces renditions of these two stories in Marathi texts between 1700 and 1800. If we approach hagiographical stories with sensitivity to how they change over time, a story about the story is revealed. In this Marathi case, part of that meta-story is that hagiographers strategically employed ambiguity to avoid answering the bhakti-caste question conclusively.

Chapter 6 follows the two stories into the 20th century, as they were represented in plays and films. Three main factors reshaped how the stories appeared on Marathi stage and screen: the narratological demands within and across media formats, equality language that had taken hold in 19th-century Marathi discourse, and the changing landscape of caste politics in the 20th century, especially with the rise of non-brahman movements. In this context, the double vision story's transgressive commensality became especially popular, and producers often sought to resolve the bhakti-caste question by depicting Eknāth as a social reformer.

Chapter 7 concludes the book by reflecting on what it means to study bhakti now in the shadow of Ambedkar, both for understanding the premodern traditions in the past on their own terms and for considering the contemporary relationships of bhakti traditions to social equality, which is one of our shared key terms in the modern world. I review examples of stories and tropes getting applied to stories about multiple saints, as a side-effect of retellings in new contexts, across media, and with different emphases. I argue that the performative nature of bhakti traditions functions as a resonance chamber of meanings, enmeshing individual stories and utterances within a narrative of social inclusivity. The semantic density of food facilitates this process especially well. In the 19th and 20th centuries, traditional strategic ambiguity and inclusive ideology did not measure up well against the standard of social equality. Although Ambedkar and others concluded that the bhakti saints did not promote social equality, neither historically nor in their own times, it remains an open question whether bhakti traditions and nondualist ethics may come to embrace it in the future. Commensality may play a vital role in this, as it did in the past.

This book is something like a meal, with the chapters being different courses along the way. Some will be rich and savory, others bitter yet nutritious, and still others voluminous but less dense. And I conclude with a dessert that, if not exactly sweet, will nonetheless leave readers with a sense of satisfaction, or so I hope. Of course, those who join in this meal come with different appetites and palates. Chapter 3, on Marathi intellectual history, may be a peculiar, acquired taste for some. Readers who relish history may find the discussion of food anthropology in Chapter 4 something they are not used to consuming. The renditions of food stories in Chapters 5 and 6 may hit the spot for those who enjoy stews of hagiographical stories, while others may struggle to stomach it. Readers who ponder the bhakti's relevance in modern times may feel that Chapters 6 and 7 lack the saltiness they crave. And to readers who are deeply devoted to and invested in the traditions I discuss, my final take on bhakti's politics in Chapter 7 may seem somehow "off," despite my best efforts to prepare it carefully. I only hope the meal is satisfying—and that part of this satisfaction comes from finding oneself implicitly in the presence of readers with very different tastes.

Conversations and contributions

This book contributes to several areas of scholarship. Above all, I offer a new perspective on bhakti and caste that is made possible by my investigation spanning three crucially distinct intellectual-cultural periods in western India: early modern, colonial, and postcolonial. Throughout these three periods, perceptions of bhakti and the contexts of those perceptions changed a great deal. In each subsequent period, new ideas and analytical lenses were developed and employed to envision the past, sometimes making it difficult to understand the perspectives of people in previous periods. This book thus offers a contextually sensitive historiography, peeling back layers of interpretation to recover earlier ways of understanding that got obscured and forgotten. In doing so, I build on work by scholars like Eleanor Zelliot,[11] David Lorenzen,[12] and Patton Burchett[13] to arrive at a broader vision of how bhakti-caste discourse changed over centuries and to identify the major role that strategic ambiguity played in premodern times.

By tracing the innovative repetition of stories across centuries, I join discussions about textual transmission practices in bhakti traditions. Philip Lutgendorf's work on the *Rāmcaritmānas* and Linda Hess's research on Kabīr poetry highlight the active use of texts by bhakti communities.[14] Christian Novetzke has made key contributions in this area, emphasizing the importance of performance above text and the significance of cultural memory as a space for considering the past alongside the discipline of history.[15] Novetzke's theories about the "bhakti public" and vernacular revolution are also important in this regard for considering how bhakti stories and songs brought people together in new ways and enabled representation of non-elite people.[16] Hess, Novetzke, and Jack Hawley all nuance our understanding of how the personae of "authors" have developed over time and among many performers.[17] I argue that this composite and long-term creation of bhakti discourse also developed a two-sided ideology of inclusion. It proclaimed radical inclusivity but preserved caste identity markers to do so.

My discussion of food and commensality in this book contributes to multiple areas of scholarship. Food has attracted attention on many fronts recently, and this book joins conversations especially about its social functions.[18] I draw on R. S. Khare's anthropological work on Hindu gastronomics and semantic density.[19] Especially in Chapter 4, I respond to Khare's call for more research into food's "long journey" across millennia of Hindu texts and paradigms.[20] My focus on food also extends Karen

Pechilis' and Barbara Holdrege's important work on embodiment in bhakti traditions.[21]

By paying special attention to portrayals of Dalits through several centuries of texts, plays, and films, I contribute to a cultural history of caste and untouchability in western India. I complement Sumit Guha's important work on the history of caste in western India, which drew mainly on courtly and imperial archives,[22] as I bring in non-courtly, bhakti-related sources to recover views of caste on a more popular level. This also supplements Anupama Rao's work on the emergence of Dalit politics in late 19th- and early 20th-century western India,[23] as well as Milind Wakankar's attempt to imagine subaltern intellectual space in premodern times.[24]

Finally, I hope this book's multi-disciplinary approach to a complex modern question contributes to the study of religion generally. Because the idea of social equality is bound up with Western political thought and expectations of secular transformation, my exploration of religion and social equality resonates beyond the study of South Asia. It is about religious traditions' roles in contemporary society, especially within political frameworks where individual citizens are said to have equal rights before the law. As we see across the globe and certainly in India, citizens still quite often behave in groups whose identities are shaped and performed through the imaginary that religion provides. Bhakti continues to play such a role for many people in India today, even after Ambedkar.

Key terms and clarifications

To avoid confusion, I want to clarify the particularities of what I mean when I use some words whose meanings have varied among scholars.

Bhakti

Chapter 2 surveys the development of bhakti in various senses and the chapter observes Marathi literature's special interest in caste, so I will not rehearse that discussion here. But some clarifications will help pinpoint the kind of "bhakti" that is at the heart of this book. Within Marathi literature, a few major traditions are commonly associated with bhakti. The largest and most visible of these is, by far, the Vārkarī *sampradāy*, whose literary corpus begins with the saint Jñāndev's Marathi rendering of the *Bhagavad Gītā* at the end of the 13th century and whose followers still today make annual massive pilgrimages to Viṭṭhal's temple in Paṇḍharpūr. Vārkarī poetry constitutes a substantial and treasured part of all Marathi literature. Likewise, stories about the four major saints—Jñāndev (13th c.), Nāmdev (13/14th c.), Eknāth (16th c.), and Tukārām (17th c.)—have circulated widely among Marathi speakers and readers. They still appear in the state's public-school textbooks as important regional history. In short, aspects of the Vārkarī tradition pervade Maharashtrian culture in very public ways, and it is because of this that I focus on them.

Beginning slightly earlier than Jñāndev and distinct from the Vārkarīs is the Mahānubhāv tradition, which looks back to the godly saint Cakradhar in the 1260s as its founder. Cakradhar's complicated relations with the Yādava rulers in western Maharashtra, which led to persecution of his followers, impelled the Mahānubhāvs to go underground. One of their tactics for self-protection was to encode their scriptures with a cipher that outsiders could not read. For centuries, Mahānubhāvs were looked down on and derided as corrupt by other Marathi speakers (including some Vārkarī authors)—a stigma that Mahānubhāvs did not refute publicly in a major way until filing a court case in 1907. Only after the Marathi scholar V. B. Kolte learned the Mahānubhāv cipher and controversially began publishing their classic literature in Devanagari in 1978 did Marathi readers outside the tradition gain access to these texts at all.[25]

Two other Maharashtrian traditions are associated with bhakti in different ways. The Datta *sampradāy* emerged in the 15th century, centered on the deity Dattātreya and two figures who are understood to be his incarnations—Śrīpad Śrīvallabha and Narasiṃha Sarasvatī.[26] Stories about the two are conveyed in the tradition's scripture, the *Gurucaritra*, which although composed in Marathi, is deeply indebted to the Sanskrit *Gurugītā* and conveys a strongly brahmanical style of bhakti toward gurus.[27] The Datta *sampradāy* has been comprised mainly of Maharashtrian brahmans who showed little interest in non-brahman affairs. This caste profile is largely true of the Rāmdāsī tradition as well. Rāmdās is remembered as a 17th-century yogi whose devotion to Rāma distinguished him from the Viṭṭhal/Kṛṣṇa-focused Vārkarīs, although some later observers regarded Rāmdāsīs and Vārkarīs as kindred spirits.[28] A common Marathi idiom expresses the two groups' supposed affinity and difference in rhyme—Vārkarīs do *vārī* (pilgrimage) while Dhārkarīs (esp. Rāmdāsīs) wield the sword. With patronage from early

Maratha rulers, the Rāmdāsī tradition established a network of *maṭhs* that were key in preserving a large archive of precolonial Marathi manuscripts, including those of Vārkarīs.

These latter three groups fall mostly outside the scope of my book. The relative absence of the Mahānubhāvs in 19th-century Marathi literature and 20th-century Maharashtrian consciousness meant that they did not feature much in public Marathi discussions of bhakti and caste. Because the Datta and Rāmdāsī *sampradāy*s maintained a strong brahmanical character, they engaged less with critiques of caste or untouchability. For them, the bhakti-caste relationship was not much of a question at all; their positions were quite clear on the matter. So, although the Mahānubhāv, Datta, and Rāmdāsī traditions all were undeniably part of the larger cultural environment in Maharashtra, I focus on the largest and most influential group, whose caste politics have seemed the most influential yet elusive—the Vārkarī *sampradāy*.

Most of the hagiographical stories in this book are about Eknāth, a boundary-crossing brahman saint-poet who lived with his wife and children during the 16th century in the ancient, orthodox town of Paiṭhaṇ (formerly Pratiṣṭhāna). This focus derives partially from my deep familiarity with Eknāth; he was the subject of my dissertation.[29] In writing the dissertation, however, it became increasingly clear to me that the extraordinary stories about Eknāth's interactions with Dalits—especially the ways in which they were repeated—deserved further analysis beyond just what they say about the saint himself. More than any other Vārkarī saint, and arguably more than any other saint in India, the persona of Eknāth came to represent the elite critique of caste and untouchability. If there is competition for the status of arch-critic of caste, it comes from Kabīr or maybe Ravidās. But Eknāth also carried the privileged burden of brahmanhood; critiques associated with him reflected on his status (and its questioning by orthodox brahmans) in a way that critiques by Kabīr and Ravidās did not. Since Eknāth illustrates the bhakti-caste tension in this way, he represents issues of religious and social change that are much larger than him.

Caste

As many modern authors do, I use "caste" as a shorthand for the notoriously complex and contested set of rules and customs that have shaped social hierarchy in South Asia over the past two millennia at least. Much scholarship has explored the historical construction of caste, in its four-fold system of *varṇa* and its more granular and regionally distinct systems of endogamy and occupation, or *jāti*.[30] Many ethnographers challenged Louis Dumont's overly neat theorization, which discussed how Hindus (and many non-Hindu Indians) positioned themselves among inherited caste structures.[31] Nicholas Dirks called attention to the British colonial administration's role in clarifying and solidifying caste boundaries,[32] and others, like Rosalind O'Hanlon, have warned against overestimating the extent of British intervention.[33] Caste's close relationship to the material and economic realities of Dalits has been a focus of much recent scholarship, including that of P. Sanal Mohan, Rupa Viswanath, and Ramnarayan Rawat.[34] And still others, like Sumit Guha, warn that no single rationale or theory can encompass the diverse political, economic, cultural, and religious forces that have shaped the realities of caste on the ground over thousands of years.[35]

Although caste is a complicated business, the Marathi materials at the center of this book bypass many of those complexities by focusing on what classical Hindu law regarded as the polar extremes of ritual purity—brahmans and Dalits. The most contentious cases of caste politics occur between groups of relatively close status, which could put them in competition.[36] In contrast, I focus on the starkest disparity, in which no one contested the relative positions of the groups involved. Whatever structural considerations figure into discussions of caste in other contexts, the caste issues at stake in my study are extremely simple because they are simply extreme. I believe that it is precisely because the brahman-Dalit relationship involves such an obvious disparity that stories about Eknāth captured people's imaginations.

It is important to note that this envisioned spectrum of ritual purity is a Hindu brahmanical one, rooted in Hindu legal texts. Dalits, including Ambedkar, have often put forward a different perspective, not just of ritual purity but of caste itself. For them, more fundamental than the divisions among castes was the dichotomy between people who have a caste and those who do not. Whatever inter-caste tensions may exist, these are less consequential than the otherness of Dalits, who the paradigm of caste accounted for but essentially marginalized. In this perspective, the caste/non-caste dichotomy explains the pattern of caste Hindus allying themselves against Dalits, such as happened with brutal and deadly results at Khairlāñjī in 2006.[37]

Dalit

The question of how to refer to groups that have long been stigmatized as having no caste (*avarṇa*) and treated as "untouchable" is a vexed one. Early references in Sanskrit law books demonstrate that some people, such as perpetrators of mild crimes or women during menstruation, were regarded as "not to be touched" (*aspṛśya*) until they underwent ritual purification.[38] (This is but one example of how the regulation of caste fundamentally involved regulating gender roles and especially the bodies of women.) Other social groups were viewed as irrevocably untouchable for the entirety of their lives, such as the category of *mleccha*—a xenological term traditionally denoting ethnicity. Under the *mleccha* umbrella came Greco-Bactrians, Turks, Afghans, Persians, Europeans, and some aboriginal tribes.[39] Although these groups were technically *avarṇa* due to their unfamiliarity with caste, they were sometimes reckoned with more sympathetically, especially if they had political and military power.[40]

Untouchability was also attached to some occupations. Hunters, leather workers, funerary service laborers, and drummers were frequently regarded as untouchable by birth. Since occupations in ancient India were mainly inherited, the stigma of untouchable labor was passed on through generations. More general categories of irredeemable untouchability were groups who were said to cook and presumably eat dogs (*śvapaca*) and those who were simply called "fierce" (*caṇḍāla*). Early Sanskrit texts do not elaborate on the origins of these categories, which suggests that they classified groups who probably carried out essential labor that nonetheless was regarded as polluting. Labels for these groups changed greatly in the past 150 years. A thorough history of untouchability across millennia is still wanting, but important pieces of it appear in scholarship on Sanskrit law books,[41] British ethnographic and census records,[42] Christian missionary archives,[43] and modern movements.[44]

Since the 1970s, some communities that were designated in modern times as "Untouchables" have adopted as a term of self-reference the label "Dalit" (Marathi for "ground down" or "broken into pieces"), especially with the rise of the Dalit Panthers and Dalit poetry movements in Maharashtra.[45] In recent decades, "Dalit" has become a standard term among scholars to name the diverse set of groups on the Government of India's list of Scheduled Castes. Adoption of "Dalit" for self-reference has not been universal across India or even in Maharashtra. Some Indians favor other terms, such as *bahujan* (majority community) or their local *jāti* names, and trends will surely continue to change over time.

In this book, I consistently use the term "Dalit" not only to refer to modern Indian communities but to encompass premodern words as well. This is a self-consciously interpretive move, synthetically gathering diverse words from diverse contexts under a single umbrella term, but I think it is justified by the conceptual and social continuity of stigmatization that endures across those diverse places, times, and words. For the sake of precision and to demonstrate the diversity of terms in use, I routinely include the Marathi and Sanskrit words that I translate as Dalit. Until very recently, the noun "Untouchable" played this translational role. Some scholars still use this term with the assumption that it is preceded implicitly by "so-called," to demonstrate that it was imposed by some people on others. Others quite reasonably continue using "Untouchable" intentionally in the way that Ambedkar did—as a provocation to remind readers of its inherent offensiveness.[46] As Simon Charsley shows, using "Untouchable" as a noun is a relatively recent practice, even though its adjectival usage is ancient.[47] I prefer the admittedly anachronistic term that at least has some current emic usage—"Dalit"—even in historical cases that predated this word. In doing so, I follow the lead of several contemporary scholars, including Sumit Guha, Anupama Rao, and Nathaniel Roberts.

Names of God

Following the precedent set by the Vārkarīs, I will shift freely among different names for God without always distinguishing among deities as if they were separate. People typically regard Kṛṣṇa as an *avatār* of Viṣṇu, yet functionally, Kṛṣṇa is more popular than Viṣṇu and sometimes is viewed as the supreme deity, such as in the *Bhāgavata Purāṇa* and in the Kṛṣṇa-centered traditions in western India. The regional deity Viṭṭhal is acknowledged to be an incarnation of Kṛṣṇa,[48] but here as well, most Vārkarīs revere him in practice simply as Viṭṭhal. Saints too are sometimes referred to as *avatār*s of one deity or another, or without a deity being specified at all. This keeps with the general Hindu sensibility that humans and deities exist on a spectrum of divinity. When I refer to "God" in this book, I have this fluid sense of divinity in mind.

Saint

Throughout this book, I use the English word "saint" to cover a fairly well-established set of highly revered individuals in bhakti traditions' histories. Many terms exist for these figures, but the most popular one in Marathi is *sant*, which comes from the Sanskrit root *sat*, meaning truth, being, and goodness. A person becomes a *sant* by virtue of popular memory making them a *sant*, not by a sanctioning body in the way that the Roman Catholic Church beatifies saints. (The Hindi use of *sant* is more limited than in Marathi, applying only to low-caste and Dalit bhakti figures like Kabīr and Ravidās who have a nondualist view of ultimate reality.) The relationship between bhakti saints and God is also fluid: saints are sometimes viewed as completely distinct from God, as semi-infused by God or semi-absorbed in Brahman, or as a human manifestation of God.

Commensality

Foreshadowing my discussion of food in Chapter 4, I want readers to note at the outset that I take "commensality" to signify a wider range of interactions than the typical western image of people eating together around a table. In Hindu contexts, the crux of the issue lies in whom one accepts food from and how that squares with codes of ritual purity. As I have said, food is a symbolically rich site that can be examined to reveal attitudes toward caste, and the implications of food's symbolisms for Hindus extend well beyond eating in the same place at the same time.

Critical commensality, as I see it, could be applied to any realm in which we find people eating together. This book deals mainly with *stories* about food and commensality rather than ethnographic observations. One reason for this is that I am concerned especially with history, for which texts and very occasional visual representations are simply the most relevant sources, especially when considering the world before 1900. Another reason for my textual emphasis has to do once again with Ambedkar and his legacy. Many Dalits in western India, and increasingly throughout the subcontinent, have distanced themselves from bhakti traditions, whether they have converted to Buddhism or not. This naturally reduces the statistical likelihood of Dalits engaging at all in inter-caste commensality in overtly bhakti settings.

Consequently, there are fewer alternatives but to analyze commensality as it is represented in texts and media. I discuss this in greater depth in Chapter 7.

Uses of theory

There is a tendency in some scholarship on India to resort constantly to conceptual frameworks that were provided by the western post-Enlightenment world, as if these lenses alone reveal how the world "really is." Such frameworks, as used in the social sciences and humanities under the heading of cultural studies, are commonly designated as "theory." I confess that I have a love-hate relationship with theory of this sort.

Coming into academia from a rural, agricultural background, I often have felt out of place when scholars fall into jargon-dense conversations. Highly specialized technical language can function as guild-speak, policing the gates to the scholarly profession, even if unintentionally, so that only the properly acculturated and high-born may enter. I do not want to reinforce this. On the other hand, I believe that theoretical conversations do help—as analytical frameworks, to some degree, but even more as ways of translating aspects of Indian history and Marathi language into forms that non-specialists might grasp more readily.

I have tried to write this book in a way that is mindful of theory while avoiding language that is unnecessarily complicated. This reflects my hope to make this book accessible to a wider audience, and it stems from my sense of scholars' responsibility to be accessible beyond just the world of the academy. This effort is also born out of an ethical concern about representation. The Marathi sources I work with here have their own logical coherence, force, and creativity—all of which are impressive in their own right. I hope that readers may encounter these Marathi sources, as much as possible, on their own terms and not buried beneath too thick a layer of theoretical analysis that comes from elsewhere.

Now let the meal commence.

PART I

Equality is *the* critical reference point when people consider the roles of caste in Hindu devotional traditions. Do bhakti traditions promote equality now? Did they do so in the past? These are two modern forms of what I call the bhakti-caste question, which aims to clarify the relationship between bhakti and caste. When people in the 20th century have closely observed the Vārkarī tradition and nearly all other bhakti traditions, most have answered "no" along with Ambedkar, and without much hesitation. Although I too am inclined toward answering in the negative, that somehow has never felt complete or satisfactory, as if more needs to be said about the answer and especially about the question. Part I does just that—investigates the bhakti-caste question in its modern configuration, to be able to think more broadly about bhakti, caste, equality, and the ways in which they shaped social behavior. With this greater clarity about the modern lens of equality, we can start to recover the emic terms that the Vārkarī tradition used to address the bhakti-caste question.

1

Religion and Social Change

Narratives of Outrage and Disappointment

In scholarship throughout the past century, the idea of equality has become something of a touchstone that authors use to discuss religious traditions. This is part of broader conversations about modernity, which wrestle especially with religion in society, its relative authority over people's lives, and its impact on matters of social and political equality.[1] This way of talking about religion in modernity has spilled over into discussions about the premodern world as well. It portrays premodern traditions in a particularly harsh light and has prompted many modern observers to feel outrage or disappointment. Outrage has come from those who see premodern religions as supporting and justifying inequality, so that religion becomes a serious hindrance to modernization that must be overcome. Other observers conclude that premodern religions held intellectual resources that could have promoted social liberation and human equality, but for one reason or another, they failed to realize this potential. Both judgments measure the premodern past of religious traditions over against the secular nation-state. The modern nation has become the standard framework within which equality is now advocated, appealed to, and sometimes instituted on legal grounds. When judgments of the past are made, what often gets overlooked is the fact that western modernity has also often failed to realize equality for marginalized groups in practice. Applying such a notion of social equality—as natural as it now seems—creates difficulties for interpreting religions in history. Bhakti in western India is an exemplary case.

One of my main concerns in this book is to explore why modern interpreters are so frequently disappointed or outraged when they envision religion's relationship to social change. What gets sidelined when equality is the aspirational standard by which groups are judged? Evaluating religion's social effects in history is difficult because religion is so multivalent, pervading many different sectors of social life and functioning in many different ways. Any attempt to narrate the social impact of religion is unavoidably

Shared Devotion, Shared Food. Jon Keune, Oxford University Press. © Oxford University Press 2021.
DOI: 10.1093/oso/9780197574836.003.0002

selective in its scope and reflects the narrator's goals. When viewed as an ideological system, as by Marx, religion legitimatizes the control of those in power and tempers the suffering of the oppressed. Viewed as a group's communal projection of itself, as by Durkheim, religion functions to draw social boundaries and nurture a sense of belonging in one's group, while excluding others. When viewed as a system of ideas, values, and practices that give order to the world (Peter Berger) or that offer people options they can rationally select to benefit themselves (Rodney Stark), religion is a cultural resource to create psychological and social stability. Viewed as an alternative source of authority that can pierce deep layers of traditional psychological control (Luce Irigaray), religion helps people to discover for themselves new subjectivities. When viewed as a social movement (Vittorio Lanternari), religion may function as a counter-ideology to mobilize protesters and insurgents with a utopian vision.

When these and other theories assess particular functions of religion, they inevitably have a field of vision within which they perceive their data and examples. Each theory involves or takes for granted a particular social location. As it does so, the analytic scope of each theory leaves at the periphery other places where religion plays quite different and even contrary roles. Narratives of outrage and disappointment about religion's failure to realize equality appear most often when scholars focus their attention on non-elite, disempowered social groups.

Religion through the lenses of history and social science

When it comes to handling religion, the modern discipline of history is particularly troubled, especially when historians move beyond the well-documented official narratives of political and institutional authorities. Since the mid-20th century, scholars who focus on non-elites (subalterns, or "history from below"), usually in the vein of social history, typically approach their studies with a set of Marxian analytical tools attuned to economic and power disparities. In the process, however, these scholars tend to plot non-elites—whose lives are recorded most richly in non-official archives that are permeated by religion—onto ready-made narratives of how religion constrains, dominates, and subjugates them. The unspoken assumption is that if the religions of non-elites had been successful, then they would have overcome their marginality and ceased to be non-elite. In this respect, as historical narratives describe a given non-elite group of people, the narratives effectively reiterate a version of the same theory about how religion functions in society, just with a different set of non-elite people plugged into it. Although the narrative seems to be about the non-elite people, it also—even primarily—rehearses a common story about religion's marginal role in modernity.

The negative account of how bhakti traditions failed to overcome caste in the past is one variation of a broader historical-sociological theme about what religion does for non-elites: it promises hope and may deliver compassion, but it ultimately fails to transform society and these people's status within it. Or in the words of Ranajit Guha, bhakti was a conservative force for maintaining the status quo—"an ideology of subordination par excellence."[2] Some scholars of social history developed more sophisticated approaches to religion,[3] but this has not much affected the ways in which modern authors have perceived precolonial bhakti traditions. In short, the narrative of outrage and disappointment has at least as much to do with modern ideas of religion and society, and with the secular discipline of history, as it does with the past world that the narrative attempts to describe. In the next section, I explain why I think this is the case.

Broadly, and at the risk of over-simplifying things, history as an academic discipline in the West has tended to follow two major streams, depending on what historians understood as their goal.[4] One stream, typified by Leopold von Ranke, aims to describe the past as it "actually was," writing history for the sake of recovering information about the past and making it legible to people in the present. Rankean positivism, as it is often called, seeks to report the past on its own terms, regardless of whether those terms may appear inferior or obsolete by contemporary standards. The other major stream, inspired by Karl Marx's historical materialism, pays special attention to class and hierarchy, with an eye to highlighting social problems and, ideally, to alleviating them. It is Marxist historiography's interest in social hierarchy that has directed historians to focus on the lives of non-elite subjects.

Deeper in this disciplinary background stands G. W. F. Hegel, whose vision of history as a dialectic process of cultural-intellectual evolution prompted both Ranke and Marx to respond. Ranke rejected Hegel's presumption that historical details should fit into a grand narrative of development. Marx accepted Hegel's developmental view of history, but he inverted Hegel's understanding of what drove that development: economic interests rather than the unfolding of the human spirit. And for Marx, history was directed toward the liberation of oppressed classes, rather than Hegel's envisioned freedom of mind.

Although Rankean and Marxist historians processed religion in different ways, both explicitly distanced themselves from an earlier European form of remembering the past—sacred history, with its expectation that superhuman forces intervene in the everyday world. Although modern historians regularly relied on historical documents written in a sacred historiographical mode, they sought to filter out references to divine intervention. This led to a troubled relationship between historians and religion throughout the 20th century, with most historians viewing religion as a peripheral concern.[5] (This neglect and uneasiness is surely one reason for the remarkable uptick in 21st-century historians' interest in religion.[6]) Many historians in the 20th century viewed religion as a stage of civilizational development; it may have served a purpose for less enlightened folk in earlier times, but modern societies were supposed to progress beyond it by adapting to scientific discoveries.[7]

In a classical Marxist perspective, religion played a more insidious role: either legitimizing subordination or comforting the oppressed in their plights rather than inspiring them to rise up and change those conditions to achieve their liberation. In this sense, religious ideas and practices are epiphenomenal with respect to the economic and material conditions that actually shape society.[8] Such Marxists see little value in tracking religious ideas and practices, since religion only reflects the forces that order society; it is not such a force itself. The flow of influence is unidirectional; material concerns shape the world of ideas.

Responding to this view, Max Weber argued for a bi-directional influence that allowed for the possibility that people's religious ideas could impact their material conditions, including wealth acquisition and capital management. For the purpose of this book, I merely note Marx's and Weber's divergent views as reference points, because they help us understand how histories of India have described bhakti traditions. When historians have been inspired to look at bhakti traditions as sources of information about non-elite people, they have usually been inspired by a Marxian approach, which carried with it preconceptions about religion's social role and inefficacy to change the economically based arrangement of society.

A Marx-inspired inclination to seek out social structures and power disparities was central to the streams of social and cultural history that emerged from the 1960s onward, focused initially on labor and economic disparity to write "history from below."[9] This approach is epitomized in E. P. Thompson's classic of social history, *Making of the English Working Class*. The same values that inspired social historians to study non-elite people in history inclined them to either look askew at their subjects' own religious expressions or to write those aspects of their worldview out of the history altogether. Although Thompson was very sympathetic and concerned about the social worlds of working-class subjects, when it came to their Methodist Christianity, he judged its effects quite harshly.[10]

Dipesh Chakrabarty offered a more nuanced approach to religion in social history, as he discussed the translation of religious (enchanted) lifeworlds of subaltern subjects into the register of secular (disenchanted) history. Two points are noteworthy here. First, translating the enchanted lifeworlds of subalterns into disenchanted history is unavoidable and an essentially modern process. Governmentality requires a disenchanted history, and it is through government, according to Chakrabarty, that subalterns have the greatest opportunities for advancement. Therefore, this translation into disenchanted terms should be welcomed, as it enables subalterns to understand and access those governmental bodies.[11] "The subaltern classes need this knowledge in order to fight their battles for social justice."[12] At the same time, the disenchanted view of history does violence to subaltern lifeworlds by rendering them inferior in the modern world, and modern secularists become so acclimated to disenchanted time that they lose their ability to imagine other ways of life. So Chakrabarty recommends retaining something "uncanny" within disenchanted narratives to remind readers of the disruptive translation that occurred.[13] This could take the form of highlighting the subaltern's unique self-understanding, such as in Ranajit Guha's exploration of Santal tribesmen in the mid-19th century, who rebelled against British soldiers and described their actions as inspired by God.[14] A sensitive historian should render such an event both in the register of disenchanted time and in the words of the Santals themselves, even though these two views of the past are not totally commensurable. This enables one to relate to the Santals in two ways: as an object to be studied and understood, and as exemplifying for us an alternative way of living and thinking.[15] Subaltern pasts thereby invite the historian to reflect on whether disenchanted history is truly as inevitable and good as it seems.[16] Ultimately, Chakrabarty argues, the "tendency to identify reason and rational argumentation as a modernist weapon against 'premodern' superstition ends up overdrawing the boundary between the modern and the premodern."[17] Religion, in the sense of enchanted lifeworlds that inspire subalterns to assert themselves, thus presents not only a problem for secular history writing but a challenge to assumptions about a secular modernity itself.[18] Ambedkar's engagement with Buddhism, including his Marx-infused reframing of classic Buddhist doctrines, as well as the impact that his conversion had on modern Dalit politics, complicates the secular/religious dichotomy even further.

I think there is a basic question at the heart of these discussions of subaltern religiosity: should narrations of a non-elite group's past portray religion more as a source of social inertia and stasis, or an instrument for assertion and change? This question about narrating stasis or change has also appeared among anthropologists. As Bruce Kapferer explains, in the last several decades, anthropologists have been guided by two paradigms for temporally framing what they observe—either as illustrations or as events/situations. Clifford Geertz's interpretive approach tends to view individual happenings as illustrations of general patterns that reveal the logic behind cultural systems. In contrast, Max Gluckman and the Manchester School focused on atypical cases, which they called "events" or "situations." For them, the occurrences that merit attention are those that interrupt everyday life, bring unresolved conflicts to a head, and thereby open up new possibilities for thinking and being.[19] By placing disruptive events at the center of anthropology through "situational analysis," anthropologists can destabilize commonly accepted interpretations of culture. While Geertz foregrounds broad-scale stability, Gluckman and company prioritize the potential for change.

As they represent the question of bhakti and caste in their writing, modern scholars make crucial choices about where to focus their attention and frame the story they want to tell. Should they emphasize broad sociopolitical patterns and structures like caste hierarchy, in which regional bhakti traditions participated alongside non-bhakti groups? Or should they focus on particular saints and traditions that, however local and individual, interrupted those patterns and prompted people to think and do something new? Should we map bhakti traditions onto a narrative of social stability or a trajectory of change? And if there is a trajectory of change, are narratives of irruption destined to result in re-institutionalization and stasis, due to the short-lived nature of irruptions themselves? All of these questions revolve around prioritizing change or pattern as one narrates the past. How one situates bhakti traditions on that stasis-change continuum makes all the difference.

One way that scholars have described the impulse for change is through the idea of the social movement. This too is conceptually loaded. Writing on the history of social movement theory, Steve Buechler bluntly states, "Social movements are distinctly modern."[20] Of course, people have gotten together and done things under the banner of a shared agenda or charismatic leader for millennia. But Buechler calls attention to the set of conspicuously modern features that qualify something as a "social movement" in the strictest sense of the term: a notion of society as a whole, a sense that collective action changes society, and a public in which an activist group can assert its voice. In other words, the nature of social movement language is limited practically by its temporal sighting; social configurations of society, collective action, and a public must already be available to be assembled in this way. Although Buechler is precise in defining social movements, his definition is conveniently well matched to the scope of his consideration: Europe and North America since the late 19th century. Where does that leave the rest of history and the rest of the world?

Martin Fuchs and Antje Linkenbach take a more expansive approach, pointing out a crucial divide among social movement theorists. Some, like Buechler, apply the term in a narrow sense, tied explicitly to modernization, while others use it more loosely to refer to any emancipatory movement that mobilizes people by appealing to cultural identifiers.[21] This is especially common among post-Marxists, the New Left, and subaltern studies scholars in India who research peasants, aboriginal groups, Dalits, and women. Although the term "bhakti movement" (which I discuss in Chapter 2) precedes social movement theory by several decades, the spread of social movement language in India from the 1960s onward gave it new significance, recasting historical bhakti traditions as social movements. Yet the full range of modern assumptions that lie embedded in the concept of social movement and the analytical tools that could be deployed because of it were never fully developed or even acknowledged when referring to bhakti traditions. In effect, social movement as a concept provides a ready-made structure for narrating the past without fully acknowledging where that structure comes from.

Drawing on such social scientific terms to explain history like this is understandable, especially since they seem to map well onto terms in historical texts that emphasize the uniqueness of traditions and their adherents. Throughout bhakti poetry and hagiography, authors have distinguished themselves in formulaic ways from other religious actors, such as Jains, sufis, yogis, tantra practitioners, and most of all, orthodox brahmans.[22] Bhakti traditions promote particular characteristics or cultural identifiers as endemic to their group, such as inclusivity and devotion to God, above all other identity markers like gender, caste, occupation, and so on. Yet there is good reason to be wary about uncritically using social movement language for the distant past. As Steven Justice shows when reviewing scholarship on John Wyclif and 14th-century English religious dissidents, modern scholars (including Justice himself, earlier in his career) often assume that it was dissidents' unorthodox religious ideas that inspired them to diverge from the mainstream and revolt.[23] This interpretation offers a temptingly simple explanation of how social change originates, but there is usually little if any historical evidence to support it. "Whatever the reason, we still have the unthinking association of revolt with heresy, a quaint habit of thought quite untouched by theoretical refinement."[24] Correlation is not necessarily causation. Justice's argument applies even better to precolonial South Asia, where the historical record is more fragmentary. When scholars write about bhakti traditions as historical phenomena, they more often are theorizing about the cultural and social past than uncovering material evidence of it. In many (most?) cases across precolonial South Asia, and especially when non-elite bhakti traditions are involved, such material evidence rarely exists at all.

In the end, we are still left with the problem of how to envision and describe crucial changes in the past. Surely, something (or many things) led to the emergence, spread, and institutionalization of vernacular bhakti traditions. But what was this historically, and what might it entail for bhakti traditions and caste relations now? I return to these questions throughout this book and especially in the final chapter. To do so, it is important to reflect on that foundational modern term that haunts our considerations of social change: equality.

Conceiving equality

In a groundbreaking article in 2000, Rogers Brubaker and Frederick Cooper argued that the notion of "identity" was not as analytically useful as its ubiquity in humanistic and social science writing would suggest. Scholars typically refer to identity either too grandly, as connoting a distinct cultural essence, or too vaguely, as a local construction that is incommensurable with other constructions. In both cases, scholars reflect insufficiently on what exactly an "identity" is.[25] I think the same is true about "equality"—a similarly widespread term whose nuances often are overlooked or taken for granted by scholars of premodern cultures. Because "equality" became so central in discussions of bhakti and caste, it is important to draw out these nuances by tracking how it was applied and eventually became standard in modern India.

When the term appeared in the deep past, equality was remarkably narrow in its application. According to the ancient Greek historian Herodotus, the city-state of Athens accorded people *isonomia* or equality before the law.[26] Yet *isonomia* applied only to men whose parents were Athenian citizens, which effectively excluded most of the population—women, resident foreigners, and enslaved people. The framers of the US Constitution held as self-evident that "all men are created equal," but they assumed also that enslaved people, women, and landless White males did not constitute "men" in this sense.[27] It ought to give us pause that these two touchstone cases of equality so readily demonstrate its limited application, especially in that over half of the population—women—are subordinated from the outset.

Modern scholars of conceptual history have noted equality's variety of meanings and applications. Raymond Williams' *Keywords* included "equality" among its 176 essential terms for social scientific and humanistic scholarship.[28] The eight-volume pioneer of conceptual history *Geschichtliche Grundbegriffe* (Basic Concepts in History) included a lengthy article on *Gleichheit* ("equality," here). Conceptual histories like this need to be taken with a grain of salt, so as not to imagine that any concept has a single, linear history. Quentin Skinner warned scholars, including Williams specifically,[29] against the "mythology of doctrines"—the tendency to read earlier texts anachronistically through the lens of a modern concept, with a mind to reconstructing a history of its supposedly organic development.[30] Even if we are wary about a straightforward history of equality, it is nonetheless helpful to observe historical examples of the term's usage, to become sensitized to the range of meanings that it has had.

According to Williams, the earliest uses of equality in English described observations about the material world, such as equal weight or length. Only in the 15th and 16th centuries, in isolated cases, was equality applied to the social world, such as an equivalence of rank. In the late 18th century, the American and French Revolutions and the subsequent motto "all men are created equal" brought the term into common use. In this context, invoking equality aimed at redressing earlier social inequalities that were enshrined in the English and French legal codes, which distinguished among royalty, aristocracy, and commoners. Two schools diverged over what this vision of equality entailed: pursuing a systematic process of equalization that proactively leveled out disparities, or removing inherited privileges so that people could "start equal" but then have equal opportunities to distinguish themselves.[31] By the 19th century, some observers argued that if economic inequalities were allowed to persist, then legal and political equality could exist only ever in theory.

Otto Dann takes a broader approach, distinguishing equality from identity and similarity. Equality (Greek *isotes*, Latin *aequalitas*, French *égalité*, German *Gleichheit*) refers to a relationship in which two objects agree in most characteristics but differ enough that they maintain separate existences ($a = b$). In the case of identity, the two objects cannot be differentiated at all ($a = a$). And similarity refers to two objects between which there is greater difference than in the case of equality ($a \approx b$).[32] To identify what kind of relationship exists between two things, one must refer to a third term of comparison (*tertium comparationis*). In *isonomia* and the US Constitution, equality is defined in terms of people's relationship to the law. In a social sense, equality refers to the relative status of groups and individuals, especially with regard to the possibility of improving one's status, in which case equality is usually paired with the concept of freedom.[33] An important semantic division appeared in the Middle Ages: *aequitas* (equity) became a strictly legal term, while *aequalitas* (equality) was applied more generally. This distinction between "equity" and "equality" remains in French and English today.[34] Historical appearances of these terms in medieval literatures reveal an important aspect of European social visions at that time: judicial equity was written about extensively, whereas the idea that people could be equal in social status was never discussed.

The notion of spiritual equality first appeared in the West in the 15th century, in critiques of Roman Catholic ecclesial hierarchy leveled by the Waldensians and followers of Jan Hus. A legal pronouncement in 1439 by the Holy Roman Emperor Sigismund imbued spiritual equality with a worldly significance, as he banned the practice of serfdom on the grounds that, "All stand in equal freedom [*glicher fryheit*] before heaven."[35] More famously, Luther asserted a notion of spiritual equality in 1520: "all Christians have a truly spiritual status, and there is no difference among them." Michael Geismayr, a leader of the Peasant Revolt, radicalized this language in his *Landesordnung* in 1526: "All city walls, along with castles and fortresses, will be destroyed, and there will no longer be cities but towns, so that no differences among men will exist. . . . Instead, there will be complete equality [*ganze Gleichheit*] in the country." Dann calls this pronouncement a "social-utopian aspiration."[36]

In the late 17th century, references to social equality began appearing in charters of some German and French civil clubs, such as the Freemasons, as well as in occasional French political tracts.[37] Thomas Hobbes in *Leviathan* (1651) argued that the "natural condition" of humans was that they were "equall" in physical and mental faculties,[38] which should be acknowledged as a "law of nature." Jean-Jacques Rousseau placed equality and liberty at the center of his program for civic reform: since people were equal by nature, they all ought to enjoy equal liberty to live as they choose, independent of rulers' wishes.[39] This contributed to the motto of the French Revolution—*liberté, egalité, fraternité.*

The same ideals were circulating at the founding of the United States of America, most famously in the Declaration of Independence, and in slightly different forms in the constitutions of Virginia (1776) and Massachusetts (1780). These too asserted equality as a natural right, which, in an American context, immediately raised the question of enslaved people's status.[40] This and many other examples of unequal rights among men and women of various ethnicities and religions, glaringly in practice if not always explicitly in theory, have persisted in nations that declare the equal rights of citizens. Thus, Charles Taylor refers to "islands of equality" within seas of hierarchy.[41]

It is also worth touching on a few other attempts to disambiguate aspects and values that the ideal of equality glommed together. As mentioned earlier, discussions about equality require a third reference point—equality in terms of something. In most cases, this something was the state's legal code, and asserting equality involved combating inequalities that had been institutionalized in the past. But "equality" may also refer to opportunity, access to resources, freedom to use resources, moral worth, wealth, social status, or power to affect politics.[42] Defining "equality" with reference to one of these does not necessarily entail a commitment to equality in the other respects. Viewing all people as having equal moral value does not necessarily acknowledge the unequal distribution of wealth. There is also the question of whether equality in a social sense is related necessarily to justice, and if so, how.[43] Should equality be promoted as a good in itself or because of the effects that it supposedly bears with it?[44] And does equality require that people commit to a project of redistribution or "leveling down" of parties that are over-privileged,[45] such as through the reservation system in contemporary India?[46]

Even when people agree that equality in some sense is a worthy aspiration, debates continue about how to define, measure, and institute it. John Arthur makes this point in relation to race in the United States after the civil rights movement: "Unlike in earlier centuries, today racial equality is *in some sense* widely accepted. But whatever consensus may exist at the abstract level evaporates when questions are raised about either its meaning or what it requires in practice."[47] What Arthur describes about race in the United States applies in many ways to post-independence India, after the Indian constitution banned negative discrimination on the basis of caste.

Given the deeply rooted ambiguity and indeterminacy of equality, we should soberly consider the consistent failure of modern democracies to realize social equality, especially among historically disenfranchised minority groups. Since practically all modern countries have not prevented extreme wealth disparities among their citizens, and most countries fall quite short of providing the equal access to and treatment within a nation's legal structure that are constitutionally promised, some major forms of equality have clearly *not* been achieved, despite western modernity's consistent discourse of equality. There is always a difference between equality as idealized within a liberal democratic system and how it is practically lived out in the world, with all its messiness, tacit hierarchies, and historically instituted inequities. If people judge that bhakti traditions failed to effect genuine social equality on the ground, it is not as if western modernity—which explicitly promotes social equality ideals—has fared drastically better. This is not to imply that modern democracies offered no improvements over traditional hierarchies for non-elite groups, but it is hard to deny that modern aspirations toward equality remain strikingly unfulfilled.

This has led some scholars, such as Anastasia Piliavsky, Jason Hickell, and Vita Peacock, to refocus on the functional hierarchies that persist within communities not as cultural artifacts but simply as part of normal life.[48] Earlier scholars' enthusiasm to study equality, as well intentioned as it was, tended to flatten the subjects that they observed and view social hierarchies as problems to be resolved. Additionally, discourse about egalitarianism and equality is still discourse. Whatever people may intend when they invoke ideals of equality, they all have their distinct contextual reasons for doing so.

Religion and equality

In his recent book on societal and religious development in human history, Robert Bellah regarded equality and egalitarianism as significant cultural milestones. Primates and hunter-gatherer societies had it, later and larger societies lost it, and societies in the post-axial age re-envisioned equality and pursued it again.[49] "The theoretical breakthrough in each axial case led to the possibility of universal ethics, the reassertion of fundamental human equality, and the necessity of respect for all humans, indeed for all sentient beings."[50] Whatever one thinks of Bellah's evolutionary theory, his use of "equality" is indicative: modern scholarship on religion often resorts to equality language when explaining religious history.

Perusing historical studies of many religious figures and traditions, it is not hard to find examples of people relying on the modern notion of equality to interpret historical actors and traditions. Some have cited Paul's Letter to the Galatians 3:28 as promoting an egalitarian social vision that refutes slavery in the United States in the 19th century,[51] or advocates for women's ordination in the mid- to late 20th century.[52] "There is no longer Jew nor Greek, . . . slave or free . . . , male and female. For all of you are one in Christ Jesus." Interpreters like Augustine, Luther, and Calvin argued that Paul referred only to followers' equal status before God, not the total obliteration of social distinctions.[53]

Two 17th-century English radical Protestant groups, the Levelers and the Diggers, attempted to establish communal work and living arrangements, citing Acts 4:32 ("they all shared with one another everything they had") as their guiding light. Marx and Engels identified these groups as proto-communist,[54] and several later Marxist historians have argued that their religious discourse and activities promoted a sense of human equality.[55] Engels also called attention to US groups like the Shakers, despite overlooking the remarkable reference to gender equality, which was instituted in 1788 after Joseph Meacham proclaimed a divine revelation of the "Perfect Equality" of men and women in all church affairs.[56]

As noted earlier, Martin Luther is often cited as a reformer who promoted social equality. The classic doctrine of "the priesthood of all believers" as well as Luther's *Freedom of a Christian* clearly support a sense of equality. If there were any question about whether Luther imagined this equality applying to society, however, his response to the Peasant Revolt made it clear. Luther unequivocally condemned the violent uprising of local reformers and peasants who cited his work to decry their subjugation to knights and princes.[57] In his Introduction to *Hegel's Philosophy of Right*, Karl Marx expressed lukewarm appreciation of Luther for emancipating people's minds, even though that proved insufficient for real revolution.[58] Friedrich Engels was decidedly less enthusiastic, casting Luther as a conservative ideologue who supported the German nobility over their oppressed subjects. To Engels, Thomas Müntzer was the more genuine social radical.[59]

Hong Xuiquan, the leader of the Taiping Rebellion in the mid-19th century, claimed that he was Jesus' brother and would usher in a new Heavenly Kingdom. One aspect of this new world order was that Chinese peasants' social standing would be transformed, away from the Qing bureaucratic state that had structured their everyday lives. Although some scholars have assumed that equality was an "axiom" of the rebellion,[60] the Taiping texts cited in support of this are less than clear. Part of this assumption about equality surely derives from Chinese historians soon after the Communist Revolution wanting to reconstruct "Taiping Ideology" as proto-socialist—a view that later scholars have rejected.[61]

Equality language has been tied up with many other traditions as well. Louise Marlow argued that egalitarian impulses were essential for the first generations of Muslims.[62] As a pilgrim in Mecca, Malcolm X was deeply impressed by what he perceived as equality among diverse Muslims.[63] Jack Goldstone cited the Taizhou school of Neo-Confucianism in 16th-century China as advocating "equality of all men."[64] Early 20th-century Buddhist leaders like Taixu, Shanui, and Lin Qiuwu in China and Taiwan brought Marxist thought to bear on Buddhist doctrinal precedents, resulting in a form of modern Buddhist teaching that promoted gender and social equality.[65] Around the same time in Japan, Buddhist monks such as Senoo Giro and Uchiyama Gudo were inspired by reading Marx to view human equality as connected to the Pure Land and Buddha-nature.[66]

In the 1920s in the United States, the African American preacher known as Father Divine made eating together a central activity in his preaching and promotion of racial equality. Father Divine and his wife hosted lavish banquets where they intentionally seated participants to ensure that Black and White people ate together and interacted. This spectacularly generous activity (which literally bankrupted the movement) was meant to symbolize people's common status before God and realize that leveling in a tangible way.[67] As I argue in Part II of this book, it is one thing to think and talk about equality in the abstract; eating together and physically demonstrating one's convictions about equality are quite another. Father Divine understood this well.

Equality has featured especially in discourse about two South Asian traditions. Among all regional bhakti groups, the Vīraśaiva or Liṅgāyata community in Karnataka is most famously associated with the idea of equality among members. As Prithvi Datta Chandra Shobhi has shown, this language of equality emerged conspicuously in the 20th century, subsuming earlier Vīraśaiva critiques of caste.[68] Gil Ben-Herut has emphasized that the earliest hagiographical texts of this tradition promote an approach of "non-discrimination" toward fellow Śiva-bhaktas, which is often interpreted in modern times through the lens of equality.[69]

Language of equality is also commonly used to describe caste and gender relations in Sikh traditions.[70] Of particular interest for this book is *langar*—the institution of free communal meals.[71] Dating to near the inception of the Sikh tradition itself, this custom of eating together in the temple is heralded as an example of inclusivity, hospitality, and equality. Some Sikhs living in North America have consciously rejected using tables and chairs, out of concern that this furniture will organize people into cliques that exacerbate social differentiations.[72] At the same time, scholars of Dalit Sikhs have argued that the dominant narrative of Sikh egalitarianism neglects the presence of a significant underclass.[73]

As should be clear from this global survey, no single summary can capture the diverse ways in which ideas of equality appear. A pattern in modern scholarship on premodern religion is notable, however. Scholars often cite equality as an aspiration that motivated religious rebels and reformers to rise up at times when traditional social stratifications were being challenged. Whether this truly constituted a struggle for social equality—through a utopian vision, proto-communist ideal, or emergent conception of non-hierarchical society—however, is almost always a matter of interpretation. When describing traditions that take an inclusive stance toward previously marginalized social groups, scholars often summarize them as struggles for equality. Thus, an operation that technically is interpretive slips into the guise of being descriptive. This is understandable for those who want to identify premodern precedents for pursuing contemporary goals, but as a way of writing history, it is hardly transparent.

As noted earlier, references to equality in modern times are no less complicated. Equality can be a philosophical concept, a political aspiration, or an ethical principle. As it is invoked in conversation and media, it is literally a term of discourse. Diverse advocates for equality do not necessarily envision it in the same way. What people perceive in equality as an ideal, and how they understand its relevance to them, is closely tied to the social circumstances in which they dwell. The changes toward which they aspire reflect specific contexts: what are perceived as their problems, who comprises their constituency, who seems to obstruct positive change, and what rights and privileges they seek over against other groups, some of whom may also be invoking equality to protest their own situations. Visions of equality may come into conflict. For those who want to mobilize diverse groups under a single banner, this becomes the challenge of cross-sectional solidarity.

Leaders from different caste groups at the turn of the 20th century appealed to equality to reposition their own relative statuses. Upper-caste non-brahmans and Dalits both criticized the privilege of brahmans, but they did not share the same vision of equality. They had different ideas about what the desired changes would entail, whose disproportionate privileges must be curtailed, and who stood to benefit. Viewed as a discursive term, it is at least as important to identify the context in which equality is invoked as it is to understand what equality abstractly signifies. For example, Hindu nationalists and Indian secularists criticize caste hierarchy and promote a vision of social equality, but they have quite different agendas, opponents, and imagined outcomes in mind.

When it comes to using equality language for interpreting historical religious traditions in India, one common comparative point of reference is surprisingly apt. In the early 20th century, authors regularly applied the label "Luther of India" to saints and religious leaders, including people as diverse as Chaitanya,[74] Kabīr,[75] Karsandas Mulji,[76] and Dayananda Saraswati.[77] Modern scholars now rightly criticize this comparison as ill informed and superficial. But the comparison of Luther and the bhakti saints was prescient in a way that the early comparativists surely did not intend. Modern scholars who viewed Luther and the bhakti saints as potential agents for change concluded with a similar sense of disappointment in both cases: although the German and Indian reformers may have believed in spiritual equality, they did not apply this to reorganizing society. Just as Engels and later Marxists viewed Luther in this negative way, Ambedkar (among others) likewise perceived the bhakti saints.

In essence, this is a rehearsal of the classical Marxist view of religion in society. Marxist critics of religion tend to view it as mere superstructure, reflecting basic suffering and legitimatizing power disparities without changing them. A Weberian approach to religion in history could have interpreted this differently, allowing for greater possibility of religion and society shaping each other. As we will see in the chapters ahead, scholars have had many views on the bhakti-caste question, but I think their major difference in opinion can be meaningfully compared to the difference between Marx's and Weber's views of religion's social effects. In a Marxian vein, bhakti legitimizes and supports social subjugation by encouraging loyalty (Ranajit Guha), or it makes difficult life more bearable (G. B. Sardar). In a more Weberian perspective, bhakti's critique of caste helps unify people into what could become a political force (M. G. Ranade).

Although Ambedkar diverged from Marx in many ways, his assessment of the bhakti saints would have resonated: bhakti beliefs about spiritual egalitarianism did not transform social reality. Clear enough. But what then should we make of all the stories about bhakti saints transgressing caste boundaries and getting into trouble for it, whatever their historical veracity may be? Why do so many people tell such stories, and more pointedly, why do they go on repeating them? We know that Ambedkar was a skillful rhetorician, social reformer, and political leader in modern times, but how perceptive is his view of bhakti as an interpretation of the premodern past?

The notion that spiritual egalitarianism does not change the social order has many advocates among anthropologists who favor explanations that highlight resilient social structures. Louis Dumont is the paradigmatic example of this, as he described Indian society as essentially structured by caste. Dumont set off this Indic *Homo hierarchicus* over against *Homo aequalis*—humans who live in the kind of egalitarian social order toward which western societies aspire. In a classic orientalist move, Dumont hoped that his consideration of India's hierarchical culture would inspire western individuals to reflect more clearly on their own incomplete task of achieving egalitarianism.[78] In an appendix, Dumont acknowledged bhakti as a counter-force or "non-Brahmanic formation" alongside Hindu renunciants and tantric traditions that relativized caste as a merely worldly institution, subordinate to the spiritual path that was open to all.[79] Bhakti, tantra, and other renouncers did not alter the structure of Hindu society, which remained intensely caste bound and hierarchical.

Among Dumont's critics,[80] Jonathan Parry took issue both with his overly stark *hierarchicus-aequalis* binary and his characterization of bhakti. How could Dumont be so certain that bhakti adherents in the past never rejected caste in their social lives?[81] After all, bhakti traditions had welcomed low-caste and Dalit members, which was made possible by egalitarianism in the spiritual realm. Surely, some historical adherents must have connected the dots: "it is hard to believe that the religious egalitarianism they preached was not among the principal attractions of their teaching for the vast majority of followers, or that its social implications were ignored."[82] Following Parry, the burden of proof would seem to lie less with the anthropologists than with the historians.

However, historians have not been very helpful in this regard, often referring uncritically to "equality" to narrate anti-establishment messages in the past. There is no question that insurgent, revolutionary, and socially critical movements existed in the past. But challenging inherited social structures does not necessarily entail promoting equality. Historians thus often take for granted that social equality could have even made sense to someone living in the premodern past. Or if "equality" is an academic shorthand or heuristic for naming diverse protests against social structures, then historians who use the term usually fail to flag this interpretive move for their readers.[83] We have seen many such examples throughout this chapter. All of this scholarly activity is premised on a modern typology of social organization that is left assumed and implicit rather than brought to light and thoughtfully examined. So how might a careful historical investigation of "equality" and its premodern precedents in bhakti traditions proceed?

I think that stories about Eknāth, Dalits, and food offer us an ideal case study, since they very clearly demonstrate the competing values of spiritual equality and caste hierarchy. After all, it was a close, sustained reading of these stories that prompted me to rethink the bhakti-caste question and inspired me to write this book. Observing changes in renditions as the stories were retold over several centuries offers windows into the cultural history of caste—not as it was prescriptively laid out in Sanskrit legal texts, but as it was remembered, narrated, and negotiated on a popular, vernacular level.

My approach

Throughout this book, I am concerned mainly with how the bhakti-caste question got formulated in modern times and what lay behind it in the deeper past. A full exploration of this requires a combination of historical sensitivities. In tracing the usages of bhakti and equality in Marathi over the centuries (as I do in Chapter 3), I am doing something of a conceptual history that attends to how meanings of key terms changed over time. I am especially interested in how the figure of the Dalit appears and changes over time in non-official (non-courtly) sources. In this respect, I am partially pursuing social history, which is attuned to hierarchies, even as I acknowledge the elite status of these sources' authors.

A concern that runs throughout the book is historiography—how the past of bhakti and caste is narrated—and how those narrations reflect the concerns of their composers as well as the earlier past they aim to describe. This leads to a sensitivity to the narrative dimension of history. Narratives about the past are, after all, stories told by people who want to convey something that is usually more than the words alone state. This is especially important in the case of hagiographical stories, which I regard as a narrative medium through which the bhakti-caste question is worked out. In this sense, I again take inspiration from Quentin Skinner (and J. L. Austen and Ludwig Wittgenstein) in emphasizing the illocutionary force of a text. Bhakti poetry and stories not only say things to people and convey information; these utterances do something to their audiences as well.[84] As I will argue in Part II, the illocutionary force of bhakti texts may well be more important than what the texts say.

Hagiographical stories make up the main corpus that I draw on to make my arguments in this book. This is important for the reader to keep in mind. Using hagiography as a source of information about the past is challenging, especially if one is trying to learn about the saints who are the subjects of those stories. The appearance of miracles and divine interventions are difficult to parse through the instruments of secular history writing.[85] I do not aim in this book to uncover the historical people who are the subjects of these stories, if that were possible at all. Hagiography may or may not tell us about historical figures, but it certainly reveals something about hagiographers and their concerns while crafting and recrafting stories. As Massimo Rondolino has demonstrated, one can fruitfully trace the "hagiographical process" at work in iterations of stories over time, by which a standardized rendition of the saint's life and significance develop.[86] In a parallel and more synchronic view, Novetzke discusses the "*sant* function" along Foucauldian lines—that the saint (*sant*) is, at the least, a persona that emerged in the communal and reenacted memories of devotees.[87] I appreciate both of these perspectives and add my own further nuances in Chapter 5. This is why I think that stories about Eknāth, Dalits, and food are so valuable for understanding the bhakti-caste question. The historically tricky and speculative issue of discerning what the 16th-century Eknāth may or may not have done can wait for another day; this book explores how the memories of saints guided later generations of devotees to ruminate on bhakti and caste.

Hagiography is important for two more reasons as well. First, since the stories are about embodied saints and their everyday activities, audiences could use their own bodies as frames of reference for experiencing the impact of the stories. Hagiography is not abstract philosophical discourse, although it can convey philosophical messages. Scholars since Karen Pechilis have acknowledged the importance of the body in the experience of bhakti;[88] I think the embodied nature of hagiography and corporeal narratology is equally important, albeit less explored.[89] Second, since the Marathi bhakti traditions rarely enjoyed patronage from rulers and wealthy donors, their hagiographies represent an alternative archive of memories about the past. (Admittedly, this is not true of some other traditions, whose processes of institutionalization were tied closely to courtly politics.) Novetzke has emphasized the quotidian nature of Marathi bhakti, inscribing the characters and concerns of non-elite folk who were left out of official histories and political chronicles.[90] The Vārkarī hagiography that I rely on throughout this book likewise offers glimpses into a non-official history of caste and untouchability—something that is otherwise very difficult to recover. I thus agree with Anna Schultz, who detects subaltern histories being expressed through song to listeners who are affected not only mentally but through hearing and feeling their effects.[91] An overriding question that guides my view of history and the past is this: how can we understand past events on their own terms to understand what goes into present interpretations of them, while avoiding what E. P. Thompson called "the enormous condescension of posterity?"[92] When equality is in the picture, there is indeed a great risk of such condescension. When it is engaged by figures like Ambedkar, who were historically marginalized, this involves justice and not haughty condescension.

Imagining the thought worlds of people in other times and cultures can be very abstract, and interpreting religious texts as evidence of such thought can be criticized as speculative. I address this by focusing on instances of embodied memory, in which authors invoked ideas and values to narrate a physical event and communicate the gist of those ideas tangibly to their popular audiences. So, the archive of evidence at the center of Part II consists of stories about sharing food and eating together.

The commensality depicted in bhakti stories reflects Indic contexts, but eating together is a global phenomenon that scholars have been discussing for well over a century. As I consider in Chapter 4, since food consumption is essential to survival, cultures have naturally invested it with great significance. Religious traditions develop rules and boundaries to regulate how people interact with food and its life-giving power. Food is deeply enmeshed within economic and logistical networks. When people interact with it by growing, selling, buying, sacrificing, cooking, giving, receiving, and eating it, food inevitably marks people's social locations and culturally developed tastes.

The near global ubiquity of rules that regulate food in societies around the world naturally attracted attention from social scientists, who sought to identify underlying structures and values that inspired these rules. Some emphasized food's economic and material roles in gift exchanges, enforcement of labor hierarchies, and the politics of production and consumption. Others saw food as a means of establishing basic distinctions of pure and impure as a means of organizing communal life. In light of Bruno Latour's actor-network theory, activities involving food do not simply appear on a social stage that already exists; food creates and mediates the social stage itself.[93] Concrete, material concerns, such as what and with whom one may eat, effectively define people's rights, privileges, dependencies, and roles among each other—rendering them as social beings. Food is a tangible example of material that helps constitute social life. Ambedkar recognized this too: the sharing and non-sharing of food and water fundamentally mark the boundaries of caste.[94] For these reasons and others that I discuss in Chapter 4, stories about food and commensality are the ideal sites for exploring how authors handled the bhakti-caste question. It is in food that the clashes of abstract values became manifest.

In the subsequent chapters, my focus will be mainly on Marathi sources between 1700 and the present since Marathi and Maharashtra are exceptionally rich for studying the bhakti-caste question. Chapter 2 shows why.

2

Sightings of Bhakti and Its Social Impact

For anyone who has spent time in or learned about South Asia "bhakti" is a basic term. For well over two thousand years, bhakti has stood for many things, although this has not been always evident to people who use it. In one sense, the word's capacious web of meanings is an advantage. It enables people with diverse interests to discuss it. But this carries with it a major drawback, especially for scholarship. When talking and writing about bhakti, people rarely point out their frame of reference for understanding it. People can easily speak past one another, implicitly having different examples in mind, despite appearing to talk about the same thing.

A single, universal definition of bhakti is elusive—and unavoidably so. As we shall see later in this chapter, this has led some to view modern scholarship on bhakti as misconstrued and speculative, not corresponding well to actual South Asian history, literature, and practice.[1] Others suggest that using "bhakti" to classify people, texts, and traditions risks closing down alternative and more enlightening analyses.[2] Given the wide range of meanings, can bhakti function as an organizing principle for research at all? My experience with the Regional Bhakti Scholars Network has shown me that it can, if we embrace it as a term with Wittgensteinian family resemblances rather than one normative definition. Working with the term in this flexible way inevitably affects how we theorize about bhakti.

To this end, I draw inspiration from Thomas Tweed, who describes theories as "sightings"—to emphasize the viewer/theorist's positionality and to lay bare the perspectival nature of the theorizing.[3] A sighting is always of something at a particular time and place, from a particular location. The same is true of theories about the world. A good theory can spark insight into cases beyond where it originated, but it will inevitably have shortcomings in those new cases too. Tweed demonstrates this by constructing his own theory of religion, based on ethnographic research among Cuban Catholic exiles in Miami. This theory of religion puts movement and change at the center of studying religion, which are important for understanding the community in exile. When applied to other contexts, Tweed's theory of religion

Shared Devotion, Shared Food. Jon Keune, Oxford University Press. © Oxford University Press 2021.
DOI: 10.1093/oso/9780197574836.003.0003

might be thought provoking, require adjusting, or not fit well at all. It would be a mistake to expect any single theory to explain all cases one encounters.

Applying this kind of methodological self-awareness to studying bhakti entails highlighting the diverse foci of people who approach bhakti (classic Sanskrit literature, vernacular textual transmission, performance, living traditions, modern semi-political reformulations, etc.) as well as the various disciplinary approaches that are most suited to each case. Like statements about religion, statements about bhakti are contextual but rarely make explicit the speaker's frame of reference so that audiences may bear in mind the speaker's peculiar scope. As we saw in Chapter 1, the same is true of statements about equality.

Any study of bhakti, from the critical to the confessional, is informed by the particular set of texts, stories, practices, and lineages that one studies. All of these represent specific languages, geographic regions, socio-political histories, and philosophical outlooks. Even the most linguistically gifted and well read scholars can possess a deep knowledge of only a few different regions and languages, such as Tamil and Telugu, proto-Hindi languages and perhaps Punjabi, or a vernacular language and Sanskrit. No one can do it all.

This chapter considers the positionality of recent bhakti scholarship: who refers to it, what they mean by it, and what purpose they claim that bhakti served historically. In the 20th century, some intellectuals and politicians depicted bhakti traditions as forces of social unification that became especially valuable in the newly independent nation. This trope of bhakti as unifying force quickly raises the bhakti-caste question in relation to equality, since the frame for considering it is the modern, democratic nation-state. Because of its already vigorous conversations about caste and untouchability in the 19th century, western India offers an especially useful vantage point from which to view these matters.

Re-envisioning bhakti studies from western India

In constant usage for well over two millennia, "bhakti" has come to mean many things. It appears in classic Sanskrit texts: most famously in the *Bhāgavata Purāṇa* (8–10th c. CE),[4] *Bhagavad Gītā* (ca. 1st c. CE), and even earlier in the *Śvetāśvatara Upaniṣad* (ca. 2nd c. BCE) and Pāṇini's *Aṣṭādhyāyī* (4th c. BCE). It was to these sources that 19th- and 20th-century European scholars turned when they sought out bhakti's deep history, perceiving it initially (if problematically) as something distinct and even somewhat distanced from other Hindu religious concerns.[5] But "bhakti" is also a common noun that non-Hindus found useful. Jains have referred to bhakti while discussing *jina* veneration since at least the 2nd century CE.[6] Early Buddhists used the word to refer to activities that commemorate the Buddha, although they gradually made it a point to emphasize how their devotionalism differed from that of Hindus.[7] Still, in the 11th century, the Bengali Buddhist scholar, Rāmacandra Kavibhāratī, composed the *Bhakti Śataka* under royal patronage in Ceylon, praising Buddhist bhakti as a virtue. This text is taught occasionally in Sanskrit classes at Sri Lankan Buddhist monasteries still today.[8] Literary, aesthetic, and architectural aspects of traditions commonly labeled as bhakti also found their way into Persian texts and received Mughal patronage.[9]

It is now impossible to know whether early Indian Christians referred to bhakti before their contact with Europeans, since Portuguese Catholics in 1599 destroyed a great deal of earlier Malayali texts and records.[10] But we do know that when European Christian missionaries became established in India, they found bhakti a useful and strategic term to translate Christian ideas, practices, and dispositions into Indic languages. The Italian Jesuit Roberto de Nobili used the Tamil *patti* (Sanskrit bhakti) in 1610 to denote Christian devotional activity,[11] such as Mary's *pattiyokam* (bhakti yoga).[12] Seven years later, the Jesuit Thomas Stephens, the first Englishman in India, used bhakti in his *Khrista Purāṇa* to portray the life of Jesus in Marathi.[13] Stephens rendered worshiping the Christian God in Marathi as "doing bhakti," and he routinely referred to the Christian faithful as "bhaktas."[14] Using "bhakti" as a common noun in this way did not imply that missionaries or Indians perceived it as a taxonomic label that could be applied to specific traditions, even if they found those traditions' devotionalism intriguing.

In the first decades of the 18th century, the German Lutheran missionary Bartholomäus Ziegenbalg noted the popularity of Tamil Śaiva poetic anthologies such as the *Tēvāram* and sought out copies for himself.[15] European missionaries and local Tamil Christians such as Vedanāyakam Śāstrī frequently drew on literary and musical components of devotional traditions, adapting them to express themselves while strategically presenting Christianity to Hindu devotees whom they hoped to convert.[16] William Ward, the most prolific and influential among the early 19th-century English Baptist missionaries, highlighted the importance of devotion to Krishna worshipers and Chaitanya followers, but he never labeled their activities or traditions as bhakti.[17] Elijah Hoole, a British Wesleyan missionary in Madras, wrote in 1844 that the devotion expressed in Śaiva poems was "truly sublime" and evoked his admiration.[18] Yet Hoole too did not think to label these Śaivas a "bhakti tradition." Congregationalist missionaries in the American Marathi Mission in 19th-century western India, frequently commented on local devotion to the god Viṭṭhal, Hindu saint-poets, and pilgrimages to Paṇḍharpūr—aspects of the Vārkarī *sampradāy.*[19] Although these same American Protestants employed the word "bhakti" in their Marathi translations of the Bible from the 1840s onward, it was not until the end of the 19th century that they labeled particular Hindu traditions as bhakti.

We can see this gradual shift appearing in the work of the Scottish Free Church missionary, John Murray Mitchell, who was based in the Bombay Presidency and published articles and books on Hinduism between 1843 and 1905. Already in 1849, Mitchell had remarked on the eminent Vārkarī saint Tukārām's popularity among Marathi speakers.[20] Mitchell began systematically working out how various Hindu communities and traditions related to one another, based on his firsthand experiences in western India, including a multi-day trip to Paṇḍharpūr during a large pilgrimage in 1881.[21]

In a letter to his mission supervisor in 1882, Mitchell assessed, "It is not Brahmanism that most powerfully sways the mind of the Marathas;[22] it is a very remarkable form of bhakti—the religion which, in Bengal, is connected mainly to the name of Chaitanya."[23] Two aspects of this statement are noteworthy. First, Mitchell substituted the word "religion" for bhakti, as he describes a distinct set of ideas and practices. In the early 1880s, the idea of religion in the sense of religious tradition was still evolving, as was the term "Hinduism."[24] Probably because he knew it cut against prevailing views of India at the time, Mitchell highlighted the popularity of bhakti over the brahman-led and "*śāstra*"-oriented traditions that Europeans called Brahmanism. Second, Mitchell took for granted that his interlocutor (Rev. George Smith, sitting in Edinburgh) was already familiar with Chaitanya's name through the work of H. H. Wilson, as we shall see later in this chapter. Mitchell felt that these religious folk in western India resembled Chaitanya's followers enough to explain them as belonging to the same "religion"—bhakti. Although Mitchell later published systematic overviews of Hinduism in which he noted bhakti's popularity,[25] he never tried to explain its historical development. The use of bhakti as a taxonomic marker was more thoroughly (if still problematically) worked out elsewhere.

As we see in discourse from de Nobili and Stephens to Mitchell, European missionaries consistently found "bhakti" to be a useful term. It translated important Christian concepts into Indic languages. And missionaries observed the popularity of vernacular devotional traditions among the people they sought to convert. This ethnographic and translational encounter with bhakti differed somewhat from ideas about bhakti that developed in orientalist circles, which were based more on reading Indic texts.

Following Krishna Sharma's pivotal book,[26] it is now well established that bhakti as a taxonomic label for traditions has a recent pedigree,[27] dating back only to 1846 and the pen of Horace Hyman Wilson, an assistant surgeon and amateur orientalist in the East India Company. While cataloging diverse Hindu traditions, Wilson described Kṛṣṇa worshipers in the lineage of Chaitanya in this way: "the whole religious and moral code of the sect is comprised in one word: Bhakti."[28] Wilson may have understood bhakti in its more traditional Hindu sense, as a component of broader Hindu practice, and he may have used the word only metonymically to stand in for something larger. In any case, Wilson's usage was very circumscribed. Although Wilson's catalog described twenty different Vaiṣṇava groups, he used "bhakti" only for this Bengali group of Chaitanya followers. Probably without intending to do so, Wilson set "bhakti" onto a new semantic track, where it came not just to connote traditional Sanskritic meanings but to label entire traditions. In the following century, the use of bhakti as a taxonomic classifier expanded through the work of orientalist scholars in Berlin and Oxford, Albrecht Weber (1867) and Monier Monier-Williams (1875 and 1891), both of whom operated with explicitly Christian frames of comparative reference. For them, bhakti came to signify Kṛṣṇa-centered and Vaiṣṇava monotheism, which they viewed approvingly as resembling aspects of Christianity. In 1909, bhakti's use as a taxonomic category gained more traction among English speakers, as the British linguistic surveyor, philologist, and prodigious author George Abraham Grierson enshrined bhakti with its own entry in the magisterial *Encyclopaedia of Religion and Ethics*.[29]

Krishna Sharma coined the term "bhakti theory" to name this lineage of modern western scholarship which, she argued, skewed understandings in some peculiar ways.[30] First, since it was crafted by non-Indian and non-Hindu authors, according to Sharma, bhakti theory relied on "alien standards" that belied Christian concerns and Western ways of viewing the world. Indian scholars like Ramkrishna Gopal Bhandarkar may have cleared up some of the distortions, such as dismissing the possibility that bhakti arose from historical encounters with Christians, but they still adopted an essentially foreign definition of "bhakti" for indological scholarship. Second, bhakti theory unconsciously adopted one tradition—Gauḍīya Vaiṣṇavism—as representing vernacular devotional traditions generally, despite those diverse traditions not sharing a common theological program or set of characteristics. In its taxonomic work, bhakti theory thus smuggled in sectarian biases, such as a strong preference for a *saguṇa* vision of the godhead over the non-attributive views of *nirguṇa* traditions and Advaita Vedanta. Finally, bhakti theory misled people to chase after a red thread that presumably ran through the subcontinent's diverse traditions and unified them as a single, multifaceted phenomenon. Fundamentally confused but logically attractive, bhakti theory grew out of the text-centered field of Indology and seduced historians with its tidy narrative of "the bhakti movement" that assumedly had shaped South Asia's past.

Sharma's historiographical excavation inspired further research on the modern construction of the idea of bhakti, adding but also overlooking important details. Although Sharma correctly highlighted the roles of orientalists like Wilson, Monier-Williams, and Grierson, she neglected important contributions from Indian interlocutors and authors. As Vijay Pinch showed, Grierson was intellectually indebted to his friend and spiritual cousin, Sītārāmśaran Bhagvān Prasād, popularly known as Rūpkalā.[31] Steeped in *rasika* tradition from an early age in a family whose bhakti roots went back generations, Rūpkalā helped shape Grierson's views on bhakti and introduced him to the treasury of hagiographical stories that Grierson regularly drew from—the 16th-century *Bhaktamāl* of Nābhādās—on which Rūpkalā himself had written a commentary. Attuned to the emergence of nationalist sensibilities among Indian intellectuals, Vasudha Dalmia has called attention to innovative ways in which bhakti was invoked in 19th-century Banaras, especially from the desk of Bhāratendu Hariścandra,[32] whom Grierson also sometimes cited as a source. Hariścandra's writings in Hindi in the late 19th century reveal a provincial slant (although Banaras surely seemed like the center to many) in the process of re-envisioning his particular Puṣṭi-mārg tradition as paradigmatic for all Hinduism and well suited to the task of unifying the new, diverse nation.

In *Storm of Songs*, Jack Hawley picked up on Sharma's critique but traced more closely the twists and turns that brought the grand narrative into being. Although presenting itself as a subcontinent-wide phenomenon, this story of "the bhakti movement" (the singular definite article "the" being crucial) has a

North Indian pedigree. In its earliest form, in the *Bhāgavata Māhātmya* (perhaps ca. 17th c.), bhakti is personified as a woman who is born in South India, grows weary as she travels westward and northward, gets rejuvenated in Vrindāvan, and ultimately arrives in Haridvār. The story held a special place in the *rasika* tradition, and it was from there that it entered English scholarship through the friendship of Rūpkalā and Grierson. When Rāmcandra Śukla translated Grierson's overview of bhakti in 1940 in what would become the modern classic Hindi literary history, he added an important semantic nuance, shifting Grierson's reference to "bhakti reformation" (with its comparative glance toward Europe) into an independent movement—*bhakti kā āndolan*. Śukla thus coined the idea of "the bhakti movement" for the first time in any language. The very term that Sharma took for granted as the subject of her critical scholarship had Hindi as well as English roots.[33]

In a somewhat different vein, Arvind-Pal Mandair challenged the idea that Indian intellectuals, through their own agency, adapted Western ideas to suit their needs. Mandair argued that this "interactionist model" is too static, since the modern concept of religion itself was developing in the late 19th century, enabled in Britain as well as in India by the colonial regime. Discourse about religion and nations, in short, was part of the conversion to modernity that gradually directed people's ways of thinking into apparently stable categories like Hindu and Hinduism. Bhakti theory was part of this larger churning of ideas that changed everyone, Indians and Europeans alike.[34]

Like Hawley and Mandair, I too find Sharma's intervention helpful, especially as she highlights the influence of Gauḍīya Vaiṣṇavism and Christianity on bhakti as a taxonomic category. Her analysis explains, for example, why Max Weber could discuss the Liṅgāyata tradition at length in his sociology of Indian religion (1916) without ever mentioning bhakti, even though he freely used that word to describe Vaiṣṇava groups.[35] Not surprisingly, however, Sharma's argument displays some of the same shortcomings that she criticized, specifically in terms of an unconscious provinciality. Sharma's concern with the *saguṇa/nirguṇa* divide is indeed important in North Indian bhakti and literary traditions. But *saguṇa* and *nirguṇa* were not seen as mutually exclusive options elsewhere in the subcontinent. Sharma does not account for how bhakti and the bhakti movement appeared differently in other regions and languages.

This would have been more evident to Sharma if she had considered the writing of someone like John Murray Mitchell, who observed that, unlike followers of the Gauḍīya tradition, self-identifying bhaktas in western India insisted that a strong moral code was central to their practice.[36] Although Mitchell envisioned a possible Christian connection in ancient history, he did not imagine that bhakti drew its morality from there. Rather, Mitchell linked this aspect of bhakti to Buddhism, whose legacy in the region was also evident in the magnificent rock-cut caves of the Western Ghats, Ajanta, and Ellora. The perceived influence of Buddhism was significant enough that Mitchell called this western Indian tradition "Bauddha-Vaiṣṇava," following the speculative precedent set by John Stephenson around 1840.[37] The Bombay-based Indian Civil Servant Leonard John Sedgwick, in his attempt at an encyclopedic article on bhakti in 1914, highlighted regional biases as well: "owing to the fact that Dr. G. A. Grierson . . . is a student of the Hindi poets, the idea is liable to arise that Hindi is the only vernacular in which there is an important 'bhakti' literature. Western scholars may hardly be aware that there exists in Marathi a 'bhakti' literature, which in age, in volume, and in quality can equal, if not surpass, the Hindi."[38] Europeans outside North India who wrote about bhakti did not always echo their colleagues in the North. While pointing out one hidden (Gauḍīya) provinciality of bhakti theory, Sharma too overlooked the peculiarity of her own North Indian perspective.

What did bhakti do?

As scholars in the past century sought to understand the historical role of bhakti, especially in its vernacular manifestations, they often focused on one aspect: bhakti brought people together in ways that other Hindu traditions had not. But they held differing ideas about what exactly was being unified and where that unification was headed. Teleology is built into such unification narratives, whether it is unconscious, implied, or explicit. Historical narration is a kind of storytelling, and stories must go somewhere. For example, hagiographical accounts of bhakti, especially in compendia of stories about many saints, could explain this unification by appealing to a higher spiritual vision of reality or to a deity's acts in diverse places and times.[39]

It is also useful to distinguish between history written in an analytic mode that seeks to reconstruct past events and understand them on their own terms versus history that is written to mobilize perceptions about the past for the purpose of supporting contemporary agendas. Uncovering what bhakti did in the past is often connected to what bhakti can do in the present and may do in the future. A closer look at some examples will bear this out.

The tradition of Tamil Śaiva devotionalism that centers on saints and poets called Nāyāṉars takes special interest in Śiva as he appears in particular locales within Tamil Nadu.[40] Between roughly the 6th through 9th centuries, individual saints operating independently praised images of Śiva at various temple and described their pilgrimages to them.[41] These were compiled in the authoritative collection of the tradition's poetry, the *Tēvāram*. Some scholars have pointed out that this tradition overlaps with and promotes a sense of consolidated sacred space, so that Śaiva bhakti supported the geopolitical unity of Tamil rulers.[42] Others highlight how Cekkiḻār's *Periyapurāṇamu* in the 12th century interwove these songs extensively with stories about the saints, constituting one grand community of Śiva devotion that is enmeshed in a network of temples, images, and pilgrimage routes, further knitting this space together.[43] Questions about the historical accuracy of these claims notwithstanding, the notion that bhakti reinforced a sense of geospatial unity and community is clear.[44]

At the turn of the 20th century, we see people taking interest in Śaiva bhakti for its potential to do things in the present. After spending three decades as a Wesleyan missionary in Tamil Nadu, George Uglow Pope became a lecturer of Tamil and Telugu at Oxford University in 1884, where he devoted much of his time to translating and popularizing early Tamil works. Pope was well inclined toward this literature because he felt that it offered an alternative to brahmanical Hinduism and caste hierarchy, and it thus could be useful to missionaries who sought to make converts among lower caste folk. Pope's major contribution of Śaiva bhakti translation was not of Nāyaṇār poetry or stories specifically, but of the songs of a saint who came shortly after them, Maṇikkavācakār. Pope's praise was effusive: "Bhakti, or loving piety, is the main idea of the Çaiva system, and the fervent self-negating love and worship of Çivan is represented as including all religion, and transcending every kind of religious observance; and, since all are capable of this, men of all castes can be received as devotees and saints in the Çaiva system."[45] This non-elitism fit perfectly with the non-brahman ideology of the nascent Dravidian movement. Building on this non-brahman ideology, the public intellectual and orator Maraimalai Adigal explicitly drew on the Nāyaṇārs' poetry, as an ancient Tamil tradition whose social inclusivity and non-Sanskritic basis made it well suited to modern needs.[46]

On the opposite side of the subcontinent, bhakti is associated with two outstanding saints, Lal Ded and Nund Rishi.[47] Here too we find scholars resorting to the trope of bhakti as a unifying force. Because Lal Ded's and Nund Rishi's compositions drew on bhakti, tantric, and Sufi themes, they have been cast as syncretic or trans-religious figures who helped create a distinct Kashmiri heritage that transcended Hindu and Muslim communalism.[48] Scholars also cite these two to explain why caste is less prominent in Kashmir than other parts of the subcontinent. Following this line of thinking, Lal Ded and her followers in the Rishi tradition taught that individuals could encounter God directly. Not only was the intermediary of the brahman priest unnecessary, he was an unwanted hindrance.[49] The perceived similarity to Muslim teachings and Islam's freedom from caste (at least theoretically) made Rishis and Sufis quite amenable to each other. So, in the Kashmiri case, people perceived bhakti's social consolidating force as crossing Hindu-Muslim boundaries and hindering caste hierarchy.[50]

As we observed earlier, the historiographical use of bhakti and the bhakti movement was usually a team effort, if sometimes unwittingly so, between orientalist and Indian scholars, each with their distinct goals. If orientalists and British administrators sought to understand and manage the internally diverse territory that they colonized, on the Indian side, the ideal of underlying unity often supported the vision of India as an independent nation. To acknowledge and integrate India's many languages and regions, people appealed to bhakti as a common heritage that India's diverse Hindu (and in some versions, also Muslim) inhabitants shared.

Bhāratendu Hariścandra demonstrates this nation-building concern as well.[51] Although he was critical of tendencies within his own Puṣṭi-mārg tradition, Hariścandra increasingly regarded it as a prototype for something larger. In the reformist Tadīya Samāj that Hariścandra had founded, he promoted Vaiṣṇavism as the center of a broadly conceived Hindu dharma, and he translated and commented on texts like Śāṇḍilya's *Bhakti Sūtra* to demonstrate what supposedly lay at the base of this Vaiṣṇavism.[52] Bhakti was India's *mūla-dharma*—its original, underlying principle that pervaded all Hindu traditions and represented its most ancient and authentic strand.[53] Shorn of any associations with *nirguṇa* and eroticism, and occasionally marshaling orientalist publications to support it, Hariścandra's vision of bhakti would not have been recognizable as proper bhakti by all who used the term. But it fit with his reformist goals of "purifying" Hindu traditions and unifying them toward a national aspiration. Hariścandra operated mainly on conceptual and ideological levels, but he made historiographical claims to do so. He drew on selected texts and claimed that the bhakti expounded therein applied to all Hindus across India, but he never undertook the challenge of reconciling the unruly details of diverse traditions and saints.[54]

Visually presaged in 1946–47 by the Hindi Bhavan murals that depict saints from across the new country all together on the walls of Tagore's Shantiniketan,[55] the clearest invocation of bhakti as a national unifier came from the great Sanskritist V. Raghavan in a series of radio lectures that was sponsored by the Indian central government in 1964.[56] Raghavan picked up on earlier ideas of bhakti and "the bhakti movement" to craft his all-encompassing story. He narrated a transit of bhakti, invoking traditional piety to support civil religion by calling bhakti's journey a *pradakṣina-yātrā* throughout Bhārata: from Tamil lands, through western India, and to the north. Yet Raghavan identified an additional leg of the journey, beyond where the *Bhāgavata Māhātmya*, Rūpkalā, Grierson, and Dvivedī left off: bhakti returned back to Tamil lands at the behest of the Tanjore Maratha king Serfojī II in the early 19th century—seeding a tradition that grew into the *Bhajana Sampradāy*, with which Raghavan himself was deeply familiar.[57] He gently reminded his listeners that bhakti had kept on flowing after it reached the North, knitting India together ever more securely, as it returned to its southern home.

In the background of Raghavan's and Hawley's discussion of how "the bhakti movement" became a prototype of national unity stands Mahadev Govind Ranade, who had made an earlier argument about bhakti's unifying civic power. But Ranade's narrative has a very different orientation from that of Hariścandra and Raghavan, which demonstrates even more clearly the situatedness of theorizing about bhakti.

Writing in English in 1900 in Bombay, as the Indian independence movement percolated in multiple locations, Ranade looked to the erstwhile Maratha/Peshwa dynasty as the precolonial Indian empire that was closest to recent memory. "The rise of Maratha Power was due to the first beginnings of what one may well call the process of nation-making."[58] For this proto-nation to develop, sparked in the late 17th century by Śivājī's successful resistance of Aurangzeb and Bijapur generals, an important intervention occurred to bring together Hindus previously divided by caste. These crucial unifiers were the Marathi saints, who bore a message of social change along with their devotional agenda. In this sense, western India witnessed something akin to the Protestant Reformation in Europe. This reformation, as Ranade called it, effectively "modified the strictness of the old spirit of caste exclusiveness. It raised the Shudra classes to a position of spiritual power and social importance, almost equal to that of the Brahmans."[59] The saints transformed caste-riven Hindu society into a civil resource that Śivājī and his successors could mobilize for self-rule and nation-building.

Ranade's focus on Śivājī, the Maratha Empire, and the Maharashtrian saints may strike some as a peculiar trajectory on which to trace bhakti's social and political effects. Hawley characterized Ranade's narrative as a "mainly regional affirmation," whereas Raghavan was overtly national in scope.[60] This presupposes, again, the modern Indian nation (post-1947), with the predominance of Hindi and political power in the north, as the default frame of reference.[61] Raghavan, speaking in 1964, could think in terms of such a nation. Writing as he did in 1900, Ranade could not. Instead, what we see in Ranade's narrative of bhakti's unifying power is a proto-nationalist view rooted in western India, envisioning the emergent Indian nation as following Maratha footsteps. Viewed from his home in Bombay, Ranade envisioned the nation differently, and the decisive bhakti reformation that sparked this nation came from the teachings and actions of the Marathi saints.

If it seems odd to readers to regard Maharashtra as the center of the Indian nation, this further proves my point about the provinciality of bhakti narratives. They are all sightings of the broader landscape, located in specific places and marshaling local knowledge to think about bhakti as a general phenomenon, and not always accounting for the diversity of other places and traditions. Even narratives about bhakti's nation-building force, with the apparently singular object of the Indian nation in view, are local and regionally sighted. It would not be surprising to find other proto-national narratives of bhakti being penned before 1947, reflecting other regional orientations in places like Calcutta, Madras, Mysore, or Baroda.

Another response to the question of bhakti's historical impact has been proposed by Christian Novetzke, who argues that bhakti's consolidating force not only brought together diverse people but created the very social spaces and mechanisms to do so. By virtue of the performative character of bhakti traditions, whose songs and stories speak to new kinds of audiences, bhakti creates publics. Novetzke cites Michael Warner's work on queer publics in the United States as a model: "a public enables a reflexivity in the circulation of texts among strangers who become, by virtue of their reflexively circulating discourse, a social entity."[62] Bhakti texts may be inscribed, remembered, and read privately, but the real action happens when they are performed for audiences. Pilgrimage venues, *kīrtan* events, and performers' working notebooks of poetry (*bāḍas*) undergird performances physically and materially, bringing people together. These audiences then could be reshaped by the performances they witnessed. This kind of public is thus located between the levels on which bhakti is usually studied: as individual experience and as social movement.[63] Not only did bhakti create new publics in the past, but as poetry and stories of the saints like Nāmdev are presented in new formats and contexts, bhakti continues to create new publics. Although these publics are all prone to their own political concerns, Novetzke suggests that bhakti sentiment tends toward inclusion.[64]

Novetzke extends this argument about bhakti as public in his second book, arguing that a key feature of a bhakti public (in its Marathi manifestations) is vernacularization—the turn toward everyday life in language and cultural references. The two earliest Marathi texts, the *Līḷācaritra* and the *Jñāneśvarī*, exemplify this vernacular turn and were "propelled by an essential critique of cultural inequity."[65] Behind both texts is the genius of spiritual innovators. The *Līlācaritra* relates stories of Cakradhār, the founder of the Mahānubhāv sect, who pointedly teaches his disciples that following him entails disregarding conventional caste and gender hierarchies. The *Jñāneśvarī* was composed by an unorthodox brahman, Jñāndev, who proudly proclaimed that he used Marathi because it conveyed the *Bhagavad Gītā*'s liberating message in a way that was open to everyone. Novetzke argues that both men operated with a vision of spiritual equality that was accessible to all, especially women, low-caste people and the like (*strīśūdrādikā*). This vision of equality did not explicitly call for social revolution, but it enabled people to conceive of new social relations and promoted a long-term revolution. The inclusive nature of bhakti theology, registering ordinary social differences yet transcending them, thus laid the foundation in 13th-century Maharashtra for a different, more egalitarian society in the future.[66] Novetzke points to hagiographies of Jñāndev as evidence that, in either the 13th-century man himself or later memories among his followers, Jñāndev began working out the social implications of spiritual equality by interacting and eating with saintly women, śūdras, and Dalits.

From the late 19th century onward, the trope of bhakti as a force for social unification and integration was widespread. The idea was attractive to Indians like Maraimalai Adigal, M. G. Ranade, Hariścandra Bhārateṇḍu, and V. Raghavan as they envisioned their own projects of people gathering, especially under the banner of the Indian nation. Scholars outside India found the idea useful too, as an aspect of historical sociology to explain a major cultural transformation in India. Yet each of these attempts glossed over the fact that the bhakti they were describing had features that were not universal. It is unavoidable: all theories about bhakti are grounded in specific places, languages, and histories.

When viewed in terms of society and politics, bhakti as a unifying force has been the most important trope. Calling this a trope does not imply anything about its accuracy for describing the past. But in Part I of this book, I want to discern how the idea of bhakti and caste became understood in specifically modern terms.

Democracy, inclusion, and equality

The trope of bhakti as unifying force is essentially linked to social change, either as an observation about the past, an aspiration for the future, or both. This change presupposes a critique, usually of brahman privilege and the legal regime of ritual purity that authorizes caste distinctions. The trope of unification also points toward a rearrangement of social relations. In modern scholarship, words like democracy, inclusion, and equality are frequently used to name this aspiration. But authors' imprecise use of these terms and casual slippage among them can be confusing for comprehending the bhakti-caste question now. It is vital for us to disambiguate these three terms.

Twentieth-century discussions of bhakti frequently refer to "democracy" and "democratic." As Hawley has shown, authors understood these terms to connote two quite different things. Bhakti-as-democratic is (1) representative of diversity and thus inclusive, or (2) intrinsically egalitarian.[67] By way of example, Hawley highlights Raghavan's statements on All-India Radio and in print that bhakti was "a democratic doctrine which consolidates all people without distinction of caste, community, nationality, or sex."[68] Of course, the idea of democratic bhakti has a deeper history. As far as I am aware, the first appearance of democracy in a bhakti-related context was in an article by British colonial administrator Charles N. E. Elliot, as he wrote in 1910 about bhakti traditions in Assam.[69] In 1917, Vasudev Balvant Patwardhan, president of the elite Fergusson College in Pune, passionately invoked democracy in his Wilson Philological Lectures at Bombay University.

> Literature was by the saints of the Bhakti school enfranchised: The literary franchise was extended to all and sundry—to the literate and illiterate alike—to the prince and pauper, to Brahmin and Śūdra, to all without distinction. Literature is and ought to be a Republic. Ekanath declared it to be so in the teeth of the Sanskrit Pandits. Ever since the days of Jnanadeva the gates of the temple of the literary Muse were thrown wide open, and a free spirit of democracy reigned that merged division and distinction. The Brahmans, the tailor, the potter, the shoe-maker, the Mahar—aye, all stood shoulder to shoulder, danced hand in hand in the free atmosphere of the liberalizing tunes of Bhakti. As on the sands of the Chandrabhaga [near the Vārkarī's main temple of Viṭṭhal in Paṇḍharpūr], so in the temple of the Muse, all castes and classes ate of the same dish and drank of the same well. Would that this democracy of Bhakti and Saraswati, of Divine Love and Divine Speech, had continued to live with unabated force.[70]

Patwardhan called attention to literary and social aspects: everyone has a voice, and all eat together. Whether this constitutes equality here is unclear. When Patwardhan returned to bhakti democracy in a later lecture, there can be no doubt.

> Here was the truly democratic spirit. The gates of the Bhakti school were ever open. Whoever entered was hailed as a brother—nay more—was honoured as a saint. He was addressed as a saint. . . . All were equals there. Love-true-genuine-pure love [*sic*] admits not of high and low, rich and poor; all is one and equal. All separatist tendencies vanished; the haughty isolation of Pride, of Heredity, of Tradition melted away, and all were but men, human, weak, frail, feeble, lame, and blind, calling on the same strength, seeking the same love, hoping the same hope, dreaming the same dream, and seeing the same vision. Before Viṭhobā or Dattātreya, or Nāganātha—call him by any name—all were equal. Age and sex, caste and class, breathed not in this equalising air. In the joy of Love, in the bliss of the service of the Lord, in the dance round the Flag of devotion—all were inspired with the same fire; they ate of the same dish, drank of the same well, bathed in the same Chandrabhāgā or Kṛṣṇa or Godā or Bāṇagangā, lay on the same sands, and waked to the same dawn. For five successive centuries, Mahārāshṭra was the abode of that noblest and truest of all Democracies, the Democracy of the Bhakti school.[71]

Patwardhan stakes out a unifying theological position as he invokes equality here, probably undergirded by a nondualist view of the world. By referring to democracy, Patwardhan also must have sensed that word's implicit referent—democracy as equal opportunity or as equal power to represent oneself, which has social and political ramifications. In any case, the theme of bhakti democracy was quickly picked up by other authors who focused on Maharashtra. A popular anonymous book on Eknāth published in 1918 concludes by stating that the diverse Marathi saints' glorification of bhakti "made the movement an essentially democratic one."[72] More influentially, R. D. Rānaḍe, a philosophy professor and spiritual guru, cited Patwardhan in a chapter entitled "Age of Namadeva: Democratic Mysticism."[73]

The association of bhakti with democracy has been around for over a century. Discussions of bhakti in other regions and languages may unfold differently, but in early 20th-century literature in Maharashtra, there is a strong sense that bhakti traditions not only include diverse voices but promote equality of status. For this reason, although Hawley's observation about the entangled double meaning of democracy is helpful, I think that references to bhakti as democratic often gesture more toward equality. I suspect that this may hold true in other regions and languages as well. In this book, it is vital to distinguish clearly between inclusivity and equality, even if modern authors are not always so explicit.

The notion of bhakti as inclusive and representing diversity emerges from the fact that bhakti traditions welcomed women, low castes, and the like (*strīśūdrādi*) into their ranks of followers and sometimes revered them as poets and model devotees. As with any set of family resemblances, one can identify exceptional cases, such as in the more caste-sensitive Vallabha or Chaitanya traditions. And examples abound of bhakti practitioners' behavior falling short of even their inclusive ideal.[74] But in general, there is ample evidence of inclusivity in most traditions' literary and hagiographic canons, and authors emphasized it as a hallmark of bhakti traditions.

The inclusivity of bhakti traditions seems to distinguish it from other Hindu streams. Passages in the *Bhagavad Gītā* (9.32–33) and the *Bhāgavata Purāṇa* (2.4.18, 3.33.6–7, 6.16.44, 7.9.10, 10.10.43, 11.14.2) emphasize that the path of bhakti is accessible to all.[75] Yet other Hindu traditions have also flirted with inclusivity for one reason or another. Many passages within and about the Purāṇas and *Mahābhārata* proclaim that these texts are meant to reach the *strīśūdrādi*, who are not supposed to hear or understand the

Vedas.[76] In his commentary on the *Ṛg Veda*, Śāyaṇa states that Purāṇas are basically the Veda of women and śūdras.[77] In the *Bhāgavata Purāṇa* 1.4.23 and 28, the sage Vyāsa is said to have composed the *Mahābhārata* specifically for *strīśūdrādi*, so that they may know proper dharma despite lacking access to the Vedas. In his authoritative treatise on pilgrimage, Nārāyaṇa Bhaṭṭa argued that pilgrimage is "better" than Vedic sacrifices and donations because people of all *varṇas* and mixed *varṇa* can perform it.[78] He also cited *dharmaśāstra* texts that stipulate that while on pilgrimage, the usual rules of ritual pollution through contact with people in an untouchable state are suspended.[79]

Some tantric texts and lineages promoted the defiance or nonobservance of caste distinctions,[80] as a marker of acceptance among the initiated,[81] as a suspension of conventional regulations during tantric worship,[82] or as a self-consciously antinomian ritual practice for obtaining extraordinary powers.[83] Yet caste boundary transgressions in tantric traditions were carefully circumscribed within ritual contexts.[84] Somewhat related to tantra, militant yogic cadres also admitted people regardless of caste background.[85] None of these examples approaches the consistency and scale of the regional bhakti traditions. What to make of all this inclusion—whether it reflects an uptick of neighborliness or a pernicious hegemonic ideology—is another question that I will return to later.

The word "equality," as we observed in Chapter 1, in modern times is freighted with political and social significance that it accrued through its role in the constitutions of representative democratic states. As a noun, "equality" still implies a referent—equal rights, equal access, equal status, equal representation, equal power, and so on. When applied to bhakti, the adjectival sense of "equality" is almost always left implicit, although its meaning is somewhat clarified by its broader discursive use. In modern discussions of South Asia, such as in Louis Dumont's famous paradigm,[86] equality and egalitarianism function as the logical opposite of caste hierarchy. Whatever else it also may connote in an Indian context, "equality" means "anti-caste." Following this logic, if equality were achieved in India, caste distinctions along with their relative sets of privileges and deprivations would disappear. But this leaves the larger frame of reference undefined. What exactly ought to be measured as equal?

Some early orientalists held that the equality promoted by bhakti traditions overcame caste completely, and in this sense bhakti teachers were similar to the Buddha.[87] Monier-Williams put it plainly in his discussion of bhakti: "every great religious leader proclaimed the complete social equality of all who enrolled themselves under his leadership,"[88] although he quickly backpedaled by warning readers not to imagine that these teachers ever completely forgot their superior brahman status.[89] Henceforth, scholars regularly distinguished between equality in a spiritual sense (God welcomes all equally, or all may equally apprehend the Absolute) over against a sense of equal social status or power. In his influential article on bhakti, Grierson wrote about the Śrīvaiṣṇava *sampradāya*: "Although teaching the theoretical equality of all castes, the teachers and leaders of his [Rāmānuja's] church were invariably Brāhmans, and persons of low caste were not even admitted as disciples."[90] Although the details vary from case to case, this criticism is typical of historical analyses of bhakti traditions. Even the oft-repeated exception of the Vīraśaiva tradition is acknowledged to observe social differences among themselves and position their community amid the caste structure of the larger society.[91]

In my view, scholarship has tended toward three ways of reckoning bhakti and equality. First, bhakti traditions were concerned only with spiritual aspirations, showing little if any regard for the material and social world.[92] So it is unsurprising to find caste persisting in bhakti traditions; only a misunderstanding of bhakti's intentions about equality leads people to expect otherwise. This was the position of Ambedkar, who condemned the confusion about bhakti equality as holding out the tantalizing prospect of social equality that in reality had never been a goal.[93] A second way is that bhakti saints promoted equality on both spiritual and social levels, but the principle of social equality could not be realized for one reason or another. For example, initially egalitarian movements in Tamil Nadu calcified and succumbed to the "decorative charm" of myth and literature over the centuries and lost their edge.[94] Or the earliest Marathi literature contained the seed for conceiving social equality, but the revolution required to arrive there moves at a glacial pace.[95] A third way is more constructive and prospective than historical-analytical. Oppressed and marginalized groups have sometimes viewed specific saints and traditions as supporting a principle of social equality that, even if it was historically unrealized, can now support contemporary programs for social change. This is especially the case with much bhakti discourse around Ravidās and Kabīr in North India, but one also sees attempts to make this connection with Marathi texts[96] and a reading of Tamil history.[97]

References to "equality" may mean different things. Even people who invoked the equality of bhakti wholeheartedly, as Patwardhan did, tended to acknowledge that this word was not perfectly suited for this use: "Would that this democracy . . . had continued to live with unabated force." Patwardhan had to admit that the world around him did not look like social equality. M. G. Ranade recognized this disparity, too, when he wrote that the bhakti movement "raised the Shudra classes to a position of spiritual power and social importance, almost equal to that of the Brahmans."[98] This is not quite equality, but Ranade suggests that the movement was on its way.

Democracy, representation, inclusivity, and equality are modern terms that attempt to describe an earlier time and, in some cases, its continued relevance for modern society. I have paid special attention to 20th- and 21st-century scholars' use of these terms when they discussed bhakti's impact on society. We are now ready to move into less widely familiar territory, in western India, to determine how equality language became widespread in Marathi and to recover emic Marathi terms that equality language displaced.[99]

3

Bhakti and Equality in Marathi Print, 1854–1950

The 19th century transformed popular understandings of bhakti literature and traditions, especially in a historical perspective. By identifying important figures who were involved in that transformation, we can appreciate how the bhakti-caste question came into its modern form, with equality at the center. Some liberal interpreters viewed premodern bhakti as a proto-egalitarian movement from which modern Hindus should take inspiration. Nationalists and literary historians saw in bhakti literature a non-sectarian cultural resource in which Marathi speakers could take pride. Subaltern critics, rationalists, and Marxist historians remained neutral toward this view but argued strongly against the liberal interpreters' view of bhakti egalitarianism. All of this played out in the growing sphere of Marathi print media, which gave rise to new kinds of intellectuals, new ideas, and even new configurations of the Vārkarī canon itself. With a clearer understanding of this, we can begin to recover precolonial Marathi ways of conceiving bhakti's social implications, as I do later in this chapter.

To contextualize publications on bhakti and caste, it is essential to ask: who is addressing whom? In Marathi publications between roughly 1845 and 1947, I think it is critical to distinguish between two major spheres. One was dominated by mostly brahman intellectuals who were engaged in some way with the British colonial administration and its educational system. Their interest in the Vārkarī tradition arose primarily because they regarded its literature as foundational for regional identity. The other sphere grew out of and addressed the Vārkarīs' living tradition. Non-brahman editors published collections of short poems that were held in local Vārkarī leaders' archives—a literary byproduct of their use for performances and preaching. This second sphere of printed discourse shadows the vibrant living tradition. It is easy to see how two spheres of literary production are situated very differently in Marathi-reading society. Fully reconstructing the process by which Vārkarī literature entered the public sphere would require an entire book. It will

Shared Devotion, Shared Food. Jon Keune, Oxford University Press. © Oxford University Press 2021.
DOI: 10.1093/oso/9780197574836.003.0004

suffice for our purposes to note some pivotal developments. Before turning to that, however, some background knowledge about print technology and manuscript traditions in western India will be helpful.

The printing press came to India in 1556 with Portuguese Jesuit missionaries in Goa, and the technology slowly spread to other mission centers in Bombay, Tranquebar, and Calcutta over the next two centuries.[1] Two notable attempts were made to print materials outside the ambit of Christian missions in western India—one in Surat, which faltered in 1674 when the British printer proved unable to fashion usable type of an Indic script, and the other in Miraj (southern Maharashtra), which produced copies of the *Bhagavad Gītā* through block printing in 1805. But for the most part, until the mid-19th century, publishing was the purview of missionaries, who produced texts that they found advantageous: the Bible, missionary tracts, Indic language dictionaries, and grammars. The American Marathi Mission Press, established in 1814 in Bombay, is the main example of this in western India. In 1854, the Americans closed their press, having recognized that local printers could do the same quality work at lower cost.[2] Two of those printers, Gaṇpat Kṛṣṇājī and Jāvajī Dādājī (founder of the Nirnayasagara Press), had acquired their training while working for the Mission Press.[3] In the second half of the 19th century, ever more presses came into operation, some of which were founded by people we will encounter in this chapter. Just as the 19th-century study of bhakti traditions was deeply entangled with Christian missionary efforts, so was the emergence of print technology.

It is also important to understand the state of Marathi manuscripts shortly before they came to print. No exhaustive study of Marathi manuscripts has yet been done, but two scholars point out key features. Christian Novetzke describes the two major formats of the Marathi manuscript world. The elaborate and carefully crafted *pothī* was used for long compositions and often produced texts that were prized for their sheer materiality. The more workaday *bāḍa* was the domain of *kīrtan* performers, who used them to jot down lyrics alongside other practical information that related to their craft.[4] Essentially, *pothī*s served more elite literary memory, while *bāḍa*s served more public memory.[5] Due to the *bāḍa*'s functional form, modern manuscript archives showed comparatively less interest in preserving *bāḍa*s than in caring for *pothī*s. But it was the *bāḍa*s that were most intimately connected to Vārkarīs' social and religious lives, as they recorded the songs that comprise most of the Vārkarī canon.

The elite realm of *pothī* creation has been explored by Veena Naregal, who investigated transcription practices among Maratha and Peshwa officials. Although Marathi appeared as a literary language already at the end of the 13th century, and brahman administrators in the Deccan Sultanates used it as an administrative language from the 15th century onward, Marathi was not adopted as a courtly language until the late 17th century. After that, courtly patrons paid greater attention to innovative pandit-poets (*pant-kavi*) whose sophisticated rhetorical styles required more refined tastes to appreciate than the more popular compositions of the Vārkarī saints (*sant-kavi*). Even then, Maratha-Peśvā courts were more keen on sponsoring the reproduction of Sanskrit texts than Marathi ones,[6] valuing them more as physical objects of prestige than as sources of knowledge and inspiration.[7] In the latter years of Peśvā rule, increased patronage flowed to followers of Rāmdās and to less overtly religious performers of *povāḍā*s (heroic ballads) and *lāvaṇī*s (passionate, sarcastic, and sometimes ribald dance routines).

In this context, Naregal contends that the dearth of Vārkarī saints after Tukārām, and Marathi elites' attention toward Rāmdāsī *maṭh*s in the 17th and 18th centuries, signifies a "decline of bhakti."[8] I disagree. Since Vārkarīs throughout most of their history enjoyed little patronage from local rulers, it is difficult to speak of a decline in patronage. And it is doubtful that courtly trends of textual reproduction are a good indication of what people were doing with bhakti on a popular level, outside those courtly environments. The Vārkarīs have always been more a tradition of non-elites. To truly determine whether there was a decline in bhakti in the 17th and 18th centuries, further research would be required on *bāḍa* production and patronage patterns of Vārkarī pilgrimage centers and *maṭh*s in places like Paṇḍharpūr, Āḷandī, Dehū, and Paiṭhaṇ.

Locating bhakti in Marathi print discourse

Colonialism and British education formed the backdrop against which vernacular cultural knowledge was recovered and re-presented. These conditions, with increasingly inclusive educational institutions, rising literacy rates, and broader access to knowledge through print, had transformative effects on society as well.[9] In the early 20th century, voices of low-caste and Dalit people increasingly joined the larger public, especially through self-published serials. Social reformist ideas about women's rights and the critique of caste became increasingly assertive. All these contributed to new paradigms for understanding bhakti. For the sake of expedient organization, I think we may provisionally distinguish four streams of published authors as they relate to the Vārkarī tradition: liberal intellectuals; nationalists and literary scholars; Vārkarī editors and leaders; and subaltern critics, rationalists, and Marxist historians.

Liberal intellectuals

This stream begins with Bāl Gangādhar Śāstrī Jāmbhekar, who is regarded as the first Marathi public intellectual in the colonial era. His short but illustrious life (1812–1846) spanned the end of Peśvā rule and the onset of British control in western India. Jāmbhekar was educated initially at home from his learned father, a *paurāṇik*. Jāmbhekar's biographer infers that the curriculum must have included Vārkarī poetry and hagiography, as well as literature by Moropant, Vāmaṇ Paṇḍit, and Rāmdās.[10] As an adult, Jāmbhekar's nightly rituals involved singing *bhajans*, probably including those of Tukārām.[11] As the first Indian professor at Elphinstone College and publisher of the first Anglo-Marathi serial, *Darpan* (1832–1846), Jāmbhekar promoted western science and reformist positions on *satī*, widow remarriage, and temple dancing girls (*nautch*).[12] Although he apparently did not otherwise refer to bhakti in his public life, Jāmbhekar organized the first printing of the *Jñāneśvarī*, in 1845, perhaps for use in teaching his students.[13]

Dādobā Pāṇḍuraṅg Tarkhadkar (1814–1882) also engaged this combination of education and reform. As a teacher in Surat, Dādobā co-founded the Mānav Dharma Sabhā (Society for the Dharma of Humanity) in 1844 to promote a new vision of society.[14] His *Dharmavivecan* (Distinguishing of Dharma), written in 1843 but not published until 1868,[15] laid out seven principles of modern dharma, emphasizing that all people belong to one deity, *jñāti* (*jāti* or group), and dharma that inspires ethical and loving bhakti to God.[16] After succeeding Jāmbhekar as headmaster of the Bombay Normal School, Dādobā founded the Paramahaṃsa Maṇḍaḷī, whose tenets were so radical at the time that they remained a secret society. Initiates pledged to abandon caste and then demonstrated their commitment by eating food from a Goan Christian bakery or a low-caste or Christian cook.[17] The Sanskrit scholar R. G. Bhandarkar later recalled how, during his initiation at age sixteen, his body trembled when he partook of this food.[18]

Maṇḍaḷī meetings opened and concluded by singing Marathi devotional poetry from a compilation, the *Ratnamālā* (Garland of Jewels), whose inclusivism was evident on the title page: "These poems of prayer to God were made by Bhāskar Dāmodar Pāḷande for people of all *jñātis*."[19] A common variant of *jāti*, the word *jñāti* can mean "category" or "group" generally, but it often denotes caste, as it did explicitly within the Maṇḍaḷī. The *Ratnamālā*'s poetry was composed by Pāḷande, not the Vārkarī saints. The Maṇḍaḷī thus took an anti-caste position and advocated a new devotionalism without invoking traditional bhakti resources. The group disbanded in 1860 when its secret membership list was leaked,[20] but some of its members and later reformers carried on its influence.

In the early 19th century, British administrators commonly believed that Marathi was an oral and functional language, lacking any significant literature.[21] Within two decades, this changed, as demonstrated by an official writing in 1845: "The true literature of the Marathas . . . is to be found *in their songs*, of which immense collections might be made if sufficient encouragement were afforded."[22] Such a sentiment led the pandit and translator Parśurām Ballāḷ Goḍbole (1799–1874) to publish the first compilation of Marathi poetry in 1854, entitled *Navnīt athvā Kavitāṃce Veṃce* (Fresh Butter, or Selections of Poetry).[23] Effectively at the vanguard of "efforts to canonize pre-colonial poetic traditions as part of the 'literary' past of modern Marathi,"[24] it sold out quickly and was revised and republished eighteen times over the next century.[25] Goḍboḷe highlighted the variety of Marathi poetic forms across centuries, and he included excerpts from Vārkarī saints alongside those of non-Vārkarī and non-bhakti authors without classifying them as such. *Navnīt*'s first three editions contained only poetry and no information about their authors. The next three editions added two long descriptive essays by Pāḷande about the poetry and its authors.[26] By the sixth edition (1882), Pāḷande's essays were replaced by short biographical sketches before each poetic excerpt. Parts of these sketches were drawn from Janārdana Rāmcandrajī's *Kavicaritra* (Lives of the Poets, 1860).

Modeled after *Navnīt*, the *Kavicaritra* was the first Marathi compilation of authors' biographies.[27] Rāmcandrajī's sources included traditional Marathi and Sanskrit sources as well as an English book, *Biographical Sketches of Dekkan Poets*, which was published in 1826 by a South Indian assistant to Colin Mackenzie, Kavali Venkata Ramaswami.[28] Ramaswami presented minimal (and often inaccurate) biographies of just over one hundred Sanskrit, Telugu, Tamil, and Marathi poets. Rāmcandrajī added seventy more poets, including some North Indians, thereby portraying a pan-Indic literary heritage. Rāmcandrajī frequently referred to bhakti in the sense of an author's worship, such as the conservative Yādava minister Hemādri showing bhakti toward Gaṇeśa.

This use of bhakti also appears in the writings of social reformer Gopāḷ Hari Deśmukh (1823–1892). A judge within the British administration, Deśmukh published his copious Marathi and English writing on contemporary social issues in a journal that he founded, *Lokahitavādī* (Advocate for the People's Good)—which became his nickname. One set of editorials between 1848 and 1850 became famous as the *Śatapatre* (One Hundred Letters), many of which translated western political ideas into Marathi, holding up casteless democracy as an ideal for Indian self-governance.[29] Lokahitavādī's occasional references to religion mainly criticized rituals and traditions he deemed obsolete, but he rarely cited the Vārkarīs. In *Jātibhed* (1877), he called attention to the Vārkarīs' abandonment of caste pride and engagement in inter-caste activities, such as eating together.[30] But such references are exceptional. For the most part, Lokahitavādī advocated for casteless democracy and religious reform without invoking bhakti traditions to do so.

In a different vein, Viṣṇu Bhikājī Gokhale (known as Viṣṇubava Brahmacārī, 1825–1871) began debating Christian missionaries in Bombay in 1856, and thus has been called a "revivalist" who anticipated Dayananda Sarasvati.[31] From a poor brahman background, Brahmacārī was mostly autodidactic, supporting himself for a time as a merchant. One biographer claims that Brahmacārī studied major Marathi texts, including the *Jñāneśvarī*, the *Eknāthī Bhāgvat*, and Eknāth's *Bhāvārtha Rāmāyaṇa*.[32] Shortly after renouncing worldly life, Brahmacārī lived in Paṇḍharpūr for three years, studying with Vārkarī leaders and ultimately writing a book that argued that vedic *jñāna* (including the *BhG* and *purāṇas*)[33] was realized in the poet-saints' lives.[34] Properly understood, this *jñāna* instilled both devotion to God and an ethical sensibility.[35] Critical of untouchability and the idea of caste as determined by birth, Brahmacārī still regarded caste as a reflection of moral behavior.[36] In one instance, he deferred to Hindus who arranged a lecture for him and barred Mahār Christians from entering,[37] but he also apparently defied caste by employing a Muslim cook and eating food from anyone.[38]

The work of Rājārām Rāmkṛṣṇa Bhāgvat (aka Rājārām Śāstrī, 1851–1908) marks an important turn in reflecting historically on the regional past. A teacher in Bombay, Bhāgvat wrote, printed, and freely distributed reading material to his students.[39] He drew from his research on Maharashtra's political and religious history to stake positions on contemporary issues. Bhāgvat adopted Rāmdās' term "Mahārāṣṭra dharma" but refashioned it to bear the Vārkarī *sants*' caste-inclusive message.[40] Bhāgvat took a special interest in Eknāth's integration of bhakti theology with a caste-critical social orientation. Bhāgvat summed this up pithily when narrating the final teaching that Eknāth supposedly received from his guru: "In God's house, there is absolutely no form of caste difference."[41] He highlighted Eknāth's "impartial vision" (*samadṛṣṭi*) toward everyone and his role in initiating a "great religion-based movement" to raise Marathi's status without royal patronage—an early version of the bhakti vernacularization thesis.[42] Bhāgvat concluded this essay with a challenge to brahmans: be like Eknāth and disregard caste, or reveal yourselves as orthodox zealots who carry out religious persecution.[43] In Bhāgvat's treatment of Eknāth, we see the most sustained early interpretation of a Vārkarī saint promoting an anti-caste vision of bhakti.

Inspired by the Paramahaṃsa Maṇḍaḷī and led by some former members, the Prārthanā Samāj became the institutional base of liberal reformist thinking in western India. Between 1867 and 1927, it maintained chapters in several cities, counting over one thousand members at its peak.[44] Along with philosophy from the Brahmo Samāj and British Unitarianism, Prārthanā Samāj leaders incorporated Vārkarī saints' poetry, especially that of Tukārām, into their prayer meetings, theology, and literature.[45] Two prominent members illustrate the group's views on the saints in quite different ways.

Mahadev Govind Ranade (1842–1901) belonged to the first batch of Indian students at Bombay University and became the Prārthanā Samāj's intellectual leader.[46] A founding member of the Congress Party, judge on the Bombay High Court, and public scholar who advised the British administration on Marathi educational matters, Ranade's influence was far reaching.[47] Ranade advocated for a "Hindu Protestantism,"[48] and he drafted the Samāj's basic credo accordingly: "A Theist's Confession of Faith."[49] Ranade frequently gave devotional talks that invoked the Vārkarī saints, whose message he termed "Bhāgavat Dharma."[50] Ranade did this to illustrate his own theist message more than to convey knowledge about the saints. Most influentially, Ranade argued that the saints' inclusive vision enabled Śivājī to rise to power to establish self-rule in Maharashtra—something that had obvious implications in a British colonial context.[51]

More than any other Prārthanā Samāj member, Viṭṭhal Rāmjī Śinde (1873–1944) embodied the connection of bhakti and social critique.[52] He was born to a Marāṭhā-Kuṇbī family of active Vārkarīs. His father was away on pilgrimage when he was born,[53] and his siblings were named after Janābāi, Muktābāi, and Eknāth. Viṭṭhal later recalled that his family never observed caste distinctions, and his father partially inspired Viṭṭhal to take up social work.[54] During a troubled period while studying in Poona and Bombay, Viṭṭhal encountered Rāmcandra Aṇṇajī Kaḷaskar, a low-caste activist who worked among Dalits.[55] Kaḷaskar brought Śinde to Prārthanā Samāj prayer meetings in Pune, which Śinde liked more than the Bombay branch that he had previously visited, which he found culturally distant from the rural Indian masses. In 1900, Śinde began giving devotional talks on the poetry of the Vārkarī saints and Rāmdās.[56]

In 1902, Śinde enrolled in Manchester College at Oxford to study comparative religion, having been inspired by Max Mueller's writings and supported financially by Sayajirao Gaekwad III of Baroda, who later supported Ambedkar's education abroad. He grew close to his Sanskrit professor Joseph Estlin Carpenter and his family, who were active Unitarians.[57] They inspired Śinde in many ways, including by bringing him to a Christian revival, where he was impressed by evangelicals' outreach to common folk. This moved him to reflect typologically on how different castes and classes of Hindus made pilgrimages to different sites: Kāśi and Rāmeśvaram drew the orthodox; folk deities at Jejurī and Saundatti attracted non-elite Maharashtrians; and the Vārkarī centers of Paṇḍharpūr and Āḷandī welcomed everyone.[58]

After returning to India, Śinde became a Prārthanā Samāj missionary, traveling widely to give lectures at prayer meetings and service programs like night schools, for which he continued drawing on Vārkarī poetry, especially Tukārām's *abhaṅgas*. In 1905, Śinde founded a night school for Dalit students in Mīṭhgañj Peṭh in Pune, where Jotibā Phule had resided.[59] This led to Śinde founding the Depressed Classes Mission in 1906. When he grew increasingly sympathetic to B. G. Ṭiḷak's nationalism, the Prārthanā Samāj cut ties with him in 1918.[60]

Śinde has received less scholarly attention than he merits, probably because his legacy was overshadowed from two sides. He was not equal to Ranade or R. G. Bhandarkar on a public intellectual level, and his activism attracted less public attention from Samāj members. On the other side, Śinde's eighteen years working among Dalits through the Prārthanā Samāj and Depressed Classes Mission were eclipsed by Ambedkar's popular leadership in the early 1920s. Based on hearsay about Śinde's testimony at the Southborough Franchise Committee, where Śinde advocated for separate voting blocs for

Dalits, Ambedkar (having heard that Śinde advocated *against* those blocs) publicly denounced Śinde for not representing Dalits' true interests.[61] V. R. Śinde thus exemplifies the uneasy place of bhakti-infused social activism in the modern world.

In this liberal intellectual stream, bhakti was not used widely to label the Vārkarīs over against other groups, although some liberals like Lokahitavādī singled out the Vārkarīs as exemplary on the social ethical front or, as Ranade did, as pivotal historical actors. All the liberals here criticized caste and untouchability in some capacity, even if they rarely (Śinde being the major exception) put those words into practice.

Nationalists and literary scholars

Viṣṇuśāstrī Ciplūṇkar (1850–1882) became extraordinarily accomplished during his brief life. His father Kṛṣṇaśāstrī was a pandit for the British and was instrumental in mobilizing support for *Navnīt*.[62] Despite his father's engagement, Viṣṇuśāstrī was stridently anti-colonial. He worked with B. G. Ṭiḷak to establish two newspapers: *Kesarī* in Marathi, and *Mahratta* in English, and he also founded two Marathi presses on his own in 1878, Āryabhūṣaṇ and Citraśāḷā. Cipḷūṇkar published Marathi literature with his own distinctive commentary in the serials *Kāvyetihās Saṅgraha* (Collection of Historical Poetry) and *Nibandhamālā* (Garland of Essays), in which he sought to nurture an appreciation of Marathi and Sanskrit literature. For Cipḷūṇkar, the Vārkarī saints illustrated Marathi literature's emotional scope, but the pandit-poets excelled in creating literature. The saints' relations to caste did not much interest him, as he was quite comfortable with his Citpāvan brahman status until near the end of his life.[63]

The leading early nationalist Bāḷ Gaṅgādhar Ṭiḷak (1856–1920) mentioned bhakti often in his *Gītā Rahasya*, but this pertained not to the Marathi saints but to Kṛṣṇa's teaching about bhakti and dharma in the *Bhagavad Gītā*. Ṭiḷak was important, after all, for formulating *deśabhakti*—devotion and allegiance to the Indian nation. Less well known than his newspaper and political activities, Ṭiḷak strongly supported *kīrtans*, even serving as president of the second Akhil Bhāratīya *Kīrtan* Sammelan (All-India *Kīrtan* Conference) in 1918.[64] Ṭiḷak recognized the power that religious ideas and traditions could have if turned toward political aims. He took special interest in *rāṣṭrīya kīrtankārs* as a way to spread nationalist messages.[65]

The historian of precolonial Maharashtra Viśvanāth Kāśināth Rājvāḍe (1863–1923) is better known for refuting British scholarship on the region's history and collecting manuscripts and historical documentation of the Maratha Empire, but he weighed in on a few historical aspects of Vārkarī literature. He claimed to have discovered an early manuscript of the *Jñāneśvarī* that was evidence of an early version of Marathi, and he used it to publish what he felt was the most original edition of the *Jñāneśvarī*. When Vārkarīs disapproved of this version, Rājvāḍe petulantly threw the manuscript in a river in southern Maharashtra.[66] In an exceptional article, Rājvāḍe applied his historical method to a hagiographic story about the minor saint Dāmājīpant,[67] who was said to have served the sultan of Bedar until Dāmājī enraged him by opening his grain treasury during a famine. When the sultan threatened to kill him unless he compensated for the lost grain, God took the form of a Dalit and delivered to the court a great sack of coins.[68] Rājvāḍe states that he encountered a copy of an official letter that bore the seal of the king of Bedar in the archive of a prominent *kīrtankār*, Sātārkar Mahārāj, testifying that one Viṭhyā Mahār paid off a debt owed by Dāmājīpant. Rājvāḍe viewed the story as an act of poetic imagination that was overlaid on a historical event. God's intervention could be understood more mundanely: "God entered the heart of a Mahār" and inspired him to intervene.[69] Rājvāḍe otherwise had little time for Vārkarīs, whom he deemed dangerously quietist and otherworldly, in contrast to Rāmdās' spiritually energized politics. Whereas Ranade argued that the Vārkarī saints had prepared the way for Śivājī, Rājvāḍe credited the "militant brahman-led revival" of Rāmdās with this.[70]

Lakṣmaṇ Rāmcandra Pāṅgārkar (1872–1941) admired Cipḷūṇkar's use of literary history for cultural regeneration,[71] but he viewed the Vārkarī saints more positively. After studying under Ṭiḷak and the rationalist Gopāḷ Gaṇeś Āgarkar at New English College in Pune, Pāṅgārkar resided in Paṇḍharpūr for extended periods. In 1904, he published an anthology of saint poetry, the *Bhaktimārg Pradīp* (Lamp for the Path of Bhakti). More famously, Pāṅgārkar edited a serial about *bhakti* and Marathi literature, *Mumukṣu* (Liberation Seeker, 1907–1932).[72] Extremely prolific, Pāṅgārkar wrote biographies of Moropant, Eknāth, Tukārām, Jñāndev, and Mukteśvar, scholarly devotional works on Rāmdās, a history of Marathi literature that totaled over 1,600 pages, and several volumes of short articles on bhakti-related topics. Late in life, he adopted the title Hari Bhakta Parāyaṇ (H.B.P., or devotee of God and bhaktas) that Vārkarī *kīrtankārs* used to signal their spiritual leadership.

Respect for tradition infused Pāṅgārkar's scholarly interests. In one reflection on his method, he discussed three qualities that an ideal biographer of saints ought to possess: sensitivity to Vārkarīs' traditional understandings of the *sants* and their writings; aesthetic appreciation of their literature's "beauty of expression and thought"; and an expansive view of history.[73] He thus regarded V. K. Rājvāḍe as a fine historian but refuted Rājvāḍe's dismissal of the Vārkarīs as pacifist and otherworldly.[74]

Jagannāth Raghunāth Ājgāvkar (1879–1955) edited Marathi newspapers in Pune and Bombay early in life, which set him on a course to becoming a prolific author. In addition to ten books on religious and cultural topics, Ājgāvkar became most well known for his eleven-volume series, *Mahārāṣṭra-kavi-caritra-mālā* (Garland of Maharashtrian Poets' Stories), which started coming out in 1908 and totaled over three thousand pages at its completion. This series included individual volumes on the major Vārkarī *sants* and *paṇḍit*-poets, as well as extensive collections of poetry by more obscure figures. Although Pāṅgārkar was no radical when it came to caste, he at least discussed it; Ājgāvkar strikingly ignored caste and untouchability altogether.[75]

In 1876, a boy named Ḍebū was born to a Parīṭ (śūdra washermen) family near Amrāvatī. Disturbed by his alcoholic father and influenced by an uncle who recited Vārkarī poetry, Ḍebū became known for his skill at singing *abhaṅgas*[76] and, more controversially, for eating with Dalits.[77] He eventually adopted a mendicant lifestyle and wandered Maharashtra, performing *kīrtans* and encouraging his audiences to change their habits, especially about hygiene and cleanliness. Dressed in rags and with a broken clay pot (*gāḍgā*) tied to his waist, he became widely known as Gāḍge Bābā or Gāḍge Mahārāj.[78]

Part of Gāḍge Mahārāj's popularity derived from his rustic background and coarse dialect; he had little formal education. Since he often preached and led *kīrtans* that had a community-building agenda, Gāḍge Mahārāj has been called a *rāṣṭrīya kīrtankār*.[79] Condemning untouchability and caste prejudice while promoting education were consistent themes in his teachings. Gāḍge Mahārāj established many hostels and schools, especially for low-caste and Dalit children, and he associated with Ambedkar later in life. Despite not writing or publishing anything, his popularity as a *kīrtankār* was immense, leading to his final *kīrtan* being recorded and transcribed before he died in 1956.[80] It is difficult to trace people like Gāḍge Mahārāj through historical documents, but he serves as a reminder that people do talk about the saints and their significance in the countryside, even if this is not recorded.

In stark contrast, Rāmcandra Dattātreya Rānaḍe (1886–1957) was a philosophy professor who wrote popular books that established him as spiritual guru. Influenced by his study of classical Greek philosophy, Rānaḍe focused on what he perceived as a mystical core of bhakti poetry that he viewed as common to all humanity. Rānaḍe published several topically organized anthologies of Marathi, Hindi, and Kannada bhakti excerpts. When writing in a historical vein, Rānaḍe credited the Vārkarī saints' integrative roles in society, quoting the material on the "Democracy of the bhakti school" from W. B. Patwardhan that we encountered in Chapter 2.[81] His disciple S. G. Tulpule (Śaṅkar Gopāḷ Tuḷpuḷe) (1914–1994) continued Rānaḍe's perennialist view of the poet-saints,[82] while carrying out deeper research on Marathi literary history. Responding to nationalist presentations of bhakti, Tulpule drew a very clear line between the spiritual Vārkarī saints and the politically activist Rāmdās.[83]

Most nationalists and literary scholars shared an enthusiasm about the value of Vārkarī compositions within Marathi literature, but this rarely implied social change for them. This is not surprising, since many nationalists and literary historians were socially conservative brahmans who were less concerned about altering a system that privileged themselves. Gāḍge Mahārāj, who was idiosyncratic in so many ways, stands out as the exception, in social activism, caste identity, and disinterest in classic literature.

Gāthā editors and Vārkarī leaders

When non-Vārkarīs first published the *Jñāneśvarī* in 1845 and excerpts of poetry in *Navnīt* in 1854, they had mainly a non-Vārkarī audience in mind. A few decades later, publishing spread to Vārkarīs themselves, as editors brought holdings of Vārkarī leaders' manuscript collections to print. Aside from a few large independent texts (the *Jñāneśvarī*, *Eknāthī Bhāgvat*, and *Bhāvārtha Rāmāyaṇa*) the majority of the Vārkarī canon are short poems like the *abhaṅgas* of Tukārām. In Vārkarī practice, these short poems were always important, and every saint is said to have composed them. I would argue that the process of compiling and editing these poems in collections (*gāthā*) is the most crucial yet under-studied way in which Vārkarī literature entered the public sphere through print. It did more than make non-Vārkarīs aware of songs that Vārkarīs knew by heart; publishing these *gāthā*s constituted a process of canonization.

Even when *gāthā* editors did not state so explicitly, they almost certainly found the songs in the collections of leaders of Vārkarī *phaḍ*s (camps or groups), many of whom maintained *maṭh*s in Paṇḍharpūr, Āḷandī, or other key places in Maharashtra. *Phaḍ*s have long been associated with Paṇḍharpūr and the Vārkarīs. A memorial from 1273 on the Viṭṭhal temple in Paṇḍharpūr refers to the Yādava king Rāmacandra as a *pāṇḍarīphaḍamuṣya* (head of the camp/group of Paṇḍarī or Paṇḍharpūr).[84] The old and contemporary meanings of *phaḍ* may differ, but the word's appearance clues us in to its importance. Indeed, the *phaḍ* is the most institutional form that the otherwise decentralized Vārkarī tradition has taken over the centuries.

The earliest of the *gāthā* compilations contained Tukārām's songs, published by Gaṇpat Kṛṣṇajī's press in 1867 without a named editor. This is probably due to Tukārām's popularity and the fact that his most important compositions were his short poems. *Gāthā*s of Jñāndev (1891), Nāmdev (1892), and Eknāth (1893) were first published by Rāvjī Śrīdhar Gondhaḷekar, and other editors soon followed suit with their own *gāthā*s of these same saints. Another prominent editor and publisher, Tukārām Tātyā Paḍvaḷ, published *gāthā*s of Nāmdev, Eknāth, and Tukārām. The various *gāthā*s usually had different numbers of poems. For example, Gondhaḷekar's Eknāth *gāthā* contained 4,141 poems, while Paḍvaḷ's edition contained only 2,703.

In 1908, Hari Tryambak Āvaṭe published the *Gāthā Pañcak* (The Five *Gāthā*s), which eventually became more widely used than its predecessors.[85] Four volumes were devoted to Jñāndev, Nāmdev, Eknāth, and Tukārām, while the fifth *gāthā* consisted of poetry by minor authors. In 1923, Āvaṭe retitled this collection *Sakalasantagāthā* (*SSG*, the *Gāthā* of all the *Sant*s).[86] The *SSG* has been reprinted by many editors and publishers since 1923, but in the versions that I have seen, the poetry has remained the same. The *SSG* came to be accepted as the standard (but not critical) edition of the Vārkarī short poetry.[87]

Notably, the three early major *gāthā* editors were all non-brahmans. Gondhaḷekar was a vaiśya and had a long history as a printer before he began publishing *gāthā*s. His Jagadhitecchu Press in Pune published a variety of books from at least 1868. Not much more is known about the man or the press. In one *gāthā*, Gondhaḷekar reveals that he and a partner collected *abhaṅga*s of Nāmdev from holy places (*kṣetra*s) like Paṇḍharpūr and

Āḷandī.[88] Poems by Eknāth were collected from Paṇḍharpūr, Āḷandī, and Paiṭhaṇ.[89] Gondhaḷekar stated his purpose clearly: "Basically, this book is for use by devotees, Bhagavad-bhaktas and others." He supported this effort by also publishing an authoritative handbook on *kīrtan* performance.[90]

Tukārām Tātyā Paḍvaḷ (widely known only as Tukārām Tātyā, 1836–1898) was a Bhandārī (śūdra) publisher in Bombay who attended a mission school briefly and went on to become a successful cotton merchant.[91] In 1861, with the help of Jotibā Phule, he pseudonymously published an extraordinary attack on caste in *Jātibhed Viveksār* (Essential Discernment of Caste Difference), which was based on the 2nd-century Buddhist scholar Aṣvaghoṣa's *Vajrasucī*. In 1880, he began corresponding with Henry Olcott and joined the Theosophical Society when they were still based in Bombay. When the headquarters shifted to Chennai, Tukārām Tātyā became the director of the Bombay branch. He also established the Tattvavivecak Press to publish Marathi and Sanskrit literature. Tukārām Tātyā was known among the Theosophical Society leadership as someone who could be counted on to support the society's projects, including financially.[92] He was less forthcoming about his purpose behind publishing *gāthā*s and the sources from which he acquired their poems.

Tryimbak Hari Āvaṭe (1868–1949) was a Maratha who worked for Cipḷūṇkar's Āryabhūṣan Press before moving to *Kesarī* and eventually founding his own press—Indirā Prakāśan in Puṇe. Āvaṭe worked closely with Nānāmahārāj Sākhre in Āḷandi to publish texts with Sākhre's critical apparatus and commentary.[93] Although Āvaṭe did not author or comment on these works himself, he provided a channel for Vārkarī voices to enter the Marathi public sphere in a way that they had not before.

In the early 20th century, three brahman Vārkarī leaders published important Vārkarī-related material. Nārāyaṇ Jośī (1828–1903), better known as Nānāmahārāj Sākhre, settled in Āḷandī after having a vision of Jñāndev there. Āvaṭe cites him as the source of the songs in the *Gāthā-pañcak*, "selected," Āvaṭe says, from Sākhre's collection of handwritten manuscripts, which he "corrected" before printing.[94] Āvaṭe does not comment on this editorial process or on how Sākhre initially acquired his manuscripts.[95] Nānāmahārāj left an indirect textual legacy by dictating a commentary on the *Jñāneśvarī* to his son Vināyak (aka Dādāmahārāj, 1867–1940), who then published it in 1905 and wrote his own commentaries on other major Vārkarī texts.[96] The *Sārtha Jñāneśvarī* remains very popular among Vārkarīs, and the Sākhres' ashram in Āḷandi continues to be a center of Vārkarī learning.

Viṣṇu Narasiṃha Jog (aka Jogmahārāj, 1867–1920) became a Vārkarī at an early age, after being inspired by a visit to Āḷandī. He became a close friend of B. G. Ṭiḷak, supporting his nationalist efforts.[97] In 1901, Jog published the first commentary on Tukārām's Gāthā, with Āvaṭe's help. But Jog was most known as a *kīrtankār* and teacher of *kīrtan*, having established the Vārkarī Śikṣaṇ Saṃsthān (Vārkarī Education Foundation) in Āḷandi—a school that continues to train *kīrtankār*s today.

Śaṅkar Vāman Dāṇḍekar (aka Sonopant, 1896–1969) succeeded Jog as the Vārkarī Śikṣaṇ Saṃsthān's principal. Dāṇḍekar had retired from teaching philosophy at a small college in Pune, where he specialized in Jñāndev's thought.[98] Cognizant of how to address multiple audiences, Dāṇḍekar wrote the first modern overview of the Vārkarīs as a tradition.[99] Dāṇḍekar's influence continues through a popular handbook of *kīrtan* themes and quotations.[100]

Bhālcandra Paṇḍharīnāth Bahiraṭ (1904–1998) also represented the Vārkarī tradition extensively in print. A student of both Dāṇḍekar and R. D. Rānaḍe, Bahiraṭ was an active Vārkarī who made regular pilgrimages; he adopted the title Hari Bhakta Parāyaṇ.[101] In 1972, he and a co-author greatly expanded on Dāṇḍekar's work on the Vārkarīs to create a book that is the most thorough overview of the Vārkarīs to date.[102] The book helpfully includes a survey of the most prominent Vārkarī leaders and *phaḍ*s around Maharashtra since the 19th century, thus pointing to the diverse Vārkarī institutions beyond the pale of the Pune-based brahman intellectuals whose publications have almost certainly overshadowed other traditional centers and leaders.[103]

Finally, S. B. Kadam was a Maratha from Nāgpūr who, decades after Ambedkar had converted to Buddhism, set out on a quest to catalog what was known about Cokhāmeḷā, having been inspired by a Mahār *kīrtankār* in Āḷandī, Śrāvanabūva Gaṅgādhar Kāmbḷe, who lamented a lack of printed resources on Cokhāmeḷā.[104] Kadam sought practical orientation from Sonopant Dāṇḍekar to set about his task. He spoke with *kīrtankār*s and others who knew songs attributed to Cokhāmeḷā, and he visited Paṇḍharpūr many times to see the small shrine to Cokhāmeḷā near the Viṭṭhal temple's entrance. Once Kadam compiled his findings into a book, Dāṇḍekar contributed a preface and published it in 1967.[105]

Considering the preponderance of brahmans among Vārkarī leaders in Āḷandī, it is remarkable that the early *gāthā* editors were non-brahmans. Following Novetzke's discussion of the difference between *pothī*s and *bāḍa*s, one could speculate that since non-brahmans operated outside the intellectual class who found *pothīs*' literary elitism attractive, they were more attentive to the popular literary worlds of the *bāḍa*s. In any case, we see in this stream not only the practical (if unintentional) canonization of Vārkarī short poetry but also the first systematic representations of the tradition itself in print, which cast it in a quite different light than scholarship by liberals and literary historians had done.

Subaltern critics, rationalists, and Marxist historians

Jotirāv Govindrāv Phule (1827–1890) launched the most sustained, intense attack on caste hierarchy in 19th-century western India, which laid the foundation for low-caste and Dalit assertion movements in the 20th century. Having attended the Scottish Mission's high school in Pune in the early 1840s, Phule creatively used western political and indological scholarship to radically reinterpret Hindu traditions. Many of Phule's arguments about caste resembled, at least initially, those of missionaries against Hinduism.[106] Through his extensive publications, educational establishments, and the Satyaśodhak Samāj (Truth-Seekers Society) that he founded in 1873, Phule was indisputably the leading advocate for low-castes and Dalits in 19th-century western India.[107]

Phule often appealed to a mythic low-caste ruler, Bali, who he claimed was the ruler of India's native people before brahmans invaded from Iran, and who manifested himself elsewhere in the world (such as in the person of Jesus) to liberate people. More importantly, Phule's religion focused on the ethical and rational, inheriting from Christian missionaries the idea that God created everyone, but was radicalized through authors like Thomas Paine (whom Phule first read in 1847 and cited often) on human equality and human rights.[108] Phule condemned the main books of "the *bhaṭs*" (brahmans) who enslave śūdras and instead embraced a teaching that "propounds that all human beings have a right to enjoy human rights in equal measure [*sārkhā upabhog*]." He vowed to fight anyone claiming religious authority to demean other people, because "this will go against the holy rule of equal rights decreed by Him [God]."[109] Phule stated that he would regard like-minded śūdras as family members and "eat food with them without any inhibitions whatsoever."[110] An initiation rite for anyone wishing to join the Satyaśodhak Samāj was that they eat a meal on the Samāj's premises alongside a Dalit, such as Gopāḷ Bābā Vaḷaṅkar.[111]

Given Phule's inclination to clear away traditional religion, he unsurprisingly had little use for the Vārkarīs. He did not directly attack the tradition, but occasional references to individual saints demonstrate that Phule perceived them as succumbing to the same brahman ploys that suppressed śūdras elsewhere. Sometimes, he viewed individual saints as representatives of their respective castes. For example, in *Śetkaryācā Asūḍ* (Cultivator's Whipcord) in 1883, as he provided a śūdra-centric view of history with Buddhists and Muslims pitched as liberators. Phule evaluated some classic Marathi authors:

> From amongst the *bhaṭ* brahmans, Mukundaraja and Dnyanoba [Jñāndev] lifted some imaginary parts from the *Bhagavat-bakhar*, and wrote tactical books in Prakrit called *Viveksindhu* and *Dnyaneshwar* [*Jñāneśvarī*] and deluded the ignorant farmer to such an extent that the farmers started to think of the Mohammadans as low, along with the Quran, and started hating them instead. After some time had passed, a saint called Tukaram was born amongst the farmers. Fearing that he would enlighten King Shivaji and remove the artificial religion of the *bhat* brahmans, one of them, a hardened Vedanti called Ramdas Swami, conspired with the wily Gagabhatta to poison the ears of the letterless King Shivaji, and did not allow any friendship to develop between the selfless Tukaram and Shivaji.[112]

As evident here, a major aim of Phule was to subvert the brahmanical story of India's past.[113] Elsewhere, Phule recounts two miracles that were performed by Jñāndev and Rāmdās, concluding, "these and some other cunning and wicked Aryan brahman saints composed heaps and heaps of new religious books to augment the stocks of similar books written by equally cunning and wicked Rishis of yore."[114] In his posthumously published *Sārvajanik Satyadharmāce Pustak* (Book of True Religion for All People), Phule commented on verses from the *Jñāneśvarī,* highlighting what he called logical inconsistencies and fallacious reasoning.[115] And one of his *akhaṇḍa*s portrays the Vārkarīs rather prudishly, stating that Paṇḍharpūr made everyone crazy and induced men and women pilgrims to intermingle shamelessly.[116]

Yet there are some intriguing connections and oversights. G. P. Deshpande suggests that Phule's blunt style of Marathi resembled that of the saint-poets, since they spoke to people on a common rather than sophisticated, intellectual level.[117] Phule called his preferred compositional form the *akhaṇḍa*, a neologism whose phonetic and semantic similarity to the Vārkarī *abhaṅga* (both mean "unbroken") is intentional.

Phule's focus on saints was uneven. Although he disparaged the brahmans Jñāndev and Rāmdās, he never mentioned Eknāth. He acknowledged Tukārām respectfully, calling attention to his śūdra status, yet he overlooked other śūdra and Dalit saints. Phule's own Māḷī community had a minor saint—Savatā Māḷī—whose poetry drew on agricultural metaphors. Yet Phule never mentioned him nor Cokhāmeḷā.[118] This too is striking, given Phule's association with Gopāḷ Vaḷaṅkar, who we will consider shortly. In a short text that was appended to the *Cultivator's Whipcord*, Phule crafted a dialogue with someone he calls a "Kabīr-panth śūdra *sādhū*" who hails from Bombay and frequently walks to Paṇḍharpūr. The *sādhū* notes Phule's reputation as an English-reading Hindu critic of Hinduism and seeks Phule's thoughts about the Vedas. Phule then leads the *sādhū* through various questions and considerations, including the problem that the Vedas are supposedly for the sake of all humans yet were composed in Sanskrit and available to only a small minority.[119] Phule asks the *sādhū* to consider why Max Mueller, who was well acquainted with the Vedas, did not renounce Christianity and convert to Hinduism. The *sādhū* opines that Mueller was put off by the thought of wearing a sacred thread and bathing three times a day in his cold European climate.[120] Phule's questioning eventually turns to the disproportionate representation of brahmans in British and princely state administrations, and he argues for improved schools for śūdras and Dalits. Ultimately, the *sādhū* requests to take leave, and he departs. In the entire dialogue, neither Phule nor his interlocutor discuss Paṇḍharpūr, Kabīr, or bhakti at all, despite Phule introducing the man in those terms.

Two modern scholars suggest that Phule overlooked bhakti as a potential ally. G. P. Deshpande points out that appealing to "the Bhakti movement" could have resonated with the low-caste audience that Phule sought to reach. He speculates that this oversight may have come from Phule's uncritical association with Christian missionaries and British colonialism, which Phule depicted as liberative in the struggle against brahman oppression.[121] Veena Naregal offers other suggestions: Phule may have felt that bhakti traditions were inextricably connected to the Hindu order that he sought to break from, he may have felt that the modern idiom of political rights was simply more powerful than bhakti discourse, and Phule distrusted liberal brahman reformers who conceived bhakti as a resource for legitimating social change without adequately calling out its shortcomings.[122] In addition to Naregal's intriguing proposals, I wonder if Phule may have seen the Vārkarī tradition as a potentially competing path toward the reforms that Phule envisioned.

Gopāḷ Gaṇeś Āgarkar (1856–1895) couched his reformist messages in strict, atheistic rationalism. In 1881, he started working with Ṭiḷak and served as *Kesarī*'s first editor, although he left the position several years later due to ideological differences.[123] Yet Āgarkar was not aligned with brahman liberal reformers either; he publicly refuted Ranade's and Bhandarkar's proposal that spiritual sentiment was good for the nation.[124] Āgarkar spoke out against untouchability and caste prejudice, which he argued was hindering India's progress,[125] but he strangely did not engage Phule or his work.[126] Āgarkar did not distinguish between the Vārkarīs and other Hindus; in nearly all of his references to the Vārkarīs, he lumped them in with other Hindus whom he criticized. He cited Tukārām a single time, to foreground an *abhaṅga* that condemned polygamy.[127] When Āgarkar did talk about bhakti, the "devotion" that he sought to criticize was to tobacco, wine, and women.

The first major Dalit leader in the modern era, Gopāḷ (Bābā) Vaḷaṅkar (often spelled Walangkar, ca. 1840–1900), served in the Mahār regiment of the British army (as did Ambedkar's father) when he joined the Satyaśodhak Samāj after meeting Phule. The two became friends by the mid-1880s, and Phule sometimes visited Vaḷaṅkar's home in Poona. Phule would test prospective caste Hindus who wanted to join the Samāj by seating them next to Vaḷaṅkar for a meal.[128] In 1890, with other Dalit members of the Samāj, Vaḷaṅkar formed the Anārya Doṣ Parihārak Maṇḍaḷ (Committee for Removing the Stigma of Untouchability or ADPM) to work for the uplift of Dalits. One of the most public manifestations of this work was a monthly magazine in 1888 (*Viṭāḷ Vidvaṃśak*, Destroyer of Pollution) and an appeal (*Vinanti Patra*) to the British, requesting they reverse their 1892 decision to disband the Mahār Regiment that had helped educate and mobilize so many Dalit leaders.[129]

Vaḷaṅkar actively drew on bhakti resources, particularly the memory of Cokhāmeḷā, as a source of inspiration for Dalit assertion. The *Vinanti Patra* set in stark contrast caste regulations endorsed by the *Manusmṛti* with the non-hierarchical devotionalism preached by Cokhāmeḷā and Tukārām. Philip Constable has argued that Dalits' views of bhakti had been "reformulated and radicalized" by their contact with nonconformist Christian missionaries, their literature, and converts like Baba Padmanji.[130] There probably is some truth to this, but it neglects the much earlier influence of Thomas Paine on Phule, who in turn was formative for Vaḷaṅkar. In the

1890s, Vaḷaṅkar and the ADPM incorporated *kīrtans* and Vārkarī poetry in their performances around western India.[131]

Two other Mahār men near Nāgpūr led similar movements around the memory of Cokhāmeḷā. Viṭhobā Rāvjī Mūn Pāṇḍe (1864–1924) was a business leader who, with help from a Scottish missionary, defied brahman obstructions to build for Mahārs a Cokhāmeḷā shrine in 1924 in the town of Rāmṭek.[132] Kisan Fāgū Bansoḍe (1879–1946) led a similar movement to honor Cokhāmeḷā in Nāgpūr, establishing shrines and other institutions in Cokhā's name. Bansoḍe joined the Satyaśodhak Samāj in 1905, at V. R. Śinde's behest. In the 1920s and 1930s, Bansoḍe went on pilgrimage to Paṇḍharpūr and collected Cokhāmeḷā's poetry. He also composed his own poetry as well as a play about Cokhāmeḷā[133] and was active in a performance troupe (*jalsa*) of the Satyaśodhak Samāj.[134] When Ambedkar called for Mahārs to abandon Cokhāmeḷā as a guiding light, Bansoḍe strongly disagreed, leading to a split between the two men.

B. R. Ambedkar (Bhīmrao Rāmjī Ambeḍkar) (1891–1956) profoundly shaped modern perspectives on caste in all of India, to say nothing of bhakti and caste in Maharashtra. Much has been written about Ambedkar's life and leadership of Dalit movements in India, his political decisions as he led the drafting of the Indian constitution, and his conversion to Buddhism shortly before his death.[135] I restrict my focus to his connections to bhakti.

When Ambedkar's father served in the Mahār Regiment of the British Army, he was known to be a follower of Kabīr. As Valerian Rodrigues has noted, "Kabīr" in this setting was not only an object of devotion but a name under which Dalits could organize.[136] The popular image of Ambedkar is that he was a strident critic of all Hindu traditions, bhakti traditions included, and there is solid evidence of this. Ambedkar discouraged his first wife from making pilgrimage to Paṇḍharpūr,[137] and he declined an invitation to be the guest of honor when a Mahār community opened a temple to Cokhāmeḷā near Pune. Ambedkar replied that such a temple was not helpful, but he would attend if they dedicated the temple to the Buddha instead.[138] Ambedkar's writings demonstrate little interest in saints aside from Cokhāmeḷā. Although Ambedkar respected the memory of Cokhāmeḷā, he criticized what he viewed as Cokhā's resignation to his lot in life. Like Phule, Ambedkar doubted brahman liberal reformers like Ranade and their speeches against caste that did not result in action,[139] although Ambedkar agreed with Ranade's assessment of the saints as a historical unifying force. "One can say that generally speaking, History bears out the proposition that political revolutions have always been preceded by social and religious revolutions. The religious Reformation started by Luther was the precursor of the political emancipation of the European people. . . . The political revolution led by Shivaji was preceded by the religious and social reform brought about by the saints of Maharashtra."[140]

Ambedkar dissented from Gandhi's hope to alter Hindu prejudices against Dalits while not allowing Dalits to represent themselves. It was in his rebuttal of Gandhi's critique of his *Annihilation of Caste* that Ambedkar's longest reflection on the Vārkarīs came, a part of which we encountered in Chapter 1.

> With regard to the saints, one must admit that howsoever different and elevating their teachings may have been as compared to those of the merely learned, they have been lamentably ineffective. They have been ineffective for two reasons. Firstly, none of the saints ever attacked the Caste System. On the contrary—they were staunch believers in the System of Castes. Most of them lived and died as members of the castes to which they respectively belonged. So passionately attached was Jnyandeo to his status as a Brahmin that when the Brahmins of Paithan would not admit him to their fold, he moved heaven and earth to get his status as a Brahmin recognized by the Brahmin fraternity. And even the saint Eknath, who now figures in the film *Dharmatma* as a hero for having shown the courage to touch the untouchables and dine with them, did so not because he was opposed to Caste and Untouchability, but because he felt that the pollution caused thereby could be washed away by a bath in the sacred waters of the river Ganges. The saints have never, according to my study, carried on a campaign against Caste and Untouchability. They were not concerned with the struggle between men. They were concerned with the relation between man and God. They did not preach that all men were equal. They preached that all men were equal in the eyes of God—a very different and a very innocuous proposition, which nobody can find difficult to preach or dangerous to believe in.[141]

For Ambedkar, the bhakti-caste question was not difficult to answer; the answer was negative. As we shall see in the next two chapters, Ambedkar was selective about which details he cited, such as about Eknāth's transgressive commensality and subsequent purification.

Yet Ambedkar was not dismissive of bhakti saints in all senses. He dedicated *The Untouchables: Who They Were and Why They Became Untouchable* in 1943 to the memory of three Dalit saints: Nandanār, Cokhāmeḷā, and Ravidās.[142] In 1952, he sent a letter congratulating a newly opened center of bhakti-related research, writing, "I am happy to know that there has come into existence the Eknath Research Society in Aurangabad. In my young days I was very fond of the literary works of the Maharashtra Saints and I can say how great a contribution the reading of this literature can make to the moral rearmament of man. I wish the Society every success and can promise all help from the Peoples Education Society."[143] An associate of Ambedkar, Sohanlāl Śārī, testified to his fondness for the saints' literature, recalling that Ambedkar often recited and translated verses from the *Jñāneśvarī* for him.[144]

Nearly fifty years after M. G. Ranade theorized that the saints' anti-caste message helped Hindus unify, Marxist historians reconsidered bhakti's social historical effects. Bāḷkṛṣṇa Raṅgarāv Suṇṭhaṇkar stated that the Vārkarī saints were social reformers (*samāj sudhārak*) who constituted a movement or agitation (*caḷvaḷ*) that opposed brahmans' monopoly of religious and social power,[145] and he marshaled citations of poetry as evidence. Unlike Ranade, Suṇṭhaṇkar issued a blunt assessment: the movement failed to overthrow the old social order, and it no longer could be turned to for inspiration. "In my opinion, whatever role the *Bhāgavat Dharma* played in history, it has now run out."[146]

Two years later, historian Gaṅgādhar Bāḷkṛṣṇa Sardar followed up, arguing that Ranade had been too coy about the conservative sentiments in some saints' writings.[147] In Sardar's opinion, the saints never sought to overthrow caste society, because they realized that the upper castes' economic and material advantage was too great to overcome. Instead, echoing Marx, Sardar argued that the saints merely softened the harshness of caste divisions,[148] although they did sow seeds that would come to fruition later. In Sardar's opinion, Eknāth's transgression of caste boundaries made him "the true founder of Maharashtra's school of liberal and moderate thought."[149]

In the mid-1950s, Damodar Dharmanand (D. D.) Kosambi introduced Marxist historiography to India in a more sustained and explicit way.[150] His reflections on bhakti appeared in a book chapter in 1962, "The Social Functions of Bhakti," in which he zeroed in on the *Bhagavad Gītā*. "The utility of the *Gītā* derives from its peculiar fundamental defect, namely dexterity in seeming to reconcile the irreconcilable. . . . This slippery opportunism characterizes the whole book."[151] This fatal flaw extended to the *Jñāneśvarī*, as well as to the entire Vārkarī tradition that revered that book. "The conglomerate *Gītā* might provide a loophole for innovation but never the analytical tools necessary to make a way out of the social impasse."[152] But the *Gītā*'s promotion of devotion did help create loyal subjects to feudal governments.[153] When Ranajit Guha labeled bhakti an "ideology of subjugation par excellence," he essentially reiterated Kosambi's Marxist critique of the Vārkarīs and applied it to Bengal.[154] The Vārkarīs could minimize caste difference during their pilgrimages, but they never challenged the feudal order and they even relied on patronage themselves in later years, which diverted them from becoming a "democratic movement."[155] To Kosambi, the *Jñāneśvarī* and other poetry held aesthetic value but ought not be used for anything else.[156]

Two Pune-based brahman intellectuals who joined the *vārī* and wrote about their experiences reinforced the idea that bhakti failed to effect social equality. Irawati Karve, a sociologist at the University of Pune, described her pilgrimage experience in 1951, highlighting ways in which entire traveling troupes (*dindī*s) that she observed were segregated by caste.[157] Marathi novelist D. B. Mokashi wrote an entire book, *Pālkhī* (Palanquin), about his pilgrimage experience in 1961.[158] He noted ways in which caste persisted among the Vārkarīs, contrary to the popular notion that they had transcended it. Both authors walked with the Tukārām and Jñāndev palanquins from Āḷandi to Paṇḍharpūr, which is often assumed (wrongly) to be the entire pilgrimage rather than a major branch of it.[159] As secular humanists, both were also socially removed from the world of the Vārkarīs, and they sought to recast the tradition as Maharashtrian heritage endangered by growing urbanization.

Eleanor Zelliot came to study bhakti only after she was well established as a scholar of Ambedkar.[160] Roughly a fifth of her 133 publications between 1956 and 2016 pertained to bhakti, caste, and untouchability. She thus paid special attention to Cokhāmeḷā and Eknāth. Cokhāmeḷā interested her as a figure of history and memory,[161] a predecessor of modern Dalit poets,[162] and a point of pride for contemporary Dalits (including Buddhists) when viewing an otherwise troubled and difficult past.[163] Zelliot's interest in Eknāth was sparked by stories of his interactions with Mahārs,[164] as well as by his metaphorical drama-poems (*bhārūḍ*s) that represent socially marginal characters, including Mahārs.[165] Yet Zelliot still noted that Eknāth never unequivocally condemned caste.[166] Ultimately, she regarded Eknāth and Cokhāmeḷā as "a potential reservoir of ideas and models that are latently shared by most Maharashtrians, that could be drawn on for urging change in the future."[167]

Jayant Lele shared this sober analysis and reluctance to foreclose on future possibilities.[168] He suggested that Vārkarī leaders tended to be "enthralled" by the "poetic merit" of *sant* literature rather than the *sants*' challenging social messages.[169] Lele practically if implicitly contradicts Kosambi, who perceived the aesthetic realm as the only valid modern engagement with saint literature; Lele perceived exclusively aesthetic engagement as a problem. In 1989, Lele and Rajendra Singh questioned whether Ambedkar and Dalits who followed him had, in asserting the uniqueness of Dalit experience, too quickly disassociated themselves from other caste-critical voices in Maharashtra. Ambedkar's critique that the Vārkarī saints had not preached equality was an anachronistic judgment, which uncharitably did not take into account the context in which the saints lived.[170] If contemporary Dalits could explore the Vārkarī saints' critical messages that were grounded in quotidian life, they may discover "far greater affinity" than they have yet admitted.[171]

Other scholar-activists have tried to reconsider and recover the radicality of some saints' teachings. Aṇṇasaheb Hariī Sāḷuṅkhe, a Sanskrit professor and Satyaśodhak Samāj member, initiated this recent trend in his book *Vidrohī Tukārām* (Tukārām the Rebel),[172] arguing that Vārkarīs have forgotten Tukārām's social critique by emphasizing spiritual platitudes. The most controversial of these elements was an oral tradition among some non-brahmans that Tukārām did not get carried off to heaven, as tradition has it, but was murdered by resentful brahmans.[173] Gail Omvedt and Bhārat Pāṭaṅkar translated a selection of Tukārām's poetry into English that they argue reflects this vision of Tukārām as radical social critic.[174] Along these lines, Dalit studies scholar Śaṅkarrāo Kharāt reads Cokhāmeḷā in a more revolutionary light as well.[175]

This stream of critical and Marxist thinkers represents the most incisive critiques of the Vārkarīs, both in what they are perceived to have accomplished historically and in how they were represented by the liberals. The formulation of the Vārkarīs as a failed social movement comes most clearly into view among these scholars. This is important to recognize, since for most scholars outside Maharashtra and non-Marathi readers, the people in this stream are the main conduit of information about the Vārkarīs.

Antecedents of equality

Equality in a social sense appears to have entered Marathi discourse explicitly in the late 19th century, when reformers like Āgarkar began using the word *samatā* to refute caste in ways that hearkened explicitly to western ideas of equality. Phule probably had a sense of this equality in the mid-19th century already, under Thomas Paine's influence, without applying a Marathi word to it. Earlier authors challenged caste hierarchy in ways that contemporary scholars often describe as arguments for equality. These scholars were not necessarily wrong, but we should acknowledge that this was an act of *interpretation*. Casting earlier concepts as promoting equality obscures them. Greater precision and sensitivity about those terms helps us see how the modern question of bhakti and caste became shaped as it was.

Dādobā Pāṇḍuraṅg challenged caste directly in the sixth tenet of his *Dharmavivecan* in 1843: the human race is of one caste/kind (*manuṣyamātrācī ek jñāti*).[176] He then named the four *varṇa*s as examples of *jñāti*s and argued that only differences (*bhed*) of virtue and merit differentiated people.[177] Although many people think that caste was created by God (*iśvarkṛt*) to govern who one eats with and marries, in fact this is only imagined (*kalpit*) by humans.[178] Cows and dogs have obviously different body shapes and dispositions, but there are no such differences among people of different castes. No caste exclusively possesses special abilities; with truly open eyes, one could observe that brahmans are not naturally wiser than śūdras.[179] Pāṇḍuraṅg discusses this at great length but still returns to the assertion that humans all belong to a single *jñāti*. To argue against caste distinctions, he rejects the multiplicity of castes, but he does not invoke western thinkers or western historical precedents to do so.

Already in 1847, Jotibā Phule was acquainted with Paine's *Rights of Man* and cited him alongside references to the revolutions of America, France, and Russia. To translate "right" into Marathi, Phule consistently used the Sanskritic term *adhikāra* (right, authority, or qualification). He was not so direct in translating equality or equal, however. Phule denounced caste difference (*jātibhed*) often, and his writings extensively condemned the brahmans whom he held responsible for creating the system. Less ready at hand was a Marathi term to denote the kind of social organization that would exist after *jātibhed* was gone. Phule resorted to the word *sārkhā* (same, like, similar) to describe humans, which translators of his works often rendered, along with critiques of *jātibhed*, with the English word "equality." It is indeed justifiable to reinsert equality into translations of Phule's writings, since his own views on the matter had been inspired by Paine's English writings, which explicitly referred to human equality and equal rights. But this may make it difficult to appreciate Phule's challenge in communicating his ideas to fellow Indians who were unfamiliar with Paine and western history. A Marathi word to designate the opposite of caste hierarchy perhaps was not clear to Phule himself.

When Lokahitavādī discussed Vārkarīs' relation to caste in *Jātibhed* (1877), he resorted to negation: the Vārkarīs did not heed caste (*mān dilā nāhī*). So far as I am aware, he did not posit a name for their alternative social arrangement. The closest he comes to such a positive assertion is in describing Eknāth: "He possessed impartial vision [*samadṛṣṭī*], and he regarded God as existing in all places."[180]

Only in Āgarkar's writing in the late 1880s and early 1890s, do we see a Marathi word get regularly used for equality. Āgarkar argues that reform will create *samatā* in society out of the *asamatā* that characterized unreformed societies.[181] The French Revolution was clearly on Āgarkar's mind when he uses these terms: "Disregard the ignorance-laden notion of *dharma*, that one meets with contentment in Paramātman or (one) obtains heaven after death through ancestral rites or shaving one's head. Hold on to the *dharma* that says protecting and preserving the common virtues of liberty, equality, and fraternity [*svātantrya, samatā, karuṇā*] lead to the happiness of all while on this worldly pilgrimage."[182]

Pāṇḍuraṅg, Phule, and Lokhitavādī had not employed this term, but from the time of Āgarkar onward, *samatā* regularly was used to translate equality. Whether 19th-century authors referred to *samatā* or not, all reckoned with *jātibhed*. Those who critiqued it pointed toward an antithesis of caste hierarchy, even if a word for it remained elusive. By the early 1930s, Ambedkar's reproach of Hinduism's inequality made good sense conceptually, whatever people thought about his assessment. As important as this critique of inequality was (and is) in India, we should note that similar conclusions about religion and inequality were being reached in many places around the world at that time. Language of equality and religion, their fraught historical relationship, and the frequent sense of disappointment that came from casting religious history as failed movements for social change were all symptomatic of societies adapting to social scientific terms, political change, and the conditions of modernity.

But what existed in Marathi bhakti discourse *before* even the notion of equality was received by Maharashtrians in the mid-19th century? This may seem like a strange question to ask, considering how frequently scholars have applied the term to describe the past. Two questionable assumptions may underlie this application. One might assume that equality is a timeless, universal concept, even if people had no word for it. As I argued in Chapter 1 and earlier in this chapter, this is not true. A somewhat more sensitive presumption could be that medieval Indian thinkers used terms that can be meaningfully translated by "equality." As we shall see shortly, I do not think this is quite right either, at least among the Vārkarī authors. This is not to imply that there was anything deficient about their intellects or imaginations; on the contrary, medieval Indian thinkers simply had a different conceptual toolkit with which they conceived and aspired to idealized social relations. Quentin Skinner's warning about the mythology of doctrines applies to this point; we ought not assume that a notion that is standard to us now was present in a nascent state earlier in the Indian past. I believe that a crucial conceptual translation occurs when rendering precolonial Marathi thought into modern English and Marathi. Some things are lost in the process of translation, but as Paul Ricoeur argued about the productive dynamism of Hebrew thought being reconstrued in Greek conceptual space,[183] translation also opens new horizons of meaning. To appreciate what this translation involved, it is important to get a sense of the thought-world of precolonial Vārkarīs and four Sanskrit terms that they regularly used to talk about religion and society: *strīśūdrādi*, *janī janārdana*, *neti neti*, and a set of words that begin with *sama-*.

Novetzke helpfully called attention to the compound *strīśūdrādika* (women, śūdras, and the like) in the *Jñāneśvarī*, arguing that it marks a vernacular turn of authors' attention toward non-elite, quotidian life. Novetzke cites the appearance of the compound in some of the *Purāṇas*, which he also views as examples of vernacularization in the Sanskrit literary register.[184] *Śtrīśudrādika* and its semantically identical twin *strīśūdrādi* are important taxonomic terms, demarcating a class of people on the basis of their exclusion from a group that is afforded religious, social, and legal privileges—men of the three upper castes. I think there is a bit more going on with this term, however.

As noted in Chapter 2, many Sanskrit texts argue for the propriety of *strīśūdrādi* having access to non-Vedic literature to gain important knowledge. Vyāsa composed the *Mahābhārata* for this purpose, and Śāyana stated that the *Purāṇas* were the *strīśūdrādi*'s Veda. The *Bhāgavat*, *Devi*, and *Narada Purāṇas* all assert that their purpose is to reach the *strīśūdrādi*.[185] The *Narasiṃha Purāṇa* states that it is even a duty of śūdras to listen to the *Purāṇas*.[186]

Others viewed this newfound accessibility as troublesome. The late 14th-century scholar Rāmādvaya argued that since the Purāṇas were the domain of the *strīśūdrādika*, brahman males ought not read them but rely on the Vedas.[187] Medieval manuals on conduct of śūdras also included discussions about the extent of the *strīśūdrādi*'s rights to hear, study, and interpret the *Purāṇas*, and whether these rights remained intact when brahmans were present.[188] As these texts debated rights and access, they still assumed that brahman men were the superior point of reference.

The appearance of *strīśūdrādi* in the *Jñāneśvarī* is different. Sanskrit texts distinguished this "everyone else" from the twice-born males who were authors' actual concern and audience. Jñāndev argues that his text's universal accessibility is no mere afterthought or accommodation to the karmically less fortunate. Accessibility is the distinguishing feature that makes the *Bhagavad Gītā*—especially Jñāndev's Marathi rendition—better than the Vedas.[189] Other Vārkarī authors continued viewing accessibility as a top criterion for judging the worth of a religious text. Intriguingly, however, *strīśūdrādika* was not a common concept in the songs of the Vārkarī poets. Although the term is valuable in illustrating a shift in attitudes from the Sanskrit *Purāṇas* to the Marathi *Jñāneśvarī*, far more often, the Vārkarī poets (and/or those who transmitted and then inscribed their poetry) resorted to other ideas.

More explicitly theological is a term that associates the mass of people with God—*janī janārdana* (God in/among people) and less often, *jana janārdana* (God is/as people). In their dictionary of Old Marathi, Feldhaus and Tulpule define *janīṃ janārdana* as "*janasvarūp parameśvar*; God in the form of people,"[190] and they cite two exemplary occurrences in early Vārkarī poetry, by Jñāndev's brother Sopān and by Nāmdev. This is only the tip of the iceberg. Nearly all the Vārkarī saints have poems that incorporate *janī janārdana* or a closely related construction like *sarva janārdana* or *avghā janārdana* (everything is Janārdana), which indicates God's permeation of the world. In searching the *SSG*, I was able to find this term attributed to Nivṛtti (in 10 poems), Sopān (2 poems), Jñāndev (1), Muktābāī (1), Nāmdev (14), Eknāth (16), Tukārām (5), and Niḷobā (3). And these numbers are a minimal estimate; I surely missed some instances in the *SSG*, which commonly exceeds 2,500 printed pages. Of these fifty-three poems, some employ the idea of a pervasive Janārdana, with slightly different nuances, such as this poem from Nāmdev (*SSG* #804):

> The glory of the Vedas is *janī janārdana*. There's no other teaching in them.
>
> Hold on to compassion for all beings. Wholehearted *bhakti* is what you should do.

> Everything, in essence, is truly Brahman. There's nothing else that we see.
> Nāma says, "Powerful is our knowledge [*ved*], always reciting the name of Rāmkṛṣna."

As we will see in Chapter 5, *janī janārdana* was an important term that hagiographers used to describe Eknāth, either his perception of God among the people that moved him to compassion, or his *being* God among the people himself, by virtue of his deeds.

Such a sacralization of "the people," which amplifies Novetzke's argument about vernacularization, not only calls attention to the masses but envisions them as something that can be mobilized. M. G. Ranade picked up on this when he argued that the saints overcame caste divisions and enabled Śivājī to draw on their united forces. Throughout the 20th century in Marathi and Hindi (and probably other languages), Indians have casually referred to *janatā janārdan* in a political sense to connote the power of voters in a democracy.[191] The idea that the majority population is "sacred" could be useful to Hindu nationalists, as is apparent in two Maharashtrian examples: the non-brahman activist K. S. Thackeray (Keśav Sītārām Ṭhākre) and the second director of the Rāṣṭrīya Svayamsevak Sāṅgh (RSS) Mādhav Sadāśiv Golvalkar.[192] But this reference to *janatā janārdan* does not seem to be a widespread trend, perhaps because of Janārdana's traditional association to Viṣṇu and Kṛṣṇa rather than the idealized warrior Rāma, who is closer to the heart of Hindu nationalism (*deśabhakti*).

As the Nāmdev song illustrates, Vārkarī saints often grounded their teachings in classic Hindu texts, especially *upaniṣad*ic notions of Brahman's ultimacy and the subtle nature of the self. With some frequency, poets refer to that philosophical touchstone from the *Bṛhadāraṇyaka Upaniṣad* (2.3.6) *neti neti*: Jñāndev (3 poems), Nāmdev (1 poem), Cokhāmeḷā (3), Bhānudās (1), Eknāth (9), and Tukārām (3). Olivelle warns that the popular translation of *neti neti* as "not this, not this" has been "overinterpreted" by Indic and western scholars as a grander claim than the words in context may merit.[193] Whatever the case may be etymologically, when the Vārkarī saints refer to it, they mean the denial of *nāmarūpā*—the world of names and forms—the overcoming of which enables greater communion with Viṭṭhal. Because of this philosophical combination, advocating both for a God with an obviously peculiar form (standing with arms akimbo in Paṇḍharpūr) as well as ultimate nonduality, they do not fit neatly in the *saguṇa*/*nirguṇa* bhakti paradigm that became more typical of North Indian bhakti. And the saints' writings certainly do not endorse Śaṅkara's notion of Īśvar as a penultimate idea that one must transcend to reach Brahman.

The relationship between Vārkarī saints and more widespread philosophies has yet to be thoroughly explored in a critical way.[194] To do so, one would probably start with the few major independent compositions by Jñāndev and Eknāth in which philosophy is most directly explored. These would reveal connections to the Nāth tradition, yoga, and Śaiva nondualism in the case of Jñāndev, and an appreciation of Śaṅkara and Śrīdhara's commentary on the *Bhāgavata Purāṇa*, in the case of Eknāth. An exploration of this is beyond the scope of this book, but Anand Venkatkrishnan has provided an excellent model for how this could unfold.[195]

More influential than both *janī-janārdan* and *neti neti* in Vārkarī discourse was the notion of impartiality, expressed through words with *sama-*: *samatā* (sameness or impartiality), *samabuddhi* (impartial consciousness), *samabhāva* (impartial feeling), and *samadṛṣṭi* (impartial vision). Impartiality and seeing past superficialities of course have been praised in many other traditions in South Asia, both Hindu and non-Hindu.[196] Nonetheless, this element was essential for precolonial Vārkarīs when they reckoned bhakti and caste.

Of all the *sama-* terms, *samatā* appears the most often, in poems attributed to Nivṛttināth and Jñāndev (each with 10 poems), Muktāī (3 poems), Nāmdev (3), Narhari Sonār (1), Eknāth (7), Tukārām (2), Niḷobā (1), and Bahiṇa (3). When this term appears, it functions similarly to advaita, in the sense that it is a spiritually advanced way of experiencing the world, beyond differences. Two songs from Nivṛttināth makes this explicit, "First discard awareness of duality [*dvaitabuddhi*], then hold on to *samatā*" (*SSG* #288) and "Break I-ness, and act with impartiality [*samatā*]" (*SSG* #319). This sense of *samatā* existing after one's egoism dissolves appears many times, as do pairings of *samatā* with "all beings" (*sarvāṃ bhūtīṃ*) in many saints' songs. Thinking back to Otto Dann's definitions in Chapter 2, this nondualist sense of *samatā* may align better with "identity" than "equality."

In my search of the *SSG*, I found *samadṛṣṭi* in the poems of Jñāndev (1), Nāmdev (2), Bhānudās (1), Eknāth (11), and Tukārām (3). The term as the Vārkarīs use it derives almost certainly from the *BhG* 5:18: "Learned men view as the same [*samadarśinaḥ*] a brahman who is endowed with knowledge and modesty, a cow, an elephant, a dog, and even a Dalit [*śvapāke*, dog cooker]." Jñāndev elaborates on this verse in Marathi further:

> So how would there be a sense of "This is a fly, and this an elephant" or "He is a Dalit [śvapacu], he is a twice-born, this is someone else's child, or this is mine?" Or again, "This is a cow, this is a dog, one is great, one is small." For one who is awake, wouldn't all these be like a dream? One sees such distinctions [*bhedu*] only if there remains a sense of I-ness. If this I-ness weren't there at the start, what difference [*viṣam*] could exist now? Therefore, know fully the secret of impartial perception [*samadṛṣṭi*]: "I am Brahman, which is without second, everywhere, always, the same."[197]

Other saints mostly follow Jñāndev's lead in using *samadṛṣṭi* this way. In a short poem attributed to Jñāndev (*SSG* #26), *samadṛṣṭi* appears in the same verse as *neti neti*. Nāmdev (*SSG* #2055) calls *samadṛṣṭi* toward all beings a great and sweet bhakti. In one of Eknāth's poems (*SSG* #369), looking at everything with *samadṛṣṭi* leads one to see Paṇḍharpūr, Viṭṭhal, bliss, and heartfelt devotion (*bhāva*) everywhere. Elsewhere (*SSG* #386), he says that *samadṛṣṭi* leads to seeing Viṭṭhal's feet standing on bricks (as his statue does in Paṇḍharpūr) everywhere. When *samadṛṣṭi* appears in a hagiography about Eknāth, it has nothing to do with caste but with the story of a man entrusting Eknāth with a touchstone (*parīsa*) while the man goes on pilgrimage. When he returns and requests the *parīsa* back from Eknāth, Eknāth states that he threw it in the river. The man is distressed, but when they both walk to the river and Eknāth scoops up a handful of stones, they all turn into touchstones by the power of Eknāth's *samadṛṣṭi*. Only later, at the end of the 19th century, Bhāgvat stated that Eknāth interacted freely with Dalits because of his *samadṛṣṭi*.

This application of *samadṛṣṭi* to caste was unusual, but it did have a precedent. In a hymn attributed to Śaṅkara (but certainly of much later provenance) called the *Manīṣapañcakam* or Five Verses on Insight, the author narrates an encounter between Śaṅkara and a Dalit (*cāṇḍāla*) with four dogs on a road. When Śaṅkara tells the Dalit to move aside, he challenges Śaṅkara to clarify what he means. If he refers to the Dalit's body, which is comprised of food like everyone else's bodies, no one's body can be subordinate to another. If Śaṅkara is referring to the Dalit's self (*ātman*), then its nondual nature renders moot the possibility of moving aside. Eventually, the Dalit reveals himself as Śiva along with the four Vedas disguised as dogs, who had come to test Śaṅkara.[198]

A related but less common term is *samabhāva* (impartial feeling).[199] One poem with this term is attributed to Jñāndev, and two each are attributed to

Eknāth and Tukārām. In content, their messages are like that of *samadṛṣṭi*. Alike in meaning and slightly more common is *samabuddhi* (impartial consciousness), which Nāmdev and Eknāth each mention in one poem, and Tukārām mentions in three songs. Three songs that use the term *samatva* are attributed to Jñāndev, while to Nivṛtti, Nāmdev, and Tukārām are attributed one song each.

Through *strīśūdrādi*, *janī janārdana*, *neti neti*, and the *sama-* terms, Vārkarīs positioned their view of bhakti by means of earlier Hindu authorities—*dharmaśāstr*ic and Purāṇic views of society, Vaiṣṇava theology, and nondualist thought. Sometimes their efforts addressed caste distinctions explicitly and dissolved them as the penultimate reality of names and forms—one way of addressing the question of bhakti and caste. This raises the question of how thoroughly nondualist philosophy shaped the Vārkarīs' idea of proper bhakti-framed human relations, even if the references we now see only hint at such a worldview rather than systematically articulate it. I explore this question more in Chapter 7.

As valuable as the quest is to work out the significance of philosophical terms in poets' compositions, this book follows a path on which it is easier to glimpse what followers of a tradition actually *did* with these ideas and where they felt the friction of conflicting values. For this, hagiography is more valuable than the saints' compositions, especially when stories involve tangible, everyday incidents like eating a meal, to which all listeners could relate and imagine the possibility of imitating.

As the liberal, nationalist, and critical streams of thinking about Maharashtrian heritage under colonialism shaped the way that bhakti was understood, critiques of caste hierarchy also developed conceptually. Critical authors, especially, found new ways to stretch existing language prior to 1880, after which the western political notion of equality rendered into Marathi as *samatā* became standard. Once equality was conceptually ready at hand for Marathi authors, it was wielded skillfully by Ambedkar and 20th-century scholars with Marxian analytical perspectives. Viewed in these ways, the bhakti-caste question was deemed either hopelessly insolvable (and thus to be abandoned) or a source of disappointment that potentially liberating ideas failed to bring about social change.

But the modern focus on equality obscured a richer history, especially before 1800, of how the bhakti-caste question was conceived. *Strīśūdrādi*, *janī janārdana*, *neti neti*, and the *sama-* terms all framed the bhakti-caste question differently, while also bearing their own cognitive and ethical tensions.

Part I explored how the bhakti-caste question came to be framed in modern terms. The idea of social equality, which emerged in western debates about nation-states, entered Marathi discourse in the middle of the 19th century. For many reformers, equality was shorthand for the negation of caste. Under colonial conditions, some Marathi intellectuals began reconceiving the Vārkarī tradition as an indigenous literary and cultural resource that offered a less hierarchical view of society. In the process, they used "equality" to translate earlier Indic religious terms like *samadṛṣṭi*, *janī-janārdana*, *samabuddhi*, and *samatā*. Traditionally, these terms resembled equality in some ways but were embedded in different theological and metaphysical worldviews. Those differences were obscured when equality language in the late 19th century became a standard way of interpreting those terms. Imagining that social equality was a historical aspiration of bhakti traditions set them up to be seen as social movements that failed either to recognize the social implications of spiritual equality or to realize their supposed theoretical egalitarianism in practice. Against the standard of social equality, bhakti traditions—and other premodern religious traditions (and if we are honest, modern democracies)—failed to measure up. Now, having clarified some of the lenses and prejudgments that guide modern scholarship, in Part II we can observe more carefully the ways that precolonial authors managed the bhakti-caste question, particularly in stories about eating together.

PART II

The next four chapters focus on the roles of food in contentious stories about eating together, because it is in Marathi hagiographers' use of food and commensality that we can observe premodern attempts to handle the bhakti-caste question. As I have been intimating throughout the book so far, sites of commensality are extremely important for learning about how people organize and regulate their communities in practice and not just theory. Abstract values are made manifest in food relationships, especially in eating together. Bodily needs and habits, emotional bonds and repulsions, and economic realities all shape the practical logics that govern how people eat together. Although I work with Marathi bhakti sources here, I believe that this analysis of "critical commensality" could be applied fruitfully to other cultures, times, genres, and contexts. Modern social scientists have long acknowledged the importance of studying food to understand culture, and critical commensality can be informed by their theories. But people outside academia and western modernity have been just as concerned—perhaps even more so—about food and its power to shape communities. We may learn from them as well, on their terms.

4

The Complications of Eating Together

This chapter sets out the ground for studying critical commensality in Marathi bhakti stories. Western scholarship on food and commensality have proposed theories of how food functions, which may sensitize us to view food more richly, even if we ultimately need not adopt any single one as normative. The benefits and limitations of social scientific theory for studying Indic cases will become clear when we look more closely at how food appears across millennia of Sanskrit literature. Marathi bhakti authors found a subset of literary themes about food especially helpful, including most surprisingly the role of *ucchiṣṭa*, or leftover food. Above all, it was food's capacity to symbolize different things simultaneously that made it so useful to saints and hagiographers, especially as they tried to work through bhakti's relationship to caste.

In addition to being necessary for life, food requires conscious and frequent effort to acquire. In cultures around the world, only marriage and sexual relations have generated as much concern as food, and even then, food is more urgent and fundamental.[1] Heavy with meaning and closely connected to the material world, food is an integral if not always well studied part of social history.

A common concern about food across cultures pertains to what a person may and may not eat. Although the origin and purpose behind food laws has been debated,[2] it is undeniable that people have put immense effort into drawing such distinctions. Food laws affect personal conduct and radiate far into other sectors of social life. For example, in 2015 the estimated sales of certified halal food and beverages, aimed at Muslim consumers, was $415 billion.[3] The very existence of organizations that certify food as halal for international markets helps to create new consumer demand, which in turn attracts investors.[4] Food laws affect economies and societies.

When people reinterpret or flagrantly disregard them, food laws can become sites of protest. The medieval Roman Catholic custom of not eating meat on Fridays set the stage for Swiss reformer Ulrich Zwingli to defiantly host a meal that became known as the Affair of the Sausages.[5] In 2012, some

Shared Devotion, Shared Food. Jon Keune, Oxford University Press. © Oxford University Press 2021.
DOI: 10.1093/oso/9780197574836.003.0005

Dalit students at a university in Hyderabad staged a beef festival to celebrate publicly their cultural practice of eating beef, which derived from the traditional demand on many Dalit groups to remove dead cattle from villages. In response, some right-wing Hindu students rioted, in a violent attempt to impose their policy of cow protection.[6] Religious food laws set cultural ground rules that people follow or resist, and they may function as flash-points of inter-communal tension.[7]

Food has great symbolic significance, such as in dishes that are associated with deities and saints. Gaṇeśa famously loves *moḍak*s—raw sugar and grated coconut steamed in a rice-flour shell. Just seeing the image of a *moḍak* reminds many Indians of the elephant-headed deity. Some Christians bake hot cross buns on Good Friday to signify Jesus' crucifixion. The special foods served on Chinese holidays and the isometric and homonymic symbolisms they evoke are virtually endless. Food can even lie at the very heart of religion for many people, especially those (often women) who were traditionally tasked with preparing it.[8]

In ritual sacrifices and offerings, food connects the human world and the world beyond. In some sacrifices, such as those of ancient Israelites and Vedic brahmans, fire completely consumed food offerings, transforming them into smoke that conveyed the sacrifice to the divine realm. In other offerings, fire consumes only part of the food for the deity, leaving behind holy leftovers for followers to consume. On a smaller scale, food may be placed before a deity on a temple altar or in a household shrine for ancestors or deities to interact with it, after which devotees partake. Some rituals, like the Roman Catholic Mass, are understood to transform the very substance of food itself. In these and many other ways, eating ritual food transports otherworldly presence across the bodily threshold, making that presence part of one's own being.

Most important for this book, food brings people together as they raise, harvest, sacrifice, trade, prepare, share, and—above all—eat. Eating together is practically universal and takes many forms, such as family meals, holiday feasts, power lunches, conversations over coffee, and parties that celebrate personal or community milestones. Rules govern, usually tacitly, who may join these events and how the meal proceeds. A poignant example of negotiating these tacit rules can be seen in Dalit poet Hirā Bansoḍe's composition "Sakhī" (Close Friend), in which she describes her initial delight at hosting a brahman friend at her home for a meal. Her soaring spirit sinks when the friend proceeds to ridicule Bansoḍe's way arranging food on the plate and complain that Bansoḍe failed to conclude the meal by serving buttermilk or yogurt, as per brahman custom. After she overcomes the initial shock of these interruptions, Bansoḍe describes to her brahman friend how her impoverished childhood severely limited her experience of food. She defiantly concludes, "Will you tell me how this is my fault?"[9] When food brings people together, the results are not always cheerful.

Since the inception of the social sciences, scholars have observed food to identify social hierarchies, kinship structures, and patterns of interaction.[10] E. B. Tylor in 1865 identified cooking as a universal human activity that set humans apart from animals. William Robertson Smith in 1889 argued that ancient ritual sacrifices were more about the communal cohesion that arose in post-ritual meals than about whatever connection it had with divine beings. In 1910, Georg Simmel reflected on how seating and serving arrangements reflect social status.[11] Emile Durkheim and Marcel Mauss developed functionalist theories of food, such as gift exchange, which dominated the study of food through the early decades of the 20th century. When Claude Lévi-Strauss theorized about the fundamental structure of myths across cultures, he observed food and cooking as basic story components.[12] Mary Douglas discussed food as a "natural symbol" that invites people everywhere to imbue it with symbolic meaning.[13] Shared opinions about what foods are tasty or disgusting reinforce among eaters a sense of trust. When people with different ingrained food aesthetics encounter each other, mistrust is a common response.[14] Food is simultaneously physical and social, just as a meal is both a material event and a site of social communication.[15]

Historians' early forays into food research were mainly quantitative, tracking patterns of production, delivery, and consumption,[16] until two books in the 1980s opened new perspectives. Jack Goody challenged symbolic anthropologists' emphasis on meaning by showing that haute cuisine cultures throughout world history corresponded to strongly hierarchical societies.[17] Sidney Mintz similarly considered food's historical and material circumstances as he documented the greater prevalence of sugar in British kitchens than in French ones.[18] Whatever sugar may have symbolized to people, its popularity in Great Britain clearly grew out of colonial trade policies. Geopolitical circumstances affect how people perceive food's significance.

Religious studies scholars shared historians' relative neglect of food as a site for interpretive analysis for most of the 20th century.[19] This changed in 1987, when Caroline Walker Bynum published her masterful book *Holy Feast and Holy Fast*. Bynum observed how European Christian mystics referred to the Eucharist, noting that women wrote about food and fasting more frequently than men did.[20] Contrary to popular modern assumptions, women mystics' fasting did not reflect body hatred or self-mortification. Instead, they used food as both a symbol and an instrument of self-control, treating their bodies as a sensory medium through which they could participate in Christ's suffering and commune with God.[21] Bynum thus revealed that medieval women mystics were far more agentive in their piety than modern readers expected.[22] Food and controlling its intake were central to this very corporeal spirituality.

Studies of commensality

Although the act of eating together occurs in all cultures, it has many different meanings and functions. For this reason, anthropologist Maurice Bloch called commensality a "semi-universal phenomenon."[23] As Susanne Kerner and Cynthia Chou argue, the communal meal is "an activity that has implications throughout society, in the economic, legal, political and religious spheres" or in brief, a "total social fact."[24] The concept of a total social fact itself was connected to food; Marcel Mauss coined the term while describing potlatch customs among Native American communities in the Pacific Northwest.[25]

Commensality's power to shape communities can be evaluated in different ways. Some scholars highlight food's role in creating and reinforcing social bonds. The act of consuming the same food, bringing something from outside the body into it, affects both the individual and community by strengthening a shared identity.[26] If the idiom "you are what you eat" holds true, then eating the same food makes people more alike.[27] Food thus may function as an "edible identity" that people take on through eating.[28] Some scholars even suggest that eating together inclines people to regard their fellow eaters as "saliently equal."[29] Sharing meals with deities and deceased ancestors compounds that unifying power further.[30]

Commensality is not only or necessarily egalitarian, such as when it marks communal boundaries and differences among participants' statuses.[31] Hierarchical distinctions are made and enforced by determining who may sit where, who may join the meal, and who is expected to prepare and serve it.[32] Within the act of unifying, primordial human impulses to distinguish and rank are almost always at work in some way. Even acts of transgressive commensality that appear rebellious in one instance may end up reinforcing the customary order if the acts later get celebrated as exceptional occurrences and carnival-like release valves of social tension.[33]

Bruno Latour's notion of an actant illuminates very well the way food materially creates, sustains, and reconstructs social relations.[34] More than merely indicating social bonds, food helps to construct them in the first place.[35] It is no accident that food is central to so many social events. Whether or not participants are actively thinking about it, the food they eat together helps to join individuals into a community.

This brings into focus the power of food to reinforce and disrupt established orders. In a world-reconstructing vein, Banu Bargu argues that anyone who values social equality should appreciate eating together as a "quotidian, micro-political, indigenous" activity that can help make that equality a reality.[36] "Commensality, then, is both a metaphor for the emancipatory potential of biopolitics and a literal rendition of one form of social practice, lodged firmly in biological needs (labour) but not reducible to them, that moves us toward the realization of that potential."[37] The initiation rites of the Paramahaṃsa Maṇḍaḷī and the Satyaśodhak Samāj, which we encountered in Chapter 3, incorporated food in just this way.

Food and commensality in South Asia

Eating together in South Asia involves a few additional considerations. The very word "commensality" reveals its provinciality, referring to a table (Latin *mensa*), which was not traditionally a common piece of furniture in the subcontinent before the colonial period. Still today, at large events like pilgrimage meals, eaters typically sit next to each other in rows (*paṅgat* or *paṅkti*) rather than on chairs around the perimeter of a large raised surface.[38] (Photo 4.1)Many spatial arrangements can facilitate commensality.

Somewhat less intuitive, our notion of eating together must also be expanded beyond the image of individuals eating in the same place at the same time. For millennia, Hindu authors have been extremely careful about food's origins, especially for brahman eaters who were concerned about maintaining ritual purity. Food connects those who prepare, serve, and receive it, regardless of whether they partake together or at all. Some scholars, like anthropologist McKim Marriott, have referred in these cases to "food transactions," by means of which villagers calculated their relative caste

Photo 4.1. Communal meal (*paṅgat*) for Vārkarīs at Kūrmadās Temple near Laūḷ.
Source: Photo taken by the author on July 17, 2010.

status, observing who could accept food from whom.[39] Although precise and analytically useful in some contexts, I find "transaction" to be coldly economic and unable to reflect food's intense social, personal, ritual, and symbolic dimensions. Therefore, I prefer to stretch the definition of commensality to encompass these Indian cases.

No one has done more for the anthropology of food in India than R. S. Khare, both through his own writing on brahmans and Dalits in Lucknow[40] and through the International Commission on Anthropology of Food and Food Problems that he founded in 1977.[41] I find especially helpful Khare's discussions of gastrosemantics and food's semantic density. Food operates within multiple symbolic systems at the same time to convey a combination of material, moral, social, and spiritual messages. According to classical Hindu thought, food has both observable (gross) and invisible (subtle) properties, so that when it crosses the bodily boundary and gets absorbed, its effects are both nutritional and social. Devotees communicate their loyalty and faith through food offerings to deities, and in return, deities communicate power and blessing through what is left over. Saints and holy figures, who are understood to dwell at the boundary between the worldly and otherworldly, can communicate things through food, in the form of spiritually charged leftovers or as prescribed medicines whose power is believed to correspond to the strength of recipients' faith. Khare coined the term "gastrosemantics" to capture this complex web of food's possible meanings.[42] Because of its multivalence, food is a powerful and malleable resource for social communication, among people and with deities.[43] This is surely one reason why it features so prominently in Hindu texts.

While surveying food's many roles in Indian society, Khare noted the lack of research on food's "long journey" throughout South Asian history.[44] In the following section, I fill a bit of this gap by observing the appearance of food in a range of classic Hindu sources and Marathi bhakti texts. These form the conceptual and narrative environment in which stories about Eknāth's transgressive commensality became charged.

Hindu gastrosemantics

Anna (food) appears in several different forms in the Vedas but most frequently as the substrate of life that flows through the cosmos. An early hymn in the *Ṛg Veda* (*ṚV* 1:187) known as the *Anna Stuti* praises food's power to bring strength, support life, and enable brave deeds. In hundreds of other Vedic passages, food is closely connected to wealth and power. Invocations of deities as givers of food are common, as are requests for them to continue their generosity. Generosity is expected of people too, such as in this ominously direct command: "The stronger man should give to one in need. He should look along the longer path, for riches turn like chariot-wheels: they come up to one man after another. The undiscerning man finds food in vain. I speak the truth: it is just a deadly weapon for him. He does not prosper in compatriot, nor in companion. Who eats alone has only evil."[45]

The *Śatapatha Brāhmaṇa* (11.6.2.6–10) portrays food flowing back and forth between the earth and the world beyond by means of sacrifices.[46] Brahman priests are enjoined in the early Vedas to partake of sacrificed meat, including that of bulls and cows, under ritual circumstances.[47] Perhaps due to the violence involved in procuring meat, verse 6 in the *Ṛg Veda* passage just quoted ties the solo eater to evil—a warning repeated in the *Taittirīya Brāhmaṇa* and *Manusmṛti*.[48]

Vedic authors perceive the importance of food moving among people and the gods, and ritual sacrifice facilitates its proper circulation. With so much at stake, humans' roles in sacrifice were scrutinized. Charles Malamoud expresses this well: "food . . . becomes charged with a social and religious symbolism so powerful and complex that there is simply no end to the number of precautions that one may take with regard to it."[49]

Vedic authors often regard ritual sacrifice as a kind of meal.[50] The popular Indian slogan that the guest is god (*atithi devo bhava*) first appeared in the Vedas (*TU* 1.11.2) as part of an injunction to respect parents, teachers, and guests. When applied to Vedic sacrifice, the meaning is quite literal: gods come to the home as guests, and humans must show them hospitality.

In addition to deities, some Vedic sacrifices are directed to deceased ancestors. As Matthew Sayers points out, early Vedic authors envisioned the dead going to an afterworld, not being reborn.[51] Already in the *ṚV* 10.16, ritual sacrifices to propitiate and feed the ancestors (*pitṛyajña*) appear in the cremation ceremony.[52] Vedic authors regarded cremation as a form of eating; Agni devours the body and conveys it to heaven as smoke. Some rituals in the *ṚV* invite the ancestors to eat some of the sacrifice,[53] including one that the *Brāhmaṇas* prescribe to occur monthly, the *piṇḍapitṛyajña* or rice-ball sacrifice to the ancestors.[54] The offering of small cakes or rice balls is understood to provide sustenance to the deceased ancestors, but the *piṇḍapitṛyajña* extends to earthly eaters too, as the priests who conduct the ritual consume the rice balls.

Perhaps responding to Jain and Buddhist critiques of violence in Vedic animal sacrifice, the later Upaniṣads referred more frequently to non-violence (*ahiṃsa*), signaling a shift in how Vedic tradition was practiced. As animal sacrifice declined, later thinkers had to reinterpret the Vedic passages that authorized it. As Brian K. Smith suggests, "Perhaps the most important device for defanging a potentially embarrassing ritual was to thoroughly metaphorize it."[55] As the Upaniṣads reflected further on the significance of Vedic sacrifice, food became the model for several abstract ideas. In the earliest and most widely accepted Upaniṣads, probably composed between the 7th century BCE and the 2nd century CE,[56] food is understood to be at or near the center of existence. The Upaniṣads refer to food in at least seven different ways.

First, food is the foundational material of life, and eating is the cosmic process by which that material transforms. For example, the *Bṛhadāraṇyaka Upaniṣad* (*BU* 6.3.13) reflects on the cycle of human death and rebirth as a circulation of food. When humans die and are cremated, they become smoke, which reaches the moon and becomes food for the gods, whose consumption transforms them into rain and wind, which become earthly food that gets eaten by women, who then give birth to new human bodies. Other Upaniṣads also identify food as one of the primary elements of creation.[57]

Second, food is routinely cited as the fruit (*phala*) or benefit that comes from understanding an esoteric teaching. This appears in a formulaic way: "He who knows this" becomes the eater of the world and the whole world is his food (*BU* 1.2.5), will possess food that never decreases (*BU* 2.2.4), will possess and eat his own food (*ChU* 1.3.7), and will become an eater of food (*ChU* 3.1.2). Food and eating here demonstrate independence, power, and dominion.

Third, because of their phonetic similarity, breath (*ana*) and food (*anna*) are frequently associated and sometimes equated with each other.[58] As Yajñāvalkya reduces the number of gods into ever more basic forces, he recognizes food and breath as the two basic deities that rest on the singularity of Brahman (*BU* 2.2.4, 3.9.8). Elsewhere, the nature of Brahman is said to be food and breath together (*BU* 5.12, 6.12). A formula that uses food as both an object of knowledge and a fruit of knowing at the same time appears in *BU* 6.2.14: "When a man knows in this way that breath is food, nothing he eats becomes an improper food." This is repeated nearly verbatim in *ChU* 5.2.1. Patrick Olivelle cautions against dismissing this wordplay as far-fetched, since the Upaniṣadic authors also demonstrate great philological sophistication.[59] He argues that such verbal equations represent the authors' attempts to create an "integrative vision of the world" by drawing out subtle connections between apparently unrelated parts of reality.[60] Food is an especially rich motif for making such connections.

Fourth, power disparities are analogized through food, as the eater dominates the eaten.[61] *BU* 1.4.6 characterizes the world as composed of food and eaters, which are like *soma* and the sacrificial fire. Most evocatively, the *Kauṣītaki Upaniṣad* (2.9) describes social relations through a food metaphor: "You are King Soma, the radiant! You are Prajapati, with five mouths! The Brahmin is one mouth of yours; with that mouth you eat the kings [*rājñaḥ*]. . . . The king is one mouth of yours; with that mouth you eat the vaiśyas." Elsewhere in the Vedas, the purpose of common people (*viś*, from which vaiśya comes) is to be "consumed" by the kṣatriyas.[62]

Three other kinds of references in the Upaniṣads appear only once but merit comment. The *Taittirīya Upaniṣad* 3.7–9 asserts rules that ought to govern people's interactions with food: one should not belittle (*paricakṣīt*) it, one should not reject food, one should prepare a lot of food, and one should never turn anyone away from one's home. One who aspires to be a "big man" (*mahān*) ought to establish himself as someone who always has food available. *ChU* 6.5 narrates the bodily process of digestion: the densest material becomes feces, middling material becomes flesh, and the most subtle material becomes mind. Thus, even the mind is made of food. Finally, the earliest historical reference to distribution of food as charity appears in *ChU* 4.1.1–2, as a wealthy householder Jānaśruti Pautrāyaṇa established dwellings (*āvasathān*) that cooked food and served it to as many people as possible.[63]

As these diverse Vedic references demonstrate, people were quite familiar with food's semantic density well over two millennia ago.

Vedāṅgas and dharmaśāstra

In the early centuries of the Common Era, literatures arose to offer supplementary knowledge that could support ritual performance. These were the *vedāṅgas* or limbs of the Veda: phonetics, prosody, grammar, etymology, ritual instruction, and astrology. Within the category of ritual instruction (*kalpa*), three divisions of texts focused on different kinds of rituals: the *Śrautasūtra*s pertained to large, public rituals that required multiple priests, the *Gṛhyasūtras* dealt with a brahman householder's domestic rituals, and the *Dharmasūtra*s prescribed broader norms for proper conduct and ritual purity. Food appears in the *Gṛhyasūtra*s and *Dharmasūtra*s in ways that are especially relevant to this book.

In the *Gṛhyasūtras*, a new rite—*śrāddha*—overtook the Vedic *piṇḍyapitṛyajña* offering to the ancestors.[64] Ritual instruction manuals differ on the details of *śrāddha* performance and the number of different *śrāddha*s that served different goals.[65] *Śrāddha* contained two major innovations. First, brahman priests became more like professional guests. They continued to carry out rituals at the ceremony, but their main purpose became serving as proxies for the ancestors, consuming the offerings on their behalf.[66] Thus, feeding brahman guests at a *śrāddha* rite was tantamount to feeding the ancestors. Second, explanations of *śrāddha* focused more on how the ritual could please the deceased ancestors and win their blessing, rather than the *piṇḍapitṛyajña*'s traditional function of sustaining the ancestors in heaven or enhancing their afterworld status.[67]

The most basic and widely attested form of *śrāddha* is the new-moon rite, at which food is offered monthly.[68] Prescriptions for this rite also differ on details: some texts state that brahmans stand in for only the sacrificer's deceased father, others state that the brahmans must be called by the deceased father's name, and still other texts specify that other ancestors' names should be invoked as well. One text shows how Vedic sacrifice was the model for *śrāddha*, clarifying that the brahman guests replace the sacrificial fire in mediating between the sacrificing householder and the ancestors.[69] As we shall see in the next two chapters, the *śrāddha* ritual remained important among brahmans, even within bhakti circles that debated its significance.

The *Dharmasūtras* also elaborated on *śrāddha* rituals, devoting entire chapters to what food should be served and which brahmans should be invited.[70] One of the oldest and widely respected texts,[71] the *Āpastamba Dharmasūtra* (ca. 200 BCE) states that sesame, beans, rice, barley, water, roots, and fruits are appropriate for the rite, and the ancestors are especially pleased if the food is prepared in a "greasy" way. Āpastamba states that offering cow's meat satisfies the ancestors for a year, which is more powerful than offering buffalo meat, but nowhere near as efficacious as offering rhinoceros meat, which satisfies the ancestors forever.[72] Āpastamba states that ideal invitees would be brahmans who are well versed in the Vedas and unrelated to the sponsor by blood or guru-disciple lineage. He specifies further that householders should prioritize inviting the most elderly and poor brahmans. In contrast, the *Dharmasūtra* of Gautama states that younger brahmans should be preferred.

The *Dharmasūtras* also laid out foundational laws of food purity—a major concern for brahman priests and the success of their rituals. Most relevant to this book is the topic of proper sources for brahmans' food. In general, brahmans may receive food from twice-born people of good standing. But a brahman student who has returned home after a period of discipleship may accept food only from another brahman. The *Dharmasūtras* differ slightly on whether and when one may accept food from a śūdra. As we shall see shortly, later *dharmaśāstra* texts elaborated on this issue much further.

Another food regulation that is important to this book deals with *ucchiṣṭa*—the food that remains after one has finished eating. The *Baudhāyana Dharmasūtra* (2.8.11) repeats a prayer that first appeared in *TU* 10.23, which states that eating *ucchiṣṭa* is one of the most serious of all dietary offenses.[73] The *Āpastamba Dharmasūtra* (1.3.36–41) specifies three ways that a brahman student may dispose of this volatile material: burying it, throwing it in flowing water, or placing it in a pot for someone less concerned about purity to throw away. A brahman ought not eat his own *ucchiṣṭa*, much less that of someone else. *Ucchiṣṭa* must never be placed in fire, as that would effectively be making a polluted offering to Agni and the gods.[74]

In some sacred contexts, *ucchiṣṭa*'s value is inverted. *Āpastamba* 1.4.1 states that a disciple ought to eat his guru's *ucchiṣṭa*. Leftover food is a material conduit for the hierarchical and commensal relationship between teacher and student.[75] In this sense, *ucchiṣṭa* may also be viewed as sacrificial food that marks a hierarchy of beneficial interactions. The leftovers of a sacrifice to the gods is *ucchiṣṭa* that has become blessed for human consumption. Since the *śrāddha* ritual usually begins with a ritual offering to the all-gods (Vaiśvadeva), the food that gets offered to ancestors is technically the all-gods' *ucchiṣṭa*. After offering this food to the ancestors, the sponsor of the ritual can benefit from consuming the *ucchiṣṭa* that remains. Thus, the *śrāddha* is a chain of blessed *ucchiṣṭa* transmission linking the gods, ancestors, brahman mediators, and ritual patrons. As Malamoud succinctly puts it, when leftovers occur outside the process of sacrifice, they are "objects of repulsion," but as the products of sacrifice, leftovers are "edible food par excellence, and play an essential role in the continuity of *dharma*."[76]

Concerns about how to eat without jeopardizing ritual efficacy carried over into the *Manava Dharmaśāstra* (aka *Manusmṛti*, ca. 150 CE) and later *dharmaśāstras*.[77] In some ways, *dharmaśāstra* texts were legal "metadiscourse" and theoretical distillations of the customs that authors sought to normalize in everyday life.[78] *Dharmaśāstra* was one of the bases on which cases of brahman conduct and social interactions were adjudicated in places like *dharmasabhās*.[79] In such settings, *dharmaśāstra* was regarded as orthopraxy but still was interpreted, debated, played off against competing claims, and sometimes quietly overlooked. As Khare wisely notes, "All textual injunctions on *anna* thus remain remote and incomplete until they filter through regionally different sectarian ideologies, holy men, and regional/local caste customs and folk practices."[80]

When it came to who may provide brahmans with food, both the *Dharmasūtras* and the *dharmaśāstras* had much to say. The *Dharmasūtras* of Āpastamba (17.1–8) and Gautama (17.1–8) are clear that brahmans may accept food from the three highest castes generally, whereas he may accept food from a śūdra only if "he is unable to sustain himself by other means." Āpastamba makes a further caveat, "This type of food is not fit to be eaten every day." Vasiṣṭha's *Dharmasūtra* (6.26–29) is more emphatically restrictive: a meritorious brahman is one "into whose stomach the food of a śūdra has never entered." A brahman who dies with food from a śūdra in his stomach will be reborn as a pig or in the family of that śūdra, and one who eats a śūdra's food cannot find the celestial path and attain heaven. When Vasiṣṭha lists unsuitable sources of food (14.1–9), he includes outcastes and śūdras, as well as thieves, liquor dealers, leather workers, arsonists, soldiers, adulterers, and others. Other ancient lists included groups that today would be classed as Dalits or, loosely, anyone at all who brahman authors deemed to be a threat to their privilege.[81]

Manu and the *dharmaśāstra*s show greater interest in cross-caste food transactions. To Vasiṣṭha's list of inappropriate food sources for brahmans, Manu (4.205–224) adds hunters, cruel men (*ugra*), singers, carpenters, sellers of rituals, weavers, wandering acrobats, goldsmiths, blacksmiths, basket weavers, washermen, those who raise dogs, and many others. Some appear on this list by virtue of misconduct (adultery, thievery, etc.) but many are occupations that overlap with low-caste *jāti*s in India. Although lacking a single authoritative set of rules about acceptable castes for food transactions, *dharmaśāstra* texts routinely portrayed the food of śūdras as being off-limits to hungry brahmans.

*Dharmaśāstra*s also consistently enjoin brahmans to share food in acts of hospitality. We have seen this concern appear in other contexts: the *Ṛg Veda*'s command to share food, Vedic sacrifice involving the deities being treated as guests, and *śrāddha*'s feeding of brahmans as proxies for the ancestors. Hospitality toward guests extends to the human realm too. Kane devotes an entire section of his *History of Dharmaśāstra* to the honoring of guests.[82] *Dharmasūtra*s and *dharmaśāstra*s observe a range of opinions about who qualifies as a guest: always brahmans, usually travelers of any caste who have no food with them and arrive at a mealtime, often kṣatriyas and vaiśyas, as well as śūdras and *caṇḍāla*s who are not known to have committed grievous sins.[83] As *dharmaśāstra* authors forbade brahmans from accepting food from śūdras and Dalits, they commanded those same brahmans to provide food to śūdras and Dalits who may come to their door. The Vedic and Upaniṣadic resonances of food, sharing, and honor are easy to see.

Epics and Purāṇas

Food appears abundantly throughout the Epics and Purāṇas in a variety of roles. One way that it occasionally appears is through a particular use of the word *bhakta*, as the root *bhaj* can connote food and eating.[84] I highlight here some food stories in this vast Sanskrit corpus as they are pertinent to later discussions of bhakti poetry. In doing so, I keep in mind that this style of narrating a story not only entertained audiences but also illustrated ethical dilemmas and ideological positions.[85]

The *dharmaśāstras* acknowledge that food regulations may be broken in extreme cases, such as when one's life is at risk. Thus, the sage Viśvamitra in the Anuśāsana Parvan of the *Mahābhārata* calculates that because he was starving and at death's door, he would be justified in stealing dog meat from a *caṇḍāla*'s home to eat.[86] As Viśvamitra approaches the home, however, the *caṇḍāla* wakes up and warns him about the gravity of his intention. The two debate the propriety of this prospective deed, and Viśvamitra eventually takes the meat and cooks it. This story is an example of improvised morality during calamitous times (*āpad-dharma*).[87] By setting out this extreme case of clashing values of survival versus eating prohibited food, the *Mahābhārata* comments on the degenerate state of the world, in which an upstanding character like Viśvamitra could be brought to such dire straits, while simultaneously reinforcing the importance of *dharmaśāstra* food laws in ordinary life.

A more complicated story appears in Section 55 of the Aśvamedha Parva of the *MBh*. The desert-dwelling sage Uttaṅka received a boon from Kṛṣṇa, with which he requested the power to summon water merely by thinking of Kṛṣṇa. When Uttaṅka tries out this new power, his request is answered in an unexpected form: a mud-covered *caṇḍāla* arrives, surrounded by dogs. He begins to urinate and beckons Uttaṅka to drink. Uttaṅka is outraged and reviles Kṛṣṇa for this apparent trick. Kṛṣṇa then explains that he had requested the god Indra to fulfill Uttaṅka's wish by bringing him immortal nectar (*amṛta*) to drink. Reluctant to share the nectar with mortals, Indra agreed to Kṛṣṇa's request on the condition that Uttaṅka would be willing to receive the nectar from a *caṇḍāla*. In effect, Indra relied on the *caṇḍāla* disguise and Uttaṅka's sense of purity to fulfill Kṛṣṇa's request while preserving the division between humans and the gods. Kṛṣṇa recasts this all as a spiritual test of discernment, which he reprimands Uttaṅka for failing. The story hinges on food (or drink, in this case) functioning within multiple frameworks of meaning, between which Uttaṅka effectively if not consciously chooses.

The *Bhagavad Gītā* offers additional considerations of food which became more influential for bhakti traditions. Verses 3:12–14 synthesize multiple Vedic views:

Enriched by sacrifice, the gods will give you the delights you desire;
he is a thief who enjoys their gifts without giving to them in return.
Good men eating the remnants of sacrifice are free of any guilt,
but evil men who cook for themselves eat the food of sin.
Creatures depend on food, food comes from rain,
rain depends on sacrifice, and sacrifice comes from action.

BhG 17:8–10 presents a typology of food tastes that accord to the three *guṇas*. *Sāttv*ic personalities prefer foods that are savory, firm, and rich. *Rājas*ic people crave bitter, sour, salty, and pungent food. And people governed by *tamas* prefer stale, spoiled, and leftover food.

Most important is Kṛṣṇa's assertion that he relishes even the humblest offering (9.26). This form of worship resembles Vedic sacrifice in that the offering communicates with the deity, but there are notable differences. The offerings that Kṛṣṇa mentions are very simple—a leaf, a flower, fruit, or water. Everyone may worship Kṛṣṇa in this way, unlike Vedic sacrifices that could be conducted only by brahmans. Notably, the *Gītā* does not employ ritual distinctions that later became standard: *naivedya*, *bhoga*, or *prasāda*. When *prasāda* appears in the *Gītā* (e.g., 18.56), it refers only to Kṛṣṇa's benevolent disposition toward devotees.

This devotion appears in the *Rāmāyaṇa* too, when a respected forest-dwelling woman, Śabarī, is delighted by Rāma's and Lakṣmaṇ's arrival (3.70). To show them hospitality, she collects various edibles from the forest. Śabarī herself embodies an unusual combination of roles. Her name derives from the Śabara tribe to which she belongs, marking her as low caste and ritually impure. Yet Śabarī also is renowned for being a devoted caretaker of the sage Mātaṅga (who also has an unusual caste background in the Epics) and his ashram. The fact that she, revered for her pure conduct despite her low status, has gathered food for the two heroes creates a narrative dilemma. As Philip Lutgendorf points out, Vālmīki's version of the *Rāmāyaṇa* conspicuously avoids mentioning whether Rāma and Lakṣmaṇ consumed Śabarī's offering. It is possible that early oral renditions of the story were actually clearer on the matter, but the scribes who wrote down the *Rāmāyaṇa* consciously omitted this detail.[88] In any case, later vernacular commentators offered further explanations, portraying Śabarī's action as a model of bhakti. One detail became especially vivid: Śabarī expressed her devotion not just by collecting food but by tasting each berry she collected, to ensure that they were all sweet enough for Rāma. Food that was sampled by Śabarī like this clearly would be *ucchiṣṭa*, yet Rāma gladly consumes it and praises Śabarī's care.[89] Despite not appearing in the Vālmīki *Rāmāyaṇa*, this detail remained popular on a vernacular level, such that the Hirā Bansoḍe could refer to Śabarī's bhakti in the poem we observed earlier in this chapter.

Several Purāṇas reveal the growing popularity of ritual worship that involves a material offering that becomes blessed. This is usually called *prasāda*. Andrea Pinkney has shown that the term *prasāda* had broad semantic range in various texts, but it was developed most intently by Vaiṣṇavas.[90] In the *Viṣṇu Purāṇa*, *prasāda* designates material and non-material offerings, and the *Kūrma Purāṇa* refers to *prasāda* as Viṣṇu's positive emotional state from which Brahmā is created. In the *Skanda Purāṇa*, *prasāda* functions like a blessed speech-act that is the antithesis of a curse.[91] As time went on, probably under the influence of Kṛṣṇa's statement about simple offerings in the *Gītā*, Vaiṣṇavas developed a formulaic pattern of ritual worship, comprised of material offerings (*naivedya*) to a deity who is understood to happily enjoy them (*bhoga*) and, by that favorable contact, transmute it into a blessed gift (*prasāda*) that devotees can retrieve. The multivalence of *prasāda* as special material, which bears contentment (*prasanna*) for both the deity and the devotee made it a vital component of worship in nearly all Hindu traditions. Although food is not the only kind of *prasāda* (Śaivas regard sacred ash as *prasāda*), it is easy to see how food, which crosses many kinds of boundaries, mediates between humans and deities especially well.

One more way that people have used the *Purāṇas*' treatment of food stories is to view them as inspiration for later reenactments, so that people may participate in the divine activity. Such reenactment occurs famously nowadays with the *Rāmāyaṇa*, such as *Rāmlīlā* plays in India and the diaspora[92] and reenactments of Rāma's exile by Maharashtrian villagers occasioned by public readings (*pārāyaṇa*) of Eknāth's Marathi rendering of the *Rāmāyaṇa*.[93] Two stories in the *Bhāgavata Purāṇa* also developed into regional customs.

BhP 10:24–25 narrates the story of Kṛṣṇa lifting Mount Govardhana to shelter his cowherding friends during a storm. Because of its association with Kṛṣṇa's time on earth, Govardhan Hill near Mathurā became a center of Kṛṣṇa ritual worship. Govardhan Pūjā, also known as the Annakūṭa (Mountain of Food) festival, has become a major ritual in this worship, in which large amounts of food are offered to Kṛṣṇa in the form of the mountain. Paul Toomey has pointed out that although both the Puṣṭi-mārg and Gauḍiya traditions celebrate Annakūṭa, they handle food offerings to Kṛṣṇa and *prasāda* distribution in different ways.[94] Toomey also highlights ritually charged food's power to signify Kṛṣṇa's bliss and to engage bhaktas in that emotion,[95] resulting in a common, nonhierarchical experience with physical and affective dimensions.[96]

The *BhP* is the scriptural basis for a quite different food custom further south, where Vārkarīs, among others, reenact a young Kṛṣṇa's playful meal with cowherd friends. *Kālā* is the name for both this event and for the mixture of curds and parched grains that comprises its focal point. *BhP* 10.5.14 and *Viṣṇu Purāṇa* 5.5.31–35 and 5.9.1–8 have been cited as precedents for this custom, but it was elaborated further by Marathi poets.[97] It remained such a common motif among *kīrtankār*s that the standard "textbook" for *kīrtan* performers in the early 20th century included it as an important theme.[98]

In this brief survey of food appearances in Sanskrit texts, we have seen it referred to as the substrate of reality, a component of hospitality, a concern for purity laws, an instrument for extreme test cases, and a medium for conveying ritual offering and blessing. In all of these examples, food is suspended between basic dualities—*pavitra* and *apavitra*, *pāpa* and *puṇya*, *maṅgala* and *amaṅgala*—that connect the material (*laukika*) and spiritual (*adhyātmika*) realms and thereby structure Hindu worlds.[99] Bhakti literature and hagiography similarly draw on food's polyvalence, within a narrower range of meanings.

Food in vernacular bhakti literature

Vernacular bhakti texts and hagiographies consistently foregrounded several themes from among the semantic range of food in classic Sanskrit literature. As I argued in Chapter 1, hagiography is a rich resource for cultural history because hagiographical stories reveal how people remembered saints' behavior and significance. Among other functions, hagiography attempts to work out conceptual and doctrinal problems in a narrative form that a wide audience could easily grasp. In summarizing bhakti stories as I do here, I am not concerned with the historicity of characters as they are represented, nor do I think that reconstructing a trajectory of stories' development is helpful. Such a historical reconstruction would require a different set of data, to ascertain the reliability of dating source materials. But my reservations are more than this: I am not sure a reliably accurate reconstruction is possible at all, at least with the Vārkarī materials. As I will argue in Chapter 7, many hagiographical stories, themes, and poems clearly changed over time and joined in a vast intertextual and intermedial network of mutual influences. Even if we could reliably specify a date for an individual text, there is no guarantee that its contents were not the product of slippage or echoes within the larger tradition of oral transmission. In short, when I summarize these stories, I do so for their value in recognizing motifs and ethical dilemmas, not for analyzing a past that they purportedly describe.

In the Vīraśaiva hagiographical corpus, Basava's camaraderie with Śiva-bhaktas leads him into the home of a Dalit (*poḷeya*) named Kambaḷiya Nāgideva. There, Basava eats food that Nāgideva had consecrated to Śiva. A Vaiṣṇava spy observes this and reports it to Basava's employer, King Bijjala, who then summons Basava to explain his actions, which are contrary (*viparīta*) to custom. Basava responds that he has not interacted with "Untouchables" (*holeyar*, literally "polluted"), but it is soon clear that by "Untouchables" he is referring to Vaiṣṇava brahmans rather than Nāgideva.[100] To prove his point about genuine purity, Basava invites Nāgideva to the court and conducts an experiment. He makes a small cut in the bodies of an unfortunate Vaiṣṇava volunteer and Nāgideva. Blood and ugly insects emerge from the Vaiṣṇava's incision, whereas Nāgideva's wound issues forth only milk. Basava felicitates Nāgideva—Dalit by birth but brahman by conduct—by parading him around town on an elephant and giving him gifts.[101]

The canon of stories about the 15th-century North Indian Dalit (*chamār*) saint Ravidās includes a narrative of commensality. An admirer of Ravidās, Queen Jhali, serves a meal to honor brahmans. Apprehensive about Ravidās' presence and hoping to avoid pollution, the brahmans ask the queen to provide them only raw ingredients that they may cook for themselves. After the brahmans cook and begin eating, they discover Ravidās replicated miraculously among them, "sitting between every two brahmans."[102] Priyadās, the brahman hagiographer who commented on the earlier rendition of the story by Nābhādās, concludes the story by having Ravidās peel back his skin to reveal a golden sacred thread, thus demonstrating his supreme qualification for partaking in the meal.[103] Khare points out that Dalit interpreters regularly "confute and reject" this final part of the story.[104]

Kabīr too is pulled into a food story, in which antagonistic brahmans conspire to ruin him by disguising themselves as bhaktas and inviting many people to join a public feast that they claim Kabīr will offer. They especially seek out low-caste devotees (*sant*, in a Hindi sense) to invite to the meal[105] in the hope that the numbers will overwhelm Kabīr's hospitality and make him look bad. As the "innumerable" *sants* arrive, Kabīr hides and does not know what to do. So, Kṛṣṇa takes on Kabīr's form and hosts the feast himself for five days, endlessly supplying whatever food the *sants* request. Eventually, Kabīr too emerges from hiding and joins the feast that had been ostensibly organized in his name.[106] Based on this story, some later traditions that revere Kabīr developed a custom of inter-caste ritual feasts (*bhaṇḍārā*), at which attendees touch each other's right hands and then proceed to eat (*angulichuman*).[107]

As we saw in Chapter 2, scholarship on Marathi bhakti has highlighted caste and untouchability more than most other regional traditions, due in part to the strong low-caste and Dalit movements in the past two centuries. It also seems that food features more prominently in Marathi traditions than elsewhere. While this may reflect the relative dearth of scholarship on food in other traditions, I think it indicates something about Marathi traditions' priorities. Food was and is an effective medium through which bhakti operated across social boundaries in stories about God and the saints. Its everyday presence made it an excellent means of easily relating stories to people. Its semantic density embedded it within broader Hindu worlds of discourse. And its nature as something easily given and received enabled it to indicate traditional and new caste relations.

Food appears in several ways in the Mahānubhāv tradition. In a crucial story of initiation, the divine human Guṇḍam Rāūḷ tosses the Gujarati prince Haripal some fried street food (*seṅgaḷe buḍḍe*) as *prasād* that effectively transmits powerful knowledge (*jñānaśakti*). Consuming the *prasād* converts Haripal into Cakradhar, the founder of the Mahānubhāvs.[108] As he starts attracting followers, Cakradhar requires they join him in begging for food and accepting whatever is offered. Brahman followers frequently struggle to overcome their caste prejudices about food, leading Cakradhar to challenge them directly with transgressive commensal scenarios. As Novetzke shows, this is one of the most consistent and long-running themes in the entire *Līḷācaritra*.[109] Cakradhar provokes outsiders with food transactions too, such as when he gives chewed *pān* from his mouth to the devoted wife of the Yādava minister Hemādri, an orthodox brahman, as an act of blessing.

The Vārkarī tradition is replete with many uses of food. Jñāndev is credited with composing an *abhaṅga* that analogizes components of a feast (flavors, vessels, *papaḍ*, *khīr*, and *pān*) to aspects of spiritual life. Enjoying sumptuous food is a metaphor for experiencing ultimate spiritual bliss.[110] The *Jñāneśvarī* uses the image of a public feast in the town square, both as a positive metaphor for the accessibility of bhakti's liberating message[111] and as a negative metaphor of worldly temptation.[112] Over a dozen *abhaṅgas* that are attributed to Janābāī involve food,[113] including one elegantly simple song about hosting the god Viṭṭhal:

> One day, Viṭho went to Janī's home.
> He gently asked for something to eat. "What should I give you, Father?" she replied.
> Taking his hand, she led him inside. She served him *pañcāmṛta* and rice.
> He belched, out of love and happiness. Janī says, "Viṭho is satisfied."[114]

Viṭṭhal's closeness to Janābāī is reflected in a related story that Mahīpati (*Bhaktavijay* 21:42–78) tells about Viṭṭhal stopping in the middle of a meal at Nāmdev's home when he sensed Janābāī's absence and sadness. Only after Janābāī is summoned to join in the meal does Viṭṭhal finish eating and feel satisfied.[115] Eknāth composed twenty-nine *abhaṅgas* about Kṛṣṇa's *kālā* with his cowherd companions. Tukārām composed over forty *kālā abhaṅgas*. One of these describes Kṛṣṇa's miracle of devouring a threatening fire: "Why do you marvel at this? No wonder Kṛṣṇa can work such miracles; after all, he is nourished by eating our food."[116]

The notion that God eats with devotees, not only out of compassion or companionship but because God is nourished by the bhaktas, resonates across many songs and stories in the Vārkarī tradition. God cannot restrain himself from eating with the bhaktas, including śūdra and Dalit bhaktas.

Vidyut Aklujkar points out that many of Nāmdev's *abhaṅgas* invert the hierarchy of devotee and deity through food.[117] Nāmdev's food, especially his leftovers, nourish God. His bhakti renders his leftovers invaluable, so much so that Viṭṭhal refuses to share Nāmdev's *ucchiṣṭa* with the other gods. A string of Nāmdev's *abhaṅgas* describes how Nāmdev would bring a food offering, *naivedya*, to the Viṭṭhal statue in Paṇḍharpūr, and he would not leave until Viṭṭhal consumed it entirely. This left Nāmdev with no *prasād* to bring home, which upset his parents.[118] In another story, from a set of *abhāṅgas* known as the *Tīrthāvaḷī*, about Nāmdev going on pilgrimage with Jñāndev, Viṭṭhal grows lonely in Paṇḍharpūr while they are away. The god longs to see Nāmdev and eat his leftovers—a sentiment that disturbs some brahmans who are Viṭṭhal's company at the time. Viṭṭhal chides them, saying that he happily sits in the same eating row (*paṅgat*) and eats with all saintly people, who are in actuality if not appearance upper-caste folk.[119] This is the same logic we saw in the Ravidās story: a brahman essence is concealed in a Dalit body.

Mahīpati elaborates on this story in his *Bhaktavijay*, describing in great detail what happens when Nāmdev returns from pilgrimage and hosts a celebratory feast.[120] Some brahmans observe God (Viṭṭhal/Kṛṣṇa) eating Nāmdev's *ucchiṣṭa* at the feast and are confounded by this apparently impure act. The brahmans initially consider just ignoring it, following a custom of not speaking about extraordinary deeds. But they also concur that this is not an extreme case of *āpad-dharma* where rules may be reasonably broken. Moreover, the brahmans note that they may incur guilt themselves if they remain silent witnesses of a truly wrong act.

So the brahmans confront God and argue that although God is not bound by caste distinctions, he ought to bear in mind that humans must abide by the earthly rules that the Vedas and *śāstras* laid out. Kṛṣṇa responds that his overriding concern is for pure bhakti from his devotees, and eating their *ucchiṣṭa* sustains his good, healthy form. The brahmans reassert that of course God is not bound by caste, but on earth, the rules are the rules, so they request that Kṛṣṇa conform, out of respect for his human companions' limitations. Additionally, the brahmans ask Kṛṣṇa to undergo ritual purification for having eaten with a low-caste person. Kṛṣna agrees, on the condition that the brahmans care for Nāmdev. Kṛṣṇa briefly offers the brahmans a lesson on four metaphorical kinds of "bathing": listening to and meditating on the Purāṇas and *kīrtans*, making oneself physically clean inside and out, controlling all sense organs, and, best of all, showing compassion to all creatures. Then the brahmans lead Kṛṣna to the river, say some mantras, and rub cow dung and ashes on him. In narrating the scene, Mahīpati repeats several times that Kṛṣṇa, although blameless, went along with the purification to put the brahmans' minds at ease.

Mahīpati probably anticipated that God's actions here would confuse his audience, so he directly gave voice to the problem within the narrative. In the divine realm, Rādhā asks Rukmiṇī why the Lord of the Universe allowed himself to be purified, despite having done nothing wrong.[121] Rukmiṇī explains that Kṛṣṇa was so absorbed in his love for Nāmdev that he forgot worldly purity rules. Like a mother who drops everything when her child cries, Kṛṣṇa had only Nāmdev's pure devotion in mind when he accepted the penance demanded by the brahmans. This is a novel argument: Kṛṣṇa actually did not care about caste. He only sought to quickly resolve the matter so he could return to Nāmdev. Rukmiṇī's explanation effectively ignores Kṛṣṇa's own justification of his actions.

Later that day, Kṛṣṇa discusses this topic with Rukmiṇī further, emphasizing that extraordinary bhakti compels Kṛṣṇa to respond, as if paying off a karmic debt he had incurred because of his bhaktas' faith. Kṛṣṇa then offers his own feast in Paṇḍharpūr, inviting the brahmans and low-caste bhaktas to eat. In an extended narration of Kṛṣṇa revealing himself in impressive *saguṇa* and *nirguṇa* ways, Mahīpati seems inclined to overwhelm his audience with awe, as Kṛṣṇa did with his hierophanic appearance to Arjuna in the *BhG*. Although Mahīpati explores various explanations of Kṛṣṇa's commensality with Nāmdev, he ultimately resorts to a divine revelation to prove his point, as if logic alone were not sufficiently persuasive.

Kṛṣṇa/Viṭṭhal sits down to eat alongside his bhaktas once more, and the brahmans finally admit that Kṛṣṇa never needed to undergo purification. They realize that it was only out of Kṛṣṇa's compassion for the obstinate brahmans that he played along with the purification. This story is the longest reflection on bhakti and caste in the entire Marathi canon.

Nāmdev's śūdra status in this story is crucial for revealing Kṛṣṇa's love. An even more extreme example of transgressive commensality appears in a story about the Mahār *sant* Cokhāmeḷā, who is said to have been Nāmdev's contemporary. Food is integral to Cokhāmeḷā's own birth. His mother, who had been barren, became pregnant after consuming a partially eaten mango given to her by a wandering holy man. The more memorable story, which we considered briefly in the Introduction, depicts Cokhāmeḷā and Viṭṭhal. This appeared in its earliest form in Eknāth's songs and was elaborated in Mahīpati's *BhV* (chapter 23). Cokhā is described as a pious bhakta who is fated to admire Viṭṭhal from afar, since his Dalit status precluded him from entering the temple. Viṭṭhal recognizes Cokhā's devotion, and one night he leads Cokhā by the hand into the temple's inner sanctum to be near him. A priest who was sleeping nearby overhears Cokhā talking inside the temple, and he summons a crowd of brahmans to reprimand Cokhā. They ban him from Paṇḍharpūr and exile him to the other side of the river. Deprived of his devotee, Viṭṭhal then crosses the river and sits down to share a meal with Cokhā. A passing brahman notices the group. Cokhā's wife accidentally spills some curds on Viṭṭhal's robes, and Cokhā scolds her. The brahman cannot fathom that Viṭṭhal might eat with Cokhā: "For how can the Lord of the World have dined with one who is an outcaste?" Convinced that Cokhā is merely acting and trying to deceive him, the brahman interrupts the meal and slaps Cokhā.

When the brahman returns to the temple in Paṇḍharpūr, however, he notices that Viṭṭhal's clothes have yogurt spilled on them and Viṭṭhal's cheek is swollen precisely where the brahman had hit Cokhā. The priest apologizes to Cokhā and, leading him by the hand, brings Cokhā into the temple to be near Viṭṭhal again. And from that time onward, Cokhā "began coming into the temple."[122]

Conclusion

There is a lot going on in these stories about Viṭṭhal and his bhaktas. Stories about holy figures convey messages to listeners that go beyond their literal significance, as Sascha Ebeling has argued.

> Discerning a particular theological (or ideological) intention may allow us to see the social *function* of the text, its "social logic." . . . It may allow us to examine how larger (religio-)political issues are negotiated through the genre of hagiographical writing, for if hagiography was never written to chronicle reality, it was also never meant *only* to provide a pleasant, edifying story. It always served very real (and this is where the truth comes back in) ideological or political purposes, such as the negotiation of power and status amongst social groups or individuals.[123]

So, what are these stories of commensality doing? Where do their social logics lead? These questions will occupy us for the remainder of the book.

Prasād, *naivedya*, and *ucchiṣṭa* are central to the stories I have examined here. *Prasād* is present in the stories, especially in the Mahānubhāv examples. Nāmdev insists that God consume his entire food offering, leaving no *ucchiṣṭa* and thus no *prasād* behind—something that confounds Nāmdev's parents. But depictions of *prasād* in Marathi bhakti literature are not so common, especially compared to its ubiquity in Hindu temples today.

For the most part, *naivedya*'s role is assumed in these stories; audiences would need no explanation of why people are offering food to a deity. People who engage in this activity, such as Nāmdev setting food before Viṭṭhal, are regarded as exemplary bhaktas. Some readers may call to mind Ravidās' famous poem about how all *naivedya* offerings necessarily have polluted origins: the calf dirtied the cow's teat from which milk came, fish swam in the water, and bees walked on the flowers.[124] The Vārkarīs are also concerned about the pollution and power of offerings, but their emphasis is quite different, particularly in the stories that invert the roles of who is creating and consuming *ucchiṣṭa*. God seeks out and benefits from eating bhaktas' leftovers. This dimension of divine-human commensality not only transcends *dharmaśāstr*ic conventions of ritual purity; it directly contradicts the classic prohibition of burning *ucchiṣṭa*, as if making an impure sacrifice. In Vārkarī discourse, this sense of ultimacy about love for devotees, causing God to break with convention and social code, is how the bhakti side of the bhakti-caste riddle pushes the boundary of what is acceptable, right, and normative. Without calling attention to it or perhaps even being conscious of doing so, this Vārkarī view of *ucchiṣṭa* resonates with the Vedic theme of *anna*'s cosmic flow, but with a surprising redirection.

A final rubric that enmeshes food into Vārkarī discourse and practice is *kālā*.[125] Commensality is built into *kālā*—as in the popular purāṇic story that the Vārkarīs sing about and in the custom they still reenact around the pilgrimage to Paṇḍharpūr and other events. This is a literary precedent for a practical divine-human engagement around food. Because of this commensal dimension, which traditionally disregards caste distinctions, it may be tempting to view *kālā* as an event of anti-structural assertion, quotidian revolt, or an institutionalization of an egalitarian impulse. Indeed, the few scholars who have studied *kālā* are inclined toward such interpretations,[126] but my reticence about equality language extends to these cases as well.

In her analysis of Tamil Śaiva hymns, Karen Pechilis emphasizes the embodied nature of bhakti. Saints sing of how it feels to adore and be absorbed in Śiva. The effects of bhakti move their bodies, which is represented in sculpture and hagiographical stories.[127] Although some sightings of bhakti are based on region-specific features, as I argued in Chapter 2, Pechilis is discussing something that is widespread and valued across regions and languages. I would add that commensality—both in its capacity of sharing and common participation and in its tangible enactment of inclusivity—is a similar example of embodiment on a social level. Nathaniel Roberts has reflected poignantly on this among Dalits in a slum in Chennai:

> Some truths can be learned simply through observation. Others require interaction—pushing and being pushed back, touching others and allowing oneself to be touched. The giving and receiving of food is among the most important ways common being is affirmed in India, and by refusing others' food that commonality is denied.[128]

Because of humans' corporeal experience of it, food is a powerful material for conveying meaning. It invokes organic and social logics that words alone cannot, which is why a critical commensality approach is so valuable.

The Marathi bhakti stories about commensality that we have considered here, especially about Nāmdev and Cokhāmeḷā, reveal hagiographers working out theological and social problems through their narrations. Mahīpati allows us access to Kṛṣṇa's private reflections on why he both should eat the low-caste Nāmdev's food as well as appease brahmans' demands for purity. The audience witnesses Viṭṭhal's inner thoughts about Cokhāmeḷā, which impel him to leave his temple to share a meal. The narrative choices that a hagiographer like Mahīpati makes—to emphasize or embellish details, to foster ambiguities, and to pass silently over cognitive tensions—are important. A sensitive reading of a hagiographical text may reveal some of these authorial inclinations. Viewing many texts together and tracking narrative patterns and variations makes these inclinations even clearer. This is especially the case with stories about Eknāth, food, and Dalits.

5

Memories of Transgressive Commensality

Stories about food have been important to bhakti traditions across India, especially in Maharashtra. And food is present in stories about many Marathi saints, and none more than Eknāth. His status as a brahman in the notoriously orthodox town of Paiṭhaṇ positioned Eknāth well to be both an authoritative teacher and an object of public scrutiny. The historical Eknāth stood at many cultural and political crossroads. His guru Janārdana worked for a Muslim ruler and associated with a god who appeared in Muslim guises. Eknāth got married, had children, and enjoyed a happy home life (aside from a stubbornly orthodox son), all while maintaining his devotional rituals and teaching. Eknāth's literary corpus crossed popular and learned genres, composed mostly in Marathi but also some Hindusthani, as well as a little Persian and Kannada. Some texts reveal familiarity with Sanskrit philosophical traditions and Persian administrative letter-writing, while others observe customs, games, and aspects of non-elite life. As a figure of history, Eknāth was a complex, multifaceted man.[1]

As a figure of public memory,[2] Eknāth is more straightforward but no less interesting. He became the epitome of a spiritually accomplished yet socially conscious bhakta—a person who was unafraid to break with tradition when his principles called for it yet who consciously strove to maintain good relations with his fellow brahmans.[3] This is most evident in the stories about him transgressing caste boundaries, especially with Dalits. Many of Eknāth's compositions, especially his allegorical drama-poems (*bhārūḍs*) demonstrate an extraordinary degree of interest in Dalits, but memory of Eknāth was shaped much more by hagiographical stories that were told about him.

As hagiographers interpret and retell saintly stories, they do so in ways that align with their own concerns. No less than works of abstract philosophical reflection and legal jurisprudence, hagiography argues doctrinal positions. But hagiography makes these arguments through narrative and thus reaches a wider audience to shape public memory more extensively than philosophical texts.

Shared Devotion, Shared Food. Jon Keune, Oxford University Press. © Oxford University Press 2021.
DOI: 10.1093/oso/9780197574836.003.0006

The popular nature of saintly stories, which are recited and enacted before diverse audiences, makes them conduits of messages about the nature of reality and proper human conduct. This chapter explores messages that were conveyed through controversial stories about Eknāth's transgressive commensality and how the stories changed over time. These stories, two of which we encountered in the Introduction, illustrate food's semantic density and highlight hagiographers' strategically ambiguous use of it to handle the bhakti-caste question. To appreciate what these stories were doing, some background information is necessary.

The sources

Six major Marathi compositions tell stories about Eknāth. The earliest one does not deal with food or inter-caste relations, so it will not be central to this chapter. This is the *Śrīkhaṇḍhyākhyān* (Tale of Śrīkhaṇḍyā), which is attributed to Eknāth's grandson Mukteśvar, a famous Marathi *pant-kavi* or pandit-poet in the mid-17th century.[4] Unlike *sant-kavis* or saint-poets like Eknāth and Tukārām, *pant-kavis* aspired to aesthetic and rhetorical excellence, rather than connecting with the masses. In just under one hundred verses, the *Śrīkhaṇḍyākhyān* depicts a single *purāṇa*-like episode, in which Kṛṣṇa is so impressed by Eknāth's devotion that he adopts the guise of a poor brahman to work as a servant in Eknāth's home. One of his tasks is to grind sandalwood (*śrīkhaṇḍa*) for ritual worship, thus giving rise to his name Śrīkhaṇḍyā. This text is noteworthy both as the origin of the Śrīkhaṇḍyā character who appears in later hagiographies and because it shows that not all hagiographers were fixated on Eknāth's caste-transgressive behavior.

The *Pratiṣṭhān-caritra* (Story of Paiṭhaṇ, abbreviated *PC*) is more relevant. The single known manuscript of the *PC* was held by a family who claim to be Eknāth's descendants in the town of Vaṭhār, roughly sixty kilometers south of Pune.[5] Composed around 1700, the *PC* did not circulate much, if at all. Only after the family was persuaded to publish it in 1948 did the Marathi-reading public learn of its existence.[6] Nothing is known of its author, Kṛṣṇadās Jagadānanda-nandan, aside from minor autobiographical comments within the text. In just over one thousand verses, the *PC* narrates nearly the entirety of Eknāth's life and highlights extreme acts of devotion to his guru and charity to people.

The more commonly known stories about Eknāth first appeared in the *Eknāthcaritra* (Story of Eknāth, henceforth *EC*), composed by Keśavsvāmī in 1760. Eknāth's descendants in Paiṭhaṇ identify him as a disciple of one of their ancestors.[7] The 2,600 verses of the *EC* circulated widely, both on their own and as they were incorporated later by Mahīpati in one of his works. The *EC* emphasizes Eknāth's semi-divine status as an *avatār* of Viṣṇu, Kṛṣna, and Viṭṭhal. It differs from the *PC* on some key details, such as how Eknāth first came to his guru Janārdana and the town where Janārdana was based. The *EC* frames stories about Eknāth and Dalits in terms of Eknāth's semi-divine salvific work.

In the latter half of the 18th century, Marathi authors began composing collective hagiographies, which compiled stories about many saints together. Early examples of such compendia by Uddhav Cidghana and Dāsopant Digambar appear now to be lost.[8] Most influential are the works of Mahīpati (1715–1790), who lived in the hamlet of Tāhārābād, north of Ahmadnagar.[9] Mahīpati was a *kīrtan* performer and thus well versed in Vārkarī songs and lore. He gathered his capacious knowledge about Marathi and North Indian saints into four massive collective hagiographies, loosely weaving their stories into a grand meta-narrative about Viṣṇu sending gods and sages as *avatārs* to the world. To justify his profligacy and inclusion of variant stories, Mahīpati pointed out some precedents: the Purāṇas' diversity, the Vedas' fourfold structure, the *Rāmāyaṇa*'s seven divisions, and the *Mahābhārata*'s sheer immensity.

Eknāth appears in two of Mahīpati's works: the *Bhaktavijay* (Victory of the Bhaktas, *BhV*) and the *Bhaktalīlāmṛt* (Essence of the Bhaktas' Divine Play, *BhL*), composed in 1762 and 1774 respectively. The *BhV* contains over ten thousand verses about more than fifty different saints. The roughly four hundred verses that describe Eknāth overlap slightly with some *PC* stories but not enough to demonstrate a clear line of influence. A quarter of the *BhL*'s 10,800 verses are about Eknāth, which Mahīpati drew extensively from Keśavsvāmī's *EC*, sometimes verbatim and often with embellishments. The *BhV* and *BhL* contain variant renditions of some stories. Mahīpati apparently was more intent on archiving all the stories he encountered rather than attempting to identify a preferred rendition.

The final hagiography about Eknāth comes from outside the Vārkarī orbit. The author, Bhīmasvāmī (also called Bhīmakavi), was the head of a maṭh in the town of Śirgāv that venerated the late 17th-century *sādhu* and poet Rāmdās.[10] Among other compositions, Bhīmasvāmī composed a collective hagiography in 1797 entitled *Bhaktalīlāmṛt* (*BhL2*), probably in the hope of connecting with or even superseding Mahīpati's *BhL*. Many of his renditions and even entire stories diverge from previous hagiographies and show greater concern about caste hierarchy and Muslims. The *BhL2* seems not to have circulated much.[11] More than a third of the text's 3,721 verses are about Rāmdās and his followers, but Eknāth also receives substantial attention—417 verses—which probably reflects a memory in Rāmdāsī community that Rāmdās and Eknāth were distantly related.[12] Stories about Eknāth, food, and transgressive commensality thus come from five main sources:

Date	Author	Title	Abbreviation
ca. 1700	Kṛṣṇadās	*Pratiṣṭhāncaritra*	*PC*
1760	Keśavsvāmī	*Eknāthcaritra*	*EC*
1762	Mahīpati	*Bhaktavijay*	*BhV*
1774	Mahīpati	*Bhaktalīlāmṛt*	*BhL*
1797	Bhīmasvāmī	*Bhaktalīlāmṛt*	*BhL2*

One approach to reading hagiographical stories would be to seek out what they mean. What did authors hope their audiences would take away? To nudge their audiences toward emotional responses and cognitive lessons, hagiographers rely on literary devices: narrative pace, diction, intertextual references, and strategic depictions of a saint's opponents and allies. By consistently using certain devices within a text, a hagiographer systematically portrays a saint and orients audiences toward a preferred significance or meaning. In this way, hagiographers shape the public memory of saints and suggest how followers ought to respond: through emulation, worship, commemoration, and so on. Food stories in the *PC* and *EC* demonstrate this well, as they are embedded in two quite different frames of meaning.

Food as signifier of extreme bhakti

In the *PC*, Kṛṣṇadās uses food to illustrate the extent of Eknāth's devotion to Janārdana, which was so strong that it compelled him to ignore social, religious, and even hygienic norms. In all hagiographies, Eknāth reveres his guru as practically divine—an association that is easy to make, since Janārdana is a common epithet of Viṣṇu and Kṛṣṇa.[13] Eknāth even incorporated his guru's name into the moniker that he used to conclude his compositions—Ekā-Janārdana or some variant thereof. Although bhakti to one's guru is prominent in every hagiographer's stories about Eknāth, Kṛṣṇadās emphasizes its radicality by dwelling on the shocking nature of Eknāth's acts.

In one story (*PC* 4:2–45), Eknāth cleans Janārdana's pit toilet by hand, working intimately with the highly polluting product of food consumption. Eknāth overhears Janārdana instruct a servant to summon some people to clean out his full toilet-mound. Eknāth thinks to himself, "Another person should not be allowed to touch my *svāmī*'s feces. . . . Only fools would call a place where Janārdana defecates unholy."[14] So he does the work himself, stunning onlookers as well as the cleaners who eventually arrive. Kṛṣṇadās narrates the process extensively, specifying eight different hand tools that Eknāth used and highlighting how his body became covered with the reeking muck. Two later hagiographies mention this episode very briefly; only Kṛṣṇadās delves into the finer details of cleaning the toilet.[15]

Eknāth's extreme devotion more often involves food before it is digested, especially the question of what qualifies as *prasād* and how one should behave toward it. Kṛṣṇadās gives one especially startling example. To assist Janārdana with his morning self-care routine, Eknāth sets out a stool and a basin so that Janārdana can wash his mouth and clear his lungs. Eknāth thinks to himself, "Of course I revere the water that washes his feet (*caraṇodak*), but I'll also worship the water that comes from the Lord's face—his mouthwash, sweat, saliva and spittle" (3:19). Kṛṣṇadās comments, "Who would touch such water in a basin? But going to hide behind the *tulsī* altar, Eknāth gulped it down out of devotion. Saliva, spit, phlegm and bile became just like water. There, Ekā joyfully drank it as if it were guru-*prasād*" (3:21–22). By posing the rhetorical question, specifying the effluvia, and pointing out that Eknāth hid himself from view while doing this, Kṛṣṇadās clearly expected his audience to be shocked. Also in this case, only Kṛṣṇadās revels in such details; two later hagiographies mention it only briefly.[16]

In a story that was never repeated, Janārdana hosts a large, elaborate meal for some brahmans. At the meal's conclusion, Eknāth sees Janārdana's leftover food, and he cannot restrain himself. "Abandoning all shame, Ekā became a cow-mouth [*gomukhī*].[17] Without hesitation, Ekā ran to receive the *ucchiṣṭa*. Along with the *ucchiṣṭa*, he also licked and swallowed the plates made of stitched leaves as *prasād* from his guru. Then women began to talk. He had done something extraordinary" (3:51–53). As the women discuss Eknāth's behavior with the *ucchiṣṭa*, they reveal that Eknāth had not discarded

Janārdana's spittle-water that morning but drank it. Janārdana listens and responds, "This devotion [*bhajan*] is extremely profound" (3:55).[18]

Janārdana does not mean this in an entirely positive way. Kṛṣṇadās comments that although Janārdana appreciated Eknāth's fervor, he worried that such behavior would create "burdens" [*vojheṃ*] that would result in "shame in all respects" [*lāj sarvathā*] (3:58).[19] So Janārdana issues a stern warning: "You collected the leaves and leftovers and licked them without hesitation. And you drank defiling [*amaṅgal*] water.[20] Who gave you this idea? To hell with your body-consciousness [*dehabuddhi*]; you have thrown away your own purity [*śuddhi*]. From now on, hold firm to a right consciousness [*sadbuddhi*] and always act according to the three purities [*triśuddhi*].[21] You too should take the paths that people take" (3:72–74).

Kṛṣṇadās may have had his rhyme scheme at least partially in mind when he chose these words, but they create a logical problem. Body-consciousness (*dehabuddhi*) is usually a spiritual hindrance to overcome. This is not Eknāth's issue. Perhaps Janārdana was referring elliptically to Eknāth's lack of body-consciousness, or maybe he meant, "Sure, to hell with your body-consciousness—fine and good—but don't forget . . . ." Whatever Janārdana might mean here is beside the point; Kṛṣṇadās conveys his real message through Eknāth's rebuttal.

Rather than touch Janārdana's feet and meekly accept his advice, Eknāth sidesteps the argument and focuses instead on how radical bhakti is actually unselfish and even more—it is done for the public good (3:75–91). To walk on the "paths that people take" would be misguided, because those paths tempt the senses and lead to drowning in the sea of worldly existence. Instead, Eknāth argues, people should be pushed off their paths to discover Janārdana, "who is the very source of their humanity" (3:76). He points out that since Janārdana pervades everything, nothing is utterly unclean. Concern about impurity arises only if one fails to understand the world's true nature. Eknāth insists that his extreme acts are based on truly apprehending reality and being a role model to less enlightened folk.

One more act of extreme devotion appears in the *PC*'s ninth chapter, after Janārdana had died and Eknāth settled in Paiṭhaṇ as a householder. Eknāth hosts a feast for brahmans to honor his guru's death anniversary, but he runs out of ghee. After trying in vain to acquire some from his neighbors, Eknāth creates ghee miraculously from buckets of water. The brahmans find it so tasty they empty their drinking cups and fill them with ghee to take home when they depart (9:64). Amid the remnants of the feast's wondrous conclusion, another strange scene occurs:

> Then Eknāth rolled in the *ucchiṣṭa* without hesitation. Eknāth rolled in the brahmans' leftovers. Other guileless people who understood rolled in the leftovers too. . . . Because of Eknāth's actions, leftovers were on his whole body. Putting aside status, he eagerly rolled. . . . He and others threw (*ucchiṣṭa*) at each other and ran. They happily sang the stories of Kṛṣṇa. Then they all danced. . . . They picked up morsels of *ucchiṣṭa* and threw them at each other. . . . Then they reached the bank of the Gaṅgā (Godāvarī), where they played *humbarī* and began to bathe.[22] (9:67–73)

I am not aware of any precedent in Marathi literature or custom for rolling in leftover food. It somewhat resembles the controversial practice of *made snāna* in Karnataka, during which Dalits customarily rolled on food left over from upper-caste people's meals,[23] but such an inter-caste dimension is not present here. The food fight scene almost certainly hearkens to *BhP* 10.5.14, in which Kṛṣṇa plays with his cowherd companions.[24] In the Chapter 4, we observed people's interaction with Kṛṣṇa's food mountain in Jatipurā, which was also based on a story from the *BhP*. In that case, the food was fresh, awaiting consumption. In this story, however, the food is explicitly *ucchiṣṭa*. Kṛṣṇadās notably repeats phrases about Eknāth rolling in *ucchiṣṭa* many times, even though his audience would have understood if he had written it only once. Kṛṣṇadās knew his audience would find the scene shocking, and he sought to enhance that feeling.

The astonishing quality of the extreme devotional acts—cleaning the toilet, drinking the spittoon's contents, becoming a cow-mouth, and rolling in leftovers—is a theme that runs throughout the *PC*. Kṛṣṇadās' message comes across explicitly when Eknāth justifies his behavior to a concerned Janārdana. In the *PC*, true bhakti cannot be restrained by conventions of purity, social acceptability, or self-image. To convey this lesson, Kṛṣṇadās routinely resorts to food: what qualifies as edible, how one handles leftovers, and how one regards its eventual excretion from the guru's body. It is in this perspective of extreme bhakti, I believe, that the most acute episode of social tension in the *PC*—the story of the *śrāddha* meal that I discuss later in this chapter—ought to be read as well.

Compassionate hospitality

Food stories in Keśavsvāmī's *Eknāthcaritra* (*EC*) emphasize Eknāth's generosity and compassion, rather than extreme devotion. This is readily apparent in the epithets that Keśavsvāmī uses for Eknāth. Over fifty times, Keśavsvāmī describes him with the word *avatār*, either by itself or as part of a compound. Keśavsvāmī portrays Eknāth carrying out a divine purpose in the world and embodying divine presence as a *jagadoddhārak* or "uplifter of the world."[25] This and closely related terms appear twenty-five times in the text, often when describing Eknāth performing a *kīrtan*.[26] Slightly less often, Keśavsvāmī applies the terms *dīnoddhāra* (upliftment of the lowly) and *dīnadayāḷ* (compassionate to the lowly), and he often describes Eknāth's compassion toward people who are *patita* (fallen) and *anātha* (protectorless or orphaned). All of these are common epithets for Kṛṣṇa, with lowliness referring to spiritual conditions. In the *EC*'s narrative, they are applied almost always to low-caste, Dalit, or poor people whose caste is not identified.[27] A few episodes demonstrate this salvific frame of meaning.

Chapter 11 contains a chain of stories about food that all stem from a vow of hospitality that Eknāth takes. After he finishes a *kīrtan* during which he read out the *BhP* in Marathi so that women, śūdras, and the like (*strīśūdrādi*) would understand,[28] Eknāth's reputation spreads and the way of bhakti (*bhakti-panth*) increases. Local brahmans grow concerned: "Where has this Eknāth come from? Because of him, all the people have become *bhagavad-bhaktas*. So many have abandoned the ways of earthly life and think now only of their spiritual state! They no longer revere us brahmans. The stability of the world is ruined. . . . Where did this useless man Eknāth come from? All the simple and foolish people have been enchanted by him" (*EC* 11:36–41).

The brahmans recall Eknāth's public vow to feed any guests who arrive at his home without asking them about their family or *jāti*.[29] As in the story about Kabīr in Chapter 4, the brahmans scheme to exploit this generosity. First, they make a pact to never again eat at Eknāth's home so that he may no longer earn merit by feeding them (brahmans). Then, they start sending crowds of beggars to Eknāth's home at all hours, telling them that Eknāth is a generous patron who gives out food. Finally, the antagonists guide four brahman travelers to Eknāth's home late one night after a thunderstorm had drenched the entire town and made food scarce. When Eknāth's servant finds no dry firewood to cook with, Eknāth breaks apart his own furniture to use as fuel. Despite the brahmans' daily torments, Eknāth remains calm, compassionate, and empathetic (11:53–69).

The *EC* contains two vignettes in which Eknāth gives food to Dalit thieves. In the first story (20:2–45), Eknāth arrives home late after performing a *kīrtan*. Four thieves had broken into his home, but they fail to discover any valuables and wonder if God is tricking them. Eknāth pities the thieves, commenting that only people who are truly desperate would be out so late. This unexpected compassion moves the thieves to repent and ask Eknāth to forgive them. More boldly, they ask him to give them his *prasād*. So Eknāth wakes his wife and servant to prepare food. The Dalit thieves circumambulate Eknāth and say, "We're saved, we're saved [*uddharloṃ*]. We were fallen [*patita*], but you are purifying [*pāvan*]." Keśavsvāmī concludes by commenting that Eknāth demonstrates how a bhakta should observe no differentiation (*viṣamatā*).[30]

In the second episode (21:5–38), Keśavsvāmī introduces a "nameless" (*anāmik*) or Dalit thief whose body had wasted away in prison. The man somehow manages to escape but is too weak to go far.[31] He hears Eknāth performing a *kīrtan* in the distance and crawls nearer to listen. He is so deeply moved that he returns the next night.[32] He enters Eknāth's courtyard, sits in a solitary place, and eventually faints from exhaustion. After finishing his *kīrtan*, Eknāth notices the man and offers to help. He wakes up his family to cook food that befits the man's weak condition. Eknāth listens to the man's story and invites him to remain as a guest for as long as he likes, eating Eknāth's food until his body recovers. Keśavsvāmī concludes by commenting, "Compassion [*dayā*] should be placed at the head of all dharma—this was the mark of Śrī Nāth's nature."[33]

The episode of the *anāmik* thief concludes, but its significance carries into the subsequent episode, in which Eknāth encounters a brahman *rākṣasa* (demon) who begs Eknāth to share his surplus merit and release the *rākṣasa* from the bonds of past sins. Eknāth asks for clarification—should he transfer the merit he accrued by carrying out daily rituals, or the merit from feeding the poor Dalit man. The *rākṣasa* opts for the latter and is immediately is freed (21:44–59). When Eknāth returns home, his guest feels strong enough to depart (21:61). In case the rightness of Eknāth's action toward the Dalit thief were not clear enough, Keśavsvāmī ratifies it with the subsequent *rākṣasa* story.

When Mahīpati incorporated the *EC* into his *Bhaktalīlāmṛt* (*BhL*), he embellished these stories of compassionate food sharing, both to close gaps in Keśavsvāmī's narratives and to elaborate on them. When orthodox brahmans complain about Eknāth, they specify that they were especially unhappy with Eknāth's use of Prākṛt (Marathi) and the way his *kīrtans* lured away their wives (17:32–45). To prepare food for the four brahman travelers on a stormy night, Eknāth takes apart not only his bed but even parts of his walls to start a fire for cooking (17:55–66). Whereas in the *EC*, four thieves in Eknāth's home were strangely unable to locate any valuables, Mahīpati states that God struck them blind (20:142). Eknāth unlocks his treasury and offers it to them, and he then serves food to them by hand, physically helping the blind men to eat (20:161). Mahīpati adjusts Keśavsvāmī's story of the fugitive thief, stating that prison guards released him. Eknāth's wife prepares specifically a gruel of wheat flour, milk, and sugar for the man, which Eknāth feeds to him by hand, from Eknāth's own dish. Mahīpati concludes, "He ate Eknāth's food. His evil mind left his body. He began affectionately worshipping Śrī Hari" (20:201).

Food stories reveal Eknāth as the embodiment of divine compassion. If the *PC*'s Eknāth demonstrates extreme bhakti by consuming surprising forms of *prasād* from others, the *EC*'s Eknāth is an *avatār* who charitably serves his *prasād* to others. Food fits in still other frames of meaning in these texts as well.

Food in Eknāth's encounter with Dattātreya

One of the most controversial historical aspects of Eknāth's life is the identity of his *paramaguru*, or guru of his own guru Janārdana. Major hagiographies narrate the meeting slightly differently, but all concur that he first appears to Eknāth in the form of a Muslim. This figure eventually reveals himself as the god Dattātreya, which is what Eknāth's followers today emphasize: Eknāth's guru was Janārdana, and his *paramaguru* was God himself. Some historians, however, have argued that this historical figure was Muslim. This provocative claim merits a brief side note, before turning to stories of commensality.

In 1958, the Marathi historian V. S. Bendre published a novel theory that behind the story of Dattātreya and Eknāth was a historical Muslim man.[34] Two other leading scholars, R. C. Ḍhere and S. G. Tulpule, repeated this argument, lending it further credibility. By correlating several pieces of information, the scholars calculated that the Dattātreya figure was actually a *ṣūfī* of the Kādirī order who was popularly known as Cānd Bodhle.[35] The scholars pointed to a couple of appearances of Janārdana's guru, where Cānd Bodhle and very similar names appear. Many scholars now cite this tantalizing theory about a hidden *ṣūfī* connection. The Slovakian historian Dušan Deák, however, has pointed out several flaws in this precise identification of a Kādirī *ṣūfī*. One overriding problem is that regional *ṣūfī* orders around Eknāth's time (such as in nearby Khuldābād) were institutionally rigid and based in towns, unlike the mendicant, heterodox figure who appears in the stories.[36] So if Eknāth's *paramaguru* is identified with some Cānd Bodhle, Deák argues that we should envision someone like a non-institutional, yoga-practicing, *bhāṅg*-consuming, idiosyncratic religious itinerant who freely adapted whatever ideas and practices suited him.[37] I think Deák's caution here is wise.

Whoever Eknāth's *paramaguru* may have been (and I doubt we can know for certain), what is most relevant to this book are the stories of Eknāth eating with him. These illustrate two additional roles of food—as an instrument for unlocking higher levels of consciousness, and as a site for testing one's spiritual development.

In Kṛṣṇadās' short rendition (*PC* 2:67–71), Janārdana brings Eknāth to a secluded place within his compound in Ahmadnagar and shares secret knowledge.

> While Janārdana was instructing Eknāth, Cānd Bodh Candraśekhar arrived, the great *sādhū* and famous *avatār* of Dattātreya. He was extremely tall.[38] He saw Janārdana and began to laugh. He approached them, along with two dogs, who were Kāmadhenu himself. He stopped near where Janārdana was sitting. Seeing his sadguru Candraśekhar, Janārdana did *namaskār*. Janārdana reported all the news (about Eknāth), and Candraśekhar was pleased. Candraśekhar chewed some *pān* and placed it in Eknāth's mouth. He said, "You will become eloquent in the knowledge of Brahman." Having said this, he disappeared. Janārdana prostrated himself and said to Eknāth, "My *svāmī* has given you *darśan* and disappeared. Today you received fruitful knowledge." Janārdana was pleased and embraced Eknāth. At that moment, Ekā was transformed, and the sound of Kṛṣṇa-worship fell on his ears. He saw Kṛṣṇa clearly everywhere: in people, in the forest, and in uninhabited places [*janī, vanī, vijanī*].

Kṛṣṇadās' rendition is unique in mentioning the figure's extraordinary height and placing the encounter in Ahmadnagar. Dattātreya shares food intimately by transferring it directly from his mouth into Eknāth's. God creates *ucchiṣṭa* (*prasād*), proactively blesses Eknāth with it, and thereby alters Eknāth's vision of the world.[39]

Keśavsvāmī renders the encounter quite differently, and in two episodes. In one, Eknāth encounters his *paramaguru*, and in a later story, he meets a wise guru named Cānd while traveling to Tryambakeśvar, near Nāśik.[40] The *paramaguru* encounter (*EC* 3:4–51) occurs when Janārdana, who in this text worked in Devgiri/Daulatābād for a Muslim ruler who gave his officers Fridays off, takes Eknāth to a mountain lake north of town. Keśavsvāmī explains that Janārdana regularly went to this place to commune with Datta. On this occasion, Datta arrived with "his body clothed with leather, looking and eating like a *fakīr malaṅg*" and accompanied by Kāmadhenu in the form of dogs. Datta gives Janārdana a pot and tells him to milk the dogs, while Datta takes food out of a sack he was carrying. Datta mashes the food into the dog milk, and he and Janārdana eat "without hesitating, from the same bowl." After finishing, Datta tells Eknāth to wash the vessel, which Keśavsvāmī explains is a test. Eknāth happily takes the bowl and thinks, "God himself changed his dress and came here." Eknāth consumes the leftover food that he recognizes as *prasād*, washes the dish, and returns. Datta comments appreciatively, "This one is an *avatār* of Viṭṭhal, who will be a blessing for many people. Through his books and speech, beings will find the path of bhakti. . . . Eknāth's style of *kīrtan*s and writings will save countless people. . . . Having drunk everything, he stands before us in glory" (*EC* 3:42). Datta embraces Eknāth and reveals his true form, with lotus eyes, a mouth like the moon, and six arms.

When Mahīpati repeats this story (*BhV* 45:74–82), he enhances food's role as an instrument of testing and complicates Eknāth's response. Janārdana brings Eknāth to a jungle to meet Dattātreya, and he cautions Eknāth not to be scared, since Datta "assumes a form that ignorant people revile." Janārdana also instructs Eknāth to eat whatever Datta offers him. Eknāth confidently agrees. But then he sees Datta.

> Suddenly a Muslim [*avindha*, one with unpierced ears] arrived, seated on a horse. When Eknāth beheld his form, fear gripped his stomach. Eknāth said, "He looks like a real *yavana*. I think what Janārdana told me was false." His forehead was broad, and eyes were bloodshot. He held weapons while riding the horse. He got down, and Janārdana revered him. Janārdana and Dattātreya sat down and began speaking *yavana* language. Witnessing this,

> Eknāth was greatly surprised. The sadguru told Janārdana, "I am hungry. Let's eat." He prepared a variety of dishes and displayed a wondrous sight. He served the six rasas on a golden plate adorned with jewels. Janārdana sat down near him, and they ate together.

When Datta invites Eknāth to join, he wonders, "How can I eat food of a *yavana*?" and runs away. Datta vanishes, and Janārdana chastises Eknāth for being misled by appearances and missing a great opportunity.

Later, Janārdana and Eknāth return to the jungle. This time, Datta appears in the form of a mendicant (*malaṅg*), accompanied by a woman and a dog, whom Mahīpati identifies as Māyā incarnate and Kāmadhenu in disguise. Datta again announces that he wants to eat. This time, he takes out a clay pot, milks the dog, and puts food into it, which Janārdana and Datta share. When Datta again summons Eknāth to eat, Eknāth again holds back. "He clearly seems like a *fakīr*. How can I do such an improper [*anucit*] act?" Janārdana places a bite of his own *ucchiṣṭa* in Eknāth's hand, and the terrified Eknāth runs away. After Datta departs, Janārdana asks Eknāth what he had done with his *prasād*, and Eknāth confesses that he threw it away. So Janārdana transfers some of the *pān* directly from his own mouth into Eknāth's.

Bhīmasvāmi tells the story very briefly in his *Bhaktalīlāmṛt* (6:1–10),[41] mostly following Keśavsvāmī's rendition. However, Bhīmasvāmi introduces the vignette by saying that Janārdana was dreaming. This new frame is not surprising, given Bhīmasvāmi's pervasive anxiety about Muslims. The image of Eknāth and Janārdana eating food from a Muslim—even one who is God in disguise—was apparently too much for Bhīmasvāmi to stomach.

Thus, we see how a single story about Eknāth and food can be imbued with different meanings when it is retold. As *ucchiṣṭa* and *prasād*, food may illustrate extreme devotion of the receiver, or it may reveal the compassionately salvific nature of the server. Food may unlock new levels of consciousness, strengthen the guru-disciple bond, or serve as an instrument to test spiritual discernment. It is not surprising that different authors craft their renditions to reflect messages that they think are important. This is, after all, a basic function of hagiographic narrative—to embed the saint's stories within a larger framework of meaning. But more is happening here than authors simply leaving their distinctive mark on stories. Food's semantic density makes it especially pliable. Sometimes, authors consciously exploit this polyvalence, as we can see in the two most-repeated stories about Eknāth and food—the *śrāddha* meal and the double vision. Observing variations in renditions can yield for us another kind of knowledge about hagiography as it develops over time.

The *śrāddha* story

All five major hagiographies contain a version of the story of the Eknāth serving a *śrāddha* meal, which we encountered in this book's introduction. Eknāth prepares the meal to commemorate his ancestors and invites brahmans to carry out the rituals and eat. Before the brahmans arrive, interlopers ask Eknāth to eat and he agrees. Eknāth prepares a second meal, which the outraged brahmans refuse. Eknāth's deceased ancestors then miraculously arrive and eat the food themselves.

Several key details change when the story is retold. The interlopers' identities are inconsistent. Eknāth's justification for serving them changes. What prompts the ancestors to arrive is inconsistent, as is the way the brahmans respond to the miracle. Of course, these changes correlate to hagiographers' different frames of meaning. But I will argue that there is something more subtle and powerful at work, which becomes apparent if we observe the many renditions in rapid succession. The hagiographers consistently leave the bhakti-caste question unresolved—evidence that a practical logic of strategic ambiguity is at work.

The longest rendition, part of which we encountered in the Introduction, happens to be the earliest. It comprises an entire chapter of the *PC* and includes a remarkable side story about a bold Dalit woman that no hagiographer repeated.[42] Kṛṣṇadās sets up the story by describing how Eknāth's nondualist vision fits with the *śrāddha*.

> The ancestors were essentially [*svarūpī*] Janārdana. Janārdana is also brahmans (or Brahman).[43] Eknāth had a deep understanding that everyone should be regarded the same [*sarvāsī jāṇ sārikhā*]. By nature, Eknāth had a feeling of impartiality [*samabhāva*] in all places. Listen to the marvel of that day. On the memorial day of the ancestors, if anyone new arrives, they should be given food. The ancestors would be completely pleased. If a cat came into the house, it should be given food immediately. If it were beaten and put outside, the ancestors would be angry. If a dog came to the door, it should be offered food there. One should not look away. One should be full of a feeling of God. If someone with matted hair, or a shaved head, a *fakir*,

or a very low, destitute beggar comes respectfully to the door, do not throw a stone at them. You should honor them by saying "One who is essentially a brahman [*vipra*] has come to my house." Food should be given. The one who eats is the god Brahmaṇ [*dev brāhmaṇa*].[44] He should be offered food. If one deceives, the ancestors will be disturbed. One should act without guile toward guests and ancestors. One should act with great humility. The ancestors are pleased by this. On that day, whatever person may come, *namaskār* should be done to him. Thus honored, he should be felicitated in a way that is full of joy and sweetness. On that day, one should be full of the feeling of God. Because of Janārdana, in the form of the ancestors, contentment is everywhere. One should observe that sense of divinity, which was established day and night in Eknāth. In all beings exists one God—this is the behavior of service. Whoever should come is verily Janārdana. The service that one renders to a guru should be done similarly to everyone. On the *śrāddha* day, Eknāth behaved in the same way to everyone. Whoever has this intent likewise brings satisfaction. (*PC* 8:6–19)

I quote this repetitive passage to show how much emphasis Kṛṣṇadās puts on Eknāth's vision of sameness. Elsewhere in the *PC*, Kṛṣṇadās refers to this spiritually accomplished vision with the term *janī-janārdana* (Janārdana in people), which frames the *PC*'s version of the *śrāddha* story.

As we observed in the Introduction, a group of Dalits carry firewood to Eknāth's kitchen, are enchanted by the food's fragrance, and ask to eat. Ignoring his servants' concerns, Eknāth agrees, saying, "Janārdana is in all beings. The enjoyer is one. Imagining divisions is foolish."[45] After the meal concludes, Eknāth warns everyone not to tell the brahmans, but a Dalit woman either ignores this or had taken her food and left before Eknāth made his request. When brahmans challenge her at the riverbank to leave, she stands up to them, saying, "Eknāth served us. Becoming the ancestors, we went to his house. He satisfied us all. Now you too should go (to the *śrāddha*) for food. The cooking is finished. I'll eat my food peacefully, here on the riverbank. Today we are Eknāth's ancestors. Why are you intimidating me? I just thought to eat my food on the riverbank, so I came."

Unaware of this interaction at the river, Eknāth tells a brahman servant to summon the brahman guests to eat. In a fury, the brahmans at the river beat him. The servant runs home crying and reports to Eknāth. Eknāth commands him to try again, but to no avail. So Eknāth decides to forego the brahmans' rituals and just serve the *śrāddha* meal without them. He says a quick prayer and calls out to the ancestors directly. A great crowd of ancestors then appear, glowing with their own light. Eknāth reveres many of them by name, including his father, grandfather, and great-grandfather. As they begin to eat, news of the wonder spreads. The brahmans who spurned the invitation cannot resist checking out this marvelous scene, and they are shocked to recognize some of their own ancestors sitting there too. The ancestors then disappear, and Eknāth rolls in the leftover food. He then extends a third invitation to the brahmans to eat, which they finally accept, persuaded by the wonder they had witnessed. Kṛṣṇadās concludes the episode by commenting, "Eknāth's greatness is miraculous. His way of relating to ritual injunctions is incomprehensible."

Keśavsvāmī renders the story much more briefly and uses it to close out a four-episode set in which brahmans test Eknāth's hospitality. Keśavsvāmī says little about Eknāth's nondual vision, although the notion is not entirely absent. Whereas *janī-janārdana* in the *PC* referred to Eknāth's perception of God in people, Keśavsvāmī views Eknāth himself as an *avatār* of God who moves among the people. Yet Keśavsvāmī returns to the first sense of the term in the *EC*'s conclusion (31:40–41), as Eknāth sings before dying: "When I looked at the people, I saw Janārdana" (*avalokitāṃ jana dise janārdana*).[46]

Eknāth hosts a *śrāddha* and invites local brahmans, who go to bathe in the river. "Suddenly, the *trimūrti* arrived, dressed as *malaṅg*s. They said, 'We are hungry, please serve us. You are renowned for your generosity. Don't hesitate for a moment'" (*EC* 11:76–77). Keśavsvāmī notes that Eknāth responded with "no hint of differentiation [*viṣamatā*]." The three men eat and then reveal themselves to Eknāth as Brahmā, Viṣṇu, and Śiva. When the brahmans arrive, they see only three *malaṅg*s belching after the meal and blessing Eknāth "in their own language." The brahmans condemn Eknāth for allowing *mleccha*s to eat the *śrāddha* meal. The family priests (*upādhyāya*s) among them rule that Eknāth must now be put out of caste for this action. They then mock him, saying, "The merit of your deed has gone to your ancestors in heaven. Serve the food to them yourself. We will do no rituals" (11:94).

Eknāth treats their sarcasm as a literal blessing. He vocally invites his ancestors, calling them by name. From the sky then descend three ancestors, wearing pure dhotis and reciting Vedic mantras. Eknāth thanks the brahmans for having enabled this miracle, and he apologizes to them for his offense (*aparādh*). Some proud brahmans return silently to their homes, while others remain to do the rituals and eat with the ancestors. Those who departed begin to worry: "Now life is cursed, and karma has been turned upside down.[47] We didn't understand Eknāth's ideas, and something otherworldly (*alaukik*) occurred. Nothing like today's event has ever happened before. In effect, a great deal of fame has gone to Eknāth." At the end of the meal, the ancestors vanish, and Eknāth gives the brahmans gifts as they go on their way (*EC* 11:119).

Mahīpati in the *BhV* adds some different nuances to the *śrāddha* story. Immediately before the *śrāddha*, he narrates the arrival of Kṛṣṇa at Eknāth's home, disguised as a brahman servant known as Khaṇḍyā (*BhV* 46:7–44). Mahīpati notes that Khaṇḍyā especially enjoyed serving brahmans and cleaning up after their meals. "That god took infinite pleasure in removing their *ucchiṣṭa*" (46:42). When Eknāth invites brahmans to his *śrāddha*, Mahīpati highlights the divine presence that already exists there: "What could possibly lack in a place where Kṛṣṇa serves, in the form of a brahman?" (46:47).

In this story, Eknāth accompanies the brahmans to bathe in the river but returns home early. While hanging his wet clothes on the roof to dry, he overhears a conversation between a Dalit (*aṇāmik*) man and his wife who are sweeping the alley below. They smell the fragrant food, and the wife laments that she will never get to taste such things. The man says, "Why develop this useless hunger? Such warm, fine food is not for people of our birth. Today there is a *śrāddha* in Eknāth's home. Even the *ucchiṣṭa* they will bury afterwards. Foolishly not knowing this, your mind is longing for something that is impossible."

Moved by his accidental eavesdropping, Eknāth discusses with his wife what to do. She notes that since they have prepared plenty of food, they should invite the entire community of Dalits (*atiśūdra*), because if they fed only the couple, then all the other Dalits (*anāmik*) would remain hungry. Eknāth comments that since Janārdana is in all beings, the Dalits (*anāmik*) should be made satisfied. So Eknāth invites everyone to come and sit down in the street. He reveres the *anāmik*s with a ritual that is usually used for brahmans (*brāhmaṇpūjan*), using flowers, sandalwood paste, and colored rice grains. "Understanding clearly that Janārdana is in all people [*janī janārdana*], Eknāth abandoned misconceptions and regarded the eaters as Kṛṣṇa himself" (46–62). After eating, the Dalits express awe and gratitude for being served food that they had never experienced before. They depart, carrying leftover food in the folds of their clothes. Eknāth cleans the doorway to his home along with all the vessels, and they cook a second meal that is ten times larger.

The brahmans arrive and are outraged, and they vow to reject any food from Eknāth. They march to his home, and one cries, "Evil-doer! You've played an unimaginable trick on us. You didn't feed brahmans, and you worshiped Dalits [*antyaj pujle*]. This is the day for remembering your ancestors. What, were they Dalits [*anāmik*], so that you worshipped these Dalits [*atiśūdras*]—the very ones whom the Vedas and *śāstras* revile? Look, your actions have brought about a mixing of castes. You have destroyed proper brahman behavior and committed an evil act" (46:73–75). They conclude by casting Eknāth out from the brahman community. Hearing of this, Eknāth "sat quietly, his mind pained by concern" (*BhV* 46:85).

At this point, Khaṇḍyā (Kṛṣṇa in disguise) arrives and reassures Eknāth. He instructs Eknāth to prepare for another set of guests, so Eknāth lays out rows of places to eat. Then "he" (probably Khaṇḍyā) respectfully says, "Come,"[48] at which point the ancestors suddenly appear. Eknāth gives them food and precious gifts, and the meal satisfies them. Brahmans who happen to be nearby overhear Eknāth speaking with his ancestors. When they peek inside the compound and witness the ancestors eating, the divine guests quickly vanish. The brahmans are astounded. "Eknāth is not human; he is an *avatār* of Viṣṇu. Holding on to our pride in karma, we vainly tormented him. His companion, Kṛṣṇa, is pleased with him and saves him from falling into trouble" (46:97–99). Yet, despite this confession, the brahmans demand that Eknāth undergo purification before he can be restored to full social standing. "If we regard him already as pure, then our egotism [*ahaṃtā*] will be in vain. If we punish him, then he will be put back on the path of good action." The next day, they invite Eknāth to come with them to the river. They explain that because Eknāth had "unknowingly" committed an offense, he should follow a customary ritual penance. To fully grasp what happens next, we should follow Mahīpati closely:

> Hearing this, Eknāth said, "I absolutely will not take purification. With Kṛṣṇa as my refuge,[49] how should I do what is inappropriate [*viparīt*]?" The brahmans said, "Be reasonable. Heed our words. Without purification, your body is full of impurity." Then, quickly bathing Eknāth in the river, they administered the purification. They put ashes and cow dung on him and said a Vedic mantra. Then a brahman from Tryambakeśvar suddenly arrived there. (47:105–08)

Despite Eknāth's adamant protest, the purification somehow just happens. Mahīpati ignores this cognitive tension, leaving the subsequent story to explain further. A leprous brahman from Tryambakeśvar appears, having been instructed by Śiva in a dream to come to Paiṭhaṇ. Śiva told him that Eknāth accrued great merit by feeding the Dalits at the *śrāddha*, and if Eknāth would transfer some of it to the brahman, he would be healed. The brahmans of Paiṭhaṇ are incredulous and accuse the newcomer of lying. Some say, "In which *śāstra* does it say that abandoning brahmans in order to feed Dalits [*antyaj*] generates merit?" When Eknāth heals the leprous brahman, his antagonists have a change of heart: "The pride we took in karma spoiled us. For us to purify a Viṣṇu-bhakta was actually an evil act. You indeed are an *avatār* of Viṣṇu and not some human hero. . . . You do not need purification. We understand now" (47:121–24). They all return to Eknāth's home, where he reveres them and gives them gifts. They say, "Blessed is this Viṣṇu-bhakta, who is very diligent in serving brahmans. He lovingly worships God according to ritual custom" (47:128).

Mahīpati offers a second rendition of the *śrāddha* story in his *BhL*, which follows Keśavsvāmī's *EC*. Mahīpati omits Keśavsvāmī's prelude about nondual vision and instead devotes two dozen verses (*BhL* 17:30–54) to describing the brahmans' displeasure over Eknāth's rising popularity and use of Marathi. Incidentally, although tension over poets using Marathi for religious compositions is a frequent theme in Marathi literature (evidenced in the *Jñāneśvarī*, *Līḷācaritra*, and *Eknāthī Bhāgavat*), it is remarkable that Mahīpati had to go out of his way to include this tension when he repeated the *śrāddha* story in the late 18th century. The trope of linguistic tension is missing from most hagiographies about Eknāth, including in the *EC* that Mahīpati was recycling and the *BhV* that Mahīpati himself had composed only twelve years earlier.

In the *BhL*, the brahmans lodge several complaints: Eknāth's *kīrtan*s cast a spell over people's minds, his respect for the *Bhāgavata Purāṇa* overshadows the other *purāṇa*s, he relies more on Prakrit (Marathi) texts than Sanskrit sources for knowledge, patrons who had been generous to brahmans now lose interest, and Eknāth's influence diverts people from karma to the path of bhakti. The envious brahmans devise schemes to exploit Eknāth's generosity. This prompts Mahīpati to rehearse the *EC*'s set of generosity tests, concluding with the *śrāddha* story.

As in the *EC*, the *trimūrti* arrive in the form of Muslims while the brahmans are at the river. Mahīpati elaborates: the *fakīr*s have heavy beards and bloodshot eyes; they wear animal skins and anklets with bells and crystals; they carry rosaries; and they have long, matted hair. They request food, and

Eknāth provides it. Mahīpati explains, "Thus they tested Eknāth's conviction that God was in every creature" (17:77). They briefly reveal their true forms to Eknāth but then transform back into *fakīrs*.

The brahmans arrive and see three *fakīrs* blessing Eknāth in *yavana bhāṣā* (17:79). The brahmans protest that Eknāth has mixed the castes, and they say, "Today on the *śrāddha* of your ancestors, you did not first feed us with untouched [*anasūṭ*] food,[50] but you gave it to the *yavanas*." The brahmans refuse Eknāth's replacement meal and instead fetch the head of the town's brahman council (*dharmādhikārī*). They return and say, "Were your ancestors Muslim by *jātī*, so that you fed the *yavanas*?" The *dharmādhikārī* states that the brahmans need not conduct the *śrāddha* rituals, for if Eknāth's ancestors were pleased, then they would do it themselves. Whereas Keśavsvāmī in the *EC* stated merely that Eknāth took this comment literally, Mahīpati's Eknāth expounds at great length about the power that brahmans' words have to make wondrous things occur.

Bhīmasvāmi's rendition in the *BhL2* is fourteen terse verses long. It roughly follows the plot of Mahīpati's *BhV*, with a few different points of emphasis. The brahmans are away at the river when Dalits (*antej* or *antyaj*) smell the food and request it. Eknāth tells his servant Kṛṣṇa to feed them rather than doing it himself. When the angered brahmans refuse to eat, Kṛṣṇa summons Eknāth's ancestors. The brahmans proclaim that gods come to eat at Eknāth's home, and they praise him. It is risky to derive much from this very short story, but it is intriguing that Bhīmasvāmi emphasizes Kṛṣṇa's role, making it less about Eknāth's virtues and more about God's activity in the world.

The *śrāddha* story resonated beyond the borders of Maharashtra, into the Dakṣiṇa Bhajana Sampradāya of Tamil Nadu. In a compendium of stories about the Tamil saint Śrīdhara Veṅkaṭeṣa Dīkṣitār (known as Ayyāvāḷ, 1635–1720), Ayyāvāḷ prepares a *śrāddha* ceremony and invites brahmans. As Ayyāvāḷ goes to the Kaveri River to bathe beforehand, he encounters a Dalit (Parāiyār) who was starving and near death. Ayyāvāḷ feeds him some of the *śrāddha* food, and the Parāiyār reveals himself as God (Mahāliṅgasvāmi). The brahmans demand that Ayyāvāḷ purify himself by going on pilgrimage and bathing in the Gaṅgā River. Ayyāvāḷ prays to Śiva to relieve his plight, and Śiva makes the Gaṅgā emerge from Ayyāvāḷ's well to demonstrate his purity.[51] There may be a good reason for this story's uncanny similarity to Eknāth's *śrāddha*. Popular memory associates Ayyāvāḷ with Śāhujī I, the ruler of the Marathas' southern outpost in Tānjāvūr at the turn of the 17th century.[52] The Sārasvatī Mahāl Library in Tānjāvūr holds many manuscripts of texts by Eknāth, Keśavsvāmī, and Mahīpati (among other Marathi authors). The Bhajana Sampradāya in Tamil Nadu self-consciously inherited aspects of the Vārkarī tradition, even if not specifying the debt in the case of this story.[53]

Five variations across renditions of the *śrāddha* story are noteworthy. First, the identities of the interlopers switches between Dalits (*caṇḍālas*, *anāmiks*, or *antyaj*) and figures who appear as Muslims (*fakīrs* or *malaṅgs*). As I have argued elsewhere,[54] this swapping of "others" is the result of a narrative logic that regards the other's identity as less important than its function as an extreme counterpart to Eknāth's brahman-ness. Second, Eknāth's justification to serve the "wrong" people the *śrāddha* meal shifts between Eknāth's vision of sameness that sees God in everyone and a vow of generous hospitality. Third, the stories differ on what prompts the ancestors to arrive: Eknāth invites them, Khaṇḍyā/Kṛṣṇa invites them, or the brahmans' sarcastic mockery has a literal effect. Fourth, the brahmans respond differently to the miracle, especially concerning whether they demand that Eknāth undergo purification and how it is accomplished. Finally, each story has other peculiarities too, such as the assertive Dalit woman who resists the brahmans' reprimand. Table 5.1 lays out these differences visually.

Food's semantic density is pivotal in this story, embedding characters within two different and mutually exclusive systems of meaning. On one hand, the *śrāddha* meal is a vital component of a classic ritual. The sequence of events, the people who may be involved, and rules that govern *śrāddha* are clearly fixed and well known. For the ritual to be regarded as a success, food must be prepared and served to brahmans. On the other hand, food is an instrument for showing hospitality. Although the *śāstric* injunction that brahmans provide food and water to a traveler may have been in the background, the stories that we have observed make it clear Eknāth was motivated by compassion and the sense that God is in everyone. The *śrāddha* story thus hinges on a dilemma, to choose one of those paradigms over the other. By choosing to serve his unexpected guests, Eknāth must diverge from the ritual. The mutually exclusive paradigms for understanding food are held together by the miraculous arrival of the ancestors. If the goal of the *śrāddha* is to satisfy the ancestors, the story about Eknāth innovatively asserts that this can be accomplished by providing hospitality toward non-brahmans. Essentially, hagiographers of the *śrāddha* story must negotiate the two levels of food's semantic density in this story, and they did this in different ways.

Table 5.1 *Śrāddha* story renditions

Text	Interlopers	Eknāth's justification for serving interlopers	Prompt for ancestor arrival	Brahmans' response	Peculiarities
PC	Dalit wood haulers (*caṇḍālas*)	Janārdana is within the people (*janī janārdana*); impartial vision	Eknāth prays to his ancestors	Marvel at Eknāth's greatness and relation to ritual (*vidhi*)	(1) Dalit woman & brahmans converse at the riverbank (2) Eknāth rolls in leftovers
EC	*Malaṅgs*/ *trimūrti*	Eknāth's vow of hospitality to all visitors; no distinctions (*viṣamatā*)	Brahmans' sarcastic insult	Some regret misunder-standing; others receive gifts from Eknāth	
BhV	Dalit sweepers (*anāmiks*)	Janārdana is in all beings; Kṛṣṇa is the eater	Khaṇḍyā/ Kṛṣṇa is instrumental in summoning	Put Eknāth out of caste, express wonder, yet carry out purification ritual	Add-on story of leprous brahman who seeks merit transfer
BhL	*Fakīrs*/ *trimūrti*	Generosity to guests	Brahmans' sarcastic insult	Some regret misunder-standing because they look bad	Brahmans displeased with Eknāth's Marathi and popularity of his *kīrtans*
BhL2	Dalits (*antej*/ *antyaj*)	(none stated)	Kṛṣṇa directly summons ancestors	Admire and praise Eknāth	

The double vision story

The details of the double vision story remained more stable across renditions than those of the *śrāddha* story. Eknāth accepts an invitation from a Dalit couple to eat at their home. Brahmans try to catch him in the act. But they witness Eknāth simultaneously eating in the Dalits' home and sitting at his own home. The many renditions fleshed out various details of the story. Why did Eknāth accept the invitation in the first place? Who exactly ate with the Dalit couple? What accounts for the double vision? As this story was retold, some authors tried to fill in these gaps. In the process, although the story remained the same, hagiographers used the story for different purposes while preserving its basic ambiguity.

One reason for this story's relative stability across retellings is that it did not appear in the *PC* and *BhV*. The absence of such an important story may seem surprising, but in terms of hagiographic narrative, it was not technically necessary. Both the *śrāddha* and double vision stories are modular, self-contained episodes whose presence in or absence from a text do not affect the overall flow of the text. Such modular episodes are non-essential to the lifespan of a Hindu saint, in contrast to chronologically anchored stories of Eknāth's origins, discipleship, marriage, and death.

Perhaps because of their modular, optional nature, the *śrāddha* and double vision stories are more flexible for conveying different teachings. One could draw a parallel with some of Jesus' most famous teachings, such as the Sermon on the Mount, which appears in only one of the four canonical gospels (Matthew). This inconsistent appearance did not hinder such texts from becoming important to later followers. Although the double vision story was not present in all hagiographies, something about it captured the imagination of later Marathi audiences so that it became even more central to what people remembered of Eknāth's persona than details about his birth, marriage, and death. This speaks to the importance of hagiography for shaping popular understandings.

The *EC*'s rendition of the double vision story (17:19–84) coheres with that text's portrayal of Eknāth as a semi-divine salvific figure, but other elements also come to the fore. Keśavsvāmī begins by describing Eknāth's main interlocutor at length. He is a faithful Dalit (*antarniṣṭha anāmik*), who has mature knowledge and lives with his wife in Paiṭhaṇ. One day, he approaches Eknāth while he is walking to the river for his bath. Eknāth is pleased with the encounter and shares with the man spiritual knowledge (*ātmajñān*) (17:23). Some brahmans object. "We hear that you were talking about *jñāna* with an *anāmik*. This is wicked behavior." Eknāth challenges them, "But you have the same form/body [*ākṛti*] as he does. By what marks do you identify him certainly as an *anāmik*?" (17:25). Eknāth puts a finer point on the issue in the next verse: "I don't recognize any *anāmik*-ness in his knowledge. What I see is the utterly same Self as mine—fully alike in every way."[55] The brahmans are disturbed by this response but cannot find a way to refute it. So, they simply dismiss Eknāth's question: "To hell with this idea. You're utterly corrupt. We know that *anāmik*s should not be enlightened" (17:28).

Eknāth does not protest but merely asks their forgiveness for his offense. Keśavsvāmī does not clarify what exactly this "offense" was, but it did not restrict Eknāth from continuing his contact with the Dalit man. The brahmans decide that, for being near the Dalit (*antyaj sannidha*), Eknāth must undergo purification by bathing with his clothes on and allowing the brahmans to rub *pañcagavya* on him and say a mantra. Eknāth silently goes along with the exercise and then returns to his daily rituals.

The Dalit man goes home and tells his wife about the conversation with Eknāth. She too had wished to meet Eknāth but despairs at the social chasm between them. Her husband reassures her, "The great one does not know high and low. Such is Śrī Nāth's impartial consciousness [*samabuddhi*]" (17:38). The reassured woman assembles things for a meal, while her husband goes to invite Eknāth to eat with them. Eknāth respectfully accepts. A brahman spy overhears the invitation and informs his fellow brahmans. They assemble angrily around the Dalit man's home in such numbers that they fill the alley. Meanwhile, Eknāth goes about his rituals, bathes, and listens to the *purāṇas*.

When the cooking was finished and the *anāmik* man summons his guest, Eknāth tells him to go ahead and set out the vessels. Keśavsvāmī then describes Eknāth walking to the man's house, past the suspicious, whispering brahmans (17:58). Some brahmans witness Eknāth sit down in the *anāmik* couple's home, where the two worship him with incense and flowers, and then serve him their food. News of this reaches some brahmans who are at Eknāth's home, but they too are seeing Eknāth, seated and eating in front of them there. So brahmans rush back and forth between Eknāth's and the Dalit couple's home, observing Eknāth in both places, until they exhaust themselves. The brahmans wonder how Eknāth managed this double vision, and some float sinister theories: it was dark magic, a visual trick, something done with the help of a ghost, or the result of Eknāth allying himself with the demon-king Veṭal (17:69–70).

The Dalit couple show their appreciation for Eknāth's visit, saying that they had been poor and protectorless (*anātha*), and Eknāth had uplifted them (*uddharileṃ*). Eknāth responds, "You are pure and therefore have had this insight. Because your affection was boundless, I have done this deed." Eknāth accepts *pān* from the couple, and they both consume his *ucchiṣṭa* as *prasād*. Eknāth then gives them a Sanskrit verse (*vyāsavāṇi śloka*) that Keśavsvāmī describes as "authorized for brahmans and those who possess the six qualities."[56] The reference to a Sanskrit verse is inconsequential here, but Mahīpati in his *BhL* would shift it to a different place in the story and make it into a crucial plot twist. Keśavsvāmī concludes, "Eknāth's grace enabled this knowledge to take place here. Back at Eknāth's home, he carried out *brāhmaṇpūjā* as usual, and after finishing, Eknāth too ate *prasād*" (17:83).

When Mahīpati recycled this story from Keśavsvāmī, he added forty verses that cast it in a different light (*BhL* 19.137–239). He gives the Dalit man who had been literally *anāmik* in the *EC* a name—Rāṇyā Mahār. In his former life, Rāṇyā was a *yogabhraṣṭa*—someone who fell from discipline and was thus reborn with low status, despite being an essentially virtuous person. The *yogabhraṣṭa* is a common trope in Indic literature (cf. *BhG* 6:37–44) to justify why bad things happen to good people and to explain why low-status people may be spiritually advanced. Rāṇyā is identified as a very devout and pious man, having vowed to avoid meat, take regular ritual baths, keep a clean home, and attend Eknāth's *kīrtans*. One evening, Eknāth performs a *kīrtan* on the section of the *Jñāneśvarī* in which Kṛṣṇa reveals his divine glory to Arjuna. This inspires Rāṇyā to ask Eknāth, "When Śrī Hari, who pervades all things, took on his universal form, at that moment where was I, someone of low caste [*jātihīn*]?" Eknāth responds that he too was present within Kṛṣṇa. This sends Rāṇyā into a state of nondual contentment (*kalyāṇādvait*), in which he forgot all distinctions, including those of varṇa and *jāti*.

Later, Rāṇyā invites Eknāth for a meal, and Eknāth accepts. Mahīpati describes how Rāṇyā and his wife, although impoverished, prepared for the visit by gathering food and undertaking pious Vaiṣṇava practices: they put a *tulsī* altar by their door, wash all their clothes and vessels, bathe routinely, constantly recite God's name, observe fasts, and listen to Eknāth's *kīrtans*. Finally, Rāṇyā's wife decides that they are ready to host Eknāth,[57] so Rāṇyā meets Eknāth one day while he is walking to his bath and invites him.

Eknāth accepts, saying, "You are a loving Vaiṣṇava bhakta. Śrī Kṛṣṇa-nāth has certainly witnessed your sincerity and has been pleased. Brahmans who are proficient in the Vedas and *śāstras* may be turned away from devotion to Śrī Hari. They may be completely adorned with the twelve virtues, but a Dalit [*antyaj*] may indeed be superior to them. Someone may be of low caste, but God has great respect for him" (19.169–70). Eknāth then recites a Sanskrit precedent for this idea in the *BhP* (7.9.10). "A dog-cooker [*śvapaca*, Dalit] who has offered his mind, speech, efforts, wealth, and life to God is regarded as superior to a brahman who has the twelve qualities but is turned away from the lotus-feet of Viṣṇu. He (the Dalit) purifies his family, unlike the one (brahman) who has great arrogance."[58]

Some brahmans overhear Eknāth's conversation. Whereas in the *EC* the brahmans condemn Eknāth for sharing knowledge with the Dalit man, the brahmans in the *BhL* protest Eknāth's sharing of the verse itself. One of them claims that this verse was from the Vedas (*śruti*), which Dalits have no right to hear.[59] The brahmans demand that Eknāth undergo purification. Eknāth responds that Rāṇyā Mahār is a spiritually accomplished Vaiṣṇava bhakta whom they should not call a Dalit (*antyaj*) (19:178). "Not one mark of a Dalit [*anāmik*] appears on his body. He indeed possesses everything that the Bhāgavat dharma has said. I am certain that he has a right to this knowledge. Because of the strength of Rāṇyā's devotion, Śrī Hari became obedient and gave him an unmediated vision of his supreme form. Seeing his great longing, I spoke something that was relevant here.[60] Please excuse this offense, powerful ones" (19.178–81). In the *EC* rendition, Eknāth asked the brahmans how they ascertained that the man was a Dalit, and Eknāth countered with his own nondual vision. In the *BhL*, Eknāth articulates a more thoroughly theological response, even quoting the *BhP* to justify himself.

The brahmans ignore Eknāth's argument and press on with the need for purification, which Eknāth undergoes without resistance. Rāṇyā witnesses the purification, feels terrible, and goes home to inform his wife. She despairs that their caste differences may prevent the meal from ever happening, but Rāṇyā reassures her: "Eknāth is an ocean of grace; he will not disregard the poor" (19:191). Rāṇyā meets Eknāth again, invites him to come later that day, and Eknāth accepts. The brahmans respond, "He has resolved to commit a defiling act. By his deed, a mixing of castes will occur" (19.196).

Mahīpati goes beyond Keśavsvāmī and explains how the two simultaneous appearances of Eknāth was accomplished. "What did that Pāṇḍuraṅg (Viṭṭhal) do? He took the form of Eknāth and appeared at the *anāmik*'s home" (19.211). Mahīpati makes a philosophical comparison: like the oneness of an object and its reflection, the sun and its brilliance, or a flower and its honey, so too Eknāth and Pāṇḍuraṅg appeared the same (19:225). A divine act like this was a major addition, which proved very popular in later renditions of the story. Mahīpati provides another embellishment in the story: when Rāṇyā's wife feeds Eknāth, she explicitly states that the eater is Janārdana—the same idea that inspired Eknāth to feed unexpected Dalit guests at his *śrāddha* in the *PC*.

The two simultaneous images of Eknāth frustrate the brahmans' hope of censuring the saint, while also giving the event a divine stamp of approval. Mahīpati's revision leaves some troubling gaps in the narrative, however. Eknāth agreed to come to Rāṇyā's home, but then Pāṇḍuraṅg-as-Eknāth showed up instead to eat with them. So, did Eknāth break his promise to come? Was he aware of Pāṇḍuraṅg's covert activity?

Perhaps Mahīpati hoped that his audience would connect this double vision to his motif of Eknāth being an *avatār*, or Mahīpati may have been making a point about Viṭṭhal's inclusivity. It is impressive, after all, that God personally visited the Dalit couple. But by narrating the story in this way, Mahīpati effectively releases Eknāth from the question of ritual impurity, so that the human Eknāth could not be given full credit for the act. Is this transgressive commensality a divine miracle or the bold act of a human reformer? Is Mahīpati teaching a spiritual lesson with God or a social lesson with Eknāth? This ambiguity would make the double vision story the most repeated yet troubling scene in the entire hagiographic corpus about Eknāth. For modern critics like Ambedkar, this story showed the dangerous haziness of bhakti's spiritual and social message, which could disapprove of caste while still accommodating it.

In addition to the major hagiographies we have considered in this chapter, the double vision story appears in one small composition that merits attention—the *Eknāthcaritra* of Khaṇḍerāya.[61] The entire text of twenty-eight verses narrates only this story. Khaṇḍerāya was a minor poet who died in 1766 and is known to have composed short hagiographical episodes about Nāmdev and Tukārām.[62]

Khaṇḍerāya introduces Eknāth as an *avatār* of Jñāndev who came to uplift the lowly in the world. While performing a *kīrtan* one day, Eknāth uses a metaphor that compared water, which takes on the color of its container, to a devotee who takes on the qualities of a holy man (*sādhu*) whom he reveres. A man named Viveknāk Mahār attends the event and is impressed,[63] so he invites Eknāth to eat at his home. But Eknāth is skeptical, "How can food be taken at the home of an *anāmik*?" (7). Viveknāk then reminds Eknāth of his own *kīrtan*'s metaphor, which prompts Eknāth to change his mind and agree. Viveknāk happily goes home to prepare with his wife, while Eknāth returns to his *maṭh*.

When Eknāth's disciples hear of his plans, they fear that a calamity will arise. They scheme to distract their guru by inviting him to listen to them reading from the *BhP*. Eknāth' recognizes their ploy but goes along with the ruse. When it becomes mealtime, Khaṇḍerāya narrates that Eknāth travels to Viveknāk's home "internally" (*antargatineṃ*) by virtue of his "yoga" or spiritual power (16). There, Eknāth eats the food and belches in satisfaction. As he departs, he leaves behind his walking stick and *gītā*.[64] Viveknāk's wife points out that Eknāth forgot his belongings and departed without taking *pān*, so Viveknāk delivers everything to the maṭh. The disciples meet Viveknāk in the doorway and ask him disrespectfully about why he has come. Eknāth stuns them by explaining that he had forgotten some things at Viveknāk's home after eating there. The disciples are confused, because Eknāth had been sitting and reading the *BhP* with them the whole time. Khaṇḍerāya concludes, "No one can comprehend the greatness of a *sādhu*."

This is a peculiar rendition. Eknāth initially resists the invitation and must be persuaded. Eknāth's own disciples try to prevent the meal. And Eknāth appears in two places simultaneously by virtue of his own power, not God's. Through Khaṇḍerāya's pen, Eknāth comes to represent the miraculous power of yoga rather than the transgressive impulse of bhakti.

Bhīmasvāmi's terse rendition of the double vision episode (*BhL*2 27:1–20) is also idiosyncratic. A Dalit devotee (*śvapac bhāvik*) who worked in Eknāth's home conveyed an invitation from his wife to join them for a meal at their home. Eknāth accepts, and she prepares accordingly. But when she (not the man) goes to summon Eknāth, his disciples tell her that he had already eaten and had fallen asleep. Bhīmasvāmi does not clarify whether this was Eknāth's oversight or his disciples' deception. The couple despairs that Eknāth forgot them, but God (*dev*) takes Eknāth's form and eats at their home. A single brahman who happens to walk by their home witnesses the meal and says, "Defilement!" (*bhraṣṭākār*). He continues walking to Eknāth's home, where he then sees Eknāth leading a *kīrtan*, which leads him to realize that the first image of Eknāth had been God. The author concludes, "Bhīma gladly sings the story of the great bhakti that Nārāyaṇa did." Table 5.2 summarizes the differences among renditions.

As in the *śrāddha* renditions, several different words—often within a single story—get used to refer the Dalit man: *caṇḍāḷa*, *anāmik*, *antyaj*, Mahār, and *śvapaca*. Two renditions give him conspicuously Dalit names: Rāṇyā Mahār and Viveknāk. Some renditions emphasize the Dalit man's virtuous qualities. The renditions differ on whether Eknāth takes the initial invitation as an opportunity to teach a theological lesson. The most elaborate rendition, in the *BhL*, depicts Rāṇyā thoughtfully raising a tough question: how can caste difference be reconciled with Kṛṣṇa's pervasion of the universe? In one rendition, the man outsmarts Eknāth, challenging him to practice what he had

Table 5.2 Double vision story renditions

Text	Description of Dalit man	Dalit's engagement with Eknāth	Prompt of brahman outrage	Lead up to double vision	Explanation	Peculiarities
PC	—	—	—	—	—	Story not present
EC	Faithful *anāmik* who has mature knowledge	Approaches Eknāth and impresses him	Overhears Eknāth talking about *jñāna* with him	Eknāth walks past brahmans to man's home	No explanation; brahmans speculate wildly	Eknāth gives *vyāsavāṇi śloka* to couple after meal concludes
BhV	—	—	—	—	—	Story not present
BhL	Rāṇyā Mahār, a *yogabhraṣṭa* and reformed bhakta	Asks Eknāth where he as low-caste man was in Kṛṣṇa's universal form	Eknāth quotes *BhP* verse that brahmans misidentify as Vedic	Man invites Eknāth twice, before and after Eknāth's purification	God took Eknāth's form and ate with Rāṇyā and wife, like object and reflection	Brahmans force Eknāth to undergo purification for talking with Rāṇyā; couple eats Eknāth's leftovers as *prasād*
EC2	Man who attends Eknāth's *kīrtan* and is impressed	Invites Eknāth, rebuts Eknāth's initial skepticism by citing *kīrtan* example	Eknāth's disciples worry about his reputation	Disciples try to distract Eknāth by reading *BhP*	Eknāth uses yogic power to go "internally" to couple's home while sitting with disciples	Eknāth = Jñāndev's *avatār*
BhL2	Simply a "Dalit devotee"	Man's wife asks him to invite Eknāth	None mentioned	Eknāth's disciples claim that Eknāth fell asleep and cannot go	God eats with the Dalit couple	Man's wife invites and personally goes to summon Eknāth

preached by not heeding caste difference. Who is concerned about the meal's propriety also varies across renditions: from antagonistic brahmans who disapprove of Eknāth sharing either knowledge or a Sanskrit verse, to sympathetic disciples who worry about Eknāth's reputation, to Eknāth himself who initially struggles to fathom eating with a Dalit.

Most strikingly, all the renditions mention the double vision but differ over how it is accomplished and who deserves the credit. In this respect, there is more at stake in the double vision story than in the *śrāddha* story. If Eknāth eats with the Dalit couple in some manner, then he is on the hook for knowingly breaking purity rules, but he also gets credit for acting on the understanding that bhakti non-differentiation takes priority over caste-based rules. The earliest hagiographer left the double vision a mystery, which in turn left audiences with the challenge of working out the implications themselves. A much clearer but radical variation was that Eknāth possessed yogic power to be in two places simultaneously, which also demonstrates that Eknāth transcends caste restrictions but on the basis of yogic power. The renditions in which God intervenes teach something about God's compassion and justice to pious Dalit bhaktas. But where does that leave Eknāth, aside from being just another actor in God's whimsical, divine play of *līlā*? God's intervention could even implicate Eknāth: after the human Eknāth accepted the Dalit man's invitation, why did he not follow through? This is obviously not the focus for the hagiographers who depict God eating with the Dalit couple. But it does have ramifications for audiences as they try to discern what this story implies for their own behavior and social relations. This problem became especially pointed for modern thinkers who wrestled with the bhakti-caste question.

The crux of the double vision story hinges on food being able to illustrate the clash of two competing value systems. Rules of brahman purity clearly prohibit brahman-Dalit commensality except in cases of extreme emergency or *āpad-dharma*.[65] Eknāth was not under such critical duress; he freely chose to eat with the Dalit couple. For Eknāth as a brahman within a *dharmaśāstr*ic paradigm, this meal should not occur. But in terms of bhakti ethics, in which virtuous Dalits merit reward, *avatār*-like saints uplift the lowly, and spiritual prodigies see beyond worldly distinctions, sharing food reinforces core teachings about compassion and hospitality. When those values are foregrounded, the meal must go forward, despite the brahmans' opposition. In the double vision story—as in the *śrāddha* story—food's semantic density renders abstract competing value systems in vividly material terms. And as in the story about the *śrāddha* meal, hagiographers rectify the competing paradigms of meaning and value through a wondrous event. Eknāth miraculously manages to eat with and maintain distance from the pious Dalit couple, thereby fulfilling the expectations of both paradigms.

Conclusion

I expect that some readers will find these many variations of renditions dizzying and difficult to keep straight, which is why I included the two tables. There is value in tracing variations in retellings of stories like this. It helps us identify which texts were most influential in shaping how Eknāth was remembered. Paying attention to the details helps us identify each hagiographer's peculiar perspective and emphases. For understanding how texts were transmitted and received over time and for appreciating what texts are doing while they say things, such historical critical research is essential. There are limitations, of course. Comparing renditions of stories will never completely uncover a text's contextual circumstances or reveal all the illocutionary forces its stories may have. Still, recognizing narrative fault lines, cognitive dissonances, and idiosyncrasies of individual texts provides us some sense of this.

Viewing multiple renditions yield another kind of knowledge too. It makes a difference whether we read a rendition as a self-contained snapshot versus as one scene in a sequence of film frames. Viewing a hagiographical story as a snapshot leads to defining its features only in relation to other aspects of that same story. This is the typical mode of hagiographical analysis—seeking the meaning of the story within the story itself, cued in by an author's narrative devices. I was taking this approach early in the chapter, analyzing functions of food by situating their stories within the broader framework of their respective texts. Interpretation can proceed like this, but its significance is confined to the single rendition.

More interesting, I think, is regarding an entire rendition as a film frame and placing multiple renditions or frames next to each other to observe what changes over time. This knowledge is not derivable from reading one rendition in isolation. Doing this with multiple stories can bring dependencies among texts into sharper relief, enabling a scholar to reconstruct recensions, uncover historical disagreements, and so on. The film frame approach accounts for the effects of time and changing context on how a story gets told. We might call this film frame approach "hagiography in 4D"—reading hagiographies with careful attention to the temporal (fourth) dimension. Reading a sequence of story renditions to watch for changes yields meta-knowledge about its transmission—a story about the story.

One such meta-story revealed by doing hagiography in 4D puts into a new perspective the dizziness that was brought on by encountering all the story variations. Observing how controversial stories about food, bhakti, and caste changed over time—without resulting in a single authoritative rendition—reveals the capacity of the Vārkarī tradition to hold the door open to interpretation. Authors and audiences continued understanding and repeating these stories in different ways. This fluid inconsistency did not result from misunderstandings or a mere accident of history; it is a feature of Marathi bhakti. When it comes to the thorny question of how bhakti relates to caste, Marathi authors participated in, employed, and benefited from strategic ambiguity. They knew that the implications their audiences would find vital in these stories would also be difficult to pin down conclusively. That was the point. Hagiographers strategically deployed ambiguity as they communicated with their audiences.

Foreshadowing my longer discussion of strategic ambiguity in Chapter 7, a few preliminary comments about it are helpful here. The miracles in the *śrāddha* and double vision stories get preserved in retellings, although different hagiographers offer their distinct takes on them. No hagiographer crafts a narrative that conclusively resolves the tensions within the story, particularly between caste purity and bhakti inclusivity. On one level, I think that individual hagiographers—Kṛṣṇadās, Keśavsvāmī, Mahīpati, and others—quite intentionally maintained a degree of caste-bhakti friction within the stories. This ambiguity allowed various audiences with various understandings of the bhakti-caste question in precolonial times to engage these stories and, thereby, to be included within the larger tradition.

Many readers expect hagiographies to involve divine activity, but from a narrative perspective as well, the miracles in these stories were essential and could not be omitted. The *śrāddha* story would not work if Eknāth had offered a persuasive argument that convinced the reluctant brahmans to eat his food. There would have been no story at all if people had persuaded Eknāth not to serve the non-brahman interlopers. Both the sanctity of the classic *śrāddha* meal and Eknāth's hospitality-driven transgression of convention are endorsed in these stories. The miracle allows this cognitive dissonance to be both preserved and accepted, even if it creates additional dissonance on the question of whether Eknāth must or should undergo purification. Similarly, the double vision story hinges on its being inexplicable. If Eknāth had simply eaten with the Dalit couple and everyone had straightforwardly seen him do so, the story would have rendered a clear judgment: bhakti supersedes caste. That none of the precolonial renditions of the story opted for that route is important for understanding precolonial Marathi bhakti—strategic ambiguity was built into its ethos. After the onset of secular methods of viewing the saints, western notions of equality that displaced or imperfectly overlapped with Indic ideas about sameness, and new intellectual and social crises brought about by colonization, bhakti's traditional strategic ambiguity became less palatable and harder to maintain. This becomes clear as we observe how Eknāth's life and the double vision story were depicted on Marathi stage and screen in the 19th and 20th centuries.

6

Restaging Transgressive Commensality

The strategically deployed ambiguity that hagiographers used in the 18th century, along with the miraculous events that facilitated it, became more problematic in the 19th and 20th centuries. In Chapter 3, we considered how British colonization, its education system, and emerging Indian nationalism all reframed perceptions of religious traditions and their literatures. Another more tangible factor was also instrumental in these changes: the new media forms of theater and film, which used new technologies and convened new kinds of audiences. Portraying the saints on the Marathi stage and screen made them subject to different narrative demands.

The field of transmedial narratology has been especially sensitive to how stories change when they move across media,[1] potentially leading us to a more holistic understanding of how poetry and stories flowed—and still flow—through Indian society. Modern bhakti scholarship conventionally prioritized written texts, both because these were the most immediately available sources of information and because, for most of the 19th and 20th centuries, religious studies as a field was predisposed to view texts as the true heart of religious traditions. But as Novetzke and others have demonstrated, written texts are not so much final crystallizations of tradition as they are points of reference for living traditions. Viewing a story in isolation, instantiated in a single text or performance, neglects its dynamism and vitality as it moves across many media and the realms of writing, orality, memory, and performance.

Scholars such as Marie-Laure Ryan highlight the complexities involved in this. Different forms of media foreground different communicative elements—images, sounds, language, and movement—to convey messages in different ways. Each of these is based on distinct technologies and the requisite training to use them. The communicative elements and technologies all operate in cultural contexts that have customs for producing and consuming messages.[2] When stories make the intermedial journey from one media form to another, they must be reconfigured to fit new communicative, technological, and cultural demands.[3] Artists who regularly engage in transporting

Shared Devotion, Shared Food. Jon Keune, Oxford University Press. © Oxford University Press 2021.
DOI: 10.1093/oso/9780197574836.003.0007

stories like this develop transmedial strategies for how to do it well. In addition, within each media form (print, image, television, etc.) exist multiple genres or styles of presentation that also shape how a story is rendered.[4] Tracking hagiographical stories across media forms and genres is much more challenging than merely identifying what is left out or added to a given story.

Narratological sensitivity can sharpen our analysis of stories that we have already encountered in this book. Inscribing orally recited poetry and stories onto paper to create the *gāthā*s (Chapter 3) and transmit hagiographical stories (Chapter 5) is essentially an intermedial process. *Kīrtan* performance and the workly, ephemeral quality of the *bāḍa*s are even more vivid examples, since they cross back and forth between oral and literary forms.[5] When stories pass among different media forms, they may leave traces—things that served a purpose in the earlier medium but are less important in the latter. For example, Maḥīpati's written hagiographies often use casual diction and have a repetitive quality that would engage an audience to respond to the author—vestiges of Mahīpati's career as a *kīrtankār*. The circulatory flow of saints' stories across medial boundaries, taking on different inflections as they go, is aptly described as transmedial. It makes a difference if we regard a story as a nebulous entity that is always on the move, instead of identifying an original rendition from which everything else derived. The *śrāddha* and double vision stories as we encounter them thus have always been intermedial phenomena, even if we have not marked them as such. This is another reason why viewing the stories in isolation is misleading. The flow of narratives across media forms has been endemic to bhakti texts from the start, and the effect of that flow continually alters the stories.

When stories cross media forms, new narrative and technical concerns pull it in different directions. These material and technical demands, along with the changing social and political climate, reshaped the ways in which Eknāth was depicted in theater and film. As this was happening in the early decades of the 20th century, artists drew deeply on new kinds of biographical scholarship that had emerged slightly earlier.

Early biographical scholarship, 1860–1931

Marathi scholarship on Eknāth's life at the turn of the 20th century prepared the way for plays' and films' distinct interests. In this biographical literature, concern about social ethics gradually became more prominent, for a time. It was only in 1878, in *Navnīt*'s fifth edition, that Eknāth's social concern was first expressed in modern terms.[6] The anonymous author of the introduction cited two examples to illustrate what he called Eknāth's "philanthropic" (*pāropakārik*) orientation: the *śrāddha* story and Eknāth rescuing a lost Dalit (*cāmbhār*) boy. The author summarized, "It is clear that in Eknāth's heart, there was a feeling of love for people of low *jāti*."[7] Hagiographers depicted Eknāth as being remarkably kind to Dalits, but they never explicitly stated that he had a special place in his heart for them.

The first comprehensive modern biography of Eknāth was published in 1883, by a brahman schoolteacher in Pune, Dhoṇḍo Bāḷkṛṣṇa Sahasrabuddhe. In it, he recast Janārdana's esoteric final teaching to Eknāth thusly: no deed is more meritorious than working for the welfare of other people.[8] Sahasrabuddhe described the *śrāddha* story as a "miracle" of compassion. He introduced the double vision story with the title "Caste Distinction" (*jātibhed*),[9] and as he described that episode, he called *janī-janārdana* a "great sentence" (*mahāvākya*), boldly placing it alongside classic *upaniṣad*ic formulas.

Social ethics were the single overriding concern of Rāmśāstrī Bhāgvat's essay on Eknāth in 1890, which he wrote for his high school students. Bhāgvat sharpened Sahasrabuddhe's version of Janārdana's teaching: people of all *jāti*s have the right (*adhikār*) to seek refuge in and show devotion to God. "In fact, in God's home there is no caste difference whatsoever."[10] Bhāgvat claimed that Eknāth both taught and demonstrated that God cared only about *bhakti* and not *jātī*.[11] He argued that the *BhP* was unique among the *purāṇa*s in that it promoted impartial vision (*samadṛṣṭī*) toward people. Bhāgvat devoted an entire section of his long essay to Eknāth's impartial vision,[12] which explained Eknāth's readiness to distribute food in the *śrāddha* story.[13] When narrating the double vision story, Bhāgvat rephrased Rāṇyā's question to focus on brahman chauvinism: "If brahmans and I were together in Kṛṣṇa's universal form, why do brahmans regard me and my *jāti* as untouchable?"[14] Most radically, Bhāgvat removed God entirely from the story of the double vision. Eknāth simply eats at Rāṇyā's home; there is no second image.[15]

The next generation of scholarly interpreters were more conservative. Lakṣmaṇ Rāmcandra Pāṅgārkar refuted what he saw as Bhāgvat's "undue liberality" in casting Eknāth as a social reformer. Pāṅgārkar insisted that Eknāth actually was not fond of mixing castes (*saṃkarpriya*); rather, he was an exceptional great soul (*mahātmā*) who had achieved an impartial vision toward both brahmans and Dalits (*cāṇḍāḷ*s).[16] To Pāṅgārkar, Eknāth demonstrated spiritual achievement, not social protest. Pāṅgārkar's social conservatism shaded his retelling of the *śrāddha* and double vision stories too, for which he followed Mahīpati's *BhL* closely. When he narrated the brahmans' demand that Eknāth be purified in the river, Pāṅgārkar stopped short of saying whether the ritual occurred, and he conspicuously avoided denigrating the brahmans. In describing the double vision story, Pāṅgārkar amplified Mahīpati's emphasis on the Dalit hosts' purity.[17] "In body, they were Mahārs; but in all of their conduct they were like brahmans! Their *jāti*-fellows teased them as 'the brahmans among us.'"[18] No hagiographer ever went this far. Pāṅgārkar also depicted the double vision story's brahmans in a more restrained manner. He omitted the details of the brahmans' frantic attempts to catch Eknāth and stated that when the brahmans saw the two images of Eknāth, they quickly concluded that God had worked a miracle.[19] Notably, Pāṅgārkar and Ambedkar were in agreement that the saints concerned themselves with spiritual and not social matters, but they drew very different conclusions from this observation.

Jagannāth Raghunāth Ājgāvkar mostly followed Pāṅgārkar's socially conservative lead in describing Eknāth, although Ājgāvkar went a step further by simply omitting any references to Eknāth's interactions with Dalits, including the *śrāddha* and double vision stories. Ājgāvkar also introduced readers to an unprecedented rendition of Eknāth's encounter with Dattātreya—a story that Ājgāvkar said "some people" described in a "somewhat different fashion."[20] In Ājgāvkar's rendition, a group of suspicious brahmans follow Eknāth and Janārdana to the meeting place, scandalized by the rumor that Janārdana eats with a Muslim. Datta appears as a Muslim, accompanied by dogs and a wife, and he tells his wife to prepare a stew in a large cauldron. He instructs her to butcher several chickens and throw them in the pot and then to do the same with a large goat.[21] Then he points to the brahmans, telling her to add them to the stew too. After the brahmans run for their lives, Datta reveals his divine form and the meal proceeds. No hagiography of Eknāth contained such a tale. However, this is uncannily similar to a story about Rāmdās and Dattātreya found in a non-Vārkarī hagiography, the *Hanumansvāmīñcī Bakhar*.[22] The appearance of Datta in both figures' hagiographies seems to have allowed this non-veg vignette to jump across the cultural memory of saints, from Rāmdās to Eknāth, three centuries after Eknāth lived.

Although authors in the late 19th century took a special interest in Eknāth's social ethics, Marathi scholars of the saints between 1900 and 1940 mostly avoided the bhakti-caste question.[23] This may have reflected a difference of personality and outlook among these brahman men. In any case, at the same time that scholars withdrew from Sahasrabuddhe's and Bhāgvat's view of Eknāth as a social reformer, the world of Marathi theater and film embraced that interpretation and ran with it.

Eknāth in theater and film, 1903–2005

On the scholarly value of film, Rachel Dwyer argued, "If we want to study various imaginaries in the Indian context, the best place to start is with film, as it presents us not only with images and symbols of the public and the popular but also with their consumption by the audience."[24] I think that an even better place to start historically would be theater. At least in the Marathi world, plays at the beginning of the 20th century established narrative precedents that film productions followed. Indeed, the silent motion picture *Pundalik* in 1912 could be regarded as the first film in India, but since it was simply a musical play that was recorded on film, scholars have not accorded *Pundalik* this distinction.[25]

Because of their popular reach, Marathi plays and films surely shaped public impressions of Eknāth more broadly and viscerally than scholarly literature did. Although the black-and-white film *Dharmātmā* attracted some scholarly attention because of the controversies that surrounded it,[26] this film was only one instance of a broader pattern of representing Eknāth's inter-caste relations between 1903 and 2005. For the sake of space, I focus on the four most important productions, historically, marked with asterisks in the list of films and plays with their authors and directors.

1903*	*Śrī Eknāth*	Vināyak Raṅganāth Śirvaḷkar	Play, Marathi
1926	*Sant Eknāth*	Dādāsaheb Phaḷke (dir.)	Feature film, silent
1927	*Ekanath*	Harindanath Chattopadhyay	Dramatic poem, English
1933*	*Kharā Brāmhaṇ*	Keśav Sītārām Thackeray	Play, Marathi
1935*	*Dharmātmā*	V. Shantaram (dir.)	Feature film, Marathi
1938	*Ekanāthār*	Harshadrai Sakerlal Mehta (dir.)	Feature film, Tamil
1964*	*Bhāva Toci Dev*	Gopāl Govind Śirgopīkar	Play, Marathi
2004	*Sant Eknāth Mahārāj*	Rājū Phulkar (dir.)	VCD film, Marathi
2005	*Sant Eknāth*	Rājeś Limkar (dir.)	VCD film, Marathi

The first dramatic production of Eknāth's life appeared when Marathi theater was still in its infancy. There were precedents in early 18th-century Tanjore Maratha dramas, Viṣṇudās Bhāve's singular *Sītā-svayamvara* (1843), Marathi translations of Shakespeare and Kālidās, and the synthesis of Parsi-Gujarati and Urdu theater that led to the Marathi musical genre of *saṅgīt nāṭak*.[27] Audiences of those productions remained relatively exclusive, however, due to the price of entry, limited advertising, and expectations of social affiliation.[28] This changed in 1892, with the acclaimed production of *Rānā Bhīmdev* (King Bhīmdev) by Vināyak Raṅganāth Śirvaḷkar, a high school teacher in Pune.[29] The play's success prompted him to write seven more plays and two novels over the next twenty years, all of which were based on regional interests: the Maratha army's unexpected defeat at Panipat, the Peśvā general Mahādjī Śinde, and the major Vārkarī *sants*. Of the *sant* plays, *Śrī Tukārām* (1901) was the most popular, followed by those about Eknāth and Nāmdev (1903), and Jñāndev (1904).[30] Meera Kosambi has described Śirvaḷkar's oeuvre as "lowbrow," with people like mill workers being their primary audience. She does not explain the basis of this judgment, nor does she pay much heed to Śirvaḷkar's work generally.[31] Although Śirvaḷkar did initiate a turn to wider audiences, I think his work demonstrates greater sophistication and creativity than the "lowbrow" label suggests. As Śirvaḷkar's work popularized Marathi theater,[32] it helped shape popular memory of the saints, decades before cinema.

Śrī Eknāth (1903)—V. R. Śirvaḷkar

Śirvaḷkar was personally familiar with the living Vārkarī tradition. His father had made over fifty pilgrimages to Paṇḍharpūr, and Śirvaḷkar wrote that it was a relative in Paṇḍharpūr, a "famous *sādhu*," who inspired him to write "bhakti-filled plays."[33] For *Śrī Eknāth*, Śirvaḷkar carefully documented his sources of information, which included Mahīpati, Sahasrabuddhe, Bhāgvat, and three English histories of India.[34] Śirvaḷkar had done his homework, and it spanned traditional and modern modes of remembering Eknāth.

By Śirvaḷkar's time, social critiques had begun to spread from groups like the Prārthanā Samāj and Satyaśodhak Samāj and people like Jotibā Phule and G. G. Āgarkar. Socially inclined plays about *sants* fit well in this zeitgeist. As a reviewer in the Marathi newspaper *Kesarī* (not known for progressive politics) opined, such plays were "extremely important in today's social situation."[35]

To fit the technical form of theater as a medium, Śirvaḷkar integrated many hagiographic episodes into a single, flowing narrative. To accomplish this, he reworked two traditional characters. A mute, dull brahman boy named Gāvbā appeared in some hagiographies as an unlikely disciple of Eknāth.[36] Śirvaḷkar transformed him into a jester or *viduṣak*, whose witty comments kept the play lighthearted. In one tense scene about a financial crisis, Eknāth's wife hands Gāvbā her jewelry to sell. He looks down at them and quips, "Honestly, these aren't worth much. They don't even look real, like that fake jewelry that actors wear in plays."[37]

More importantly, Śirvaḷkar wrote Rāṇyā Mahār into all stories that involved Dalits, which comprised over half of the play. This move corresponded to Śirvaḷkar's portrayal of Janārdana's final lesson to Eknāth: "Distinctions like *jāti*, family, *gotra*, high, and low aren't real. A Mahār has the same right to undertake selfless devotion as the highest brahman. Viṭhobā revealed himself directly to Cokhāmeḷā, while the pious [*karmaṭh*] brahmans couldn't catch even a whiff of Viṭhobā's scent. Remember: in God's home, *bhakti* is supreme, not *jāti*."[38] Echoes of Sahasrabuddhe and Bhāgvat are impossible to miss.

The most sustained narrative about Rāṇyā appears in Acts IV and V, which were cobbled together from independent episodes. The first scene opens in a cave, where five thieves wrestle with the ethics of stealing to feed their families.[39] They fixate on a new target: the wedding party of Eknāth and his new wife, Girjā. The head thief is Rāṇyā.[40] Śirvaḷkar took great poetic license to make Rāṇyā into a thief. Although there was no precedent for this, it served the media form well by tying together the many scenes about Dalits. Soldiers eventually catch and beat Rāṇyā, but he escapes prison and encounters Eknāth.

Eknāth takes pity on him, and Girjā serves him food. Rāṇyā vows to never steal again, and he marvels at Eknāth's kindness despite their caste difference.[41] Eknāth explains, "The distinction that you are a Mahār and I am a brahman didn't come to my mind. In God's home, we both are one."[42] Later that day, Rāṇyā invites Eknāth for a meal. Eknāth accepts, on the grounds that God cares about bhakti, not caste.

Śirvaḷkar offers a novel twist on the double vision: Eknāth seeks Śrīkhaṇḍyā's advice about whether he should go eat at Rāṇyā's home or send a proxy.[43] Śrīkhaṇḍyā replies that both options are equally good, but he then suggests—for no apparent reason—that Eknāth go home and be confident that if Rāṇyā's heart is pure, God will take Eknāth's form and eat. After all,

Śrīkhaṇḍyā notes, Pāṇḍuraṅg is used to eating with Mahārs; he did so with Cokhāmeḷā in the past.[44]

This sudden reference to God taking Eknāth's form would have seemed strange to anyone who was unfamiliar with the double vision story. But it is clear why Śirvaḷkar did this: the extra dialog tries to balance the competing values of bhakti, caste, and personal integrity. It shows Eknāth's goodwill toward Rāṇyā, his disregard of caste, his intention to follow through with the visit, and his concern for maintaining good relations with fellow brahmans—all while staying relatively true to the traditional story's plot. The scene closes as Eknāth heeds Śrīkhaṇḍyā's advice, and they both return to Eknāth's home.

The next scene opens at Rāṇyā's home, where he and his wife despair that Eknāth is late and may never arrive. Rāṇyā's wife laments, "You've listened to so many *pothī*s and *purāṇa*s, but have you ever heard in them that a brahman ate at a Mahār's home? Viṭhobā will eat in our home, but never, ever a brahman."[45] Rāṇyā works through the cold logic of the situation: "Nāth Mahārāj said that all *jāti*s are alike to Viṭhobā, who only cares about bhakti. *Jāti* depends on people's behavior. We don't eat any meat. We fast on the eleventh day [*ekādaśi*]. We make the annual pilgrimage with Eknāth to Paṇḍharpūr. Day and night, we do what he instructs. After all this, if Eknāth still won't come to break his fast at our house, then what difference does it make if we live or die?"[46] The couple tie nooses and place them around their necks. As they prepare to leave the world, they sing a song that is based a famous *bhārūḍ* of Eknāth, "Open the door, woman, open the door."[47]

This *bhārūḍ* invokes the goddess by many names, highlighting her fierce forms and beseeching her to reveal herself. Some modern Marathi interpreters have argued this was a covert protest against Muslim rulers at the time, inviting the goddess to come and set things right.[48] As Śirvaḷkar uses it in the play, I think he intends it more mundanely: once the door is open, the spurned couple can leave this world. Of course, Śirvaḷkar may have used the *bhārūḍ* here precisely because of its capacity to convey multiple meanings simultaneously. Suddenly, outside their home, Eknāth's voice starts singing a *bhārūḍ* with the opposite message: "Woman, close the door."[49] This *bhārūḍ* seeks to pacify the goddess. By using two of Eknāth's own compositions, Śirvaḷkar thus brings the play to a climax.

Eknāth (actually Viṭṭhal in Eknāth's form) removes the nooses from their necks and asks them to fill his plate. The brahmans burst in and one says, "You enjoy eating the Mahār's food so much, why not just fill your belly with dung? Low one, you're now put out of caste forever. Marry your sons to Mahār girls and give your daughters to Mahārs. You vile one [*adhmā*], *cāṇḍāḷ*, affliction to my body—you've become a Dalit [*ḍom*]!!!"[50]

Eknāth explains that he eats the rice of faith (*bhāva*), the lentils of renunciation, and the ghee of peace—all of which the brahmans too would enjoy, if they would only try them. Another brahman retorts that Eknāth is not a real brahman and is speaking nonsense. At this point, Śirvaḷkar executes a creative masterstroke. Eknāth replies that the brahmans are behaving like Arjuna in the *Bhagavad Gītā*, plagued by doubts about their who they are and what they should do.[51] Then, as if to emulate Kṛṣṇa revealing his universal form to Arjuna, Eknāth sings a famous *bhārūḍ* that adopts the voice of a Mahār: "*Johār māybāp johār*. You're a Mahār from what town? If you're truly asking, then respectfully listen. My native place is Nirākār (Formless), but I left it for the sake of bhakti. Now, I dwell in Kāyāpūr (Body-town)."[52] It describes how God, who is ultimately without qualities, adopts a name and form to give people an object for their devotion. In this case, that form is Eknāth, who Viṭṭhal/Kṛṣṇa, evoking Kṛṣṇa's hierophany in the *Gītā*. This interweaving of mythic stories and bhakti songs all have the effect of presenting to the audience the image of a Mahār who reveals himself as Kṛṣṇa.

Śirvaḷkar takes more liberties with the *śrāddha* story. The hagiographies place this episode before the double vision story, but Śirvaḷkar situates it immediately after it. And although Śirvaḷkar's play mostly follows the plotline of Mahīpati's *BhL*, for this story he adopted the *BhV*'s rendition, portraying the uninvited guests as Dalits rather than *fakīr*s (as they were in the *BhL*). The decision was small but significant: Śirvaḷkar synthesized traditional sources to portray Eknāth more systematically as engaged with Dalits. Later playwrights and filmmakers would follow suit and further consolidate Eknāth's persona as a brahman who freely transgresses caste by interacting with Dalits.

Eknāth's relations with Dalits are central to Śirvaḷkar's play. By rearranging the scenes and making Rāṇyā Mahār the quintessential Dalit, Śirvaḷkar ensured that the issue of untouchability pervaded the entire play. Yet despite his interest in a social message and reliance on Bhāgvat's essay, Śirvaḷkar left the story's ambiguity intact. If it were equally good for Eknāth to eat at Rāṇyā's home or remain home, then why should Śrīkhaṇḍyā recommend going home? After taking so many other narrative liberties, Śirvaḷkar resisted revising this crucial plot point. Rāṇyā's wife poignantly confirms the problem: "You've listened to so many *pothī*s and *purāṇa*s, but have you ever heard in them that a brahman ate at a Mahār's home?" By the end of the play, Śirvaḷkar's audience had not witnessed such a brahman either.

Kharā Brāmhaṇ (1933)—K. S. Thackeray

Eknāth was invoked for a quite different end by Keśav Sītārām Thackeray (Ṭhākre), who led the *brāhmaṇetar* ("non-brahman") movement in the 1920s and 1930s and, later, the *Saṃyukta Mahārāṣṭra Sabhā* that lobbied for the creation of a state along linguistic boundaries.[53] Thackeray belonged to the *jāti* cluster Cāndrasenīya Kāyastha Prabhū or CKP, who historically were immigrant scribes and administrators in western India and thus had long-standing tensions with brahmans.[54] Thackeray's non-brahman activism focused on the grievances of his almost-brahman community and thus had a different political edge than Phule's and Ambedkar's non-brahman activism, which arose from śūdra and Dalit concerns. *Kharā Brāmhaṇ* (True Brahman) displays Thackeray's politics clearly, and the reception of its roughly one hundred performances was very contentious. Brahman groups petitioned British authorities to ban the play on the grounds that it spread hatred of brahmans.[55] Even the play's name, with the colloquial and less respectful term "Brāmhaṇ," signaled Thackeray's intent.[56]

Kharā Brāmhaṇ paid little heed to precedent; few characters and stories resemble those in the hagiographies. Thackeray's messages were overtly political and bluntly criticized brahman privilege. Yet Thackeray followed Śirvaḷkar's lead in interspersing Eknāth's songs throughout the play, and he noted that when troupes omitted the songs, the play lacked zest (*rasa*).[57]

The play begins at a Rāma temple in Paiṭṭhaṇ, with Viṭhū Mahār standing outside with his widowed daughter-in-law Sītā, whose soldier husband died in battle.[58] When brahmans emerge from the temple and leer at her, Viṭhū advises her to go home. Viṭhū prays about his desire to enter the temple, which a passing brahman and Maratha man overhear. They comment to each other that Viṭhū is wearing a *mālā*, identifying him as a Vārkarī. They note that Eknāth taught the Bhāgavat Dharma and opened the door of liberation to non-brahmans (*brāhmaṇetar*).[59] One brahman mockingly bows to Viṭhū and prods him to enter the temple. Other brahmans, including Gāvbā (an eccentric fool with a very dark sense of humor in this play), come out of the temple and demand that the first brahman bathe in the river with his clothes for having touched a Mahār. Things go downhill from there. The brahmans complain that Mahārs have become a nuisance, now that Eknāth inflated their pride.[60] If Mahārs were to be admitted to temples, then they would want to eat with brahmans, marry brahmans' daughters, and destroy *sanātana dharma*. Viṭhū politely requests them not to defame Eknāth. They decry Viṭhū's insolence and goad the Maratha man into striking Viṭhū on the forehead with his staff. Bleeding profusely, Viṭhū loses consciousness, and everyone walks away.[61] Eknāth's wife Girjā arrives and brings Viṭhū into their home, which angers the brahmans further.

The next act opens with Gāvbā dressed as a Muslim soldier (*paṭhāṇ*), talking with the temple priest. The priest is surprised but patient, aware of Gāvbā's mental instability. Gāvbā states that he converted after Eknāth and Girjā were outcasted for hosting Viṭhū in their home. Since Eknāth and Girjā became regarded as Mahārs, they moved from the brahman part of town into the Mahār neighborhood. In solidarity, Gāvbā decided to stop being a brahman too, but he chose to become a Paṭhāṇ instead, because they do not fear brahmans. Gāvbā offers some frank advice, "Everyone must become a Mahār, Māṅg, Dheḍ, Cāmbhār or Muslim, otherwise tribes of Paṭhāṇs from Peshawar need to come and stand on the chests of Paiṭhaṇ's *bhaṭs*. There is no other path for uplifting the Dalits."[62] The priest calls Gāvbā a lowlife (*pājī*) and walks away.

The play contains many other unprecedented plot twists. A deadly cattle disease spreads through Paiṭhaṇ, and the Mahārs protest by refusing to remove the carcasses, whereas Eknāth undertakes the labor to prevent humans from getting sick.[63] To protect their interests, the brahmans summon a religious official from Kāśī to put Eknāth on trial. They also complain to the local ruler, claiming that Eknāth and the Mahārs were poisoning cows themselves to spread unrest. A police force is dispatched to Paiṭhaṇ, where they torture Viṭhū Mahār, seeking a confession.[64]

The final act portrays Eknāth's trial before a *svāmī* from Kāśī, who initially challenges Eknāth for rendering the *BhP* into Marathi. The local brahmans commandeer the trial and accuse Eknāth instead of destroying *sanātana* dharma by interacting with Mahārs.[65] Eknāth agrees that this was his intention, since no genuine dharma could exclude a large portion of humanity.[66] "I'm ready to destroy brahman privilege [*brāhmaṇya*] for the sake of uplifting Mahārs."[67] A brahman asks what will remain if brahman privilege is destroyed, and Eknāth responds, "Hindutva! Strong, unified Hindutva. To preserve it, we need to bring the untouchables [*aspṛśya*] near. Even more, the time has come to offer up brahman privilege as a sacrifice for the sake of Hindutva."[68]

As the brahmans sense that the trial is turning against them, a fire mysteriously breaks out in the Mahār neighborhood and claims the life of Viṭhū's dear daughter-in-law. The *svāmī* sees this and says, "Damn our brahman-knowledge and our egoistic brahman privilege!"[69] When the local brahmans ask what he means, the *svāmī* snaps, "Shut up, fools." Eknāth continues his previous argument, saying that there is no other way to liberate Hindus from untouchability. The *svāmī* embraces Viṭhū Mahār and calls him a true brahman. The play ends with the whole cast saying, "Tathāstu, Tathāstu, Tathāstu" (Let it be so).[70]

Thackeray took enormous liberties in this play. The brahmans' treatment of Viṭhū is vicious. Eknāth does not care at all about what the brahmans think of him. Throughout most of the play, Eknāth lives contentedly as a Mahār. Eknāth's startling declaration of Hindutva as the true nature of dharma is revealing, if not overly surprising in the context of Thackeray's play. V. S. Savarkar's influential book by that name had been published one decade earlier. When Thackeray's Eknāth fights for a casteless society, his invocation of Hindutva carries strong political undertones. Savarkar's Hindutva ideology also endorsed equality but extended it only to a select group (Hindus) and quite intentionally marginalized others, especially Muslims. As we observed in Chapter 1, this was often a feature of equality in a conservative democratic mode, premised on the exclusion of people who were deemed not to belong.

Conspicuously absent in Thackeray's play are the *śrāddha* and double vision stories. Thackeray may have excluded the two stories because supernatural occurrences were essential to both. Thackeray's Hindu nationalism did not entail reverence for miraculous powers. Allowing deities to intervene could even detract from the urgency of *deśabhakta*s carrying out the work of nation-building themselves. Or we could say that in Thackeray's hands, the story of Eknāth moved across a boundary between fields (to invoke Bourdieu), out of the traditional field of religious devotion and into the socio-political field, so that it abided by different rules and adhered to different values. Thackeray's play is about Eknāth, but in terms of its illocutionary force, his goals were clearly political.

Another possibility for Thackeray's omission relates to the semantic density of food stories that enabled hagiographers' strategically ambiguous portrayals. The inherent ambiguity in the food stories does not suit Thackeray's political program, which required clarity of message and purpose. What had been discursive advantages to the hagiographers would have been disadvantageous for Thackeray's aims. The stories sustained an open-ended negotiation of bhakti and caste, whereas Thackeray wanted to move on to other goals. This speaks to the nature of storytelling itself. If one is trying to evoke outrage and anger in one's audience, ambiguity is a difficult instrument to wield. To promote an overtly political program like his, Thackeray had no desire to be ambiguous with his audience.

Dharmātmā (1935)—Prabhāt Film Company

The most widely known production of Eknāth's life on stage or screen was the Prabhāt Film Company's *Dharmātmā*.[71] Prior to *Dharmātmā*, Prabhāt was already a leader in the growing Marathi and Hindi film industries, as they shot their early films twice, once in each language.[72] Their *Amṛtamanthan* (Churning of the Nectar) was the highest grossing film in 1934.[73] Riding on that film's success, the thirty-three-year-old director Shantaram Rajaram Vankudre (known as V. Shantaram) wanted to make a film about a Marathi *sant*, so he hired K. Nārāyaṇ Kāḷe to write the script.[74] Shantaram's initial wish to focus on Tukārām was vetoed by Kāḷe, who felt that Tukārām was too otherworldly. Kāḷe recommended that Eknāth was a timelier subject because of the stories about him associating with Dalits.[75] While supporting Kāḷe's endorsement of a social message, Shantaram resisted Kāḷe's wish to omit miraculous stories completely. With an eye to the film's commercial viability, Shantaram also added a scene of *apsaras* dancing suggestively to engage a wider audience.[76]

While the film was being produced, the most exciting aspect of it by far was the casting of Marathi theater superstar Nārāyaṇ Śrīpad Rājahaṃs, better known as Bālgandharva. In 1935, Bālgandharva had come into difficult financial straits due to some poor investments, so Prabhāt reached out to him with a deal, banking on his stardom to attract audiences. This film was the first time that Bālgandharva appeared in a role as a man; he had made his name by portraying women characters on stage. Prabhāt released the film strategically under the name Bālgandharva-Prabhāt Productions and promised the actor half of the film's earnings.[77] *Dharmātmā* was ostensibly a film about Eknāth, but from the start, its main selling point was Bālgandharva.[78]

Marathi productions were some of the earliest and most outstanding examples of the Indian devotional film genre.[79] Predisposed toward social issues, devotional films in the 1930s often took inspiration from Gandhi,[80] despite his low opinion of film.[81] Shantaram hoped that his audience would associate Eknāth's attitude on untouchability with Gandhi's campaigns.[82] The film's original title *Mahātmā* was changed because of objections from the Bombay Board of Film Censors (comprised of British and Indian members),[83] who sought to prevent seditious messages being spread through depictions of religious and mythological themes.[84] Novetzke points out that *Dharmātmā* made a point about regional identity too: in the figure of Eknāth, Maharashtrians had a proto-Gandhi of their own.[85] But contemporary politics was only one of the censors' many concerns.

The completed film was rejected by the Board of Film Censors in Bombay in September 1935 on the grounds that "it treats a sacred subject irreverently and deals with controversial politics."[86] The board demanded four main alterations: change the title, cut two untraditional scenes of Eknāth interacting with Dalits, emphasize the divinity of Eknāth's servant Śrīkhaṇḍyā, and change the name of the brahman judge in the final scene to avoid alluding to contemporary Hindu leaders.[87] Somehow, these issues did not disturb the Bengal Board of Censors, who approved the film's Hindi version immediately, with its original name intact.[88] So, *Mahātmā* in Hindi was screened in Calcutta in October 1935, two months before the edited and renamed *Dharmātmā* in Marathi hit theaters in Bombay.[89]

Kāḷe repurposed Śrīkhaṇḍyā (rather than Gāvbā) for the jester role in the film and encapsulated brahman antagonism in the novel figure of a brawny, arrogant holy man named Saccidānanda and his coterie of dull-witted disciples. Kāḷe made Rāṇū the quintessential Dalit and created a charming young daughter, Jāī, who is affectionately close to Eknāth throughout the film. The impact of this endearingly cheerful character (skillfully performed by the child actress Vāsantī) was so great that many Maharashtrians today assume that Jāī had always been present in hagiographical stories. Jāī's innocent actions advance the film's plot by bringing social tensions into the open. Eknāth's son, Haripaṇḍit (played by Kāḷe himself), was another prominent character.

The plot of *Dharmātmā* focuses on a short period in Eknāth's adult life. The *śrāddha* story is included, but everything flows toward the double vision story. *Dharmātmā* made caste and transgressive commensality the basis of the entire film, thereby extending the pattern of narrative consolidation.

The film opens with Saccidānanda in his *maṭh*, sitting on a traditional swing as two women attendants wash his bare arms and chest. Townsfolk take the water that drains off and drink it devotedly as *prasād*. One exclaims, "Saccidānanda! Oh, what divinity! Unlike that wretched Eknāth. Always making a fuss about equality [*samatecī baḍbaḍ*]." Saccidānanda hears his adversary's name and shouts, "Ugh, Eknāth! Infidel!" A follower concurs, "Yes, that Eknāth sees no difference between brahmans, merchants, oil-pressers, tobacco-sellers, Mahārs, Māṅgs, women or men." Another interjects, "Anyone at all can approach Eknāth. [sarcastically] He's become a *mahātmā*!"[90] A disciple flings a banana peel out the window, which lands outside at the feet of a shirtless sweeper who we later learn is Rāṇū. He looks up and says, "Nāth," and slowly turns to his companion as a sarangi plays mournfully in the background. Speaking in dialect, he says, "Nāth is God to us. We fall and touch his feet. Because of Nāth, we were able to see our little girl again. Otherwise she would have died on the hot sand, writhing in agony."[91] A hagiographical story portrayed Eknāth picking up a lost Dalit boy on a riverbank; Kāḷe applied it to Jāī.

In the next scene, Eknāth and his wife patiently listen to Haripaṇḍit complaining about his father's behavior. Such instances recur periodically throughout the film until Haripaṇḍit's shame finally impels him to fully dissociate himself from his parents. In another scene, Haripaṇḍit storms off to air his grievances to Eknāth. Haripaṇḍit opens a door and pauses when he finds Eknāth seated in prayer, singing an *abhaṅga*, "Passionate faith is God, passionate faith is God (*bhāva toci dev*).[92] Have no doubts about this. Through passionate faith comes the fruit of devotion, through passionate faith one obtains God."[93] Haripaṇḍit is visibly moved and calms down.

Viewers first encounter Jāī in the next scene, being chased by two of Saccidānanda's disciples who call her a thief. They throw stones at her and eventually knock her unconscious outside Eknāth's door. He emerges, and the disciples demand that Jāī be punished for stealing flowers from their trees. Eknāth responds, "Lashes of a whip for stealing flowers! If God would measure our sins by this standard, what tortures await us!"[94] The disciples walk away in shame. Eknāth cares for her until she regains consciousness and her parents fetch her. Jāī asks Eknāth to offer her flowers to God in his worship. Eknāth accepts and sings a traditional *abhaṅga*: "Those who are called *strīśūdrādi*—God dwells in all beings. Lowliness has no place."[95]

In the next scene, Eknāth invites Saccidānanda and his followers to his *śrāddha* ceremony, but they refuse. So Eknāth then invites Rāṇū and the other Mahārs. (The hagiographies always placed the brahmans' refusal after the interlopers finished eating.) The brahmans point out that because they have not completed the proper rituals, Eknāth's ancestors will suffer. Eknāth is clearly bothered by this idea, as he was in Mahīpati's *Bhaktavijay*.

The script and film diverge at this point—the result of the censor board's required revisions. In the script, Śrīkhaṇḍyā reminds Eknāth about "his teaching" that children are simply small forms of God.[96] The ancestors could be satisfied if Eknāth would simply feed some children and pray to God. The film omits this explanation and jumps from Eknāth's worried face to a scene of Śrīkhaṇḍyā with playful children clinging to his legs. The camera cuts away again and suddenly Eknāth is praying to God while three children eat, and the images of Brahmā, Viṣṇu, and Śiva are superimposed on them. This hearkens to the *trimūrti* of the *BhL* story but with Dalit children substituted for Muslims.[97] Without the script's explanation by Śrīkhaṇḍyā, the film's flow and the feeding of three children is bewildering.

After the unorthodox *śrāddha* concludes, Saccidānanda stops two Mahār men and cunningly reminds them that Eknāth first had invited the brahmans and only after they declined did he invite the Mahārs. He plants doubts in their minds: if Eknāth truly is their ally, would he be willing to eat at their home? The Mahār men start debating but quickly stop when they see Jāī arrive. She heard enough to inspire her to invite Eknāth, which she quickly sets off to do, despite the protests of other Mahārs.

Jāī reaches Eknāth's home and jokes around with him and Girijā (spelled Girjā in other texts). This irritates Haripaṇḍit, who reminds her of the social chasm between Mahārs and brahmans. Jāī points out Eknāth's teaching that caste is unimportant, and she teases Haripaṇḍit for forgetting his own father's lesson. Enraged, Haripaṇḍit slaps the gleeful girl across the face, to the shock of everyone including himself. Jāī recoils and begins to cry, "I'm a Mahār. You are brahmans. Our home is atop a rubbish heap. Our clothes are tattered and torn. Mother and Father do filthy work in the dung and muck. We have only stale *capāti*s to eat. No, no. Brahmans and Mahārs are not alike. And I was going to invite you to our home to eat. I was sure that you'd come. But you're a brahman. How could you eat at a Mahār's home?"[98] Eknāth responds that he will gladly eat at her home. Her despair turns to joy, and she sets off, dancing through the streets and singing, "tomorrow Eknāth comes to eat at our home."

The townsfolk become agitated. Before he departs for Jāī's home, Eknāth quickly prays, "God, you are behind me, protecting." Śrīkhaṇḍyā, who was standing behind Eknāth, suddenly transforms into Viṣṇu and extends his hand in a sign of blessing.[99] A translucent image of Eknāth slowly becomes visible, superimposed on Viṣṇu. The image walks to a couch, sits down, and becomes fully opaque. Viṣṇu, who continued standing while the Eknāth image walked away, morphs back into Śrīkhaṇḍyā. In essence, Eknāth goes to eat at Jāī's home, while God takes Eknāth's form and remains at home.

In the original film, Kāḷe had followed Bhāgvat's un-miraculous rendition of the story and depicted Eknāth simply eating at the Mahārs' home without a second image. The censor board protested that this diverged too far from the hagiographical account and had to be changed. Prabhāt replied with a letter assuring the censor board that they would be faithful to Mahīpati's *BhL* account, but they conveniently glossed over one crucial detail. Mahīpati portrayed Eknāth remaining home while God-as-Eknāth ate with the Dalits. In *Dharmātmā*, it is the human Eknāth who goes to eat.[100]

As Eknāth walks to the Mahār neighborhood, the townsfolk cannot contain their curiosity. Śrīkhaṇḍyā follows behind and is stopped by a learned brahman who self-consciously asks, "So . . . Eknāth's gone out all dressed up today under the hot sun. . . . . Does he have a special invitation somewhere?" Śrīkhaṇḍyā responds, "Special? Oh, his invitation is to a place that until today no brahman has ever been invited." Someone else asks, "Is Eknāth *truly* going to eat at the Mahārs' home?" Śrīkhaṇḍyā replies, "What else, sir? Is it possible to eat falsely?"[101] Although the play on words is comedic, it highlights the genuine physical investment of eating together. It is not something one can fake.

The film dwells on people's reactions to seeing Eknāth eat in the Rāṇū's home, as the collage in Photo 6.1 shows.

The second image of God-as-Eknāth sitting in his own home appeared only briefly—the result of extra footage that got spliced into the film to align it with the traditional story. This is why no one in the film comments on the miraculous double vision. In the original script, no one had to wrestle with the ambiguity about where Eknāth was; he clearly ate at Rāṇū's home. This is another instance in which the censor board disrupted the smooth narrative of the film, seeking to reintroduce ambiguity where there was none.

The film's conclusion mirrors Thackeray's play, effectively putting Eknāth's transgressive behavior on trial. Saccidānanda accuses Eknāth of corrupting the *dharma* by eating with Mahārs. Eknāth argues that mixing with Dalits is fully consonant with religion, since "compassion is the foundation of *dharma*"—a very different unifying vision than Thackeray's Hindutva.[102] Eknāth then sings from a text on the ground before him, pausing to comment, "Without love, it is impossible for people to come together. Without people coming together, society will never arise. And if there is no society, then what purpose would there be for *dharma*? . . . Understand that food,

Photo 6.1. Stills from *Dharmātmā*. Eknāth eats at Jāī's home as Jāī's family, Dalit community members, and two brahmans respond.
Source: Photo by author.

clothing, wealth, and honor are only worldly yearnings. Acting kindly toward all beings—this is everyone's innate duty."[103] As Eknāth sings the final verses, the rhythm picks up, and everyone in the room, including the judge and Haripaṇḍit, break out in huge smiles, nearly swooning with bliss. In the end, the judge is convinced and jumps up to embrace him, saying, "Eknāth, you truly are a *mahātmā*." In Thackeray's play, the judge embraced Viṭhū Mahār and called him a "true brahman."

Advertising for *Dharmātmā* had built up great anticipation for the film, but when the edited film was finally screened, reviews were mixed. As we have observed, some last-minute alterations imposed by the censor board disrupted the fluidity of the narrative. Audiences and reviewers were remarkably unfazed by the treatment of untouchability in the film, which came out in the same year that Ambedkar publicly announced that he would not die a Hindu.[104]

What critics did focus on was the film's casting. Haripaṇḍit was several inches taller and appeared older than his mother—a discrepancy that was exacerbated by her way of looking up at him tenderly throughout the film and calling him Bāḷ (child or baby). The actress who played Jāī was universally praised, as was Shantaram's directing.[105] English language newspapers had generally positive reviews.[106] The film continued to be screened for at least two months after its release. Meera Kosambi describes the film as a "debacle" and "financial disaster,"[107] but I have not come across evidence of such a dire reception. *Dharmātmā* did not do as well as Prabhāt had hoped, but it did not fail at the box office either.[108]

Ironically, the film's greatest problem lay with Bālgandharva, who struggled to adjust to the film medium's technical requirements. One reviewer wrote that the superstar's performance was so bland that *Dharmātmā* seemed to lack a main character, like "Hamlet without the Prince of Denmark."[109] The film's assistant director, Śāntārām Āṭhavḷe, described the actor's plight at length.[110] Bālgandharva felt awkward in this role as a man, which involved having to sing while wearing a mustache.[111] He struggled to adjust to shooting a single scene several times in a row before moving on to the next scene.[112] He frequently lost his place and forgot his lines, which Āṭhavḷe eventually had to paint on plywood for Bālgandharva to see off-screen.[113] This deflated the actor's self-confidence. Having admired Bālgandharva's theatrical performances, Āṭhavḷe was "pained" to see how the star had fallen.[114]

Bālgandharva's mediocre performance stood out even more because Prabhāt had marketed the film extensively around him. Advertisements featured Bālgandharva prominently. Although other cast members were depicted in costume, as Photo 6.2 shows, the star was only ever shown wearing a fine turban and stately long coat—never as Eknāth.[115]

Prabhāt did this to generate suspense and pique people's curiosity about how he would ultimately appear in the film.[116] Even if Bālgandharva had performed well, he may not have been able to live up to the hype.

Because of the substantial documentation available on this film, we can see more clearly in *Dharmātmā* how material factors and transmedial strategies impacted its depictions of bhakti and caste. The film's advertisements, publicity announcements, and reviews all reveal the extent to which market concerns shaped the film's production. Viewers were enticed into the theater to see Bālgandharva, not because the film was about Eknāth and untouchability. Yet, along the way, *Dharmātmā* reaffirmed the increasingly popular view that Eknāth was an anti-caste reformer.

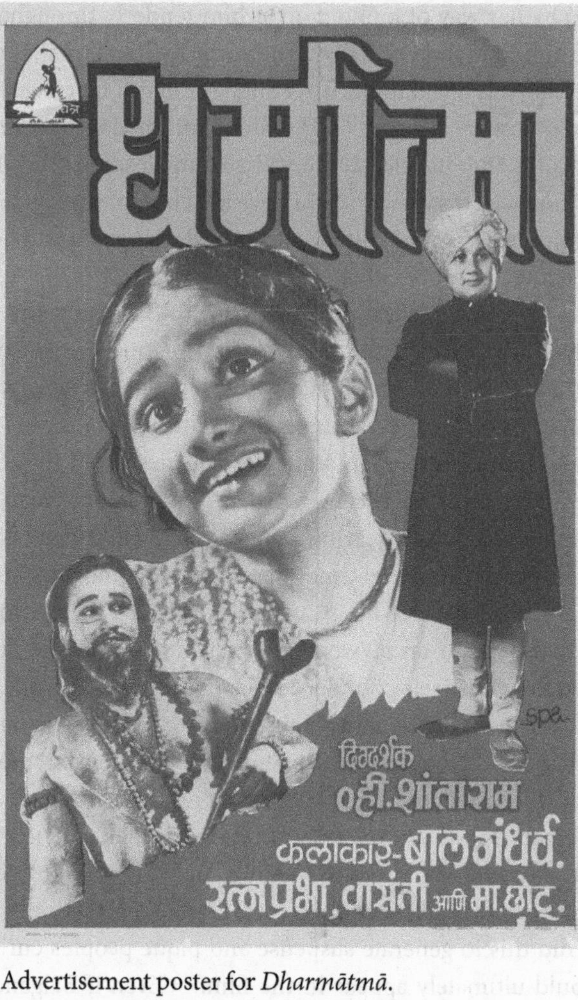

Photo 6.2. Advertisement poster for *Dharmātmā*.
Source: National Film Archive of India. Used with permission.

Bhāva Toci Dev (1965)—G. G. Śirgopīkar

Thirty years after *Dharmātmā* ceased screening, a Marathi play picked up some of its themes and adopted one of the film's most popular songs as its name—*Bhāva Toci Dev*. In the intervening three decades, India had witnessed massive changes: Gandhi's rise to fame and assassination, World War II, Indian Independence and Partition, the enshrinement of equality and reservations in the Indian Constitution, and Ambedkar's conversion to Buddhism. Marathi film and theater also underwent great changes, technologically and culturally. *Bhāva Toci Dev* reflected this cultural-political landscape, with an eye toward distinctly rural audiences.

Between 1965 and 1975, the play was performed more than 1,500 times, mostly in small towns across the Maharashtrian countryside. Although impossible to confirm statistically, it is quite likely that *Bhāva Toci Dev* eventually reached a larger audience than *Dharmātmā*. Yet, because this audience and popularity were located outside urban centers, *Bhāva Toci Dev* has been completely overlooked by modern authors who write about Eknāth.[117]

The play's author, Gopāḷ Govind (Nānāsāheb) Śirgopīkar grew up around theatrical drama. His father Govind Rāmcandra (Aṇṇasāheb) founded a children's theater troupe in 1923 that performed in Kolhāpūr and neighboring towns.[118] The troupe struggled financially until he found consistent profit through plays about deities and miracles. In 1932, Śirgopīkar founded a troupe of adults—the Ānand Saṅgīt Maṇḍaḷī (ĀSM, the Blissful Music Group)—which became famous in the following year for its musical play about Kṛṣṇa, *Gokuḷcā Cor* (The Thief of Gokula). The troupe performed this play more than three thousand times in the following three decades.[119]

Govind insisted that his son go to college before he could join the troupe, so Gopāḷ went off to earn a degree in physics in 1947. By the time he graduated, the ĀSM had developed into a disciplined, profitable business with touring routes that reached nearly six hundred towns throughout Maharashtra and Goa.[120] Gopāḷ Śirgopīkar inherited both the established troupe and good business practices from his father.[121] From 1950 onward, the troupe was in Gopāḷ's hands.[122]

Unlike Bombay- and Pune-based drama companies, such as the one that Bālgandharva founded, the ĀSM was always on the road. The troupe owned three large trucks, a custom-made cloth tent that could seat one thousand people, an electric generator and waterproof containers to carry costumes and props as they traveled.[123] During the monsoon months (late May through early September) the troupe resided at the Śirgopīkar home in Kolhāpūr, where they rested, wrote new plays, constructed sets, and rehearsed.[124] During the rest of the year, the troupe was on tour. ĀSM preferred smaller towns with fewer entertainment options to compete with for audiences. Over time, several "lines" or commercially viable touring routes developed as standard itineraries. They traveled a different line each year, so as not to revisit a region too frequently.[125] Upon arriving at a venue, they would clear a field, set up their tent, and put on seven or eight performances before moving on to the next town. News of ĀSM's performances spread mainly by word of mouth, which minimized advertising costs, and people would travel in from miles around to attend. The travel itinerary corresponded to the various harvest seasons of cash crops (rice, mangoes, millet, etc.), to attract local people when they were in a celebratory mood and had money to spend.[126]

Theater was the Śirgopīkars' livelihood and sole source of income. To remain in business, *Bhāva Toci Dev* had to appeal to a wide audience, comprised of people in rural areas who had little formal education. Essential to the play are slapstick comedy and ample interludes of song and dance. Most of all, *Bhāva Toci Dev* became renowned for its "trick scenes" that Śirgopīkar created by utilizing his physics education to design illusions.

Both the elder and younger Śirgopīkar knew that mythological and devotional plays would be popular in places where they performed. The elder's early play about Kṛṣṇa was the most successful play in the troupe's repertoire for over fifty years. The younger Śirgopīkar penned a few early dramas, but he too attracted sizable audiences only when he started writing plays about the Marathi *sants*. *Bhāva Toci Dev* was his first and most successful effort. Starting in 1963, he played the role of Śrīkhaṇḍyā and directed it over 1,500 times. Śirgopīkar also wrote relatively successful plays about Tukārām (1970 with 1,000 performances), Jñāndev (1978 with 1,000 performances) and Nāmdev (1984 with 500 performances).[127]

Bhāva Toci Dev consists of four acts and a small cast: Eknāth, Girijā, Śrīkhaṇḍyā, Rāṇū Mahār, Rādhā (Rāṇū's daughter), and two brahman antagonists. The role of Rāṇū was inspired by Rāṇū in *Dharmātmā*, and Rādhā was a slightly older version of Jāī (ĀSM was an adult troupe, after all). The two brahmans were Vicitraśāstrī, who claims to be the leader of Paiṭhaṇ's brahmans, and his enthusiastic, bumbling disciple Lokhaṇḍyā. The two try to bully Eknāth in comically ineffective ways. Even their names inspire ridicule—*vicitra* means "strange," and *lokhaṇḍa* means "iron," in contrast to the elegant sandalwood (*śrīkhaṇḍa*) from which Śrīkhaṇḍyā's name derived. Lokhaṇḍyā eagerly tries to support his guru but usually asks questions that undercut Vicitraśāstrī's arguments. Although Eknāth and Girijā are relatively staid characters, everyone else cracks jokes and teases each other, which results in a very light-hearted mood throughout the play. The content only loosely follows the double vision story as it was presented in *Dharmātmā*. A few references are made to traditional stories, but most of the play revolves around jokes and Śirgopīkar's famous trick scenes.

The play opens with Vicitraśāstrī and Lokhaṇḍyā coming to Eknāth's home to air their grievances. Eknāth is away, so Girijā offers the men a cup of milk while they wait. This sets up a conversation between Vicitraśāstrī and Lokhaṇḍyā about whether they could maintain ritual purity if they drank this milk, whether the milk contains ritually unclean water, whether the cow had ingested ritually unclean water, and so on.[128]

Later in the scene, Rāṇū tells Eknāth that he had always wanted to invite a brahman to his place to eat but was afraid to ask.[129] Eknāth responds that he and Girijā would gladly fulfill his wish. Vicitraśāstrī and Lokhaṇḍyā arrive at that moment and denounce them. Vicitraśāstrī then notices that he is standing close to Rāṇū and Rādhā. He sends Lokhaṇḍyā to fetch water to sprinkle on the ground to purify it, just as Śrīkhaṇḍyā comes by, carrying water from the river. Vicitraśāstrī asks him if this is Gaṅgā water, and Śrīkhaṇḍyā replies that since both Gaṅgā and Yamunā (rivers as goddesses) were busy, he had to fetch Sarasvatī water instead.[130] The audience would know that fetching Sarasvatī water was incredible, since the Sarasvatī River is legendarily invisible. Vicitraśāstrī is very impressed, however, and he asks Śrīkhaṇḍyā for the bucket to sprinkle water on the ground.

This sets up the first trick scene: Lokhaṇḍyā takes the bucket, but when he tips it, nothing comes out. A slat inside the bucket held the water if the bucket were tipped from one direction but would not obstruct it if tipped the other way. Śrīkhaṇḍyā says, "Oh, Sarasvatī must have vanished; she won't appear for just anyone."[131] He then takes the bucket and pours out the water. Rādhā comes near and asks if she can wash her hands, and Śrīkhaṇḍyā pours the same water on her hands. This angers Vicitraśāstrī and Lokhaṇḍyā, who then condemn Eknāth and demand that he undergo purification. Vicitraśāstrī concludes, "This brahman of southern Kāśī (Paiṭhaṇ) has become corrupted. Now the destruction of the universe [*pralaya*] will begin." Eknāth's response concludes the act: "Destruction? No, now it's time for uplifting the world. God, may my hands do service to promote the equal rights [*samān hakkā*] of all beings."[132] This is the first presentation of Eknāth that mentioned equal rights.

Śirgopīkar embellished the double vision story extensively. As Rāṇū and Rādhā prepare for Eknāth and Girijā to arrive, the brahmans stop by and warn Rāṇū that if Eknāth were to eat at Rāṇū's home, Paiṭhaṇ's brahmans may be so offended that they would attack Eknāth. Rāṇū takes this to heart and discusses it at length with Rādhā, but Śrīkhaṇḍyā eventually passes by and reassures them. Eknāth and Girijā eventually arrive, and Eknāth responds to this concern, "Although people think that I am doing *adharma* by eating at your home, I am actually doing it in order to awaken Janārdana among the people."[133] The second half of the sentence plays on the phrase *janī janārdana*, but with a different nuance. Eknāth wants to awaken a sense of the divine in people, like a general evocation of spirituality. He goes on to say that if Haripaṇḍit were amenable to it, he would even arrange for him to marry Rādhā—a completely unprecedented statement.[134] The meal proceeds peacefully. Vicitraśāstrī and Lokhaṇḍyā return to Rāṇū's home carrying sticks and try to create a commotion. But Śrīkhaṇḍyā stands watch outside, and by arguing and using his miraculous powers (being Kṛṣṇa, after all), he prevents the brahmans from entering the home.

Interestingly, Śirgopīkar opted to omit the appearance of a second Eknāth. The reason could not have been that Śirgopīkar disliked the idea of miracles; he had no qualms about depicting other miracles through trick scenes. Was this a difficult scene to portray on stage? Was Śirgopīkar simply bold in his portrayal of Eknāth? Perhaps the cultural climate had changed so much by the 1960s that inter-caste commensality was no longer anathema.

Newspaper reviews of *Bhāva Toci Dev* were quite positive. One highlighted the fact that although the action of the play moved rather slowly, this allowed the cast to vividly evoke various *rasas* (sentiments) on stage.[135] Another reviewer commented that the trick scenes aptly represented the miraculous elements of stories.[136] Yet another found the play to be a "pleasing . . . combination of message, music and miracles."[137] I have not come across reviews that mention the play's caste dynamics.

As it was in *Dharmātmā*, marketability and entertainment were central to how *Bhāva Toci Dev* was crafted. Of the few traditional stories that the play represented, the main one depicted Eknāth's transgressive commensality. This had been the double vision story, except that it portrayed a single, human Eknāth. Eknāth even comments in the play that he would gladly arrange the marriage of his son with Rāṇū's daughter if his son were willing.[138] Eknāth, Girijā, Śrīkhaṇḍyā, and Rādhā interact without heeding caste at all. At some points, Eknāth tries to persuade Rāṇū of caste's irrelevance. It is hard to know what the audience made of the play's occasional social commentary, in the face of *Bhāva Toci Dev*'s overwhelmingly lighthearted, comical presentation.

Sant Eknāth Mahārāj (2004) and *Sant Eknāth* (2005)

Four decades after *Bhāva Toci Dev*, Eknāth appeared in two low-budget films that reflected a new technology—the video compact disc (VCD) and digital video disc (DVD)—and the more informal audiences that were not bound by performance times and locations. These years also witnessed the rise of Marathi Dalit literature, the Dalit Panthers, and the continued conversion of Dalits to Buddhism. People were finding their own answers to the bhakti-caste question.

These two films were produced by companies that specialize in Marathi devotional films about saintly figures, intended not for public screening but for sale as inexpensive VCDs in music shops and stalls outside temples and pilgrimage sites. Despite being produced only one year apart, these two films depict Eknāth in very different ways.

Sant Eknāth Mahārāj (2004), directed by Rājū Phulkar, features actors from the Marathi theater scene and takes a very lighthearted approach.[139] Many traditional episodes appear in this film, including the *śrāddha* and double vision stories. As others before him did, Phulkar situates Rāṇū Mahār in all stories that involved Dalits. The antagonistic brahmans are led by a portly, saffron-clad *svāmī* with a bushy mustache and a bejeweled earring. Although the brahmans criticize Eknāth's friendship with Rāṇū, and although they refuse to join his *śrāddha*, there is rarely a sense of tension or threat about their actions. Usually, they appear as bumbling opponents whose plans backfire amusingly, as they did in *Bhāva Toci Dev*.

Phulkar handles the *śrāddha* and double vision stories with great sensitivity. On the *śrāddha* day, Rāṇū's family passes by Eknāth's home, and they smell the food cooking. Rāṇū's small son glimpses a plate of sweets in Eknāth's home and throws a very public tantrum because he wants to have one. Śrīkhaṇḍyā walks by and explains to the boy that the food is for brahmans, whose customs the boy would not understand. Eknāth intervenes, rebukes Śrīkhaṇḍyā, and invites Rāṇū's family to eat. Eknāth and Śrīkhaṇḍyā conspicuously avoid calling Rāṇū and his family by any word other than the pronoun "them" while discussing the situation. Context makes it clear that Rāṇū's family are Dalits (outraged brahmans later call them *aśpṛṣya*s and *śūdra*s). That Eknāth and Śrīkhaṇḍyā do not refer to caste-related terms may have arisen from 21st-century sensitivities about untouchability and names.

Later, when Eknāth prepares to go to Rāṇū's home for a meal, Śrīkhaṇḍyā approaches Eknāth and asks if he intends to skip performing a *kīrtan* in the temple today. Eknāth smiles and responds, "What difference is there between Rāṇū's home and a temple?" As Eknāth departs, Śrīkhaṇḍyā looks directly at the camera and says mischievously, "Now let's have some fun with the brahmans." He adopts Eknāth's form and walks off to the temple. The audience is left to imagine Eknāth eating at Rāṇū's home, because the film completely ignores that event and focuses instead on Śrīkhaṇḍyā-Eknāth making mischief with the temple brahmans, with much singing and dancing. In Phulkar's film, Eknāth transgresses caste boundaries, but because of the film's lighthearted mood, inter-caste tension is more a source of comedy than of suspense or concern.

In Rājeś Limkar's *Sant Eknāth* (2005), Eknāth appears very human and emotionally fragile.[140] The *śrāddha* story comes across as a genuinely educational experience. A family of Dalits cut grass outside Eknāth's home when they smell the cooking food. The young boy among them says that he is hungry, and his father responds, "Yes, you're hungry. I'm hungry too, but these brahmans can't understand our hunger. We're Mahārs. It's our fate to eat scraps, crumbs and rough things. We can't go in there and eat their food." The boy's mother adds, "Just wait, maybe they'll throw out some leftover food with their leaf-plates once they're finished."[141] Eknāth happens to be standing just around the corner from them, listening in. He had been about to summon the brahmans back from the river to eat, but he is stunned by the Mahārs' conversation. He stands for some time and thinks to himself, "Eknāth, you always say that there is no caste difference. . . . These people are hungry. Action is greater than just words. Consider this." He eventually invites the Mahārs in to eat. This is one of only two scenes about Eknāth's relations with people of lower social status in Limkar's three-hour film. The double vision story is absent.

Phulkar attends instead to stories that earlier productions never depicted, such as one about a wonder-working yogi named Daṇḍavat-svāmi (in Mahīpati's *BhL*) who accidentally resurrects a dead donkey.[142] Eknāth is disturbed by this pointless miracle, so he recommends that Daṇḍavat take *samādhi* by being buried alive. Daṇḍavat reluctantly agrees, and as Eknāth places the final bricks in the wall to seal the tomb, a very fearful Daṇḍavat peers out from inside. Another scene portrays something that hagiographies never mentioned: the death of Eknāth's wife.[143] When Eknāth discovers her lifeless body, he walks closer as suspenseful music swells. The camera zooms in on Eknāth's increasingly distraught face, spending an entire minute on the tears that well up Eknāth's eyes as he sits with his wife's corpse. Śrīkhaṇḍyā lets out a howl of despair. This death saps Eknāth's will to live, and he prepares for his death.

The emotional tone of Limkar's film is incredibly different from that of other plays and films. Advertisements for other films, which appear periodically in intermissions on the VCD, suggest why this is the case. One ad, for a film about the saintly potter Gorā Kumbhār, shows a clip in which Gorā kneads clay in a pit with his feet, repeating Viṭṭhal's name as he works. Two small legs stick up out of the mud; Gorā unwittingly had trampled his own child to death while he was absorbed in bhakti.[144] Clips from the film *Dhanya Dhanya Pativratā* (Blessed Is the Dutiful Wife) depict a destitute, leprous husband requesting his dutiful wife to find a prostitute for him. To advertise *Śivabhakta Cāṅguṇā*, a clip shows an ascetic demanding a young mother to kill and cook her young son to satisfy his hunger.[145] There is an obvious pattern here. Limkar transposed the story of Eknāth into a different filmic genre, whose appeal lay less in evoking reverence to the saints or making audiences laugh than with filling them with shock and suspense through somber stories of extreme bhakti—something more typical of traditional stories about Tamil Śaiva saints.[146]

Conclusion

Staging the life of Eknāth in plays and films placed new intermedial demands on traditional stories, resulting in some semiotic changes. Since plays and films (lasting usually only a couple of hours) were temporally bounded and unidirectional, characters had to be easily identifiable and narratives made seamless so that audiences could easily follow the plot. This had a consolidating effect. Hagiographies consistently depicted Eknāth interacting with Dalits, but the plays and films standardized his persona into that of a caste-transgressing brahman reformer. If Kabīr in the 20th century became the "apostle of Hindu-Muslim unity" in North India,[147] Marathi plays and films recrafted Eknāth into an advocate for social equality in Maharashtra. What had been separate Dalit characters in different stories crystallized into a single Dalit man (Rāṇyā, Rāṇū, or Viṭhū) in the plays and films. To focus their audiences even more, playwrights and filmmakers created a compelling young Dalit girl character (Sītā, Jāī, or Rādhā) to embody the innocence and injustice of caste oppression. The use of a girl character for this purpose is notable and reflects the social aesthetics of 20th-century theater and film. No premodern hagiographer depicted vulnerable young women in this way. A jester character also consistently appeared in plays and films, cracking jokes, and making fun. More than mere products of artistic creativity (although they were that too), these changes resulted from intermedial adjustments that situated traditions stories in new media forms.

Plays and films brought Eknāth to new kinds of audiences, which entailed new financing structures. Far from the model of a single royal patron who a court poet needed to please, theater and film productions rely on ticket sales and a very different set of popular tastes. Devotional and mythological stories were good business in the 20th century, as Śirvaḷkar's and Śirgopīkar's plays and Prabhāt's films demonstrate. Yet all of these were also modern entertainment. The fascination with a superstar actor could reorient an entire production around him. Some media forms, like the low-budget VCD, developed new genres as they incorporated traditional stories on the periphery and outside of the Vārkarī tradition. A single saint could be drastically different when their story moved across genres.

Although late 19th-century biographers highlighted the *śrāddha* and double vision stories as indicators of Eknāth's socially impartial vision, early 20th-century authors showed less interest, due either to their more conservative political views or the fact that they wrote in a more literary rather than social historical mode. In contrast, all the plays and films about Eknāth in the 20th century focused on Eknāth's interactions with Dalits, and the double vision story took center stage in their plots. The early plays were explicitly indebted to late 19th-century scholars for their social views of Eknāth, but as time went on, other important contemporary events impacted the depictions. Eknāth advocated for equality in *Kharā Brāmhaṇ* (1933) in the name of Hindutva, pulling bhakti into the field of non-brahman caste politics. In *Dharmātmā* (1935), Eknāth became a proto-Gandhi.

As these early plays and films represented Eknāth as a social reformer, there is no obvious indication that they reckoned with the more strident message of Ambedkar, whose *Annihilation of Caste* was published in 1936. In his rebuttal letter to Gandhi, Ambedkar specifically criticized *Dharmātmā*'s portrayal of Eknāth as misleading. *Bhāva Toci Dev* was first performed in 1964, eight years after Ambedkar's conversation to Buddhism. The effects of Dalit assertion were surely on some audience members' minds, even if the play did not directly address them. And the two VCDs of the early 2000s were produced in the shadow of Ambedkar, with increased sensitivity to portrayals of Dalits and a preference to focus on aspects of Eknāth's life that did not have to do with caste. Throughout the long 20th century, films and plays (with the exception of Thackeray's) regularly treated caste tensions as something to laugh about, and increasingly, to laugh at.[148] On one level, this modulation had something to do with the medial requirement that presentations be entertaining and marketable. But laughter was also a coping mechanism, however imperfect, to deal with intractable social issues that were hard to ignore but even harder to address directly.

What happened to food and ambiguity in all these changes? Although the *śrāddha* story was not regularly repeated, the double vision story became standard. Both stories were affected by the palpable unease among playwrights and filmmakers, most of whom were socially liberal and highly educated brahmans, about how to handle the miraculous in general. The double vision story indicates this well. Some plays and films omitted the second Eknāth completely, rendering what had been a miraculous event into a straightforward human act of transgressive commensality. For reasons that I explore in Chapter 7, modern Marathi audiences seem to have lost their appetite for ambiguity.

7

Bhakti in the Shadow of Ambedkar

> As I ran through this bounteous, plentiful land
> my feet burned, my mind wept.
> I ran, yelling for my life, hoping to meet someone like Eknath.
> I met quite a few who revered Eknath.
> They were engrossed in their *kīrtan*.
> My cry didn't enter their hearts.
>
> Tryambak Sapkale, "Angulimala"

This book began with the question of how bhakti relates to caste. We have examined why the term "social equality" is problematic for appreciating bhakti traditions' premodern pasts. For that historical task, emic terms like *janī-janārdana* and *samadṛṣṭi*—especially as they were invoked when eating together—are more illuminating. Those terms reveal the nondualist and theological frames that bhakti traditions used to handle the bhakti-caste question. Coming to terms with the anachronism of equality discourse for doing premodern history is one aspect of studying bhakti now, in the shadow of Ambedkar. We reckon with the shadow to do history better, especially when dealing with periods before that shadow existed. Another aspect hits closer to home: what does Ambedkar's quest for social equality and his critical assessment of bhakti traditions mean for those traditions today? Social equality is, after all, an emic term in our modern vocabulary and worldviews; we need not shy away from it in the present. This chapter's epigraph illustrates one fallout of Ambedkar's critical assessment: most of his Mahār followers in Maharashtra now have little interest in Marathi bhakti traditions. Does taking seriously Ambedkar's sober view of caste in bhakti traditions rule out ever answering the bhakti-caste question in new ways? And how does this all affect social relations today—between caste Hindu and Dalit adherents within bhakti traditions and between Dalits who do and do not follow Ambedkar in rejecting bhakti? In this chapter, I offer some reflections.

Shared Devotion, Shared Food. Jon Keune, Oxford University Press. © Oxford University Press 2021.
DOI: 10.1093/oso/9780197574836.003.0008

An unexpected encounter in Paiṭhaṇ inspired me to see inter-caste connections among the Vārkarī saints differently than I had before. Outside the Eknāth Samādhi Mandir that commemorates Eknāth's earthly departure, the owner of a devotional trinket stall pointed me toward a small Cokhāmeḷā shrine nearby, off the main road.[1] No scholarship on Eknāth had ever mentioned this Cokhāmeḷā shrine, pilgrims to the Eknāth temple appear unaware of it, and Eleanor Zelliot, who did substantial research on both saints and visited Paiṭhaṇ several times, also had never heard of it. The occluded proximity of these two sites memorializing saints on opposite ends of the caste hierarchy was uncanny—in plain sight yet easy to overlook. It raised questions about how saints of different castes figured into the Vārkarī tradition as a whole.

It is, of course, difficult to speak of "the whole" of a tradition like the Vārkarīs, who have no centralized institutional authority or strictly orthodox canon. Although the boundaries of the tradition are not strictly defined,[2] the coherence of the tradition appears in other ways. These include the many intertextual references among saints' poetry, collective hagiographical projects like those of Mahīpati, *kīrtankār* performance traditions, local groups of devotees who follow a leader or *mahārāj*, and modern traditions of writing about the Vārkarīs for non-sectarian audiences. As nebulous as this whole will ever be, sympathizers and critics alike have talked about it in just that way—as a whole. The systemic aspect, even if coalesced informally and without an institutional framework, is hardly unique to the Vārkarīs. It is what makes bhakti traditions into traditions at all.

Bhakti as resonant manifold

This approach to studying bhakti traditions as systematized wholes is essential for appreciating how literary and cultural elements flow within and among them, sometimes existing independently of the saintly personae who come to host those elements. Aditya Behl recognized this dynamic at work between North Indian *ṣūfī* and bhakti texts, which he described as "best understood as a historical dialogue, a call and response. Rather than bearing witness to presence, we need to think of an echo chamber or a hall of mirrors reflecting (and thus responding to) each other."[3] If the idea of an echo chamber is helpful for recognizing *ṣūfī*-bhakti interactions, it is even more applicable among and within bhakti traditions themselves. For example, we have a story about a *parīsa* or philosopher's stone that changes whatever it touches into gold. Someone entrusts a *parīsa* to a saint for safe-keeping, but the saint discards it as useless, and when the original owner is alarmed to discover his *parīsa* is gone, the saint miraculously materializes endless *parīsa*s, thereby teaching the owner about non-attachment to wealth. This story has circulated through the hagiographies of Ravidās,[4] Nāmdev,[5] and Eknāth,[6] and probably beyond them too. We should not be surprised to find other stories with straightforward morals that circulate in the same way. The story of antagonistic brahmans scheming to exhaust a saint's hospitality and ability to offer food, which we observed earlier in stories about Kabīr and Eknāth, is another case. The *śrāddha* story of food for brahmans being given to interlopers, which obviously spread from Eknāth in Marathi to Ayyāvāḷ in Tamil. Stories and tropes echo across different saints' biographies, either because saints themselves may have modeled their actions after those of their predecessors or because hagiographers depicted a given saint as emulating another. This is a well-recognized dynamic in story-telling traditions around the world. It inspired some scholars to compile indices of such occurrences across cultures.[7]

But I think something more complex than just traveling motifs is happening in the coherence of bhakti traditions. Literary critic George Steiner illustrates this when he describes the sensitivity of a reader who picks up on intertextual references. "The classic reader . . . locates the text he is reading inside a resonant manifold. Echo answers echo, analogy is precise and contiguous, correction and emendation carry the justification of accurately remembered precedent. The reader replies to the text out of the articulate density of his own store of reference and remembrance. It is an ancient, formidable suggestion that the Muses of memory and of invention are one."[8] More than just an echo as repeated sound, bhakti poetry and stories *resonate* in their listeners, evoking connections to other things they have heard. More than an echo, resonance creates sounds beyond the original sound that initiated it. Classical Indian musicians understand this: the sitar, sarod, and sarangi acquire their rich timbre from a set of sympathetic strings that the performer typically does not touch. When the performer plays certain pitches directly on the main strings, those frequencies cause the sympathetic strings to vibrate, producing their own complementary sounds.

Through performances across media, contexts, and generations, bhakti stories and literature start to resonate in their audiences. A story about one saint inspires an informed audience to think of other saints, songs, poems, or themes. Sometimes this resonance is explicit, as in intertextual cases of a saint praising and telling stories about saints who had come before. Christian Novetzke describes how Nāmdev relays stories about Jñāndev. Eknāth's short poetry includes songs about Cokhāmeḷā, some of which echo and resonate with poetry that is attributed to the Mahār saint. Tukārām praises various saints who came before him, as do Bahiṇabāī and Mahīpati. All of them repeat things from the Epics, Purāṇas, and Upaniṣads.

If it were possible to take the historicity of poetic and hagiographical compositions at face value, such as by believing that a poem attributed to Nāmdev in a late 19th-century compilation indisputably reproduced the voice of the 14th-century śūdra poet and tailor by that name, one might try to reconstruct ur-texts and identify later echoes and intertextual references. In the Vārkarī tradition, such an archive of clearly discernible historical layers does not exist, or at least no one has discovered it yet. Instead, nearly all the poetic compositions (with the prominent exception of the *Jñāneśvarī*) and hagiographical stories of the tradition are the products of oral transmission, occasional written manuscripts, and quite late printed editions and compilations. And as Novetzke has shown so well, even written documents of the Vārkarīs are closely bound to performance. This being the case, I argue that a great deal of resonance has occurred within the Vārkarī tradition, by which some stories and motifs became attached to particular saints but actually belong to the larger tradition as a whole.

Thus, we could observe several parallels between the poetry of and stories about Cokhāmeḷā and those of Eknāth. Stories about how Viṭṭhal rescues Cokhā and, separately, Eknāth's great-grandfather Bhānudās from execution after being falsely accused by brahmans are quite similar. The epithets that Cokhāmeḷā uses for Viṭṭhal resemble those that hagiographers apply to Eknāth. And Eknāth's distinctive *bhārūḍ*s that represent Mahār characters are more articulate about the everyday lives and duties of Mahārs than Cokhā's own poetry. Given the fuzzy historicity of these stories and compositions over centuries of performance and repetition, I suspect that the personae of Cokhāmeḷā and the Dalit figures in Eknāth's stories and poetry resonated with each other. For example, the figure of Cokhāmeḷā may have initially inspired Eknāth to compose Mahār *bhārūḍ*s, and after those *bhārūḍ*s were composed and performed, they fed back into what people thought about Cokhāmeḷā. Things that seem uncannily similar are actually not so coincidental; they result from thematic resonance that occurred over centuries.

This leads me to wonder: might the story of Eknāth eating with Dalits have resonated with the story of Viṭṭhal eating with Cokhāmeḷā? This could have happened as either Eknāth or his hagiographers intentionally modeled the commensality episode on a preexisting story of Cokhāmeḷā and Viṭṭhal. After both the Cokhāmeḷā-Viṭṭhal and Eknāth-Dalits stories became widely known, it is not hard to see how people could conflate the two or even mistake one story for the other. This happened in one of Eleanor Zelliot's essays, which included a photo of the Cokhāmeḷā shrine in Paṇḍharpūr. Above the shrine hangs a painting that we see in Photo 7.1—Cokhāmeḷā's wife serves food to Viṭṭhal and other luminaries who sat in a row, as Cokhāmeḷā looks on proudly and outsiders peer with amazement through the window and doorway.

Perhaps she viewed the painting only from a distance and thus did not see the names on the painting itself, because Zelliot's caption states that the

Photo 7.1. Painting of Cokhāmeḷā and his wife hosting Nārad, Nāmdev, Viṭṭhal, Rukmiṇī, and Indra.
Source: Photo taken by Wasim Maner, July 2019, in Paṇḍharpūr.

painting depicts Rāṇyā Mahār and his wife feeding Eknāth and guests.[9] Yet, even as Zelliot mislabeled this particular painting, she did accidentally touch upon a genuine connection to Eknāth. On the painting is the verse, "They sat at *paṅgat* in Cokhā's home, the woman who served them was Cokhā's." This song came from Eknāth's *Gāthā*, which is the place in which this story about Cokhāmeḷā first appeared.[10]

This is my hypothesis. I cannot point to irrefutable evidence of where and how stories of Eknāth and Cokhāmeḷā resonated at some point over centuries of performances. This evidence does not exist because those occurrences were not documented or recorded. And due to the performed nature of the saints' short poetic compositions, little evidence now exists about how they circulated and developed before editors compiled and printed them at the end of the 19th century. However, I think that my theory of bhakti's resonance chamber is more than sheer speculation. Representations of saints' voices in poetry that is attributed to them and hagiographical stories about them were crafted, to some extent, to situate their personae within the saintly constellation of the tradition as a whole. By putting all these saints together, from Dalits to brahmans, the Vārkarī performative tradition as a whole managed the bhakti-caste question. Because of this, the personae of Eknāth, Cokhāmeḷā, and other figures whom we now witness in bhakti poetry, reach us only after centuries of resonance and systematization. And it is in the systemic capacity of this discourse that what we might call the Vārkarī tradition's ideology of inclusive difference comes into view.

Ideology of inclusive difference

Clearly, a strong socially inclusive ethos pervades the Vārkarī tradition, even as it preserves caste markers in its classic texts and hagiographies. To call attention to the double motion of including yet differentiating, I refer to this as ideology of inclusive difference, or for the sake of brevity, inclusive ideology. We will not find Vārkarī inclusive ideology codified in any single text or doctrinal formulation; it is implied through stories and remembered associations more than it is rendered explicitly. It appears most clearly from the 18th century onward in the composite memory of many saints together, such as in the collective hagiographies of Mahīpati. But this ideology was active before Mahīpati too, as literature by and about various saints was repeated over generations—a process that created and then magnified a series of distinctive resonances. As I argued in Chapter 6, the process of transmedial circulation itself has an integrating effect on stories that are repeated among diverse audiences, centuries ago and still today.

That the Vārkarī tradition actively reveres saints of many castes is often interpreted as evidence of its inclusivity. How did this diversity develop? Novetzke has argued that the process of vernacularization brought representations of non-elite people into early Marathi literature to create a new and much broader public than had existed before.[11] That may be, but it does not address why so many early saints of Dalit and low-caste background are remembered to have composed their own songs. I want to suggest a different theory, which peers back into the past from the inclusive perspective that characterized later Vārkarī practice. What if the diversity of figures in bhakti traditions reflects a historical development, as more and more communities came to participate? Saints of particular castes and occupations—Mahārs, barbers, potters, gardeners, and so on—gave particular communities a special seat at the *paṅkti* and nurtured a sense of belonging in the Marathi bhakti world.[12] Especially since the poetry of many low-caste saints creates allegories out of their work and tools, bhakti poetry based on particular occupations could have appealed to people who did those jobs. This may not have occurred necessarily at the time when the low-caste and Dalit saints are purported to have lived, around the 13th and 14th centuries, or maybe it could have. Whatever the historical status of original saints may be, the representation of diverse saints would have built diverse constituencies in later generations. This would find parallels in the structures of some Vārkarī pilgrim groups (*diṇḍī*s) today. The saint represents, among other things, the community.

As pilgrims would sing and hear the songs of saints from other castes, they might come to feel just a little closer to fellow Vārkarīs. And as pilgrimages to Paṇḍhaṛpūr proceed through towns that are associated with different saints, the bodily act of walking interweaves sacred space with diverse saints' stories and caste representations. For example, if one walks with the Eknāth *pālkhī* from Paiṭhaṇ, the path brings pilgrims to stop for a meal at the temple of Kūrmadās, a paraplegic saint (a photo of which appeared in Chapter 4), and an overnight in the town of Savatā, the gardener. One would encounter *pālkhī*s of other saints and their constituencies along the way too. And everyone would at least walk by the Cokhāmeḷā shrine outside the Viṭṭhal temple in Paṇḍharpūr. The Vārkarīs' caste inclusivity is reinforced both in song and in pilgrimage.

Amid these cohesive forces, the Vārkarīs' inclusive ideology also preserves caste designations. Savatā's bhakti is praiseworthy and is remembered to have been so great that Viṭṭhal traveled from Paṇḍharpūr to meet him when he could not leave his work. But Savatā is still a śūdra gardener, which makes Viṭṭhal's actions all the more remarkable. Likewise, Cokhāmeḷā's Mahār status is never erased when he enters the constellation of saints; quite the contrary. Viṭṭhal's care is astounding, and bhakti's inclusivity is shockingly radical precisely because these saints belong to the castes that they do. The character of Viṭṭhal as universally inclusive, welcoming devotees of all castes and genders, would have been undermined by erasing the social differentiations that distinguish the devotees. A god who strives to include the weak, poor, and marginalized—all relative designations that require hierarchy—is obviously compassionate and loving. James Laine has argued that bhakti "defers" resolving the tension between perspectives that transcend and preserve caste.[13] I think this was not so much a deferred choice, postponed until the future, nor was it the result of unfinished thinking or unprincipled practice on the part of the Vārkarīs. Rather, this differentiation and emphasis on the marginalized is an integral part of the Vārkarīs' inclusive ideology, which has maintained the bhakti-caste relationship as a riddle.

Viewed from a more stereotypically North Indian formulation of bhakti, the Vārkarīs' way of rendering the bhakti-caste relationship may stem from their promotion of both *saguṇa* and *nirguṇa* visions of ultimate reality. In this North Indian paradigm, *saguṇa* traditions tend to preserve caste distinctions, while *nirguṇa* ones seek to erase them.[14] Vārkarī theology thus results in something between preservation and erasure. But a North Indian lens is not necessary; the complex theological landscape of the Vārkarīs can be viewed on their own terms. Among the Vārkarīs, especially in literature by and about Eknāth, we can see a variety of tactics deployed to reconcile bhakti and caste.

One way is to hearken to a classic *dharmaśāstr*ic distinction between laws that apply to all people (*sādhāraṇa* or *sāmānya dharma*) and those that apply to particular castes and stages of life (*varṇāśramadharma*).[15] An example of this appears in Keśavsvāmī's hagiography of Eknāth: "The superiority of compassion [*dayā*] should be established as the head of all *dharma*—this was the mark of Śrī Nāth's essential nature" (*EC* 21:40). This is used to justify Eknāth bringing an emaciated Dalit thief into his home, preparing food for him, and nursing him back to health. Manu 10:63 lists nonviolence, truth, purification, and suppression of sensory temptation as incumbent on all four castes, and he notes in 6:8 that the duties of a brahman householder include being compassionate to all living things. Gautama's *Dharmasūtra* (8:22–25) elevates compassion to one of the eight basic virtues of the self, and he specifies that possessing these virtues is required—even more than fulfilling sacramental duties—for a person to obtain union with Brahman.[16] And the *Anuśāsanaparva* of the *Mahābhārata* (141:25–26) lists compassion for all beings (*sarvābhūtānukampanam*) as one of the highest duties of a householder.[17] In common practice, however, brahman councils regarded *varṇāśramadharma* as taking precedence over *sādhāraṇa dharma.*[18] For Keśavsvāmī to justify Eknāth's sustained, intimate interaction with a Dalit thief on the basis of compassion, *sādhāraṇa dharma*, is a strong claim for the priority of bhakti over caste.[19]

Another way of reckoning is to flip the script of caste and invert its hierarchy. We witnessed this in Basava's justification for accepting food from a Dalit Śaiva bhakta: the true Untouchables were orthodox Vaiṣṇava brahmans. In the *Līḷācaritra*, brahmans who harass a pious Cāmbhār Mahānubhāv preacher eventually repent and call themselves *cāṇḍāls.*[20] There is even a codified term for this upside-down language in the poetry of Kabīr—*ulaṭbāmsī.*[21] Eknāth's *bhārūḍ*s that are solely in the voices of Mahārs revel in such inversions as well, as they begin by emphasizing their lowliness but conclude by revealing their great wisdom and bhakti.[22] Two of his dialogical *bhārūḍs*—between a brahman and a dog, and a brahman and a Mahār—also depict this inversion, as the brahman haughtily denigrates his interlocutor at first but ends up chastened by their superior knowledge. To assert the superiority of bhakti and knowledge as they do, all these examples require specifying hierarchical distinctions, like caste.

A third traditional way of reconciling bhakti and caste is apparent in Mahīpati's story about Nāmdev and Kṛṣṇa, which we reviewed in Chapter 4. In fact, that story includes multiple attempts at reconciliation, as different human and divine figures try to fathom why Viṭṭhal/Kṛṣṇa was keen on eating Nāmdev's leftovers. Kṛṣṇa tells the brahmans that his desire for bhakti overrides other concerns, and eating the food of his bhaktas, regardless of their caste, keeps him in good shape. Rukmiṇī's reasoning is similar: Kṛṣṇa was so absorbed in love for his bhaktas that he paid no heed to purity laws, and he underwent purification rituals only because this was the quickest way to resolve the conflict and get back to Nāmdev. In short, God cares only about bhakti, not caste. But these are divine characters talking among each other, as deities justify Kṛṣṇa's actions. On the human side in the story, the brahmans who sparked the controversy argued that although God need not observe caste distinctions, humans are still subject to Vedic and *śāstric* law. What may make sense to the gods is not reasonable for humans. This earthly mode of reasoning was hardly unique to the brahmans in Mahīpati's story. In the 1880s, Rev. John Murray Mitchell visited Paṇḍharpūr and asked pilgrims why, if Viṭṭhal was willing to carry dead cattle with Cokhāmeḷā, Mahārs now were prohibited from entering Viṭṭhal's temple. He received this response: "That was all very well for the god; he may do as he pleases. But men must obey the rules of caste."[23] Just because God can choose to ignore caste does not imply that people may do likewise.

The fourth way of reconciling caste and bhakti—strategic ambiguity—is the most important and least appreciated. Chapters 5 and 6 examined stories that were retold and reinterpreted many times in ways that allowed the bhakti-caste tension to remain. I believe that this was a feature of the Vārkarī approach, not a flaw. It is worth reflecting on strategic ambiguity more thoroughly with other theories about the unresolved bhakti-caste tension.

In his analysis of mythology, Claude Lévi-Strauss argued that the reason mythic stories kept getting retold, with many variations, is that they cope with deep-seated problems that cannot be solved intellectually.[24] In Lévi-Strauss' structuralist view, such problems are unavoidable; humans cannot help but perceive the world through binary oppositions like nature/culture, hunting/cultivating, and life/death, even though these binaries fail to grasp complex human experiences. Myths manage the impossible reconciliation of binaries by transposing them into a narrative form that expresses their cognitive dissonance. Following Lévi-Strauss, the food stories about Eknāth and Dalits may be understood as reckoning two competing social visions (caste/bhakti, or following Victor Turner, structure/anti-structure). It is the narration of Eknāth's actions that holds them together without resolving them. This could explain why so many renditions of the *śrāddha* and double vision stories remained ambiguous about bhakti and caste. This mythic "solution" is not intellectual. In terms of logic, it is positively unsatisfying.

But bhakti and caste are not an inevitable binary in the way that Lévi-Strauss intended. They do not represent a basic structural relationship of human thought; indeed, bhakti adherents and authors had a wide variety of views on bhakti and caste, many of which were not terribly oppositional. Furthermore, caste institutions and bhakti traditions have both changed over time. Lévi-Strauss' theory does not account for such historical change, which has been a major focus of this book. So, although Lévi-Strauss offers an intriguing theory about the use of story to manage cognitive tensions, I think that strategic ambiguity is a more incisive way of understanding the food stories in question, as well as bhakti literature more generally. Unlike mythic binary oppositions, the bhakti-caste question sometimes can be resolved for particular people and cases, but not universally. To see things in terms of strategically deployed ambiguity captures the non-finality of this handling of the bhakti-caste question and calls attention to the ways in which authors and traditions carry it out.

In Part II, I have shown how food has semantic density, evoking multiple meanings simultaneously. This made it an ideal substance for stories about Eknāth and Dalits. When it is given to travelers or the needy, it is a performance of *śāstra*-sanctioned hospitality. When it is offered to the ancestors and fed to their brahman proxies in *śrāddha*, it fulfills an ancient ritual formula. When it creates a site of transgressive commensality, it may demonstrate bhakti's preeminence over caste. When it takes the form of *ucchiṣṭa*, it becomes dangerously polluting under most circumstances but revered as *prasād* if the first eater is God. And when God relishes the *ucchiṣṭa* of devoted humans, it demonstrates bhakti's incredible power, to which even God submits.

Because food symbolizes and communicates so many things, stories about food get reinterpreted in different directions. Food stories are very easily ambiguous, at conscious and subconscious levels. This is a power of food and a reason why it is involved in so many rituals. Scholars often highlight the importance of ambiguity and space for multiple understandings of ritual.[25] In the words of Catherine Bell, "symbols and symbolic action not only fail to communicate clear and shared understandings, but the obvious ambiguity or overdetermination of much religious symbolism may even be integral to its efficacy."[26] A major feature of Vārkarī inclusive ideology is that it is ambiguous about how it handles bhakti and caste, not only in story but in action and practice. Anna Schultz describes Marathi *kīrtan* performance in similarly dense terms: "it is a complex semiotic system of rhetorical tropes and song genres, it is an embodied experience, and it is a communicative event."[27] Bodily experience, multi-sensory engagements, and emotional participation are central to bhakti. This materiality is inevitably open to interpretation; it is unavoidably ambiguous.

To say that ambiguity is strategic implies intentionality of some sort. So who devises and executes the strategy? Who or what is responsible for constructing the Vārkarīs' inclusive ideology? Depending on where we focus, I think three aspects of agency are at work.

At an authorial level,[28] those who compose bhakti literature may and often do deliberately invite multiple and even competing interpretations about the relationship of bhakti and caste. South Asia has a long history of poetry that conveys multiple meanings simultaneously. Prowess in this form of rhetorical fireworks—*śleṣa*—was a mark of distinction among elite Sanskrit poets.[29] In the more quotidian, pragmatic realm of Marathi bhakti, polysemy took a less overtly sophisticated form, functioning more as a mundane communicative instrument than as an aesthetic achievement. The goal is to convey key teachings (about Viṭṭhal devotion and ultimate nonduality) in ways that reach a diverse audience of people with high, low, and no caste. Novetzke's idea of the "brahman double"—brahman authors representing despicable brahmans to portray their own brahman-ness more palatably to non-brahman audiences—is one example of such an illocutionary effect. I think this sensitivity to caste dynamics between author and audience should be expanded to cover the bhakti-caste riddle more broadly. Bhakti authors and performers of all and no caste needed to know their audiences and how to relate to them. Unless we are to imagine that bhakti audiences were typically comprised of people of one caste (which I find unlikely), preaching bhakti involved speaking across caste lines, both performing and promoting inclusivity. Enabling people to interact with a message by holding open multiple interpretations about the bhakti-caste tension was valuable.

A second aspect of bhakti's strategic ambiguity about caste is the reliance on a religious dimension. The stories in Chapters 5 and 6 show how the semantic density of food was a narrative component and the irruptive site of miracles in the narratives effectively avoided making a conclusive judgment about the role of caste in the Vārkarī tradition. The propriety of Eknāth feeding Dalits the *śrāddha* meal or eating at a Dalit couple's home is ratified by miraculous appearances. Deceased ancestors arrive, or Eknāth appears in two places simultaneously. When the religious dimension of bhakti gets pared away or is refashioned in modern Marathi literature, the capacity for strategic ambiguity is lost. Both the Vārkarī inclusive ideology and the strategic ambiguity that maintain it appear obsolete and undesirable in a modern, secular paradigm.

A third aspect is the blunting of localized radical critique. Jonathan Parry argued that there is no reason to imagine that historical proponents of bhakti could not have creatively applied bhakti's spiritual egalitarianism to caste and social relations.[30] I wholeheartedly agree. The cultural and social worlds of the past were surely no less complex than our own, even if a dearth of material evidence makes it difficult for us to imagine them. Given South Asia's incredibly rich cultural and intellectual diversity, we ought to *assume* that there were radical voices in the Marathi past, especially among subaltern groups in Maharashtra, who made the step that we see clearly in Ravidās, Kabīr, and Basava—that bhakti erases caste or at least offers a strident critique of social hierarchy. On an individual and local community basis, this almost certainly happened, with a very different effect than strategic ambiguity and inclusive ideology. Maybe even Cokhāmeḷā, if he was an actual person in the 14th century, was more radical than he came to be remembered as. But those more radical voices and actions are not evidently available to us.

As Cokhāmeḷā's and others' voices were harmonized with the larger tradition as it coalesced, as their songs were recited and adapted, new songs were composed in their names. And as stories about them were retold and refashioned by brahman hagiographers like Mahīpati,[31] the agents of inclusive ideology rounded off the sharpest edges. The most radical voices, if they did exist in the past, may have disappeared entirely, perhaps because the audiences they appealed to were too small and ephemeral in Maharashtra to remember them. The weight of more explicitly inclusive and ambiguous options restrained radical critique from taking hold or becoming normative. In traditions elsewhere (some Vīraśaivas, the Mahānubhāvs, some followers of Ravidās, and the Satnāmīs), erasing the caste of bhaktas created more socially egalitarian communities that became distanced from the larger society. To recall a distinction made by Michel de Certeau, bhakti asserted as a *strategy*, such as in the larger Vārkarī tradition, led to inclusive ideology. Bhakti deployed as a *tactic* could be more radically subversive, but it lacked the power to become normative.[32]

Another alternative theory to what I am arguing about strategic ambiguity appears in Christian Novetzke's *The Quotidian Revolution*. He too observes bhakti-caste tension and innovative social inclusivity in Marathi bhakti literature, especially in the *Jñāneśvarī*'s ambivalence about caste, but he explains it in a different way. Early chapters of the *Jñāneśvarī* assert bhakti's superiority over caste, while the references in the latter half not only preserve caste distinctions but even repeat disparaging tropes about lower caste people. Novetzke argues that the text was ambivalent because although Jñāndev may have envisioned social equality, he was bound by caste-based idioms to communicate his ideas to a Marathi speaking audience.[33] For Novetzke, this illustrates the "glacial pace" by which the process of vernacularization unfolds on the path toward social equality.[34]

It seems to me that two problems arise from this interpretation. On a conceptual level, as I showed in Chapter 1, referring to equality in discourse before the 19th century skews the worldview of earlier authors, such as Jñāndev in the 13th century. Referring to equality "heuristically" or "strategically," as Novetzke does, only slightly wards off readers from anachronistic interpretation, and it leaves them with the burden of imagining on their own historical worldviews that resemble but do not quite reach equality. On a social level, I do not see how social equality can result from a sociological process without intentionality and an ideology that some group aims to institutionalize.[35] Perhaps I am simply more pessimistic about human societies naturally becoming more egalitarian without trying. So, as I read it, the *Jñāneśvarī*'s ambivalence about caste is not a side effect of glacially slow social change but rather a conscious decision by Jñāndev (or perhaps his redactors, including Eknāth). Like stories about Eknāth, the *Jñāneśvarī* also was strategically ambiguous about the bhakti-caste question, which enabled a wider audience to engage the text and derive different interpretations.

Throughout this book, I have tried to strike a certain balance in analyzing bhakti's ideology of inclusive differentiation. On one hand, I want to recognize the relative innovation of bhakti traditions' inclusivity as a genuine inspiration for creating social connections through shared devotion. This is not social equality in a modern sense, but it truly was remarkable in itself, against the much more hierarchical and segregated social structures that characterized most of the premodern Indian world. On the other hand, inclusive ideology cannot but retain caste differences that were the former basis of distinction, ranking, and exclusion. Preserving caste markers was essential to demonstrating how radically inclusive and universal bhakti traditions could be.

Stories about Eknāth figure into this too, as he needs Dalit figures to fully offset his brahman-ness and demonstrate his inclusivity. Projecting a brahman double is not enough, by itself. Cokhāmeḷā needs brahman figures, too, and not only the oppressive ones who castigate and exile him. Anant Bhaṭ, a brahman who appears in some hagiographical stories as a scribe for Cokhāmeḷā, and Eknāth, who praises Cokhāmeḷā in his own songs, both serve to ratify the Dalit poet's message.

Given the way in which Indian conceptions of social difference developed, caste structure is essential for bhakti inclusivity. Yet, while bhakti's inclusive ideology may have been jarringly prosocial and generative of change in some contexts, it is also a source of social inertia. How does one practically erase caste distinctions among followers if the stories one tells involve, or even require, repeating the saints' caste identities? This returns us to the question that Ambedkar raised about bhakti: can it ever truly overcome caste, especially when there are so many motivations to preserve it? Could bhakti's spiritual egalitarianism actually lead to social equality on a wide scale? These were pointed questions for Ambedkar, who understandably answered them in the negative. But there are other perspectives on this problem.

As I discussed in Chapter 1, defining equality hinges on a referent, in relation to which equality is measured—equal rights, equal standing before the law, equal opportunity, and so on. One's sense of equality does not entail other senses; in fact, if one brings multiple senses of equality together, philosophical disparities and problems quickly arise. This is, essentially, the crux of the problem with talking about bhakti and equality. Theological egalitarianism did not bring about social egalitarianism. This is well established among scholars and critics, and I agree. What does not get asked, however, is why those two equalities should be expected to go together at all. A particular equality in one conceptual framework does not imply other kinds of equality. Equal standing before the law, which in modern nation-states is constitutionally foundational, rarely entails individuals having equal opportunities, social status, or political power, despite how much social activists may argue it should. There is no reason to expect bhakti traditions to have applied equality across sectors of life more effectively than constitutional democracies have.

A growing stream of research in anthropology has recently begun reconsidering the "sacred secular" status of equality. In this vein of thought, the unexamined assumption that equality is a normative political and social benchmark hinders people both from grasping how equality gets used in practice, and from recognizing how other, unequal relationships also yield social cohesion and belonging.

Anastasia Piliavsky reflects astutely on this. A widely held "egalitarian fantasy" among social scientists and journalists has led them to view democracies in places like India, Brazil, and South Africa as immature, since those societies seem based more on patronage and clientelism than on a belief in the egalitarianism of all voters.[36] Groups in developed western countries, too, as is readily apparent in resurgent nationalist movements, also promote majoritarian and socially hierarchical worldviews, often under the banner of equality insofar as they seek to extinguish any legal provisions that are specially made for historically underprivileged minorities. Piliavsky argues that blind faith in the idea of equality has obscured ways that it goes together with hierarchy in people's actual practice. She recommends that social scientists take a more self-consciously ethnographic approach to egalitarianism, observing how people refer to it in practice, as they maneuver around the hierarchical structures in which they live. In this perspective, both bhakti traditions and modern Indian democracy have failed to eradicate caste and establish social equality. But this says at least as much about the unexamined ideal of equality as it does about bhakti traditions and Indian democracy. And a sober view of Western nations and modern Christian groups would discover that, although they talk more regularly about equality, they too have failed thus far in achieving it. Bhakti traditions and India are not so unique in this.

Nondualist social ethics?

In Chapter 3, I presented evidence for why I think it is incorrect to identify the nondualism of Vārkarī authors with "equality." In strictly historical terms, "sameness" is a better translation of the Marathi and Sanskrit words that connote nonduality. It is worth reflecting further on what relation sameness, equality, and nonduality may have to erasing and preserving caste distinctions.

A good deal has been written about whether a nondualist view of reality may serve as a basis for social ethics. In the late 19th century, Indologists Paul Deussen and Max Müller and, more famously, Swami Vivekananda argued that it did, and they cited the Upaniṣadic formula *tat tvam asi* (translated by them as "that thou art") as the basis.[37] P. V. Kane repeated a version of this argument in 1941 in his survey of *dharmaśāstra*: Hindus should practice compassion and nonviolence because of *tat tvam asi*. "This is the highest point reached in Indian metaphysics and combines morality and metaphysics."[38] As evidence, Kane cited the *Dakṣasmṛti* and *Devalasmṛti*, which in turn claimed to base their arguments on human conscience and Vedic revelation.[39] Sarvapelli Radhakrishnan argued for a nondual worldly ethics as well, pushing back against Christian missionary critiques.[40]

In 1965, Paul Hacker rejected this claim as made by Vivekananda, arguing that it was based more on Arthur Schopenhauer and Deussen's interpretation of nondualism than on Śaṅkara himself. Hacker leveled a version of an argument that we have seen several times in this book: Advaita Vedānta was concerned with nonduality on a metaphysical level only, with no carryover into ethical or historical practice.[41] Having enthusiastically converted to Roman Catholicism only three years earlier,[42] Hacker gave his arguments a comparative and even polemic edge: Hindus lacked something like Christian *Nächstenliebe* or love of one's neighbor. Hacker's student, Wilhelm Halbfass, concurred with this reading of Śaṅkara, pointing out that traditional Advaitins perceived nondual truth as irrelevant to social relations.[43]

Although Hacker did not explicate this, perhaps he was influenced by a taxonomy that distinguished between prophetic and mystical traditions (Western monotheism and "Eastern religions"), such as proposed by his contemporary, Gustav Mensching, a Protestant theologian and student of Rudolf Otto.[44] After all, Hacker disagreed quite strongly with the evaluation of Vaiṣṇava inclusivism that Mensching published thirty years earlier.[45] If this were the case, then one decisive difference would be the position from which a judgment about equality is made. If the perception of non-difference (which we may translate as "equality" in this experiment) is held up as a desirable spiritual achievement, the perception is based in the eyes of the perceiver, even if abstractly nonduality is taken as true in an ultimate sense. A spiritually accomplished saint can perceive non-difference in the diverse people around her, and people may praise her for that accomplishment. But less accomplished people do not yet have and may never attain that enlightened perspective. This differs substantially from a view of human equality that is grounded in an authority outside of personal perception, such as a nation-state's constitution or legal code, which is authoritative and enforceable regardless of how one perceives it.

Hacker's critique also has come under question more recently. Andrew Nicholson reprimands Hacker for doing "sloppy intellectual history" when he called Vivekananda's thought "pseudo-Vedānta," as if Śaṅkara alone possessed the genuine version of Advaita Vedānta.[46] James Madaio points out that Hacker's argument overlooked an entire millennium of Indian thought that would have complicated his false binary assumption that Vivekananda could follow either Śaṅkara or Deussen. Little scholarship has yet been done on the history of Vedānta after Śaṅkara, during which ideas surely developed further, and vernacular versions of Vedānta would also have fostered distinct positions.[47] Hugh van Skyhawk points out one such example, citing statements from Eknāth's commentary on part of the *BhP* as evidence that

Eknāth connected the metaphysical and the ethical.[48] And the stories that we observed in the previous two chapters, especially when Eknāth says that he perceives the same self in his Dalit interlocutor as in himself, present further counter-evidence to Hacker on this point. Whatever Eknāth himself may have thought, later Vārkarīs remembered him as justifying caste-transgressive actions on the basis of perceiving non-difference.

Another example of Hacker's neglect of vernacular ethics is his discussion of the story of the demon-boy Prahlāda in the *Viṣṇu Purāṇa*, which Hacker identified as an alternative basis for Hindu ethics. Although born into a demon family, Prahlāda perceives Viṣṇu in all beings and is thus an exemplary bhakta. Hacker felt that this "personalist orientation" was only a brief exceptional case in Indian intellectual history, and it never became the basis of a Hindu ethical system.[49] But as we saw in Chapter 3, in terms like *janī-janārdana*, the perception of God's existence in people as a basis of social respect, was indeed a theme in Marathi bhakti literature. The figure of Prahlāda was not as forgotten as Hacker assumed. Most of the Vārkarī *sant*-poets composed short songs about Prahlāda (rendered by them as Pralhād), routinely citing him as an exemplary bhakta. This bhakti-tinted perspective on society may seem essentially based on a *saguṇa* vision of reality that runs contrary to the aforementioned nondualism. But the fact that Vārkarīs have so often held bhakti and nondualism together in practice should prompt us to question not the Vārkarīs' logic but our presuppositions about it. Or perhaps Vārkarī inclusive ideology forced inter-caste relations to be a perennial issue, and individual authors drew on whatever conceptual resources they could find to handle it in popularly accessible ways.

Vedāntic thought continues to be a resource that Hindus can develop and apply in new ways. Hacker's critique of Vivekananda's socially-turned Vedānta notwithstanding, it became a core doctrine for the Ramakrishna Mission that he founded. And Hindu thinkers, especially in diaspora settings, also bring new perspectives. Anantanand Rambachan strongly argues, from a normative and constructive position as a Hindu thinker, that traditional philosophers are to blame for not applying nondual thought to worldly problems; it is not the philosophy's fault. Rambachan soberly acknowledges the dominance of the traditional disconnect between advaita metaphysics and social ethics,[50] yet he argues, "there are not insurmountable philosophical reasons for this indifference and many more good ones exist that would justify such concern and action."[51] In his most recent book, Rambachan carries out this project, arguing that nondualist arguments can be made to critique patriarchy, heteronormativity, caste, and other social injustices.[52]

Rambachan is not alone in this. Sadhana, the US-based progressive Hindu network of which Rambachan is a member, also marshals Hindu intellectual resources to combat caste. In 2017, the group released a "Hindu Apology for Caste and Untouchability,"[53] which began with a quote from Ambedkar's call in *Annihilation of Caste* for Hindus to find doctrinal bases that accord with liberty, equality, and fraternity: "it may not be necessary for you to borrow from foreign sources. . . . You could draw for such principles on the Upanishads."[54] Sadhana's apology did not explicitly note what Ambedkar thought this change would entail for Hindus: "a complete change in the fundamental notions of life . . . in the values of life . . . in outlook and in attitudes towards men. . . . You must discard the authority of the Shastras, and destroy the religion of the Shastras."[55] Clearly, Ambedkar did not imagine this would be easy for Hindus to accomplish, and as evidenced by his later call for conversion to Buddhism, he did not recommend that Dalits wait around to find out.

Ambedkar and bhakti

Ambedkar's assessment that the bhakti saints did not promote social equality encapsulates the bhakti-caste question in modern times. His intellectual engagement with the saints was not confined to this judgment, however. We observed examples of this in Chapter 3: his father's affiliation with Kabīr, dedicating *The Untouchables* to the memory of three Dalit saints, encouraging the newly opened Eknāth Research Center in Aurangabad, his enduring fondness of bhakti poetry's literary qualities, and objections to Mahārs' reverence of Ċokhāmeḷā.

As I see it, the disagreement about how to regard Cokhāmeḷā in practice—either as a saint to be revered or as a historical Dalit to be honorably yet cautiously remembered—hinges on a judgment about Cokhāmeḷā's place among other bhakti saints. Could the Cokhāmeḷā that modern Dalits inherited be anything beyond the crucial role that he played in the larger Vārkarī tradition's inclusive ideology? As I argued earlier in this chapter, inclusive ideology requires the preservation of caste identity markers, because it is low-caste and Dalit figures who best demonstrate the tradition's radical inclusivity. I suspect that Ambedkar recognized that Cokhāmeḷā would never be the sole property of Mahārs or Dalits; he was too inextricably bound up with the larger tradition. This is why the voice of Cokhāmeḷā in his poetry acquiesced to caste hierarchy in a way that Ambedkar found counterproductive for the purpose of Dalit assertion. Cokhāmeḷā differed in this respect from Ravidās and Kabīr, who have more peripheral roles in the Vārkarī tradition and thereby more independence from it. Yet Ravidās and Kabīr were also not local saints with substantial followings in Maharashtra, which made them less immediately present for bhaktas there. In asserting independence from the inclusive ideology of Vārkarī bhakti, Ambedkar and his followers were operating with a local sighting of bhakti that would not necessarily have appeared in the same way elsewhere.

Another aspect of Ambedkar's thought about Hinduism that merits consideration is that Ambedkar himself lived, thought, and acted in an intellectual shadow—that of modernity, by means of which social equality became a standard part of discourse about religion. Ambedkar approached the bhakti-caste question as part of his program for improving the lives of Dalits, with the conceptual tools that he had at hand. This included early 20th-century theories of religion. Scott Stroud has shown that Ambedkar drew a great deal on his teacher at Columbia University, John Dewey.[56] I would add that Dewey's pragmatic ideas for analyzing religion came with some baggage, especially a Protestant bias toward prioritizing ethics and ideas over ritual and practice. By contrasting Hinduism as rule-bound and unreflective, against a vision that Buddhism was based on principle and rationality, Ambedkar's argument paralleled the stereotypical Protestant critique of Catholicism. This is not surprising, since Ambedkar had initially learned about Buddhism through western scholarship, which for most of the 19th and early 20th centuries was mainly an idealized reconstruction based on philosophical texts that ignored living Buddhist traditions. Western scholars often invoked the Protestant Reformation to illustrate what they imagined was the Buddha's relationship to brahmanical traditions.[57] More research is needed to appreciate fully all of the ideas about Buddhism that were circulating in India in the 19th and early 20th centuries, including among Dalit groups,[58] but surely the Protestant bias that pervaded the entire field of religious studies at the time must be taken into consideration.

I make this point cautiously, realizing that it may seem as if I am undercutting the importance of social changes that Ambedkar was so pivotal in enacting. My point here is not to refute Ambedkar's view of Hinduism, including of bhakti, but to contextualize it. It is worth reflecting on how the concepts that he used to analyze religion carried their own presuppositions. As scholars reevaluate earlier theories of religion, this has ramifications for how we understand Ambedkar in his own context and in ours.

Historical imagination, hagiography, and food

Throughout this book, I have argued that the peculiarly modern, secular way of describing the past skews our perception of religious traditions. Especially when it comes to understanding non-elite people and the ideal of social equality, religions cannot but fall short of the mark. Reformers and insurgent groups who try to reorganize the social order ultimately appear as social movements that failed to realize their utopian visions. I argue that this has less to do with the traditions than with the idea of social equality, which is a problematically anachronistic concept for understanding the past unless its role as a shorthand or conceptual translation is fully explained. A lack of clarity about this has plagued the study of bhakti traditions, which has led to many scholars unconsciously reciting a narrative about religion's place in modern society as they aim to be describing the premodern past. With a clearer view of the concepts that are so close to us now as to feel natural, we can develop a more nuanced understanding of bhakti's social history, such as by studying critical commensality.

A crucial question at the heart of this social history is whether the ideas that people hold can disrupt and reorient their behavior. When adherents of bhakti traditions grasped that God welcomes everyone, did they ever see any implications in this for how they related to each other, even if that was not exactly social equality? I believe that the hagiographical materials I examined in Chapter 5 show that at least some people did make this connection, perhaps Eknāth himself in the 16th century (although we cannot know for certain), but certainly some later hagiographers and their audiences. Due to the limited historical evidence available before the mid-19th century, I am not sure that this question can be answered conclusively. The dots of historical data are too few and far apart to confidently connect. What guides us in drawing these connections and reconstructing past conditions, then, is our historical imagination and sense of how humans operate.

It seems to me that Marx and Weber offer the two major options for approaching the bhakti-caste question. Following Marx, religious ideas are part of the superstructure that legitimatizes existing economic relations. And there is no denying that at a granular level of historical practice, caste has strong ties to economy,[59] being involved with hereditary occupations, discounted labor, and even slavery.[60] Following Marx in this way, bhakti and any other religious program cannot possibly overcome caste; superstructure simply does not alter the base. In a Weberian bidirectional view, it is at least conceivable that bhakti-infused concepts could reshape adherents' attitudes toward caste, even if it was rare and difficult. Most scholars writing in a social historical vein, focusing on non-elite people, have taken more of a Marxist approach to the bhakti-caste question. Readers have probably detected by now that I am more Weberian in this respect, perhaps at least in part because I am a religious studies scholar who thinks that religion is not always only epiphenomenal. How we orient ourselves between these options not only influences what we can imagine is possible of humans in the past but bears directly on living bhakti traditions and how they could change in the future.

Similarly, the goal of someone who is describing the history of bhakti traditions strongly shapes the way they view change over time. An approach that aims to describe long-term patterns and developments will tend to foreground that which endures. And although caste has undoubtedly changed along the way, it has also certainly endured in some form across millennia. An approach that seeks to highlight ways the status quo is disrupted and challenged will focus on irruptive events, revolutionary figures, and counter-hegemonic ideas, even if the glimmer of irruption is the exception rather than the rule within the broader scope of time. In this case, one's orientation leads one to take a more activist path, acknowledging the preponderance of social stasis but always seeking opportunities to change. For the study of bhakti, it is important to distinguish between these two oversimplified paths. The intellectual values that inform them relate to how keenly one seeks a socially emancipatory vision. This has as much to do with hope for the future as it does with concern for the past.

This book has looked closely at stories about Eknāth and the Vārkarī saints, and my approach in this is a bit different from other ways of analyzing hagiography. I have argued that most scholars treat hagiographical stories as narrative snapshots, in that a given rendition of a story hangs together, bearing an author's distinct imprint. A single rendition nudges its audience to find a particular significance in the saint whose life is narrated. A different kind of knowledge can be found by placing many renditions next to each other and recognizing each rendition as if it functioned as a frame in a film. The film frame offers an image that could make sense by itself, but its significance is more than what the individual frame portrays. Just as multiple frames go by and depict movement in the film, renditions of stories that are read next to each other yield a more dynamic representation of a saint in memory over time, what I refer to in Chapter 5 as hagiography in 4D.

A 4D approach to hagiography reveals how an individual snapshot/rendition belongs to the extended, inter-generational flow of narration. The peculiarities of individual renditions come more clearly into view, allowing the reader to detect more easily how a hagiographer molded their portrayal. Greater temporal sensitivity also uncovers patterns in how some stories get repeated, sidelined, and reprocessed to convey the relevance of saint to each successive audience over centuries. The saint may come to have an enduring character, to stand for a particular message. This was the case with Eknāth and transgressive commensality. These stories got repeated regularly, yet always with some cognitive tension, due to the competing value systems of inclusive bhakti and hierarchical caste. Detecting this strange repetition was what suggested to me that the ambiguity in the stories was a feature and not a flaw. And it stood out even more when the stories got retold in the 19th and 20th centuries on the Marathi stage and screen, after the notion of social equality was added to the mix. This 4D approach to hagiography—when a sufficiently rich textual record makes it possible—may enable other perspectives on other saints and traditions. For now, I think it highlights several general points about the historical reading of hagiography.

First, hagiographical representations have a great deal of illocutionary force that is not readily evident to readers who are temporally and culturally distant from their authors and audiences. Modern readers struggle to perceive the ways in which hagiographies did and not just said something to their audiences. By viewing renditions in succession, a 4D approach calls a reader's attention to what changes. Only with awareness of such changes can one look into what may have produced them. And it is asking why that leads one to investigate and imagine a given hagiography's illocutionary force. This is absolutely crucial for handling vernacular bhakti literature—short songs, commentaries, and stories—as a source of historical knowledge. A 4D approach helps ward off problematically mistaken interpretations that are based on a single rendition of a story.

For example, one of the most learned of Marathi literary historians in the 20th century, S. G. Tulpule, interpreted a story about Eknāth in this way: "The Muslim rulers of Paithan, where he lived, had no special love for him, as is seen from an incident in his life when a rude and arrogant

Muslim had the audacity to spit on him while he was returning from a bath in the river Godavari."[61] Tulpule has misused hagiography as a source of historical knowledge here by failing to enact a 4D approach. As I have pointed out elsewhere,[62] this story is a case of "others" getting swapped in different renditions, as we saw occur with Muslims and Dalits in the *śrāddha* story in Chapter 5. In some renditions, including the earliest one, the man who spits on Eknāth is a Dalit. The renditions also differ as to whether this act was intentional, whether the spitter felt remorse, whether the spitter was even aware of what had occurred, and how Eknāth rectified the situation. Relying on one rendition of the story, as Tulpule did, to gain a sense of historical Hindu-Muslim relations in the 16th century is clearly unwarranted. It reflects the desire of the modern interpreter and the agenda of the hagiographer who repeated the story. Trying to reconstruct a cultural history of caste and untouchability by using bhakti literature without accounting for its practical logic, transmedial dynamics, and change over time is no less fraught. And I write this as someone who has hoped to read bhakti literature—with great caution—precisely for this purpose.

Second, caste identities of bhakti saints are more than just representations of historical people belonging to historical communities. In bhakti poetry and stories, caste identities always place saints in relation to others. As stories and poetry get performed repeatedly over time, it becomes more difficult and unreliable to imagine that they tell us about the "original" past in which they lived. Instead, the saints of narratives are personae—aspects of character that get represented. Saints stand for particular values, insights, and social roles. In other words, the caste identities of bhakti saints are like tropes, in that they are crafted, performed, and consumed in public. The selfhood of individual saints exists only on the broader social canvas, even as much bhakti literature seems to be about interior emotional and contemplative states. This makes it impossible to say that poetry of Dalit saints clearly or exclusively represents actual Dalits' voices. The poetry and stories that we perceive belong not to individuals but to the larger tradition. This is especially true with the Vārkarīs, the bulk of whose popular textual corpus (aside from a handful of commentarial and philosophical works by Jñāndev and Eknāth) was ephemeral and cannot be traced reliably much before the 18th century. By this, I am not at all suggesting that these texts were *composed* after the 18th century, but they were almost certainly reshaped through performance and transmedial communication along the way. So the caste identities of saints tell us more about what people found worth remembering and representing about them than about historical figures.

Third, I think it is worth reconsidering how people related stories about bhakti saints to their own lives. Saints can be examples or illustrations *of* something, like a virtue, so that people better grasp what it means. Saints can be examples *to* people so that they may refashion their lives by following the saint as a model. Saints may be both an example-of and an example-to at the same time, and they occasionally may be neither.[63] The roles of bhakti saints can be plotted helpfully within this paradigm.

In stories of more extreme bhakti, such as the Tamil Śaiva saint Kaṇṇappar gouging out his eyes for Śiva, or Ciruttoṇṭar and his wife cooking their own child for a hungry yogi, it seems clear that these acts were not meant to be emulated.[64] This is true of the comparably tamer stories about Eknāth's extreme bhakti in the *Pratiṣṭhān-caritra*, in which he cleans out his guru's toilet by hand and drinks the contents of his guru's spittoon as *prasād*. All these stories have shock value—an illocutionary force—to grab an audience's attention and illustrate the supremacy of bhakti above all else. In a similar line, some Christian hagiographers clarified that the medieval saints were not supposed to be models of behavior that others should emulate. That was too dangerous. The point of saints was to be venerated and loved.[65]

But stories of transgressive commensality, cross-caste interaction, and radical compassion all lie more within the realm of emulation. I find it hard to imagine that some people—even if only a few—did *not* regard Eknāth's theologically inspired social acts as precedents to follow. Renditions of the double vision story especially show that authors kept repeating the story but changing their explanation of the dual appearance and the level of Eknāth's conscious involvement. Likewise, the epithets used for Eknāth are revealing, as some hagiographers (Keśavsvāmī) describe him as an *avatār* and *janī-janārdana*, effectively making Eknāth into God present among the people, while others (Kṛṣṇadās) attributed *janī-janārdana* to Eknāth's spiritually astute perception—something admirable and worth striving toward. That these stories revolve around food and commensality as they did makes them all the more relatable to everyday bhaktas' lives. This is why I think we should not dismiss too quickly the possibility that some bhaktas understood these actions of Eknāth as informative for how they themselves were to behave.

Finally, it matters that these stories are religious, involving extraordinary events and superhuman entities. In the two stories about Eknāth that I analyzed, the ambiguity hinges on divine activity overcoming the conflict between bhakti inclusivity and caste separation. That the deceased ancestors appear to eat the second *śrāddha* meal and that, in nearly all versions of the double vision story, God is involved in creating a second image of Eknāth may indicate that many Marathi authors found the bhakti-caste question impossible to resolve only on a human plane. The miraculous events ratify Eknāth's caste-transgressive choices as the right ones. But in the process, the miracles raise another question—of whether the saint was extraordinarily sanctioned to behave in this way.

Divine activity resolves the bhakti-caste tension in one way but opens a new ambiguity in doing so. So, when modern authors, operating under a more disenchanted view, grew uncomfortable with the miraculous in bhakti stories, they effectively forced a decision on what was previously allowed to be ambiguous. When, as in R. R. Bhāgvat's rendition of the double vision story, no second image of Eknāth appears miraculously, then Eknāth the man becomes a social reformer who is bent on publicly transgressing caste boundaries because it is simply the right thing to do. With that transformation, the bhakti-caste question truly gets answered, and audiences get forced to choose whether they agree. As modern renditions of bhakti stories suppress the miraculous dimension, it becomes more difficult to see and appreciate the role that divinity played in maintaining ambiguity and, thereby, this particular inclusive ideology.

Another central theme in this book has been the materiality of food, even when it appears in literature and narrative. Anthropologists, sociologists, historians, and South Asia scholars have all recognized the power of food to convey ideas about human relations. Most of the time, these ideas are not at the level of consciousness but reside more powerfully in the realm of bodily experience, emotion, and inherited understandings of how people belong and should act among other people. Khare developed the notion of semantic density to understand Hindu traditions and India, but it is clear that food in other cultures, religions, and times is similarly dense with symbolic meaning. As I argued in Chapter 4, food is one of those material instruments that facilitate the very construction of social relationships, as well as maintain and regulate them.

Recent scholarship on bhakti has foregrounded its experiential, affective, bodily, and participatory dimensions. Food stands at the center of all of these, as a nexus of social relations. This is hardly unique to bhakti. Commensality has been an important social marker throughout the 19th and 20th centuries in India. As we saw in Chapter 3, inter-caste eating became a rite for joining reformist movements in Maharashtra, including the underground Paramahaṃsa Maṇḍaḷī and the publicly assertive Satyaśodhak Samāj, as well as in Viṭṭhal Rāmjī Śinde's anti-untouchability programs. Commensality did not have to occur in an organization to be powerful. Baba Padmanji, while still a Hindu, recollected an argument among friends over caste distinctions that they all resolved by committing to eat a biscuit together.[66]

In 1891, an extraordinary constellation of Marathi public intellectuals from across the political spectrum, including M. G. Ranade, B. G. Ṭiḷak, V. K. Rājvāḍe, and G. G. Āgarkar, were invited to the Panch Howd Mission in Pune for a public lecture,[67] at which tea and biscuits were served. This put many attendees in a dilemma, as they calculated whether to partake and how others would perceive their commensality with not only Christians but also political opponents.[68] The commensal event, which became known as the Panch Howd Tea Episode, caused outrage on many fronts, in no small part because the organizer, Gopālrāo Jośī, had a predilection for stirring up controversy.[69] Orthodox brahmans, in consultation with a Śaṅkarācārya, insisted that everyone involved would be put out of caste unless they underwent purification. The rationalist Āgarkar refused outright, arguing that the *śāstra*s and traditional religious authorities were no longer valid for modern life. The conservative nationalist Ṭiḷak affirmed *dharmaśāstr*ic authority on the matter but conveniently asserted that he had undertaken purification already on his own during a visit to Varanasi and thus did not need to repeat the ritual in Pune. Some of his followers had looked askance at Ṭiḷak for convening with his liberal opponents at the event. The liberal Ranade refused purification for a year but eventually acquiesced, stating three reasons. First, if he were purified and then continued publicly in transgressive commensality, he could more effectively reveal the hollowness of purification. Second, undergoing purification would make it easier for a wider range of collaborators to pursue social reform with him. And third, he needed to address a confidential family matter that had arisen because of the event.[70] Ranade's purification, which his colleagues viewed as backsliding, was roundly and publicly criticized, especially by fellow Prārthanā Samāj members.[71] Whereas stories of Eknāth undergoing purification after transgressing caste boundaries benefited from strategic ambiguity, the climate of the late 19th century demanded more clarity.

Thirty years later, B. G. Tilak's son, Śrīdhar, took a very different view of caste and social change. In 1928, Śrīdhar established at his home a branch of the Samāj Samatā Sangh (Social Equality Assembly) that Ambedkar had founded two years earlier. Śrīdhar hosted public discussions on caste discrimination and public *saha-bhojans* (shared meals) that included Dalits. This activity was especially inflammatory because Śrīdhar's home was in Sadāśiv Peṭh, the epicenter of Pune's powerful brahman community.[72] Ambedkar himself attended one of these events and had tea with Śrīdhar.[73] When his famous father died in 1920, Śrīdhar inherited not only the family's home but also part ownership of the influential nationalist Marathi newspaper *Kesarī*, which his father had founded. *Kesarī*'s trustees were outraged by Śrīdhar's activities, so they initiated a legal battle to wrest control of the newspaper from him. Persecuted and alienated, Śrīdhar soon after killed himself. In a letter to Ambedkar that he wrote only hours before taking his own life, Śrīdhar said that he would be carrying the Dalits' grievances directly to the feet of Kṛṣṇa himself.[74] Transgressive commensality had become an act of political protest in the early 20th century, often with dire consequences.

These recent historical events vividly depict the fraught social terrain that Hindus have navigated with food in the early 20th century. Although we may question the historicity of earlier hagiographical stories, we surely ought not imagine that the times of the bhakti saints were any less complicated than these 20th-century stories whose historicity is known. I take for granted that the social lives of the saints, their followers, and hagiographers were marvelously complex—far more is evident in the texts they left behind. It is this presumption of complexity that inclines me to read bhakti poetry and hagiography in the rich, polyvocal, strategically ambiguous ways that I do. Observing food and its many significances is an excellent way to become sensitized to this complexity.

As social scientists have long observed, the fact that people come together around food means that commensality is a powerful site for creating, regulating, and sustaining social connections. Pilgrims inevitably eat together and share food, sometimes acquiring it from the communities through which they transit and thus connecting pilgrims to people around them. This is surely an important dynamic in the Vārkarī tradition, especially in its smaller branches today, as well as in its earlier forms, before the trucks and large logistical support programs characterizing the major branches that move between Āḷandī and Paṇḍharpūr developed.[75] Sharing food like this helps knit together sacred space and establish connections among people.

In a very different context, Banu Bargu has highlighted the importance of commensality for social change. Bargu argues that by not promoting eating together more often, left-wing movements have lost a valuable means for achieving the social equality that they extol. Commensality is "both a metaphor for the emancipatory potential of biopolitics and a literal rendition of one form of social practice."[76] We see an example of this in the Vārkarī leader Hari Mahārāj Babhūtkar (1885–1944) in a town in northern Maharashtra. Babhūtkar required his followers to eat and live together, to disregard their castes.[77] Of course, eating together can be mobilized to other ends as well, as Indian politicians have begun staging media events that document them eating at Dalit constituents' homes. This activity, which Indian newspapers have termed "lunch diplomacy,"[78] is carried out in the hope that shared food results in shared political allegiance.

Just because eating together could be a site for manifesting social hierarchies and making political messages does not mean that it must be so. Since eating food will continue to be a basic fact of everyday life, people ought to become more conscious about organizing commensal events for the social good. Commensality effectively "substantiates a positive horizon of emancipation at the quotidian, micro-political level, with indigenous forms of sociality which are productive of the relations of friendship and solidarity, which are in turn constitutive of egalitarian and democratic subjectivities."[79] Marathi bhakti traditions recognized the importance of food well before equality and democracy became part of their vocabulary. Now that those terms have become current, bhakti traditions could theoretically draw on them, if they wanted, to add yet another layer of meaning to the semantic density of food-related activities in which they are already engaged.

Conclusion

I have offered in this book a view of the bhakti-caste question based in Maharashtrian history and Marathi literature. Perceiving bhakti and caste from this position is helpful, since the Vārkarī tradition has an uncommonly long, complex relationship to caste, and the rise of Dalit movements in modern times has foregrounded caste hierarchy and untouchability in the region. Ambedkar's shadow is especially strong in Maharashtra. Stories about Eknāth, Dalits, and food are prismatic sites through which we can observe bhakti and secular authors from the 18th century onward wrestle with the question. Strategic ambiguity was an important yet overlooked narrative instrument that enabled many Vārkarīs to avoid answering the bhakti-caste question, thus making it into a riddle. Although I do not imagine that strategic ambiguity, like the basic North Indian *saguṇa*/*nirguṇa* distinction, is universal among bhakti traditions, we should not be surprised to find similar dynamics in other traditions and locales. Likewise, the importance of food in literature, memory, and practice will likely resonate at least somewhat in other traditions. Food is, after all, one of the most basic material interactions between the internal world of the bhakta and the world outside.

Another aspect of bhakti that should hold true across regions is its transmedial character—organically changing as it moves across various media. I strongly suspect that, in many regions, local bhakti traditions' literatures were appropriated as classical vernacular literature in the late 19th and early 20th centuries in ways that resemble the Marathi case. The pervasion of Marxian ideas and equality language around the world in the early 20th century probably became a reference point for modern historiography of regional traditions across India. The intermedial shift from bhakti literature to theatrical or filmic productions probably bears some resemblances to the Marathi case, due to the common technologies that were used and mass inter-regional markets that developed, even if not all regional film industries were as developed early on as the Marathi one. The correlation of "equality"—a Western term that took root in India through British education and reading—with local vernacular words likely resulted in similar issues of semantic proximity but imperfect overlap, especially if the vernacular tradition was drawing on Vedāntic terminology.

There are surely major differences in how regional traditions have handled the bhakti-caste question too. The presence of Ravidās in the life and memories of many North Indian (and some Maharashtrian) Dalit communities certainly leads them to construe the bhakti-caste question differently. Performing and transmitting bhakti in more socially homogeneous settings would have less need for strategic ambiguity. This holds true of some exclusively *nirguṇa* traditions that grew up around Kabīr in North India as well; the question of bhakti and caste will look quite different to them. In Tamil Nadu, the figures of Periyar and Iyothee Thass cast a different shadow on the study of bhakti than Ambedkar does in Maharashtra. Although not so visible in Maharashtra, Gandhi's shadow surely influences the interpretation of bhakti strongly in other parts of India, especially Gujarat. And the bhakti-caste question certainly looks different when sighted from Karnataka and Punjab, where Liṅgāyats and Sikhs often emphasize their difference from Hindus. Sightings of the bhakti-caste question in other regions and languages will—and *must*—differ from what I have presented in this book. I hope that my way of exploring bhakti and caste may inspire others to do similar research, especially of the prismatic 19th century, in other languages and regions.

Further research on the bhakti-caste question could be carried out in Maharashtra and Marathi too. A natural extension of this book's consideration of food would be to observe ethnographically how Vārkarīs today talk about bhakti and caste, especially in relation to Dalits within and outside their ranks. I admire Paul Toomey's astute observations of how food functions differently in the various traditions that carry out Annakūṭa celebrations, and I regret that my family circumstances have not allowed me to return to India to be among the Vārkarīs often enough to do a similar ethnography among them. I would like to make a few comments, as provisional as they are, with the hope that others would follow up with more ethnographic research in Maharashtra.

First, discussion of caste with contemporary Vārkarīs (and many other Hindus) is obviously quite emotionally and politically fraught, and the most reliable observations of such difficult matters would require spending significant time with people. What devotees might say and even truly believe about bhakti and caste, and what they practically do in the complex social contexts where they dwell, may not always overlap. This is not to imply that, for those who view bhakti as a thoroughgoing challenge to caste hierarchy (which not all bhaktas do), it is impossible to refashion lives and even communities around radical principles. It can and does happen. But one ought not be surprised that among large-scale religious traditions, religion in everyday life is negotiated differently. Discourse about human equality, in both religious and non-religious contexts, is unavoidably shaped by the situations in which it occurs. Recent research on the ethnography of equality is very helpful in sensitizing us to what exactly people mean when they appeal to equality.[80] I would expect that further ethnography among the Vārkarīs and Mahānubhāvs would be no different.

Second, the time that I have spent among Vārkarīs, especially at celebrations of Eknāth's birthday (Eknāth Ṣaṣṭhi) in Paiṭhaṇ and while walking on pilgrimage with the Eknāth palanquin for eighteen days from Paiṭhaṇ to Paṇḍharpūr, already shows well that Vārkarīs continue to differ on what the bhakti-caste relationship should look like. And those who endorse a non-caste vision of bhakti struggle to live it out. Scholars nowadays tend to dismiss Victor Turner's discussion of the Vārkarī pilgrimage as a liminal space in which caste distinctions break down, usually citing D. B. Mokashi's and Irawati Karve's one-time experiences of the pilgrimage in the 1960s.[81] In my pilgrimage experience fifty years later (and on a different branch than the Āḷandī-Dehū-Paṇḍharpūr that Mokashi and Karve observed), I witnessed a few examples of brahman Vārkarīs quietly avoiding eating with śūdra Vārkarīs, despite walking alongside them for weeks. Much more often, however, I observed brahmans freely eating with and accepting food from everyone. Focusing on caste's continued influence among Vārkarīs, especially on an institutional level, ought not be the only way that people perceive Vārkarīs managing bhakti and caste. Such a casual dismissal does a disservice to those (even if they are in the minority) who change their everyday social interactions to become not only more inclusive but more egalitarian.

Third, any contemporary ethnography must acknowledge the impact of Ambedkar's legacy on bhakti in Maharashtra, which for many Dalits today (especially the majority Mahār community), renders affiliation with bhakti traditions undesirable and even impossible. Indications of the gap that has grown between Marathi bhakti traditions and Mahārs can be seen in the infrequent and irreverent references to the Vārkarīs in Marathi Dalit literature that arose in the 1970s. This chapter began with an excerpt from a poem by Tryambak Sapkale. It is worth considering the poem in its entirety, as it draws creatively on the ancient Buddhist story of Aṅgulimāla as a motif for expressing Sapkale's sense of marginality.[82]

When I came into this world I was crying, the world was laughing.
Two hands caressed me, on my back, on my stomach.

When I was crawling, I used to fall, then get up,
supported by the little fingers of those hands.

When understanding came, I cried. The world only laughed.
Two hands raised the whip to my back, to my stomach.

As I ran through this bounteous, plentiful land
my feet burned, my mind wept.
I ran yelling for my life, hoping to meet someone like Eknath.

I met quite a few who revered Eknath.
They were engrossed in their *kīrtan*.
My cry did not enter their hearts.

Even the Sahara has an oasis.
I ran in search of something like an oasis.

I tried to catch hold of this turning earth.
My hands were brushed off. I fell.
The world laughed, pointing its fingers at me.

Tears dried. Feet froze.
Gathering all my strength, I laughed at this world.
Ha . . . Ha . . . Ha . . . Ha . . .
There was a tremor in the earth when I laughed.

Hey—how come you rabbit spawn aren't laughing anymore?
Those fingers that point at me
will become fingers dangling from the garland around my neck.

Angulimal
I am Angulimal . . .
I am Angulimal—[83]

It is hard to imagine an easy rapprochement between Dalits who share Sapkale's feelings and practicing Vārkarīs. Yet Dalits, especially outside urban areas, do have to interact with low-caste Vārkarī and other Hindu neighbors on an everyday level. How does this happen, especially among Dalits who converted to Buddhism? Additionally, Maharashtrian Dalits who are not Mahārs often have a different relationship to both bhakti and institutional manifestations of Ambedkar's legacy. Cāmbhārs often retain a close affiliation to Rohidās (Ravidās or Raidās, in North India) as their saint. No saint has been connected to the Māṅg or Mātaṅga community, who have also been wary of Dalit organizations that they perceive as dominated by Mahārs. How these communities' relationships to bhakti and Ambedkar continue to evolve is worth exploring.

The largely unstudied worlds of the Vārkarīs as a living tradition do not always resemble their textual corpus. Given the deeply un-institutional, local, and decentralized nature of Vārkarī practice, it should be clear that observing the words of those *mahārājs* (traditional local leaders) and those who claim to advocate for a Vārkarī contingency in the Maharashtrian political sphere is not like taking the pulse of "the Vārkarīs" in general. Even joining the pilgrims to walk from Āḷandī to Paṇḍharpūr offers only a partial view of Vārkarī practice. And in light of the recent institutionalization of that branch of the *vārī*, it sheds little light now on how the pilgrimage was practiced historically.

The annual major *vārī* in June and July regularly attracts now between seven hundred thousand and a million pilgrims, which is surely a fraction of the total, diffuse population who are engaged with Vārkarī texts and practices in some way. What does bhakti in the shadow of Ambedkar look like to them? Has the Marxian critique of bhakti as subjugation or unsuccessful ideology reached them at all? Perhaps Marx casts little if any shadow on bhakti in the Maharashtrian countryside. Given the continued incidents of anti-Dalit violence and the fractious politics around government reservations in recent years, Ambedkar's legacy in the countryside and among rural Vārkarīs is not always well received. Further ethnographic research among the Vārkarīs, to get a taste of their everyday lives, join them as they eat, and observe who is and is not among them at meals will surely reveal different new perspectives, add nuance to arguments that I have made here, and maybe even refute them. I would welcome this, especially from those who are engaged in the tradition itself and wrestle with what has become the question of bhakti and caste in the 21st century.

Lest my critical approach lead readers to suspect otherwise, I want to state clearly that my goal in this book has *not* been to question whether social equality is a worthwhile goal for us today. And I do not imply that we ought to prefer unequal and hierarchical social structures for organizing society. We live now under the sign of modernity, and social equality language—as fraught and aspirational as it may be—is part of our world. Nor do I mean to question or criticize efforts of those who are disempowered to assert themselves and strive for positive change. Yet recognizing that the scope of a particular struggle for equality is always limited (equality of *something*), even as activists refer to it as if it were an objective and ultimate virtue, may be helpful in understanding how the word's significance slips as it moves across contexts and discursive spheres.

I do maintain, however, that scholars must be careful about referring to "equality" when studying history and texts before the 19th century. Conflating premodern Indic terms, especially of nondualist philosophy, with equality can give the misleading impression that the worlds of people in the past are more familiar to us than they actually are. And this can lead us to flatten the richness of bhakti texts and contexts, to overlook how they fit with past practical logics of authors and audiences, and to miss out on subtle features that do not actually align with terms like equality. Ultimately, I am arguing for a more sophisticated, nuanced, and sensitive approach to reading bhakti literature as a source of cultural, social, and conceptual history. For that historical project, modern social equality language obscures more than it reveals. A deeper understanding of this will expand our vision of how living bhakti traditions functioned then and continue to change today. Now, social equality, enshrined in the kind of constitutional democracies that Ambedkar helped create, has become normative and even impossible to think without as we orient ourselves in the world.

What is the point of writing history? If it is to document the past and understand the lives of people who lived then, sensitivity to conceptual history and different thought worlds is required. If the point is to invoke and use the past to orient oneself in the present, whether by positively inheriting or critically rejecting traditions, then a more overtly political and practice-oriented skill set is called for. How we handle the bhakti-caste question, and whether the door is left open for imagining that traditions may change to adopt more proactively egalitarian attitudes, is strongly tied to how we view the goal of scholarship.

As she reflected on the memory and history writing about the Holocaust, Gabrielle Spiegel argued for a new "historical ethics" that foregrounds a concern for representing trauma. This entails "a turn from epistemological to ethical commitments in the study of the past" in ways that respect the reality of traumatized people's memory without immediately interrogating, abandoning, or reducing it to its correspondence with the verifiable past.[84] I think studying bhakti now, in the shadow of Ambedkar, could benefit from this approach. For it is certainly true of contemporary bhakti traditions and South Asia generally that the present is "haunted by the past, and the past is modeled, invented, reinvented and reconstructed by the present."[85] After Ambedkar especially, we know that caste and untouchability have created trauma. Where bhakti has contributed to that trauma, it must change.

Finally, let us return to food. In a time of rapid climate change, we witness increasing worries about food scarcity and spates of farmer suicides, especially in India. As we have seen throughout the book, bhakti has dealt extensively with food. Historically, it offered narrative models for adherents to emulate on pilgrimages and in festivals, and it highlighted how transgressive commensality could be a micro-tactic for building community. Universal commensality, which bhakti traditions recognized from early on, is vital for this project. Whatever our relation to bhakti and scholarship may be, this is a lesson that applies to everyone. If we are to eat, as the future unfolds, we should eat together.

Notes

Introduction

1. Charles Taylor, *A Secular Age* (Cambridge MA: Belknap Press of Harvard University Press, 2007), 160.
2. For more on this meal, see Claudia Marra, "Fucha Ryori: The Monastic Cuisine of the Obaku-Zen School," *The Journal of Nagasaki University of Foreign Studies in History* 15 (2011): 215–32.
3. Kṛṣṇadās Jagadānanda-nandan, *Pratiṣṭhāncaritra*, ed. Raghunāth Hamaṇpanth Koṭnīs (Mumbaī: Trinity Publicity Society, 1948), 75–83. A version of this story will appear in *Sources of Indian History*, ed. Rachel McDermott, Vidya Dehejia, and Indira Peterson, 3rd ed. (New York: Columbia University Press, Forthcoming).
4. Saints' behavior is not always understood as something to emulate, as Hawley's discussion of two divergent senses of "example" shows. John Stratton Hawley, ed. *Saints and Virtues* (Berkeley: University of California Press, 1987), x–xvii.
5. B. R. Ambedkar, "A Reply to the Mahatma," in *Annihilation of Caste* (London: Verso, 2014), 336.
6. This letter was published serially in three issues of *Harijan* in 1936: July 11, July 18, and August 15.
7. I am grateful to an anonymous reviewer for proposing the term "critical commensality" to encapsulate my scholarly approach to people eating together.
8. Pierre Bourdieu, *An Invitation to Reflexive Sociology* (Chicago: University of Chicago Press, 1992), 22.
9. A current example of this is the journalist-turned-*kīrtankār* in Mumbai, Śyāmsundar Sonnār Mahārāj, parts of whose *kīrtans* can be found on YouTube. I am grateful to Smita Pendharkar for making this connection. See also, Linda Hess, *Bodies of Song: Kabir Oral Traditions and Performative Worlds in North India* (New York: Oxford University Press, 2015), 257–73; Jayant Lele, "Community, Discourse and Critique in Jnanesvar," *Journal of Asian and African Studies* 15, no. 1–2 (1980): 183–84.
10. Samuel Moyn, *The Last Utopia: Human Rights in History* (Cambridge: Harvard University Press, 2010), 21–23.
11. Eleanor Zelliot, "The Early Voices of Untouchables: The Bhakti Saints," in *From Stigma to Assertion: Untouchability, Identity and Politics in Early and Modern India*, ed. Mikael Aktor and Robert Deliége (Copenhagen: Museum Tusculanum Press, 2010); "The Medieval Bhakti Movement in History," in *Hinduism: New Essays in the History of Religions*, ed. Bardwell L. Smith (Leiden: E. J. Brill, 1976).
12. David N. Lorenzen, ed. *Bhakti Religion in North India: Community Identity and Political Action* (Albany: State University of New York Press, 1995); "The Lives

of *Nirguṇi* Saints," in *Bhakti Religion in North India*; "The Historical Vicissitudes of Bhakti Religion," in *Bhakti Religion in North India*; "The Social Ideologies of Hagiography: Sankara, Tukaram and Kabir," in *Who Invented Hinduism? Essays on Religion in History* (New Delhi: Yoda Press, 2006).

13. Patton Burchett, "Bhakti Rhetoric in the Hagiography of 'Untouchable' Saints: Discerning Bhakti's Ambivalence on Caste and Brahminhood," *International Journal of Hindu Studies* 13, no. 2 (2009), 115–41.
14. Philip Lutgendorf, *The Life of a Text: Performing the Rāmcaritmānas of Tulsīdās* (Berkeley: University of California Press, 1991); Hess, *Bodies of Song*.
15. Christian Lee Novetzke, "Religion and the Public Sphere in Premodern India," *Asiatische Studien—Études Asiatiques* 72, no. 1 (2018), 147–76; "Bhakti and Its Public," *International Journal of Hindu Studies* 11, no. 3 (2007), 255-72; *Religion and Public Memory: A Cultural History of Saint Namdev in India* (New York: Columbia University Press, 2008).
16. *The Quotidian Revolution: Vernacularization, Religion, and the Premodern Public Sphere in India* (New York: Columbia University Press, 2016).
17. "Divining an Author: The Idea of Authorship in an Indian Religious Tradition," *History of Religions* 42, no. 3 (2003), 213–42; John Stratton Hawley, "Author and Authority," in *Three Bhakti Voices: Mirabai, Surdas, and Kabir in Their Time and Ours* (New Delhi: Oxford University Press, 2005).
18. Claude Grignon, "Commensality and Social Morphology: An Essay of Typology," in *Food, Drink and Identity: Cooking, Eating and Drinking in Europe since the Middle Ages*, ed. Peter Scholliers (New York: Berg, 2001); R. Kenji Tierney and Emiko Ohnuki-Tierney, eds., "Anthropology of Food," in The Oxford Handbook of Food History, ed. Jeffrey M. Pilcher (Oxford: Oxford University Press, 2012); Alice P. Julier, *Eating Together: Food, Friendship, and Inequality* (Urbana: University of Illinois Press, 2013).
19. R. S. Khare and M. S. A. Rao, eds., *Food, Society and Culture: Aspects in South Asian Food Systems* (Durham, NC: Carolina Academic Press, 1986); R. S. Khare, "Food with the Saints: An Aspect of Hindu Gastrosemantics," in *The Eternal Food: Gastronomic Ideas and Experiences of Hindus and Buddhists* (Albany: State University of New York Press, 1992).
20. "Anna," in *The Hindu World*, ed. Sushil Mittal and Gene R. Thursby (New York: Routledge, 2004), 49.
21. Barbara A. Holdrege, "The Gauḍīya Discourse of Embodiment: Re-Visioning Jñāna and Yoga in the Embodied Aesthetics of Kṛṣṇa Bhakti," *The Journal of Hindu Studies* 6, no. 2 (2013), 154–97; *Bhakti and Embodiment: Fashioning Divine Bodies and Devotional Bodies in Kṛṣṇa Bhakti* (New York: Routledge, 2015); Karen Pechilis, *The Embodiment of Bhakti* (New York: Oxford University Press, 1999).
22. Sumit Guha, *Beyond Caste: Identity and Power in South Asia, Past and Present* (Leiden: Brill, 2013); "Speaking Historically: The Changing Voices of Historical Narration in Western India, 1400–1900," *American Historical Review* 109, no. 4 (2004); "Wrongs and Rights in the Maratha Country: Antiquity, Custom and Power in

Eighteenth-Century India," in *Changing Concepts of Rights and Justice in South Asia*, ed. M. R. Anderson and Sumit Guha (New Delhi: Oxford University Press, 2000).

23. Anupama Rao, *The Caste Question: Dalits and the Politics of Modern India* (Berkeley: University of California Press, 2009).
24. Milind Wakankar, *Subalternity and Religion: The Prehistory of Dalit Empowerment in South Asia* (London: Routledge, 2010).
25. Novetzke, *The Quotidian Revolution*, 301–04.
26. Antonio Rigopoulos, *Dattātreya: The Immortal Guru, Yogin, and Avatāra* (Albany: State University of New York Press, 1998).
27. Jeremy G. Morse, "Devotion according to the Rules: Guru-Bhakti in the Texts and Practices of the Datta Sampradāya" (PhD dissertation, University of Chicago, 2017), 3–5.
28. Prachi Deshpande, *Creative Pasts: Historical Memory and Identity in Western India, 1700–1960* (New York: Columbia University Press, 2007), 128–34.
29. Jon Keune, "Eknāth Remembered and Reformed: Bhakti, Brahmans, and Untouchables in Marathi Historiography" (PhD dissertation, Columbia University, 2011).
30. Harald Tambs-Lyche, "Caste," in *Brill Encyclopedia of Hinduism*, ed. Knut Axel Jacobsen (Leiden: Brill, 2011).
31. Diane P. Mines, *Caste in India* (Ann Arbor: Association for Asian Studies, 2009); Eleanor Zelliot, "Caste in Contemporary India," in *Contemporary Hinduism: Ritual, Culture and Practice*, ed. Robin Rinehart (Santa Barbara: ABC-CLIO, 2004); M. N. Srinivas, "Caste in Modern India," in *The Oxford India Srinivas* (New Delhi: Oxford University Press, 2009).
32. Nicholas B. Dirks, *Castes of Mind: Colonialism and the Making of Modern India* (Princeton: Princeton University Press, 2001).
33. Rosalind O'Hanlon, "Caste and Its Histories in Colonial India: A Reappraisal," *Modern Asian Studies* 51, no. 2 (2017), 432–61.
34. Rupa Viswanath, *The Pariah Problem: Caste, Religion, and the Social in Modern India* (New York: Columbia University Press, 2014); Ramnarayan Rawat, *Reconsidering Untouchability: Chamars and Dalit History in North India* (Bloomington: Indiana University Press, 2011); P. Sanal Mohan, *Modernity of Slavery: Struggles against Caste Inequality in Colonial Kerala* (Oxford: Oxford University Press, 2015).
35. Guha, *Beyond Caste*.
36. For examples of tensions between brahmans, Kayasthas, and Guravs, see Novetzke, *The Quotidian Revolution*, 56–61 and 158–68. On competition among Dalit *jātis*, see Robert Deliège, "Replication and Consensus: Untouchability, Caste and Ideology in India," *Royal Anthropological Institute of Great Britain and Ireland* 27, no. 1 (1992), 155–73.
37. Anand Teltumbde, *The Persistence of Caste: The Khairlanji Murders and India's Hidden Apartheid* (New Delhi: Navayana, 2010).
38. Wilhelm Halbfass, "Traditional Indian Xenology," in *India and Europe: An Essay in Understanding* (Albany: State University of New York Press, 1988), 176–79.

39. Jon Keune, "The Challenge of the Swappable Other: A Framework for Interpreting Otherness in Bhakti Texts," in *Regional Communities of Devotion in South Asia: Insiders, Outsiders and Interlopers*, ed. Gil Ben-Herut, Jon Keune, and Anne E. Monius (New York: Routledge, 2019).
40. Julia Leslie, "Some Traditional Indian Views on Menstruation and Female Sexuality," in *Sexual Knowledge, Sexual Science: The History of Attitudes to Sexuality*, ed. Roy Porter and Mikuláš Teich (Cambridge: Cambridge University Press, 1994), 66–67.
41. Mikael Aktor, "Untouchability in Brahminical Law Books: Ritual and Economic Control," in *From Stigma to Assertion: Untouchability, Identity and Politics in Early and Modern India*, ed. Mikael Aktor and Robert Deliège (Copenhagen: Museum Tusculanum Press, University of Copenhagen, 2010), 38–46.
42. Simon Charsley, "'Untouchable': What Is in a Name?," *Journal of the Royal Anthropological Institute* 2, no. 1 (1996), 1–23.
43. Viswanath, *The Pariah Problem*.
44. Rao, *The Caste Question*.
45. Eleanor Zelliot, "Dalit—New Cultural Context for an Old Marathi Word," in *From Untouchable to Dalit: Essays on the Ambedkar Movement* (New Delhi: Manohar, 1992).
46. Jesús Francisco Cháirez-Garza, "Touching Space: Ambedkar on the Spatial Features of Untouchability," *Contemporary South Asia* 22, no. 1 (2014): 3.
47. Charsley, "'Untouchable': What is in a Name?."
48. Christian Lee Novetzke, "A Family Affair: Krishna Comes to Pandharpur and Makes Himself at Home," in *Alternative Krishnas: Regional and Vernacular Variations on a Hindu Deity*, ed. Guy Beck (Albany: State University of New York Press, 2005).

Chapter 1

1. Charles Taylor, "Modern Social Imaginaries," *Public Culture* 14, no. 1 (2002): 100; "Modes of Secularism," in *Secularism and Its Critics*, ed. Rajeev Bhargava (Delhi: Oxford University Press, 2004), esp. 40–43.
2. Ranajit Guha, *Dominance without Hegemony: History and Power in Colonial India* (Cambridge: Harvard University Press, 1997), 49.
3. David Hardiman, *The Coming of the Devi: Adivasi Assertion in Western India* (Oxford: Oxford University Press, 1987); Saurabh Dube, *Untouchable Pasts: Religion, Identity, and Power among a Central Indian Community, 1780–1950* (Albany: State University of New York Press, 1998).
4. Mark Donnelly and Claire Norton, *Doing History* (London: Routledge, 2011), 35–46.
5. C. T. McIntire, "Transcending Dichotomies in History and Religion," *History and Theory* 45, no. 4 (2006): 80–92.
6. Robert B. Townsend, "A New Found Religion? The Field Surges among AHA Members," https://www.historians.org/publications-and-directories/perspectives-on-history/december-2009/a-new-found-religion-the-field-surges-among-aha-members;

Thomas Albert Howard, "A 'Religious Turn' in Modern European Historiography?," *Historically Speaking* 4, no. 5 (2003): 24–26.

7. As he attends to the ideas and practices of early modern English peasants, Keith Thomas offers a paradigmatic example of this. Keith Thomas, *Religion and the Decline of Magic: Studies in Popular Beliefs in Sixteenth and Seventeenth Century England* (New York: Oxford University Press, 1971 [1997]).
8. Of course, some religious advocates have incorporated Marxist social analysis into their perspectives, such as liberation theologians, some black theologians, Christian socialists, some Buddhist monks in early 20th-century China and Japan, and Ambedkar himself. These fall beyond the scope of my consideration of social history as a mode of narrating the past.
9. Donald M. MacRaild and Avram Taylor, *Social Theory and Social History* (New York: Palgrave Macmillan, 2004), 23–30.
10. Roland Boer, "E. P. Thompson and the Psychic Terror of Methodism," *Thesis Eleven* 110, no. 1 (2012): 54–67.
11. Dipesh Chakrabarty, *Provincializing Europe: Postcolonial Thought and Historical Difference* (Princeton: Princeton University Press, 2000), 86.
12. Ibid.
13. Ibid., 90.
14. Ibid., 105.
15. Ibid., 112.
16. Both Chakrabarty and Guha apparently overlook the fact that the academic study of religion in the late 19th and early 20th centuries often played precisely this role of unsettling modernist assumptions and imagining alternative ways of life in Europe. Hans G. Kippenberg, *Discovering Religious History in the Modern Age* (Princeton: Princeton University Press, 2002), 192–95.
17. Chakrabarty, *Provincializing Europe*, 238.
18. A similar point has been made in Christian Novetzke, "The Subaltern Numen: Making History in the Name of God," *History of Religions* 46, no. 2 (2006): 99–126.
19. Bruce Kapferer, "In the Event: Toward an Anthropology of Generic Moments," *Social Analysis* 54, no. 3 (2010): 2–3.
20. Steven M. Buechler, *Understanding Social Movements: Theories from the Classic Era to the Present* (Boulder: Paradigm Publishers, 2011), 1.
21. Martin Fuchs and Antje Linkenbach, "Social Movements," in *Oxford India Companion to Sociology and Social Anthropology*, ed. Veena Das, Andre Beteille, and T. N. Madan (Delhi: Oxford University Press, 2003), 1530.
22. On bhakti traditions' various "others," see Gil Ben-Herut, Jon Keune, and Anne E. Monius, eds., *Regional Communities of Devotion in South Asia* (New York: Routledge, 2019). For a penetrating discussion of historical group relations, see Patton Burchett, *A Genealogy of Devotion: Bhakti, Tantra, Yoga, and Sufism in North India* (New York: Columbia University Press, 2019).
23. Steven Justice, "Religious Dissent, Social Revolt and 'Ideology,'" *Past & Present* 195, no. Supplement 2 (2007): 205–06.
24. Ibid., 210.

25. Rogers Brubaker and Frederick Cooper, "Beyond 'Identity'," *Theory and Society* 29, no. 1 (2000): 1.
26. Peter J. Rhodes, "Isonomia," in *Brill's New Pauly (Antiquity)* (Leiden: Brill), 984. For a reassessment, see Dmitriev Sviatoslav, "Herodotus, Isonomia, and the Origins of Greek Democracy," *Athenaeum* 103, no. 1 (2015): 53–83.
27. Pauline Maier, "The Strange Case of All Men Are Created Equal," *Washington and Lee Review* 56, no. 3 (1999): 873–90.
28. Raymond Williams, *Keywords: A Vocabulary of Culture and Society* (Oxford: Oxford University Press, 2015), 76–78.
29. Quentin Skinner and James Tully, *Meaning and Context: Quentin Skinner and His Critics* (Cambridge: Polity, 1988), 38, 119–32.
30. Quentin Skinner, *Visions of Politics: Regarding Method* (New York: Cambridge University Press, 2002), 59.
31. Williams, *Keywords*, 76–77.
32. Otto Dann, "Gleichheit," in *Geschichliche Grundbegriffe*, ed. Otto Brunner, Werner Conze, and Reinhart Koselleck (Stuttgart: Ernst Klett Verlag, 1975), 997.
33. Ibid., 999.
34. Ibid., 1002.
35. Ibid., 1005. (This appears in Luther's *On the Christian Nobility of the German Nation Concerning the Reform of the Christian Estate*.)
36. Ibid.
37. Ibid., 1007.
38. Ibid., 1009.
39. Ibid., 1016.
40. David Armitage, *The Declaration of Independence: A Global History* (Cambridge MA: Harvard University Press, 2007), 76–77.
41. Taylor, "Modern Social Imaginaries," 100.
42. Carina Fourie, Fabian Schuppert, and Ivo Wallimann-Helmer, eds., *Social Equality: On What It Means to Be Equals* (Oxford: Oxford University Press, 2015), 1.
43. Ibid., 6–8.
44. Jeremy Moss, *Reassessing Egalitarianism* (Basingstoke, Hampshire: Palgrave Macmillan, 2014), 24–25.
45. Ibid., 30–33.
46. Marc Galanter, *Competing Equalities: Law and the Backward Classes in India* (Berkeley: University of California Press, 1984), 41–83.
47. John Arthur, *Race, Equality, and the Burdens of History* (Cambridge: Cambridge University Press, 2007), 122.
48. Anastasia Piliavsky, "Egalitarian Fantasy and Politics in the Real World," *Anthropology of This Century* (2018), http://aotcpress.com/articles/egalitarian-fantasy/; Vita Peacock, "The Negation of Hierarchy and Its Consequences," *Anthropological Theory* 15, no. 1 (2015): 3–21; Jason Hickel, *Democracy as Death: The Moral Order of Anti-Liberal Politics in South Africa* (Berkeley CA: University of California Press, 2015), 18–26.

49. Robert N. Bellah, *Religion in Human Evolution: From the Paleolithic to the Axial Age* (Cambridge: Belknap Press of Harvard University Press, 2011), xix, 101.
50. Ibid., 606.
51. Denise Kimber Buell and Caroline Johnson Hodge, "The Politics of Interpretation: The Rhetoric of Race and Ethnicity in Paul," *Journal of Biblical Literature* 123, no. 2 (2004): 247–50.
52. Mary Hayter, *The New Eve in Christ: The Use and Abuse of the Bible in the Debate About Women in the Church* (Grand Rapids: W.B. Eerdmans, 1987).
53. John Kenneth Riches, *Galatians through the Centuries* (Oxford: Wiley-Blackwell, 2013), 204–07.
54. Many citations of Marx's and Engels' works are found in Christopher Hill, "The English Civil War Interpreted by Marx and Engels," *Science & Society* 12, no. 1 (1948): 130–56.
55. John Gurney, "Gerrard Winstanley and the Left," *Past & Present* 235, no. 1 (2017): 179–206. For a critical historiography of this interpretation, see Ariel Hessayon, "Fabricating Radical Traditions," *Cromohs Virtual Seminars. Recent Historiographical Trends of the British Studies* (2006), http://www.fupress.net/public/journals/49/Seminar/hessayon2_radical.html.
56. David Leopold, "'Socialist Turnips': The Young Friedrich Engels and the Feasibility of Communism," *Political Theory* 40, no. 3 (2012): 354, 377fn111; Christian Goodwillie and Glendyne R. Wergland, *Shaker Autobiographies, Biographies and Testimonies, 1806–1907*, vol. 1 (London: Pickering & Chatto, 2014), xv.
57. Luther's arguments in *Against the Murdering and Robbing Hordes of Peasants* (1525) strongly condemn the peasants for violent uprising. For further analysis, see Robert Kolb, "Luther on Peasants and Princes," *Lutheran Quarterly* 23, no. 2 (2009): 125–46.
58. Karl Marx, Friedrich Engels, and Robert C. Tucker, *The Marx-Engels Reader*, 2nd ed. (New York: W.W. Norton, 1978), 60–61.
59. Friedrich Engels, *The German Revolutions: The Peasant War in Germany, and Germany: Revolution and Counter-Revolution*, trans. Leonard Krieger (Chicago: University of Chicago Press, 1967), 38–52.
60. John Fitzgerald, "Equality, Modernity, and Gender in Chinese Nationalism," in *Performing "Nation": Gender Politics in Literature, Theater, and the Visual Arts of China and Japan, 1880–1940*, ed. Doris Croissant, Catherine Vance Yeh, and Joshua S. Mostow (Leiden: Brill, 2008), 39.
61. Vincent Yu-Chung Shih, *The Taiping Ideology* (Tokyo: University of Tokyo Press, 1967), 230.
62. Louise Marlow, *Hierarchy and Egalitarianism in Islamic Thought* (New York: Cambridge University Press, 1997), 14–36.
63. Malcolm X, *The Autobiography of Malcolm X as Told to Alex Haley* (New York: Ballentine Books, 2015), 347.
64. Jack A. Goldstone, *Revolution and Rebellion in the Early Modern World* (Berkeley: University of California Press, 1991), 387.
65. Charles B. Jones, "Buddhism and Marxism in Taiwan: Lin Qiuwu's Religious Socialism and Its Legacy in Modern Times," *Journal of Global Buddhism* 1 (2000): 82–111.

66. James Mark Shields, *Against Harmony: Progressive and Radical Buddhism in Modern Japan* (New York: Oxford University Press, 2017). Fabio Rambelli, *Zen Anarchism: The Egalitarian Dharma of Uchiyama Gudo* (Berkeley: Institute of Buddhist Studies and BDK America, 2013).
67. Michael Kleen, "Feasting at God's Table," https://michaelkleen.com/2016/11/24/feasting-at-gods-table/; R. Marie Griffith, "Body Salvation: New Thought, Father Divine, and the Feast of Material Pleasures," *Religion and American Culture: A Journal of Interpretation* 11, no. 2 (2001): 119–53; Judith Weisenfeld, *New World a-Coming: Black Religion and Racial Identity During the Great Migration* (New York: New York University Press, 2016), 73–86.
68. Prithvi Datta Chandra Shobhi, "Pre-Modern Communities and Modern Histories: Narrating Virasaiva and Lingayat Selves" (PhD dissertation, University of Chicago, 2005), esp. 71–80.
69. Gil Ben-Herut, *Śiva's Saints: The Origins of Devotion in Kannada according to Harihara's Ragaḷegaḷu* (New York: Oxford University Press, 2017), 93–102.
70. Louis E. Fenech and W. H. McLeod, *Historical Dictionary of Sikhism*, 3rd ed. (Lanham: Rowman & Littlefield, 2014), 108–09.
71. Michel Desjardins and Ellen Desjardins, "Food That Builds Community: The Sikh Langar in Canada," *Cuizine* 1, no. 2 (2009), https://id.erudit.org/iderudit/037851ar.
72. Ibid., 18.
73. Ronki Ram, "Social Exclusion, Resistance and Deras: Exploring the Myth of Casteless Sikh Society in Punjab," *Economic and Political Weekly* 42, no. 40 (2007): 4066–74; Rajkumar Hans, "Making Sense of Dalit Sikh History," in *Dalit Studies*, ed. Ramnarayan S. Rawat and K. Satyanarayana (Durham: Duke University Press, 2016); Harish K. Puri, "Scheduled Castes in Sikh Community: A Historical Perspective," *Economic and Political Weekly* 38, no. 26 (2003): 2693–701.
74. Pechilis, *The Embodiment of Bhakti*, 4.
75. Zelliot, "The Medieval Bhakti Movement in History," 143.
76. J. Barton Scott, "Luther in the Tropics: Karsandas Mulji and the Colonial 'Reformation' of Hinduism," *Journal of the American Academy of Religion* 83, no. 1 (2015): 182.
77. Timothy S. Dobe, "Dayānanda Sarasvati as Irascible Ṛṣi: The Personal and Performed Authority of a Text," *The Journal of Hindu Studies* 4, no. 1 (2011): 80.
78. Louis Dumont, *Homo Hierarchicus: The Caste System and Its Implications*, trans. Mark Sainsbury, Louis Dumont, and Basia Gulati, revised ed. (Delhi: Oxford University Press, 1966 [1980]), 236–38.
79. Ibid., 285.
80. See Steve Barnett, Lina Fruzzetti, and Akos Ostor, "Hierarchy Purified: Notes on Dumont and His Critics," *The Journal of Asian Studies* 35, no. 4 (1976): 627–46 and R. S. Khare, *Caste, Hierarchy, and Individualism: Indian Critiques of Louis Dumont's Contributions* (New Delhi: Oxford University Press, 2006).
81. Jonathan Parry, "Egalitarian Values in a Hierarchical Society," *South Asian Review* 7, no. 2 (1974): 116.
82. Ibid., 117.

83. I appreciate Novetzke's attempt to distinguish between the latent "sonic equality" manifested in bhakti traditions' vernacularity and later, more ideological programs of social equality that followed. Although theoretically appealing, it is speculative (and unavoidably so, with so little historical material to go on) for interpreting 13th- to 15th-century history. *The Quotidian Revolution*, 283–84.
84. Jon Keune, "Pedagogical Otherness: The Use of Muslims and Untouchables in Some Hindu Devotional Literature," *Journal of the American Academy of Religion* 84, no. 3 (2016): 727–49.
85. For helpful recent discussions of this problem, see the essays in Kerry P. C. San Chirico, Rachel J. Smith, and Rico G. Monge, eds., *Hagiography and Religious Truth: Case Studies in the Abrahamic and Dharmic Traditions* (London: Bloomsbury Academic, 2016).
86. Massimo A. Rondolino, *Cross-Cultural Perspectives on Hagiographical Strategies: A Comparative Study of the Standard Lives of St. Francis and Milarepa* (New York: Routledge, 2017), esp. 1–5, 12–17.
87. Novetzke, *The Quotidian Revolution*, 120–27.
88. Pechilis, *The Embodiment of Bhakti*.
89. For some preliminary considerations of corporeal narratology, see Daniel Punday, *Narrative Bodies: Toward a Corporeal Narratology* (New York: Palgrave Macmillan, 2003), esp. 1–15, 185–90.
90. Novetzke, *The Quotidian Revolution*, 43–47. Novetzke carefully notes the continued roles of brahman authors in modulating the quotidian world in writing.
91. Anna Schultz, *Singing a Hindu Nation: Marathi Devotional Performance and Nationalism* (New York: Oxford University Press, 2013), 2.
92. E. P. Thompson, *The Making of the English Working Class* (New York: Pantheon Books, 1964), 12.
93. Bruno Latour, *Reassembling the Social: An Introduction to Actor-Network-Theory* (Oxford: Oxford University Press, 2005), 2–5.
94. "Who Were the Untouchables," in B. R. Ambedkar, *Dr. Babasaheb Ambedkar: Writings and Speeches* (New Delhi: Dr. Ambedkar Foundation, 1979 [2014]), 7:329.

Chapter 2

1. Krishna Sharma, *Bhakti and the Bhakti Movement: A New Perspective* (New Delhi: Munshiram Manoharlal Publishers, 1987).
2. D. R. Nagaraj, "Critical Tensions in the History of Kannada Literary Culture," in *Literary Cultures in History: Reconstructions from South Asia*, ed. Sheldon Pollock (Berkeley: University of California Press, 2003), 347, 56–59; Jon Keune, "Eknāth in Context: The Literary, Social, and Political Milieus of an Early Modern Saint-Poet," *South Asian History and Culture* 6, no. 1 (2015): 70–71; Sheldon Pollock, "Literary History, Indian History, World History," *Social Scientist* 23, no. 10/12 (1995): 131–32; *The Language of the Gods in the World of Men* (Berkeley: University of California

Press, 2006), 423–24; David Gordon White, *Kiss of the Yoginī: "Tantric Sex" in Its South Asian Contexts* (Chicago: University of Chicago Press, 2003), 2–7.

3. Ibid., 13.
4. Current scholarly opinions vary widely on possible composition dates of the *BhP*, from as early the 4th century CE (Ravi Gupta and Kenneth Valpey, *The Bhāgavata Purāṇa: Sacred Text and Living Tradition* (New York: Columbia University Press, 2013), 13) to the 10th century CE (Friedhelm Hardy, *Viraha-Bhakti: The Early History of Kṛṣṇa Devotion in South India* (Delhi: Oxford University Press, 1983), 511–26). The latter gives weight to the fact that the first commentary on the *BhP* (by Madhva) appeared only around 1300. I am grateful to Aleksandar Uskanov and Abhishek Ghosh for discussion of this point.
5. John S. Hawley, *A Storm of Songs: India and the Idea of the Bhakti Movement* (Cambridge MA: Harvard University Press, 2015), 1–9; Pechilis, *The Embodiment of Bhakti*, 13–16.
6. John E. Cort, "Bhakti in the Early Jain Tradition: Understanding Devotional Religion in South Asia," *History of Religions* 42, no. 1 (2002): 72.
7. Karel Werner, "Love and Devotion in Buddhism," in *Love Divine: Studies in Bhakti and Devotional Mysticism*, ed. Karel Werner (Richmond, Surrey: Curzon Press, 1993), 37–51; Andy Rotman, *Thus Have I Seen: Visualizing Faith in Early Indian Buddhism* (New York: Oxford University Press, 2009), 39–44.
8. Rāmacandra Kavibhāratī and Haraprasād Śāstrī, "Bhakti Śataka: One Hundred Slokas on Reverence and Love," *The Buddhist Text Society of India* 1, no. 2 (1893). I am grateful to Upali Sraman for introducing me to this text and describing his encounter with it while studying in Sri Lanka.
9. Francesca Orsini and Stefano Pellò, "Bhakti in Persian," Unpublished paper given at *21st European Conference on Modern South Asian Studies* (Bonn, 2010). Also see articles in a special issue of the *Journal of Hindu Studies* 6, no. 1 (2013).
10. Email correspondence, Rich Freeman, September 17, 2017. Freeman suspects that local Christians before 1599 drew more on a Syriac than Sanskritic idiom for literary productions. Records of popular Malayalam Christian folk songs (*mārgamkaḷi*, whose exact historicity is uncertain) do not refer to bhakti.
11. Susan Bayly, *Saints, Goddesses and Kings: Muslims and Christians in South Indian Society, 1700–1900* (Cambridge: Cambridge University Press, 1989), 390.
12. Soosai Arokiasamy, "Dharma, Hindu and Christian according to Roberto De Nobili: Analysis of Its Meaning and Its Use in Hinduism and Christianity" (PhD dissertation, Pontifical Gregorian University, 1986), 251.
13. Ananya Chakravarti, "Between Bhakti and Pietà: Untangling Emotion in Marāṭhī Christian Poetry," *History of Religions* 56, no. 4 (2017): esp. 374–87; Alexander Henn, *Hindu-Catholic Encounters in Goa: Religion, Colonialism, and Modernity* (Bloomington: Indiana University Press, 2014), 65–77.
14. For example, Thomas Stephens and Nelson Falcao, *Phādar Thomas Sṭīphanskṛt Khristapurāṇa* (Beṅgaluru: Khristu Jyotī Pablikeśans, 2010), 6 (1.1.30) and 594 (2.2.29). For a discussion of Stephens' view of bhakti as a prerequisite for salvation, see

Nelson Falcao, *Kristapurāṇa: A Christian-Hindu Encounter* (Anand, Gujarat: Gujarat Sahitya Prakash, 2003), 180–87.

15. Bartholomaeus Ziegenbalg et al., *Bibliotheca Malabarica: Bartholomäus Ziegenbalg's Tamil Library*, Collection Indologie (Pondicherry: École Française D'extrême-Orient, 2012).
16. Hephzibah Israel, *Religious Transactions in Colonial South India: Language, Translation, and the Making of Protestant Identity* (New York: Palgrave Macmillan, 2011), 199.
17. William Ward, *A View of the History, Literature, and Mythology of the Hindoos: Including a Minute Description of Their Manners and Customs, and Translations from Their Principal Works*, vol. 2 (Serampore: Printed at the Mission Press, 1818), viii–ix.
18. Elijah Hoole, *Madras, Mysore, and the South of India: Or, a Personal Narrative of a Mission to Those Countries from 1820 to 1828*, 2nd ed. (London: Longman, Brown, Green and Longmans, 1844), 380. Cited in Geoffrey A. Oddie, *Imagined Hinduism: British Protestant Missionary Constructions of Hinduism, 1793–1900* (Thousand Oaks, CA: Sage, 2006), 270.
19. For example, the stories about the deity Viṭhobā and pilgrimages to Āḷandī appear with some frequency in the Anglo-Marathi serial *Dnyānoday* from 1844 onward. Gaṅgādhar Morje, *Jñānoday Lekhan-Sār-Sūcī: Khaṇḍa Pahilā Bhāg Pahilā, Jun 1842 Te Dec 1850* (Mumbaī: Mahārāṣṭra Rājya Sāhitya āṇi Saṃskṛtī Maṇḍaḷ, 1986).
20. John Murray Mitchell, "The Story of Tukaráma. From the Marathí-Prákrit," *Journal of the Bombay Branch of the Royal Asiatic Society* 3, no. 1 (1849): 1–3.
21. John Murray Mitchell, "Paṇḍharpūr," *Indian Antiquary* 11 (1882): 149–56.
22. By "Maratha," Mitchell almost certainly meant Marathi speakers and inhabitants of the erstwhile Maratha state, not the *jāti* cluster that now bears that name. See Prachi Deshpande, "Caste as Maratha: Social Categories, Colonial Policy and Early Twentieth-Century Maharashtra," *Indian Economic Social History Review* 41, no. 1 (2004): 9–14.
23. Correspondence held at the National Library of Scotland, cited in Oddie, *Imagined Hinduism*, 283.
24. Jonathan Z. Smith, "Religion, Religions, Religious," in *Critical Terms for Religious Studies*, ed. Mark C. Taylor (Chicago: University of Chicago Press, 1998), 275–80; Brian K. Pennington, *Was Hinduism Invented?: Britons, Indians, and Colonial Construction of Religion* (New York: Oxford University Press, 2005), 4–7; Daniel Vaca, "'Great Religions' as Peacemaker: What Unitarian Infighting Did for Comparative Religion," *History of Religions* 53, no. 2 (2013): 115–20.
25. J. Murray Mitchell, *Hinduism Past and Present: With an Account of Recent Hindu Reformers and a Brief Comparison between Hinduism and Christianity*, 2nd ed. (London: Religious Tract Society, 1897); *The Great Religions of India* (Edinburgh: Oliphant, 1905); John Murray Mitchell and William Muir, *Two Old Faiths; Essays on the Religions of the Hindus and the Mohammedans* (New York: Chautauqua Press, 1891).
26. Sharma, *Bhakti and the Bhakti Movement*, 8–15.

27. The collective hagiographies of Nābhādās (16th c.) and Mahīpati (18th c.) freely employ the terms "bhakti" and "bhakta" but not as labels of groups in the sense of bhakti traditions.
28. H. H. Wilson, *Sketch of the Religious Sects of the Hindus* (London: Christian Literature Society, 1846 [1904]), 82.
29. George A. Grierson, "Bhakti-Marga," in *Encyclopedia of Religion and Ethics*, ed. J. Hastings (Edinburgh: T&T Clark, 1909), 539–51. For more on Grierson and his legacy, see Vijay Pinch, "Bhakti and the British Empire," *Past & Present* 179, no. 1 (2003): 173–80; John Stratton Hawley, "The Four Churches of the Reformation," *Modern Asian Studies* 52, no. 5 (2018): 1457–85.
30. Sharma, *Bhakti and the Bhakti Movement*, 8.
31. Pinch, "Bhakti and the British Empire," 172–73.
32. Vasudha Dalmia, *The Nationalization of Hindu Traditions* (Delhi: Oxford University Press, 1997), esp. 340–81.
33. Hawley points out an isolated reference to bhakti movement by Sophia Dobson Collette in the 1870s, but this seems to have been forgotten. Hawley, *A Storm of Songs*, 264.
34. Arvind-Pal Mandair, *Religion and the Specter of the West: Sikhism, India, Postcoloniality, and the Politics of Translation* (New York: Columbia University Press, 2009), 78–84.
35. Max Weber, *The Religion of India: The Sociology of Hinduism and Buddhism*, trans. Hans Heinrich Gerth and Don Martindale (Glencoe IL: Free Press, 1958), 298–317.
36. Mitchell and Muir, *Two Old Faiths*, 50–51.
37. John Stephenson [Stevenson], "On the Ante-Brahmanical Worship of the Hindus (from P. 195 V.5 No.1)," *Journal of the Royal Asiatic Society of Great Britain and Ireland* 5, no. 2 (1839): 264–67; John Stevenson and John Wilson, "On the Ante-Brahmanical Worship of the Hindus in the Dekhan," *Journal of the Royal Asiatic Society of Great Britain and Ireland* 5, no. 1 (1839): 189–97; John Stephenson [Stevenson], "On the Ante-Brahmanical Worship of the Hindus in the Dekhan (Continued from P. 267, Vol V)," *Journal of the Royal Asiatic Society of Great Britain and Ireland* 6, no. 2 (1841): 239–41.
38. Leonard John Sedgwick, "Bhakti," *Journal of the Bombay Branch of the Royal Asiatic Society* 23 (1914): 109.
39. A good example of this is the mythological framework of Mahīpati, who depicts Viṣṇu telling deities and sages in his divine court to become incarnate on earth as various saints. Justin Abbott and Narhar R. Godbole, *Stories of Indian Saints: A Translation of Mahipati's Marathi Bhaktavijaya* (Delhi: Motilal Banarsidass, 1933 [1988]), 6–7. See also Christian Novetzke, "The Theographic and the Historiographic in an Indian Sacred Life Story," *Sikh Formations* 3, no. 2 (2007): 169–84.
40. I am grateful to Leslie Orr and Anne Monius for very insightful conversations about this topic.
41. Indira V. Peterson, "Singing of a Place: Pilgrimage as Metaphor and Motif in the Tevaram Songs of the Tamil Śaivite Saints," *Journal of the American Oriental Society* 102, no. 1 (1982): 69–71.

42. George W. Spencer, "The Sacred Geography of the Tamil Shaivite Hymns," *Numen* 17, no. 3 (1970): 234–36.
43. Indira V. Peterson, "Lives of the Wandering Singers: Pilgrimage and Poetry in Tamil Śaivite Hagiography," *History of Religions* 22, no. 4 (1983): 352.
44. Leslie C. Orr, "The Sacred Landscape of Tamil Śaivism: Plotting Place in the Realm of Devotion," in *Mapping the Chronology of Bhakti: Milestones, Stepping Stones, and Stumbling Stones*, ed. Valérie Gillet (Pondicherry: Institut Français de Pondichéry, 2014), 198–201.
45. Māṇikkavācakar, *The Tiruvāçagam*, trans. G. U. Pope (Oxford: Clarendon Press, 1900), lxvii.
46. Ravi (aka V. Ravindran) Vaitheespara, "Discourses of Empowerment: Missionary Orientalism in the Development of Dravidian Nationalism," in *Nation Work: Asian Elites and National Identities*, ed. Timothy Brook and Andre Schmid (Ann Arbor: University of Michigan Press, 2000), 76–78.
47. I am grateful to Dean Accardi for orienting me on perceptions of bhakti's impact in Kashmir.
48. George Abraham Grierson and Lionel David Barnett, *Lallā-Vākyāni: Or, the Wise Sayings of Lal Dĕd, a Mystic Poetess of Ancient Kashmīr* (London: Royal Asiatic Society, 1920), 1–3; Mohammad Ishaq Khan, "The Rishi Movement as Social Force in Medieval Kashmir," in *Religious Movements in South Asia 600–1800*, ed. David N. Lorenzen (New York: Oxford University Press, 2004), 136. For a critical historiography of the notion of Kashmiriyat, see Rattan Lal Hangloo, "Kashmiriyat: The Voice of the Past Misconstrued," in *The Parchment of Kashmir: History, Society, and Polity*, ed. Nyla Ali Khan (New York: Palgrave Macmillan, 2012).
49. Khan, "The Rishi Movement as Social Force in Medieval Kashmir," 133.
50. S. S. Toshkani, ed. *Lal Ded: The Great Kashmiri Saint-Poetess* (New Delhi: A.P.H. Publishing Corporation, 2000).
51. Dalmia, *The Nationalization of Hindu Traditions*, esp. 21–28.
52. Ibid., 370.
53. Ibid., 390.
54. Ibid., 375.
55. Hawley, *A Storm of Songs*, 275.
56. V. Raghavan, *The Great Integrators: The Saint-Singers of India*, Patel Memorial Lectures, 1964 (Delhi: Publications Division, Ministry of Information and Broadcasting, 1966), 3–7, 30–36.
57. Hawley, *A Storm of Songs*, 20–28. V. Raghavan and William J. Jackson, *The Power of the Sacred Name: V. Raghavan's Studies in Nāmasiddhānta and Indian Culture* (Delhi: Sri Satguru Publications, 1994), 317–27.
58. Mahadev Govind Ranade, *Rise of the Maratha Power* (Delhi: Ministry of Information and Broadcasting, 1900 [1961]), 3.
59. Ibid., 76.
60. Hawley, *A Storm of Songs*, 31. Of course, at the time that Sen and Dvivedī wrote, the idea of an Indian national body was still a prospect, not a reality.

61. Ibid., 232. Based on my research with Marathi public school textbooks, I think Hawley overestimates the influence that Hindi textbooks had on teaching about bhakti and the bhakti movement outside the Hindi Belt. Keune, "Eknāth Remembered and Reformed," 18.
62. Novetzke, "Bhakti and Its Public," 16.
63. Ibid., 255.
64. Ibid., 20.
65. Novetzke, *The Quotidian Revolution*, 3.
66. Ibid., 31.
67. John Stratton Hawley, "Bhakti, Democracy, and the Study of Religion," in *Three Bhakti Voices* (New Delhi: Oxford University Press, 2005), 322.
68. Raghavan, *The Great Integrators: The Saint-Singers of India*, 18.
69. Charles N. E. Eliot, "Hinduism in Assam," *Journal of the Royal Asiatic Society of Great Britain and Ireland* (1910): 161, 169, 174, 180.
70. W. B. (Vasudev Balwant) Patwardhan, "Wilson Philological Lectures, 1917, Lecture 5: Ekanath and His Circle," *Fergusson College Magazine* 9, no. 3 (1918): 97.
71. "Wilson Philological Lectures, 1917, Lecture 7: What Did the Bhakti School Do for Marathi Literature?," *Fergusson College Magazine* 10, no. 1 (1919): 34.
72. *Shri Ekanath: A Sketch of His Life and Teachings* (Madras: G. A. Natesan & Co., 1918 [1935]), 37.
73. Ramcandra Dattatreya Ranade, *Mysticism in Maharashtra* (Delhi: Motilal Banarsidass, 1933 [1982]), 209. Ranade only mentioned that the passage came from Patwardhan, without specifying where.
74. Burchett, "Bhakti Rhetoric in the Hagiography of 'Untouchable' Saints," 113; David N. Lorenzen, "Bhakti," in *The Hindu World*, ed. Sushil Mittal and Gene Thursby (New York: Routledge, 2004), 185–86.
75. Lorenzen, "Bhakti," 193.
76. The *Mahābhārata* Adīparva 1.267–68, *Bhāgavata Purāṇa* 1.4.25, *Devī Purāṇa* 1.3.21, and the *Narsiṃha Purāṇa*. Jayant Gadkari, *Society and Religion: From Rugveda to Puranas* (Bombay: Popular Prakashan, 1996), 180. Cited in Novetzke, *The Quotidian Revolution*, 311fn37.
77. Ludo Rocher, *The Purāṇas*, Vol. 2—Epics and Sanskrit Religious Literature, A History of Indian Literature (Wiesbaden: Harrassowitz, 1986), 16.
78. Nārāyaṇa Bhaṭṭa and Richard Salomon, *The Bridge to the Three Holy Cities = the Sāmānya-Praghaṭṭaka of Nārāyaṇa Bhaṭṭa's Tristhalīsetu* (Delhi: Motilal Banarsidass, 1985), vv. 37–39, 196–98.
79. Ibid., xvi–xvii, 256–57. I am grateful to Rosalind O'Hanlon for calling my attention to this text.
80. The *Bhāver Gītā* of the Kārtabhāja sect in Bengal, cited in Hugh B. Urban, *Songs of Ecstasy: Tantric and Devotional Songs from Colonial Bengal* (New York: Oxford University Press, 2001), 9.

81. The *Mahanirvana Tantra*, quoted in Wendy editor Doniger, *The Hindus: An Alternative History* (Oxford: Oxford University Press, 2010), 435.
82. Teun Goudriaan and Sanjukta Gupta, *Hindu Tantric and Śākta Literature*, A History of Indian Literature (Wiesbaden: Harrassowitz, 1981), 100; Hugh B. Urban, *The Power of Tantra: Religion, Sexuality, and the Politics of South Asian Studies* (New York: I.B. Tauris, 2010), 105.
83. Travis L. Smith, "Tantras," in *Brill Encyclopedia of Hinduism*, ed. Knut Axel Jacobsen (Leiden: Brill, 2010), 174.
84. Hugh Urban, "Elitism and Esotericism: Strategies of Secrecy and Power in South Indian Tantra and French Freemasonry," *Numen* 44, no. 1 (1997): 6.
85. William R. Pinch, *Warrior Ascetics and Indian Empires* (New York: Cambridge University Press, 2006), 44, 122.
86. Louis Dumont, *Homo Hierarchicus: The Caste System and Its Implications* (Chicago: University of Chicago Press, 1980), esp. ch1 and ch11.
87. Martin Fárek, "Were Shramana and Bhakti Movements against the Caste System?," in *Western Foundations of the Caste System*, ed. Martin Fárek, et al. (Cham, Switzerland: Palgrave Macmillan, 2017), 127–29.
88. Monier Monier-Williams, *Religious Thought and Life in India: An Account of the Religions of the Indian Peoples, Based on a Life's Study of Their Literature and on Personal Investigations in Their Own Country* (London: John Murray, 1883), 64.
89. Ibid., 114.
90. Grierson, "Bhakti-Marga," 545.
91. Chandra Shobhi, "Pre-Modern Communities and Modern Histories," esp. Introduction and ch1.
92. John S. Hawley, "Bhakti," in *Encyclopedia of Asian History*, ed. Ainslee T. Embree (New York: Charles Scribner's Sons, 1988), 156; James G. Lochtefeld, *The Illustrated Encyclopedia of Hinduism*, vol. 1, 1st ed., 2 vols. (New York: Rosen, 2002), 99.
93. B. R. Ambedkar, *Annihilation of Caste*, Annotated critical ed. (London: Verso, 2014), 337.
94. M. G. S. Narayanan and Kesavan Veluthat, "Bhakti Movement in South India," in *The Feudal Order: State, Society, and Ideology in Early Medieval India*, ed. D. N. Jha (New Delhi: Manohar, 2000), 406–07.
95. Novetzke, *The Quotidian Revolution*, 305.
96. Lele, "Community, Discourse and Critique in Jnanesvar," 104–06.
97. R. Champakalakshmi, "From Devotion and Dissent to Dominance: The Bhakti of the Tamil Alvars and Nayanars," in *Religious Movements in South Asia 600–1800*, ed. David N. Lorenzen (New Delhi: Oxford University Press, 2005), 70.
98. Ranade, *Rise of the Maratha Power*, 76.
99. For further discussions of bhakti politics, see essays in Christian Lee Novetzke et al., eds., *Bhakti and Power: Social Location and Religious Affect in India's Religion of the Heart* (Seattle: University of Washington Press, 2019).

Chapter 3

1. Anant Kakba Priolkar, *The Printing Press in India, Its Beginnings and Early Development, Being a Quatercentenary Commemoration Study of the Advent of Printing in India, in 1556* (Bombay: Marathi Samshodhana Mandala, 1958).
2. Ibid., 86.
3. For more on Marathi and Gujarati vernacular presses in Bombay, see Veena Naregal, *Language Politics, Elites, and the Public Sphere: Western India under Colonialism* (London: Anthem Press, 2002), 168–81.
4. Novetzke, *Religion and Public Memory*, 100.
5. Ibid., 124.
6. Naregal, *Language Politics, Elites, and the Public Sphere*, 22.
7. Ibid., 32.
8. Ibid., 21.
9. On British agendas within "liberalism" in colonial contexts, see Uday Singh Mehta, *Liberalism and Empire: A Study in Nineteenth-Century British Liberal Thought* (Chicago: University of Chicago Press, 1999). For more discussion of "Indian liberalism" among intellectuals in Bombay and Calcutta, see Christopher A. Bayly, *Recovering Liberties: Indian Thought in the Age of Liberalism and Empire* (Cambridge: Cambridge University Press, 2012), 2–7.
10. Ganesh Gangadhar Jambhekar, ed. *Memoirs and Writings of Acharya Bal Gangadhar Shastri Jambhekar*, vol. 1 (Poona: Ganesh Gangadhar Jambhekar, 1950), iv.
11. Bayly, *Recovering Liberties*, 123.
12. Ibid., 121; Ganesh Gangadhar Jambhekar, ed. *Memoirs and Writings of Acharya Bal Gangadhar Shastri Jambhekar*, vol. 2 (Poona: Ganesh Gangadhar Jambhekar, 1950), 2–108.
13. *Memoirs and Writings of Acharya Bal Gangadhar Shastri Jambhekar*, vol. 2, 296–98.
14. Kenneth W. Jones, *Socio-Religious Reform Movements in British India* (Cambridge: Cambridge University Press, 1989), 138.
15. J. V. Naik, "'Dharmavivechan': An Early 19th Century Rationalistic Reform Manifesto in Western India," in *Social Reform Movements in India: A Historical Perspective*, ed. G. T. Kulkarni, M. R. Kantak, and V. D. Divekar (Pune: Bharat Itihas Samshodhak Mandal: Popular Prakashan, 1991), 63.
16. Anant Kākbā Priyoḷkar, *Paramahaṃsa Sabhā va tīce Adhyakṣa Rāmcandra Bāḷkṛṣṇa* (Mumbaī: Mumbaī Marāṭhī Grantha Saṅgrahālaya, 1966), 63–122.
17. Jones, *Socio-Religious Reform Movements in British India*, 140.
18. Priyoḷkar, *Paramahaṃsa Sabhā va tīce Adhyakṣa Rāmcandra Bāḷkṛṣṇa*, 10.
19. Bhāskar Dāmodar Pāḷande, *Ratnamālā: Hī Parameśvar Prārthanecī Kavitā Sarva Jñātīñcyā Lokāṅkaritāṃ*, 3rd ed. (Puṇe: Dī-Brāñc Buddhiprakāśa Chā. Chā., 1847 [1895]).
20. Jones, *Socio-Religious Reform Movements in British India*, 141.
21. Vans Kennedy, *Dictionary of the Maratha Language* (Bombay: Courier Press, 1824), iv. Cited in Anant Kākbā Priyoḷkar and Parśurām Ballāḷ Goḍbole, eds., *Navnīt Athvā Marāṭhī Kavitāṃce Veṃce* (Puṇe: Śubhadā-Sārasvat Prakāśan, 1990), 12.

22. *Navnīt Athvā Marāṭhī Kavitāṃce Veṃce*, 13–14.
23. Naregal, *Language Politics, Elites, and the Public Sphere*, 171.
24. Ibid., 185.
25. Priyoḷkar and Goḍbole, *Navnīt Athvā Marāṭhī Kavitāṃce Veṃce*, 17–28.
26. Ibid., 17–19.
27. Janārdana Rāmcandrajī, *Kavicaritra, Mhaṇje Hindusthānātīl Prācīn Va Arvācīn Kavi Āṇi Granthakāra Yāñce Itihāsa* (Mumbaī: Gaṇpat Kṛṣṇājī Chāpkhānā, 1860).
28. Cavelly Venkat Ramaswamie, *Biographical Sketches of Dekkan Poets, Being Memoirs of Several . . . Bards Both Ancient and Modern Who Have Flourished in . . . the Indian Peninsula; Compiled from Authentic Documents* (Calcutta, 1829). For more on the work of Rāmasvāmī and his two brothers with Mackenzie, see Rama Sundari Mantena, *The Origins of Modern Historiography in India: Antiquarianism and Philology, 1780–1880* (New York: Palgrave Macmillan, 2012), ch2.
29. Mahadev L. Apte, "Lokahitavadi and V. K. Chiplunkar: Spokesmen of Change in Nineteenth-Century Maharashtra," *Modern Asian Studies* 7, no. 2 (1973): 195.
30. Lokahitavādī, *Lokahitavādī: Samagra Vāṅmay*, 2 vols. (Mumbaī: Mahārāshṭra Rājya Sāhitya Samskṛti Maṇḍaḷa, 1988), 1:198–99.
31. Frank F. Conlon, "The Polemic Process in Nineteenth Century Maharashtra: Vishnubawa Brahmachari and Hindu Revival," in *Religious Controversy in British India: Dialogues in South Asian Languages*, ed. Kenneth W. Jones (Albany: State University of New York Press, 1982), 9.
32. Matthew Lederle, *Philosophical Trends in Modern Maharāṣṭra* (Bombay: Popular Prakashan, 1976), 192.
33. Ibid., 194.
34. Conlon, "The Polemic Process in Nineteenth Century Maharashtra," 10. Conlon cites Rāmcandra Pāṇḍuraṅg Ājrekar, *Śrī Viṣṇubābā Brahmacārī Yāñce Caritra* (Mumbaī: Ātmārām Kaṇhobā, 1872). I am grateful to Frank Conlon for generously sharing with me his photocopies of some of Brahmacārī's rare publications.
35. Conlon, "The Polemic Process in Nineteenth Century Maharashtra," 22.
36. Ibid., 20.
37. Ibid., 15.
38. Tryambak Visnu Parvate, *Mahadev Govind Ranade. A Biography* (Bombay: Asia Publishing House, 1963), 40.
39. Rājārām Rāmkṛṣṇa Bhāgvat, *Lekhasaṅgraha - 1*, ed. Durgā Bhāgvat, vol. 4, *Rājārāmśāstrī Bhāgvat Yāñce Nivaḍak Sāhitya* (Puṇe: Varadā Buks, 1979), 3.
40. *Lekhasaṅgraha - 2*, ed. Durgā Bhāgvat, vol. 5, *Rājārāmśāstrī Bhāgvat Yāñce Nivaḍak Sāhitya* (Puṇe: Varadā Buks, 1979), 227.
41. "Eknāthāñce Caritra," in *Rājārāmśāstrī Bhāgvat Yāñce Nivaḍak Sāhitya - Lekhasaṅgraha - 1*, ed. Durgā Bhāgvat, vol. 4 (Puṇe: Varadā Buks, 1890 [1979]), 76. *arthāt devace gharī koṇtyāhī prakārcā jātibhed nāhī.*
42. Ibid., 110–11. *dharmasambandhi moṭhī caḷvaḷ.*
43. Ibid., 12.
44. G. M. Pawar, *The Life and Works of Maharshi Vitthal Ramji Shindé (1873–1944)*, trans. Sudharkar Marathe (New Delhi: Sahitya Akademi, 2013), 105.

45. Dvārkānāth Govind Vaidya, *Prārthanāsamājācā Itihās* (Mumbaī: Prārthanā Samāj, 1927); J. V. Naik, "Social Composition of the Prarthana Samaj: A Statistical Analysis," *Proceedings of the Indian History Congress* 48 (1987):502–11; "D. G. Vaidya and the Prarthana Samaj," in *Region, Nationality and Religion*, ed. A. R. Kulkarni and N. K. Wagle (Mumbai: Popular Prakashan, 1999).
46. Aparna Devare, "Historicity Meets Its Limits: M.G. Ranade and a Faith-Based Private/Public Sphere," *Postcolonial Studies* 12, no. 1 (2009): 47–67; *History and the Making of a Modern Hindu Self* (New Delhi: Routledge, 2011), 93–152.
47. Mahadev Govind Ranade, *The Miscellaneous Writings of . . . Mr Justice M.G. Ranade* (Poona: Ramabai Ranade, 1915); *Religious and Social Reform: A Collection of Essays and Speeches* (Bombay: Gopal Narayen and Co., 1902).
48. Ibid., 198–228.
49. Ibid., 250–78.
50. Mahādev Govind Rānaḍe and Rāmābāī Rānaḍe, *Nyā. Mū. Mahādev Govind Rānaḍe Hyāñcīṃ Dharmapar Vyākhyāneṃ*, 4th ed. (Mumbaī: Karnāṭak Press, 1940).
51. Ranade, *Rise of the Maratha Power*.
52. Śinde's family came from Kuṇbī peasant background. See Deshpande, "Caste as Maratha."
53. Pawar, *The Life and Works of Maharshi Vitthal Ramji Shindé (1873–1944)*, 32.
54. Viṭṭhal Rāmjī Śinde, *Mājhyā Āṭhavaṇī va Anubhāva* (Puṇe: Vātsala Sāhitya Prakāśan, 1940), 44.
55. Pawar, *The Life and Works of Maharshi Vitthal Ramji Shindé (1873–1944)*, 75–80.
56. Ibid., 121–26.
57. Ibid.
58. Ibid., 182.
59. Ibid., 259.
60. Ibid., 477.
61. Ibid., 423–35. Pawar surveys various opinions and the sources on the episode, and he explains why he thinks Ambedkar's attack on Śinde was unwarranted.
62. Priyoḷkar and Goḍbole, *Navnīt Athvā Marāṭhī Kavitāṃce Veṃce*, 14.
63. Hulas Singh, *Rise of Reason: Intellectual History of 19th-Century Maharashtra*, 1st South Asia ed. (Abingdon: Routledge, 2016), 94.
64. Schultz, *Singing a Hindu Nation*, 42.
65. Ibid., 47.
66. Milind Wakankar, "System and History in Rajwade's 'Grammar' for the Dnyaneswari (1909)," in *Subalternity and Religion: The Prehistory of Dalit Empowerment in South Asia* (London and New York: Routledge, 2010).
67. Vi. Kā. Rājvāḍe, "Dāmājipant Va Viṭhyā Mahār," in *Caturtha Sammelan Vṛtta*, ed. Kanderāv Cintāman Mehendale (Puṇe: Bhārat Itihās Saṃśodhak Maṇḍaḷ, 1917).
68. Abbott and Godbole, *Stories of Indian Saints*, 2:85–99.
69. Rājvāḍe, "Dāmājipant Va Viṭhyā Mahār," 56.
70. Deshpande, *Creative Pasts*, 131–33.

71. Go. Ma. Kulkarṇī, *Marāṭhī Vāṅmaykoś (Khaṇḍa Dusrā, Bhāg Ek - Marāṭhī Granthakār I. Sa. 1878 Te 30 Epril 1960)* (Mumbaī: Mahārāṣṭra Rājya Sāhitya āṇi Saṃskṛtī Maṇḍaḷ, 2003), 93.
72. Jayā Daḍkar et al., *Saṅkṣipta Marāṭhī Vāṅmaykoś* (Mumbaī: Jī. Ār. Bhaṭkaḷ Phāuṇḍeśan, 2003), 337–38.
73. Lakṣmaṇ Rāmcandra Pāṅgārkar, *Eknāth Caritra: Caritra Āṇi Vāṅmay Darśan*, 9th ed. (Puṇe: Varadā Buks, 1910 [2003]), *pāc*.
74. Ibid.
75. Keune, "Eknāth Remembered and Reformed," 248.
76. Satyavān Meśrām, *Sant Gāḍge Mahārāj: Kāl Āṇi Kartṛtva* (Muṃbaī: Mahārāṣṭra Rājya āṇi Saṃskṛtī Maṇḍaḷ, 1998), 8.
77. P. L. Joshi, *Political Ideas and Leadership in Vidarbha* (Nagpur: Dept. of Political Science & Public Administration, Nagpur University, 1980), 288.
78. Eleanor Zelliot, "Four Radical Saints in Maharashtra," in *Religion and Society in Maharashtra*, ed. Milton Israel and N. K. Wagle (Toronto: University of Toronto Press, 1987), 138–40.
79. Schultz, *Singing a Hindu Nation*, 60–64.
80. G. N. Dandekar, "The Last *Kīrtan* of Gadge Baba," in *The Experience of Hinduism: Essays on Religion in Maharashtra*, ed. Eleanor Zelliot and Maxine Berntsen (Albany: State University of New York Press, 1988).
81. Ramcandra Dattatreya Ranade, *Pathway to God in Marathi Literature* (Bombay: Bharatiya Vidya Bhavan, 1961), 165.
82. Śaṅkar Gopāl Tuḷpuḷe, *Gurudev Rā. Da. Rānaḍe: Caritra Āṇi Tatvajñān* (Nimbāḷ, Dt. Bijāpūr, India: Śrī Gurudev Rānaḍe Samādhī Trust, 2002); S. G. Tulpule, *Mysticism in Medieval India* (Wiesbaden: Harrassowitz, 1984).
83. "The Development of Mystical Thought in Maharashtra," in *Region, Nationality and Religion*, ed. A. R. Kulkarni and N. K. Wagle (Mumbai: Popular Prakashan, 1999), 208.
84. Novetzke, *The Quotidian Revolution*, 96.
85. Tryambak Hari Āvaṭe, ed., *Gāthā Pañcak*, 5 vols. (Puṇe: Indirā Chāpkhāna, 1908).
86. Gaṃ. De. Khānolkar, ed., *Marāṭhī Vāṅmaykoś (Khaṇḍa Pahilā - Marāṭhī Granthakār, I.S. 1070–1866)* (Mumbaī: Mahārāṣṭra Rājya Sāhitya Saṃskṛti Maṇḍaḷ, 1977), 16.
87. Pra. Na. Jośī, "Svāgat," in *Śrī Sakal Santa Gāthā*, ed. Ra. Rā. Gosāvī (Puṇe: Sārthī Prakāśan, 2000), vi.
88. Rāvjī Śrīdhar Gondhaḷekar, ed., *Śrī Nāmdevācī Gāthā* (Puṇe: Jagaddhitecchu Press, 1892), Prastāvanā.
89. *Śrī Eknāthācī Gāthā* (Puṇe: Jagaddhitecchu Press, 1895), Prastāvanā.
90. Schultz, *Singing a Hindu Nation*, 32–35; Rāvjī Śrīdhar Gondhaḷekar, Pāṇḍuraṅg Ābājī Moghe, and Vāman Eknāthśāstrī Kemkar, *Kīrtantaraṅgiṇī Bhāg Dusrā* (Puṇe: Keśav Rāvjī Gondhaḷekar, 1915).
91. Novetzke refers to this person (mistakenly, I believe) by the surname Gharat rather than Paḍvaḷ. Novetzke, *Religion and Public Memory*, 195.
92. N. C. Ramanujachary, "Tookaram Tatya," *The Theosophist* 130, no. 10 (2009).
93. Khānolkar, *Marāṭhī Vāṅmaykoś*.

94. Tryambak Harī Āvaṭe, ed., *Gāthā Pañcak—Śrī Jñāneśvar Mahārāj Yāñcyā Abhaṅgācī Gāthā*, vol. 1 (Puṇe: Indirā Chāpkhāna, 1908).
95. According to a descendant, Nānāmahārāj traveled around Maharashtra collecting the manuscripts and noting down songs that people were singing. Personal communication, Kisan Mahārāj Sākhre, March 5, 2009.
96. Kulkarṇī, *Marāṭhī Vāṅmaykoś*, 155–56.
97. Ibid., 63.
98. Bhā. Paṃ. Bahiraṭ and Pa. Jñā. Bhālerāv, *Vārkarī Sampradāy: Uday Va Vikās* (Puṇe: Vhīnas Prakāśan, 1972 [1988]), 269–70.
99. Śaṅkar Vaman (Sonopant) Dāṇḍekar, *Vārkarī Pantācā Itihās*, 3rd ed. (Āḷandī: Prā. Dāṇḍekar Dhārmik Vāṅmay Prakāśan, 1927 [1966]).
100. S. B. Kadam, *Śrī Sant Cokhāmeḷā Mahārāj Yāñce Caritra Va Abhaṅga Gāthā* (Mumbaī: Mandākinī S. Kadam, 1967).
101. https://en.wikipedia.org/wiki/Bhalchandra_Pandharinath_Bahirat. Accessed July 18, 2020.
102. Bahiraṭ and Bhālerāv, *Vārkarī Sampradāy: Uday Va Vikās*.
103. Ibid.
104. Kadam, *Śrī Sant Cokhāmeḷā Mahārāj*, 6.
105. Ibid.
106. Rosalind O'Hanlon, *Caste, Conflict and Ideology: Mahatma Jotirao Phule and Low Caste Protest in Nineteenth-Century Western India* (Cambridge: University of Cambridge Press, 1985 [2002]), 72–75.
107. Dominic Vendell, "Jotirao Phule's Satyashodh and the Problem of Subaltern Consciousness," *Comparative Studies of South Asia, Africa and the Middle East* 34, no. 1 (2014): 52–53.
108. Jotīrāv Govindarāv Phule and G. P. Deshpande, *Selected Writings of Jotirao Phule* (New Delhi: Leftword, 2002), 2.
109. Deshpande adds the word "equal" here. *Āplyā utpannakartyāne nirmāṇ kelelyā pavitra adhikārācyā niyamās.*
110. Phule and Deshpande, *Selected Writings of Jotirao Phule*, 98–99.
111. Philip Constable, "Early Dalit Literature and Culture in Late Nineteenth- and Early Twentieth-Century Western India," *Modern Asian Studies* 31, no. 2 (1997): 318.
112. Phule and Deshpande, *Selected Writings of Jotirao Phule*, 128–29.
113. Ibid., 7.
114. Ibid., 8–9. This section of the *Cultivator's Whipcord* is not translated by Deshpande.
115. Jotīrāv Govindrāv Phule, *Mahātmā Phule: Samagra Vāṅmay*, ed. Ya. Di. Phaḍke, 6th ed. (Mumbāī: Mahārāṣṭra Rājya Sāhitya āṇi Saṃskṛtī Maṇḍaḷ, 2006), 497–500. These sections have not been translated yet into English.
116. Ibid., 525.
117. Phule and Deshpande, *Selected Writings of Jotirao Phule*, xi–xii.
118. Cokhāmeḷā's name technically does appear in passing, but it connotes a group of Mahārs rather than the saint.
119. Jotīrāv Govindarāv Phule, *Collected Works of Mahatma Jotirao Phule*, trans. P. G. Patil. 1st ed., vol. 2 (Bombay: Education Dept., Govt. of Maharashtra, 1991), 2, 104.

120. Ibid.
121. Phule and Deshpande, *Selected Writings of Jotirao Phule*, 18.
122. Naregal, *Language Politics, Elites, and the Public Sphere*, 52–53.
123. Johannes Quack, *Disenchanting India: Organized Rationalism and Criticism of Religion in India* (New York: Oxford University Press, 2012), 62.
124. Devare, *History and the Making of a Modern Hindu Self*, 151–52.
125. For quotations of Āgarkar on caste, see Singh, *Rise of Reason*, 95–69.
126. Quack, *Disenchanting India*, 64.
127. Gopāḷ Gaṇeś Āgarkar, "Āṇkhī Ek Śahāṇyācā Kāndā," in *Āgarkar Vāṅmay*, 3 vols. (Mumbaī: Mahārāṣtra Rājya Sāhitya āṇi Saṃskṛti Maṇḍaḷ, 1974 [1999]), 2:403.
128. Constable, "Early Dalit Literature and Culture," 318.
129. Anand Teltumbde, *Dalits: Past, Present and Future* (New York: Routledge, 2017), 38–9. According to one source, M. G. Ranade also helped Vaḷaṅkar to publish the *Vinanti Patra*. Pawar, *The Life and Works of Maharshi Vitthal Ramji Shindé (1873–1944)*, 304.
130. Constable, "Early Dalit Literature and Culture," 326. Constable mistakenly identifies Padmanji as a brahman; his Tvaṣṭa Kasar (coppersmith) community was regarded commonly as vaiśya.
131. Ibid., 332; Rao, *The Caste Question*, 51–53.
132. Constable, "Early Dalit Literature and Culture," 336.
133. Eleanor Zelliot, "Chokhamela and Eknath: Two 'Bhakti' Modes of Legitimacy for Modern Change," *Journal of Asian and African Studies* 15, no. 1–2 (1980): 141.
134. Ibid., 302fn61.
135. *From Untouchable to Dalit: Essays on the Ambedkar Movement* (New Delhi: Manohar Publications, 1992); A. K. Narain, "Dr. Ambedkar, Buddhism, and Social Change: A Reappraisal," in *Dr. Ambedkar, Buddhism, and Social Change*, ed. A. K. Narain and D. C. Ahir (Delhi: B. R. Publishing Corporation, 1994); Bhagwan Das and S. Anand, *In Pursuit of Ambedkar* (New Delhi: Navayana Pub., 2009); Christoph Jaffrelot, "Dr. Ambedkar's Strategies against Untouchability and the Caste System," *Institute of Dalit Studies Working Paper Series* 3, no. 4 (2009), http://dalitstudies.org.in/wp/0904.pdf; Aishwary Kumar, *Radical Equality: Ambedkar, Gandhi, and the Risk of Democracy*, Cultural Memory in the Past (Stanford: Stanford University Press, 2015).
136. Valerian Rodrigues, "Kabir as Ambedkar's Guru: Complex Mediations," Unpublished paper presented at *Dalits and Religion Conference* (Erfurt, 2017).
137. Dhananjay Keer, *Dr. Ambedkar: Life and Mission*, 2nd ed. (Bombay: Popular Prakashan, 1962), 247.
138. Eleanor Zelliot, "Sant Sahitya and Its Effect on Dalit Movements," in *Intersections: Socio-Cultural Trends in Maharashtra*, ed. Meera Kosambi (New Delhi: Orient Longman Limited, 2000), 190.
139. B. R. Ambedkar, "Ranade, Gandhi, and Jinnah" (Bombay: Thackeray and Co. Ltd., 1943).
140. *Annihilation of Caste*, 224, 2:21.
141. B. R. Ambedkar, "A Reply to the Mahatma," in *Annihilation of Caste*, 336–38.
142. "Ranade, Gandhi, and Jinnah."

143. *Eknāth Darśan Khaṇḍa 1-Lā* (Auraṅgābād: Eknāth Saṃśodhan Mandir, 1952), unpaginated preface page.
144. Salim Yusufji, *Ambedkar: The Attendant Details* (New Delhi: Navayana, 2017), 104.
145. Bāḷkṛṣṇa Raṅgarāv Suṇṭhaṇkar, *Mahārāṣṭrīya Sant-Maṇḍaḷāce Aitihāsik Kārya* (Mumbaī: Lokvāṅmay Gṛha, 1948 [2008]), 32–33.
146. Ibid., 132.
147. Gaṅgādhar Bāḷkṛṣṇa Sardār, *Sant Vāṅmayācī Sāmājik Phalaśrutī*, 7th ed. (Mumbaī: Lokvāṅmay Gṛha, 1950 [2006]), 2.
148. Ibid., 20.
149. Ibid., 82.
150. Damodar Dharmanand Kosambi (1907–1966) should not be confused with his father, Dharmanand Damodar Kosambi (1876–1947), who was a prominent Sanskritist and Buddhist convert.
151. D. D. Kosambi, *Myth and Reality* (Bombay: Popular Prakashan, 1962), 17.
152. Ibid., 35.
153. Ibid., 32.
154. Guha, *Dominance without Hegemony*, 39.
155. Kosambi, *Myth and Reality*, 35.
156. Ibid., 37.
157. Irawati Karve, "'On the Road': A Maharashtrian Pilgrimage," in *The Experience of Hinduism: Essays on Religion in Maharashtra*, ed. Eleanor Zelliot and Maxine Berntsen (Albany: State University of New York Press, 1988). Karve published this article in Marathi in 1951 and in English in 1962. Irāvatī Karve, *Paripūrtī* (Puṇe: Deśmukh āṇi Kampanī, 1951); Irawati Karve, "On the Road," *Journal of Asian Studies* 22, no. 1 (1962): 13–29.
158. D. B. Mokashi, *Palkhi: An Indian Pilgrimage*, trans. Philip Engblom (Albany: State University of New York Press, 1964 [1987]).
159. For an alternative view of *vārī* that traverses more rural territory and is less rigid toward caste, see Jon Keune, "Vārkarīs in Rural Western India," in *Contemporary Hinduism*, ed. P. Pratap Kumar (Durham, UK: Acumen Publishing, 2013).
160. Joel Lee, "In Memoriam: Doyenne of Dalit Studies—Eleanor Zelliot (1926–2016)," *Biblio: Review of Books* 21, (September–October 2016).
161. "Chokhamela: Piety and Protest," in *Bhakti Religion in North India: Community Identity and Political Action*, ed. David N. Lorenzen (Albany: State University of New York Press, 1995); Eleanor Zelliot and Vā. La. Manjūḷ, eds., *Sant Cokhāmeḷā Vividh Darśan* (Puṇe: Sugāvā Prakāśan, 2002).
162. Zelliot, "Sant Sahitya and Its Effect on Dalit Movements."
163. "Dalit—New Cultural Context for an Old Marathi Word," 79–80; "The Indian Rediscovery of Buddhism, 1855–1956," in *Studies in Pali and Buddhism*, ed. A. K. Narain (New Delhi: D. K. Publishers' Distributors, 1978), 102.
164. "Four Radical Saints in Maharashtra."
165. "Eknath's Bharude: The Sant as a Link between Cultures," in *The Sants*, ed. Karine Schomer and W. H. McLeod (Delhi: Motilal Banarsidass, 1987).
166. Ibid., 108.

167. "Chokhamela and Eknath," 153.
168. Lele, "Community, Discourse and Critique in Jnanesvar," 106.
169. "Jñāneśvar and Tukārām," 122; "Vārkarī Sampradāyātīl Krāntikārak Āśay," *Samāj Prabodhan Patrikā* (October–December 1991); "From Reformism to Interest Group Pluralism: The Relevance of the Non-Brahman Movement for an Understanding of Contemporary Maharashtra," in *Writers, Editors and Reformers: Social and Political Transformations in Maharashtra*, ed. N. K. Wagle (Delhi: Manohar Publishers, 1999).
170. Jayant K. Lele and R. Singh, "Language and Literature of *Dalits* and *Sants*: Some Missed Opportunities," in *Language and Society: Steps toward an Integrated Theory*, ed. J. K. Lele and R. Singh (Leiden: E. J. Brill, 1989), 131.
171. Ibid., 134.
172. Ā. Ha. Sāḷuṅkhe, *Vidrohī Tukāram* (Sātārā: Rākeś Ā. Sāḷuṅkhe, 1997 [2008]).
173. Gail Omvedt and Bhārat Pāṭaṅkar, *The Songs of Tukoba* (New Delhi: Manohar Publishers & Distributors, 2012), 41.
174. Tukārām, *The Songs of Tukoba*, trans. Gail Omvedt and Bhārat Pāṭaṇkar (New Delhi: Manohar Publishers & Distributors, 2012).
175. Śaṅkarrāv Kharāt, *Cokhobācā Vidroha* (Puṇe: Sugāva Prakāśan, 2002).
176. Priyoḷkar, *Paramahaṃsa Sabhā Va Tīce Adhyakṣa Rāmcandra Bāḷkṛṣṇa*, 91.
177. Ibid.
178. Ibid., 92.
179. Ibid., 94.
180. Lokahitavādī, *Lokahitavādī: Samagra Vāṅmay*, 1:199.
181. Āgarkar, "Taruṇ Suśikṣitāṃs Vijñāpanā," in *Āgarkar Vāṅmay*, 1:46.
182. Āgarjarm "Śahāṇyāñcā Mūrkhapaṇā Athvā Āmce Pretasaṃskār," in *Āgarkar Vāṅmay*, 1:153.
183. Paul Ricœur, "From Interpretation to Translation," in *Thinking Biblically: Exegetical and Hermeneutical Studies*, ed. André Lacocque and Paul Ricœur (Chicago: University of Chicago Press, 1998), 337.
184. Novetzke, *The Quotidian Revolution*, 15, 311ch37.
185. Gadkari, *Society and Religion: From Rugveda to Puranas*, 180.
186. Ibid.
187. Lawrence McCrea, "Freed by the Weight of History: Polemic and Doxography in Sixteenth Century Vedānta," *South Asian History & Culture* 6, no. 1 (2015): 92.
188. Theodore Benke, "The Śūdrācāraśiromaṇi of Kṛṣṇa Śeṣa: A 16th Century Manual of Dharma for Śūdras" (PhD dissertation, University of Pennsylvania, 2010), 117–22.
189. Novetzke, *The Quotidian Revolution*, 239.
190. S. G. Tulpule and Anne Feldhaus, *A Dictionary of Old Marathi* (Oxford: Oxford University Press, 2000), 250.
191. I am grateful to Rajiv Ranjan and Sujata Mahajan for discussing the modern Hindi and Marathi uses of this term. On the phrase's use in early 20th-century Hindi, see Hajārīprasād Dvivedī, *Hajārīprasād Dvivedī Granthāvalī*, 11 vols. (Nayī Dillī: Rājakamala, 1981), 9:445.
192. Ṭhākre concluded his play on Eknāth with *janatā janārdanārpaṇamastu* (dedicated to the people). Keśav Sītārām Ṭhākre, "Kharā Brāmhaṇ," in *Pabodhankār Ṭhākre*

Samagra Vāṅmay (Mumbaī: Mahārāṣṭra Rājya Sāhitya āṇi Saṃskṛtī Maṇḍaḷ, 1999), 338. In a short speech to RSS members in Ṭhāṇe in 1972, Golwalkar asserted, "God's form is the people–this ultimate vision is the core of our idea of nation" (*janatā hī janārdanācec svarūp āhe, hī śreṣṭhatam dṛṣṭi hā āplyā rāṣṭrakalpanecā gābhā āhe*) http://www.golwalkarguruji.org/mr/Encyc/2017/10/25/JanataJanardan.html. Accessed December 30, 2018.

193. Patrick Olivelle, ed. *The Early Upaniṣads: Annotated Text and Translation* (New York: Oxford University Press, 1998), 501–02.
194. Existing surveys casually assume an indebtedness to Śaṅkara, but a critical analysis of intellectual heritage and reception history may reveal otherwise. Ramcandra Dattatreya Ranade, *Mysticism in Maharashtra* (Delhi: Motilal Banarsidass, 1982); Bhalchandra Pandharinath Bahirat, *The Philosophy of Jñānadeva* (Delhi: Motilal Banarsidass, 1956).
195. Anand Venkatkrishnan, "Philosophy from the Bottom Up: Eknāth's Vernacular Advaita," *Journal of Indian Philosophy* 48, no.1 (2020): 9–21.
196. Kamban lauds King Daśaratha for possessing this quality in his Tamil *Rāmāyaṇa*. A. S. Gnanasambandan and Gomati Narayanan, "An Excerpt from 'Kamban—Putiya Parvai': An Ideal Monarch," *Indian Literature* 29, no. 5 (1986): 225. For a tantric example, see Urban, *The Power of Tantra*, 120.
197. Jñāndev, *Śrījñāneśvarī* (Mumbaī: Mahārāṣṭra Śāsan, Śikṣaṇ Vibhāg, 1977 [1991]), 82.
198. I am grateful to Anand Venkatkrishnan for calling attention to this text. Śaṅkara, "Manīṣā Pañcakam," in *The Works of Sri Sankaracharya*, Vol. 2—Miscellaneous Prakaranas (Srirangam: Vani Vilas Press, 1910), 55–56. This hymn may have arisen pseudonymously from a hagiographical story about Śaṅkara that appears in Madhva's *Śaṅkaradigvijaya* in the 14th century. Madhava-vidyaranya, *Sankara-Dig-Vijaya: The Traditional Life of Sri Sankaracharya*, trans. Swami Tapasyananda (Madras: Sri Ramakrishna Math, 1986), 59–61. Rich Freeman suggests that elements of the story may have Dalit origins. Rich Freeman, "Untouchable Bodies of Knowledge in the Spirit Possession of Malabar," *Paragrana* 18, no. 1 (2009): 135–64.
199. *Samabhāva* may be a more famous term due to Gandhi's use of it in a popular saying: *sarva dharma samabhāva*—impartiality toward all religions.

Chapter 4

1. Audrey Isabel Richards, *Hunger and Work in a Savage Tribe* (London: G. Routledge & Sons, 1932), 1.
2. Victor Benno Meyer-Rochow, "Food Taboos: Their Origins and Purposes," *Journal of Ethnobiology and Ethnomedicine* 5, no. 1 (2009): 1–10.
3. *State of the Global Islamic Economy Report 2016/17* (Thomson Reuters in collaboration with DinarStandard, 2016). http://13.251.163.42/wp-content/uploads/2019/02/ThomsonReuters-stateoftheGlobalIslamicEconomyReport201617.pdf. Thanks to

Shaheed Tayob for this reference and consideration of the trade group that produced this estimate.

4. Shaheed Tayob, "'O You Who Believe, Eat of the Tayyibāt (Pure and Wholesome Food) That We Have Provided You': Producing Risk, Expertise and Certified Halal Consumption in South Africa," *Journal of Religion in Africa* 46 (2016): 73–76.
5. Carter Lindberg, *The European Reformations*, 2nd ed. (Malden, MA: Wiley-Blackwell, 2010).
6. "Violence Breaks Out at Indian Beef-Eating Festival," BBC, April 16, 2012, https://www.bbc.com/news/world-asia-india-17727379, accessed May 11, 2019.
7. Arjun Appadurai, "Gastro-Politics in Hindu South Asia," *American Ethnologist* 8, no. 3 (1981): 494–511.
8. For example, Vasudha Narayanan, "Diglossic Hinduism: Liberation and Lentils," *Journal of the American Academy of Religion* 68, no. 4 (2000): 761–79; Shampa Mazumdar and Sanjoy Mazumdar, "'Women's Significant Spaces': Religion, Space, and Community," *Journal of Environmental Psychology* 19, no. 2 (1999): 159-70; Corrie E. Norman, "Food and Religion," in *The Oxford Handbook of Food History*, ed. Jeffrey M. Pilcher (Oxford: Oxford University Press, 2012).
9. Translated by the author from Hirā Bansoḍe, *Phiryād* (Puṇe: Samāj Prabodhan Saṃsthā Prakāśan, 1984). For another translation, see Eleanor Zelliot and Mulk Raj Anand, eds., *An Anthology of Dalit Literature* (New Delhi: Gyan, 1992), 27–29.
10. Robert Dirks and Gina Hunter, "The Anthropology of Food," in *Routledge International Handbook of Food Studies*, ed. Ken Albala (London: Routledge, 2013), 3–5.
11. Georg Simmel, "Sociology of the Meal," in *Simmel on Culture: Selected Writings*, ed. David Frisby and Mike Featherstone (Thousand Oaks: Sage Publications, 1997).
12. Claude Lévi-Strauss, *The Raw and the Cooked*, trans. John Weightman and Doreen Weightman (New York: Harper & Row, 1969), 1.
13. Mary Douglas, *Natural Symbols: Explorations in Cosmology* (New York: Routledge, 2003).
14. Peter Scholliers, *Food, Drink and Identity: Cooking, Eating and Drinking in Europe since the Middle Ages* (Oxford: Berg, 2001).
15. Mary Douglas, "Standard Social Uses of Food," in *Food in the Social Order*, ed. Mary Douglas (New York: Russell Sage Foundation, 1984), 12.
16. Scholliers, *Food, Drink and Identity*, 10.
17. Jack Goody, *Cooking, Cuisine and Class: A Study in Comparative Sociology* (Cambridge: Cambridge University Press, 1982).
18. Sidney W. Mintz, *Sweetness and Power: The Place of Sugar in Modern History* (New York: Penguin, 1986).
19. Michel Desjardins, "Religious Studies That Really Schmecks: Introducing Food to the Academic Study of Religion," in *Failure and Nerve in the Academic Study of Religion*, ed. Russell T. McCutcheon, Willi Braun, and William Arnal (Sheffield: Equinox, 2012).
20. Caroline Walker Bynum, *Holy Feast and Holy Fast: The Religious Significance of Food to Medieval Women* (Berkeley: University of California Press, 1987), 1–5.
21. Ibid., 289–95.

22. Ibid., 75–93.
23. Maurice Bloch, "Commensality and Poisoning," *Social Research* 66, no. 1 (1999): 133–49.
24. Susanne Kerner and Cynthia Chou, "Introduction," in *Commensality: From Everyday Food to Feast*, ed. Susanne Kerner, Cynthia Chou, and Morten Warmind (London: Bloomsbury Academic, 2015), 2.
25. Marcel Mauss, *The Gift: The Form and Reason for Exchange in Archaic Societies* (London: Routledge Classics, 2002), 100.
26. Simmel, "Sociology of the Meal."
27. Claude Fischler, "Commensality, Society and Culture," *Social Science Information* 50, no. 3–4 (2011): 533.
28. Ingvild Sœlid Gilhus, "Ritual Meals and Polemics in Antiquity," in *Commensality*, ed. Susanne Kerner, Cynthia Chou, and Morten Warmind, 203.
29. Carolyn Korsmeyer, *Making Sense of Taste: Food and Philosophy* (Ithaca: Cornell University Press, 1999), 200.
30. Gilhus, "Ritual Meals and Polemics in Antiquity," 206.
31. Ibid.
32. Grignon, "Commensality and Social Morphology: An Essay of Typology."
33. Ibid., 31.
34. Latour, *Reassembling the Social*, 54.
35. Ibid., 4–5.
36. Banu Bargu, "The Politics of Commensality," in *The Anarchist Turn* (London: Pluto Books, 2013), 36.
37. Ibid., 41.
38. This arrangement by rows differs from the apparently more widespread global practice of eaters sitting in circles, facing each other. Fischler, "Commensality, Society and Culture," 534.
39. McKim Marriott, "Hindu Transactions: Diversity without Dualism," in *Transaction and Meaning: Directions in the Anthropology of Exchange and Symbolic Behavior*, ed. Bruce Kapferer (Philadelphia: Institute for the Study of Human Issues, 1976).
40. R. S. Khare, *Culture and Reality: Essays on the Hindu System of Managing Foods* (Simla: Indian Institute of Advanced Study, 1976); *The Hindu Hearth and Home* (New Delhi: Vikas, 1976); *The Untouchable as Himself: Ideology, Identity, and Pragmatism among the Lucknow Chamars* (Cambridge: Cambridge University Press, 1984); Khare and Rao, *Food, Society and Culture*; R. S. Khare, "A Paradoxical Gift of Memory: The Pain, Pride, and History of an Untouchable 'Kitchen Poetess,'" *Anthropology and Humanism* 21, no. 1 (1996): 19–30.
41. Khare and Rao, *Food, Society and Culture*; Khare, *Culture and Reality* ; *The Eternal Food: Gastronomic Ideas and Experiences of Hindus and Buddhists* (Albany: State University of New York Press, 1992).
42. Ibid., 27.
43. Ibid., 39.
44. Ibid., 41; "Anna," in *The Hindu World*, ed. Sushil Mittal and Gene R. Thursby (New York: Routledge, 2004), 409.

45. Stephanie W. Jamison and Joel P. Brereton, *The Rigveda: The Earliest Religious Poetry of India*, vol. 1 (New York: Oxford University Press, 2014), 1587.
46. Brian K. Smith, "Eaters, Food, and Social Hierarchy in Ancient India: A Dietary Guide to a Revolution of Values," *Journal of the American Academy of Religion* 58, no. 2 (1990): 181–82.
47. D. N. Jha, *The Myth of the Holy Cow* (London: Verso, 2002).
48. J. C. Heesterman, *The Broken World of Sacrifice: An Essay in Ancient Indian Ritual* (Chicago: University of Chicago Press, 1993), 202.
49. Charles Malamoud, *Cooking the World: Ritual and Thought in Ancient India* (New York: Oxford University Press, 1996), 7.
50. Matthew R. Sayers, *Feeding the Dead: Ancestor Worship in Ancient India* (New York: Oxford University Press, 2013), 3.
51. Ibid., 1–2.
52. Ibid., 28.
53. Ibid., 38.
54. Ibid., 21; David Knipe, "Sapindikarana: The Hindu Rite of Entry into Heaven," in *Religious Encounters with Death: Insights from the History and Anthropology of Religions*, ed. Frank E. Reynolds and Earle H. Waugh (University Park: Penn State University Press, 1977).
55. Smith, "Eaters, Food, and Social Hierarchy in Ancient India," 201.
56. Olivelle, *The Early Upaniṣads*, 12–13.
57. *ChU* 6.2.1–3; *TU* 2.1–2.
58. H. W. Bodewitz, *Jaiminīya Brāhmaṇa I, 1–65 Translation and Commentary with a Study Agnihotra and Prāṇāgnihotra* (Leiden: Brill, 1973), 285n25, cited in Olivelle, *The Early Upaniṣads*, 526.
59. Olivelle, *The Early Upaniṣads*, 25.
60. Ibid., 26.
61. Smith, "Eaters, Food, and Social Hierarchy in Ancient India," 186–90.
62. Ibid., 189fn22.
63. Michael Christian Linderman, "Charity's Venue: Representing Indian Kingship in the Monumental Pilgrim Rest Houses of the Maratha Rajas of Tanjavur, 1761–1832" (PhD dissertation, University of Pennsylvania, 2009), 14.
64. Sayers, *Feeding the Dead*, 70.
65. Ibid., 84–85.
66. Ibid., 70.
67. Ibid., 73.
68. Ibid., 71.
69. Ibid., 76.
70. See Āpastamba Dharumasūtra 16.23–17.10, Gautama Dharmasūtra ch15, Baudhāyana Dharmasūtra 14.1–15.12, and Vasiṣṭha Dharmasūtra 11.16–44, translated in Patrick Olivelle, *Dharmasūtras: The Law Codes of Āpastamba, Gautama, Baudhāyana, and Vasiṣṭha* (Oxford: Oxford University Press, 1999).
71. On the dating the *Dharmasūtras*, see ibid., xxvi–xxxiv.
72. Āpastamba Dharmasūtra 16.29–17.1.

73. Malamoud, *Cooking the World*, 8.
74. Ibid., 9.
75. Ibid., 12–13.
76. Ibid., 21.
77. Patrick Olivelle and Donald R. Davis, *Hindu Law: A New History of Dharmaśāstra* (Oxford: Oxford University Press, 2018), 20–28.
78. Ibid., 4.
79. Rosalind O'Hanlon, "Narratives of Penance and Purification in Western India, C.1650–1850," *Journal of Hindu Studies* 2, no. 1 (2009).
80. Khare, "Anna," 409.
81. Ibid., 24.
82. Pandurang Vaman Kane, *History of Dharmaśāstra*, vol. 2, Pt. 2 (Poona: Bhandarkar Oriental Research Institute, 1941), ch21.
83. Ibid., 751–52.
84. *Bhakta* as literal food appears occasionally throughout Sanskrit literature. Novetzke, *Religion and Public Memory*, 19; Vaman Shivaram Apte et al., *Practical Sanskrit-English Dictionary* (Poona: Prasad Prakashan, 1957), 1181; Heesterman, *The Broken World of Sacrifice*, 206; Monier Monier-Williams, *A Sanskrit-English Dictionary* (Oxford: Clarendon Press, 1956), 742–43.
85. Romila Thapar, "Society and Historical Consciousness: The Itihasa-Purana Tradition," in *Interpreting Early India* (New Delhi: Oxford University Press, 2001); Velcheru Narayana Rao, "Purāṇa as Brahminic Ideology," in *Purāṇa Perennis: Reciprocity and Transformation in Hindu and Jaina Texts*, ed. Wendy Doniger (Delhi: Sri Satguru Publications, 1993).
86. David Gordon White, *Myths of the Dog-Man* (Chicago: University of Chicago Press, 1991), 75–78.
87. Ibid., 77.
88. Philip Lutgendorf, "Dining Out at Lake Pampa: The Shabari Episode in Multiple Ramayanas," in *Questioning Ramayanas: A South Asian Tradition*, ed. Paula Richman (Berkeley: University of California Press, 2001), 120–22.
89. Ibid., 126–28.
90. Andrea Marion Pinkney, "Prasāda, the Gracious Gift, in Contemporary and Classical South Asia," *Journal of the American Academy of Religion* 81, no. 3 (2013): 748–50.
91. Ibid., 751.
92. Lutgendorf, *The Life of a Text*; Sherry-Ann Singh, "The Ramayana in Trinidad: A Socio-Historical Perspective," *The Journal of Caribbean History* 44, no. 2 (2010): 201–23.
93. During my fieldwork in 2008–2010, I observed these temporary mendicants, who wore sackcloth and would "wander" from town to town around the time of Eknāth's birthday celebration. That this was a custom in some Maharashtrian villages was confirmed by conversation with Marathi literary scholar Kalyan Kale. Personal conversation, February 1, 2009.
94. Paul Michael Toomey, *Food from the Mouth of Krishna: Feasts and Festivals in a North Indian Pilgrimage Centre*, Studies in Sociology and Social Anthropology (Delhi: Hindustan Pub. Corp., 1994).

95. "Krishna's Consuming Passions: Food as Metaphor and Metonym for Emotion at Mount Govardhan," in *Religion and Emotion: Approaches and Interpretations*, ed. John Corrigan (Oxford: Oxford University Press, 2004), 225.
96. "Mountain of Food, Mountain of Love: Ritual Inversion in the Annakuta Feast at Mount Govardhan," in *The Eternal Food: Gastronomic Ideas and Experiences of Hindus and Buddhists*, ed. R. S. Khare (Albany: State University of New York Press, 1992), 137.
97. Erik Reenberg Sand, "The *Gopālakālā* as Reflected in the *Pāṇḍuraṅgamāhātmya* of Pralhāda Mahārāj and the *Abhaṅgas* of Tukārām," in *Studies in South Asian Devotional Literature, 1888–1991*, ed. Alan W. Entwistle and Francoise Mallison (Delhi: Manohar, 1994), 126.
98. Gondhaḷekar, Moghe, and Kemkar, *Kīrtantaraṅgiṇī Bhāg Dusrā*, 76–83.
99. Khare, "Anna," 412.
100. Personal communication, Gil Ben-Herut, December 24, 2018.
101. Ben-Herut, *Śiva's Saints*, 131–32.
102. This story is found in Text 59 of Nābhādās' *Bhaktamāl*, translated into English in Nabhādās, *Śrī Bhaktāmāla Compiled by Śrī Nābhā Goswāmī with Commentary by Śrī Priyādāsa*, trans. Bhumipati Dāsa (Vrindaban: Rasbihari Lal & Sons, 2017), 200–01.
103. Khare, *The Untouchable as Himself*, 44.
104. Ibid., 46.
105. Note that *sant* in Hindi tends to connote low-caste location, while the same word in Marathi implies nothing about caste.
106. Nabhādās, *Śrī Bhaktāmāla Compiled by Śrī Nābhā Goswāmī with Commentary by Śrī Priyādāsa*, 206–07. The translator of this text notably chose to translate Prīyadās' *sant* as "saintly persons" and avoid the issue of caste. For the rendition of the story as told by Anantdās, see David N. Lorenzen, *Kabir Legends and Ananta-Das's Kabir Parachai* (Albany: State University of New York Press, 1991), 115–17.
107. Purnendu Ranjan, *History of Kabirpanth: A Regional Process* (New Delhi: Anamika, 2008), 156–58.
108. Kolte, Vi. Bhi, ed. *Mhāiṃbhaṭ saṅkalit Śrīcakradhar Līḷācaritra.* 2nd ed. (Mumbaī: Mahārāṣṭra Rājya Sāhitya Sāṃskṛti Maṇḍaḷ, 1982), 14–15, *Pūrvārdha* 20. I am grateful to Anne Feldhaus to clarifying this story and sharing the reference.
109. Ibid., 134–36, 41, 43–45, 50–53, 74, 95, etc.
110. Ra. Rā. Gosāvī, ed. *Śrī Sakal Santa Gāthā* (Puṇe: Sārthī Prakāśan, 2000), 118, 273. Cited in Vidyut Aklujkar, "Sharing the Divine Feast: Evolution of Food Metaphor in Marathi Sant Poetry," in *The Eternal Food: Gastronomic Ideas and Experiences of Hindus and Buddhists*, ed. R. S. Khare (Albany: State University of New York Press, 1992), 98–100.
111. *Jñāneśvarī* 18.1452, cited in Novetzke, *The Quotidian Revolution*, 240.
112. *Jñāneśvarī* 17.293–97, cited in Novetzke, *The Quotidian Revolution*, 273–74.
113. Some Gāthā editors devote a separate section—*thālīpāk* (plate of food)—to Janābāī's food-related songs. Gosāvī, *Śrī Sakal Santa Gāthā*, 752–53, #317–30.
114. For another translation, see Jacqueline Daukes, "Female Voices in the Vārkarī Sampradāya: Gender Constructions in a Bhakti Tradition" (SOAS, University of London, 2014), 213.

115. Abbott and Godbole, *Stories of Indian Saints*, 341–44.
116. Gosāvī, *Śrī Sakal Santa Gāthā*, 2:1034, #3729; Aklujkar, "Sharing the Divine Feast," 106.
117. Ibid., 100.
118. Ibid., 101.
119. Gosāvī, *Śrī Sakal Santa Gāthā*, 1:416, #963; Aklujkar, "Sharing the Divine Feast," 103.
120. Abbott and Godbole, *Stories of Indian Saints*, 1:219–33.
121. For more on Kṛṣṇa-related mythology in Pandharpur, see Novetzke, "A Family Affair."
122. *sadā rāuḷīṃ yeu lāglā. Bhaktavijay* 23:85. That Cokhāmeḷā was allowed into the temple in this story did not lead to the temple allowing other Dalits in. As noted in Chapter 2, Christian missionaries in the 19th century observed that Dalits were prohibited from entering the Viṭṭhal temple in Paṇḍharpūr, and the reformer Sāne Gurujī famously staged a fast at the temple in 1947, to force the temple to admit Dalits.
123. Sascha Ebeling, "Another Tomorrow for Nantaṉār: The Continuation and Re-Invention of a Medieval South-Indian Untouchable Saint," in *Geschichten und Geschichte: Historiographie und Hagiographie in der Asiatischen Religionsgeschichte*, ed. Peter Schalk (Uppsala: Uppsala University, 2010), 438. Emphases in the original.
124. John S. Hawley and Mark Juergensmeyer, *Songs of the Saints in India* (New Delhi: Oxford University Press, 1988 [2004]), 26.
125. A book on *dabbawalas* (lunch deliverers) in Mumbai discusses Vārkarīs' presence in the business. Many explanatory details about the Vārkarīs here are inaccurate, however, so I am cautious about drawing on it. Sara Roncaglia, *Feeding the City: Work and Food Culture of the Mumbai Dabbawalas*, trans. Angela Armone (Cambridge UK: Open Book Publishers, 2013).
126. Aklujkar, "Sharing the Divine Feast," 104; Erik Reenberg Sand, "Gopālpūr-*Kālā*: Some Aspects of the History of the Sacred Places South of Pandharpur," in *Folk Culture, Folk Religion, and Oral Traditions as a Component in Maharashtrian Culture*, ed. Günther-Dietz Sontheimer (New Delhi: Manohar, 1995), 125.
127. Pechilis, *The Embodiment of Bhakti*, 153.
128. Nathaniel Roberts, *To Be Cared For: The Power of Conversion and Foreignness of Belonging in an Indian Slum* (Berkeley: University of California Press, 2016), 245.

Chapter 5

1. Keune, "Eknāth in Context."
2. On public memory in Marathi bhakti, see Novetzke, *Religion and Public Memory*, xi, 14–30.
3. Novetzke, *The Quotidian Revolution*, 57–67.
4. I find persuasive L. R. Pāṅgārkar's arguments for 1599 as Eknāth's final year of life. Pāṅgārkar, *Eknāth Caritra*, 141. Regarding Mukteśvar's dates, see Khānolkar, *Marāṭhī Vāṅmaykoś*, 231.

5. Eknāth's descendants in Paiṭhaṇ dispute this claim. The Vaṭhār group cite an official letter (*sanad*) from the Marāṭhā ruler Śāhujī (Śivājī's grandson) to their family as historical evidence. Jagadānanda-nandan, *Pratiṣṭhān-Caritra*, Pariṣiṣṭha, 7–8.
6. The *PC*'s unusual reception history may raise suspicions about authenticity, but I am inclined to trust the story of its heritage. Keune, "Eknāth Remembered and Reformed," 80.
7. Ibid., 102.
8. Ibid., 137.
9. "Gathering the Bhaktas in Marāṭhī," *Journal of Vaishnava Studies* 15, no. 2 (2007): 169–87.
10. On the Rāmdās *sampradāy*, see James W. Laine, Shivaji: *Hindu King in Islamic India* (Oxford: Oxford University Press, 2003), 52–62; Deshpande, Creative Pasts, 183–91; Wilbur S. Deming, *Rāmdās and the Rāmdāsīs* (London: Oxford University Press, 1928).
11. Bhīmasvāmī Śirgāvkar, "Bhaktalīlāmṛt," in *Rāmdās āṇi Rāmdāsī: Bhāg Dusrā—Śrīsamarthāñcī don Junīṃ Caritreṃ* (Dhuḷe: Satkāryottejak Sabhā, 1906).
12. Rāmdās' mother apparently came from a family of Vārkarīs who revered Eknāth. Khānolkar, *Marāṭhī Vāṅmaykoś*, 306. Two early hagiographies of Rāmdās include a childhood episode in which he was brought to hear Eknāth's *kīrtans*, but the commonly accepted dates of Eknāth and Rāmdās make this unlikely. Deming, *Rāmdās and the Rāmdāsīs*, 28, 68. A Rāmdāsī poet in Maratha-ruled Tānjāvūr claimed to be Eknāth's grandson, although some scholars have argued that this was Eknāth of Bīḍ, whose guru was one Janī-Janārdana. Shankar Gopal Tulpule, *Classical Marāṭhī Literature* (Wiesbaden: Harrassowitz, 1979), 413. Whatever their veracity, these associations demonstrate that Eknāth's reputation was well established soon after his death. Keune, "Eknāth Remembered and Reformed," 187–93.
13. Janārdana is a common epithet of Viṣṇu in Pañcarātra texts, the Vaiṣṇava Purāṇas, and the *Devī Bhāgavata Purāṇa*. In the *MBh* and *BhP*, "Janārdana" refers to Kṛṣṇa. Due to the range of meanings of *ārdana* (moving, exciting, watching over, agitating, tormenting, killing), the epithet has been interpreted variously. Śaṅkara noted two meanings in his gloss on the Viṣṇusahasranāma: "Tormenter (ārdana) of Wicked People (*jana*)" and "He to whom people (*jana*) pray (*ārdana*) for prosperity and happiness," Śaṅkarācārya, *The Vishnu Sahasranama with the Bhasya of Sri Sankaracharya* (Madras: Theosophical Publishing House, 1927), 51. Neither Eknāth nor his hagiographers explicitly discussed the name's meaning.
14. Two important *Dharmasūtras* (Gautama 2.32 and Baudhāyana 1.3.25), state that a disciple's duties include assisting the guru in getting dressed, helping with his bath, rubbing his body, and eating leftovers. Cleaning the guru's toilet seems to fall beyond the scope of these injunctions.
15. *BhL* 13:149 and *BhL2* 2:8–13.
16. *BhV* 45:24 and *BhL2* 5:1–4.
17. The *PC*'s editor suggests that *gomukhī* refers to a holy river site (*tīrtha*) called Gāyamukhī near Amrāvatī in northern Maharashtra, and eaters of Janārdana's leftovers are like the pilgrims there. I find this unlikely. *Molesworth's Marathi-English*

Dictionary defines *gomukhī* as someone who takes a vow to pick up his food with his mouth without using his hands. But the *PC* mentions nothing about such a vow. In one kind of *śrāddha* rite, "glad-faced" (*nāndī-mūkha*) ancestors are invited to partake of the meal. Sayers, *Feeding the Dead*, 73. An imprecise scribe or pronunciation imaginably could modify this word to *nandi-mūkha* (calling to mind Śiva's bull). But this story does not specify that Janārdana's meal as a *śrāddha*. I find most plausible a suggestion by Sucheta Paranjpe—*gomukhī* evokes the image of a cow grazing on the leftover food and leaf-plates after a meal.

18. *Bhajan* in contemporary Marathi commonly refers to a call-and-answer style of devotional song, but it is often used in the *PC* interchangeably with *sevā* or *bhāva* to name the activity of devoted service.
19. It is unclear whether Janārdana is worried more about Eknāth's reputation or his own.
20. There are good reasons to be cautious about conflating the oppositional pairs of purity (*śuddha/aśuddha*) with auspiciousness (*maṅgal/amaṅgal*). See Frédérique Apffel-Marglin, "Types of Opposition in Hindu Culture," in *Purity and Auspiciousness in Indian Society*, ed. John Braisted Carman and Frédérique Apffel-Marglin (Leiden: Brill, 1985), 65–83. Kṛṣṇadās draws that connection, however; consuming *amaṅgal* water adversely affects bodily purity (*śuddhi*).
21. The "three purities" connote body, mind, and speech (*kāyā-mana-vāca*)—a conventional Marathi way of saying "in complete and total purity." See *Mahārāṣṭra Śabdakoś*, ed. Yaśvant Rāmkṛṣṇa Dāte and Cintāmaṇ Gaṇeś Karve (Puṇe: Varadā Buks, 1932 [1995]), 4:1585.
22. Both Molesworth and Tulpule/Feldhaus define *humbarī* as a play or game among cowherd-children. Its name probably derives from the verb *humbarṇe*—to moo or bellow loudly.
23. G. K. Karanth, "*Made Snana*: Indignity in the Name of Tradition?," *Economic and Political Weekly* 47, no. 13 (2012): 27–9.
24. "The merry cowherds joyously sprayed and besmeared one another with curds, milk, ghee and water and they threw (balls of) butter at each other." *The Bhāgavata Purāṇa*, Part IV (Skandha X), trans. G. V. Tagare (Delhi: Motilal Banarsidass, 1978 [2002]), 1285.
25. As with *avatār*, these two terms involving *uddhār* are commonly used to describe the work of Marathi *sants*.
26. In its Maharashtrian form, a *kīrtan* involves a liturgy of textual reading, devotional singing, and an exposition of that text by the *kīrtankār* (performer of the *kīrtan*). For more on Marathi *kīrtans*, see Anna Schultz, "From Sants to Court Singers: Style and Patronage in Marathi Kirtan," *Journal of Vaishnava Studies* 17, no. 2 (2009): 127–46; Novetzke, *Religion and Public Memory*, 81–82.
27. Two exceptions to this pattern are a story in which Kṛṣṇa attends Eknāth's *kīrtans* in the form of a poor brahman, describing himself as *anātha*, and the concluding statement after Chapter 27 in the Gosāvī edition of the *EC*, which summarizes a story about Eknāth persuading a merchant to engage in spiritual practices as an example of purifying (*pāvan*) the fallen (*patita*).

28. This may hearken to Eknāth's Marathi commentary on the eleventh skandha of the *BhP*, known as the *Eknāthī Bhāgavat*.
29. The vow's language parallels an *abhaṅga* attributed to Janārdana, in which he implores Eknāth to maintain a nondual vision of the world and give food without regard to *jñāti* (*jāti*). Eknāth and Nānāmahārāj Sākhre, *Śrī Eknāth Gāthā, Śrī Bhānudās Mahārāj Āṇi Śrī Janārdana Mahārāj Yāñcyā Abhaṅgāsahit* (Puṇe: Varadā Buks, 1990 [2002]), 33, #26.
30. Compare with *Jñāneśvarī* 5:94, which comments on the *BhG* 5:18: "If the experience of egoism remains, then one sees the world with (such) distinctions [*bheda*]. But if it is not there at the beginning, how can there be any difference [*viśama*]?" Translation from Novetzke, *The Quotidian Revolution*, 253.
31. The text says nothing about how the thief suddenly became free.
32. Here too Keśavsvāmī ignores some obvious details: where did the emaciated thief go on the first night and how did he sustain himself before returning on the second night?
33. These episodes about Eknāth's compassion toward thieves are embellished alongside other stories in Mahīpati's *BhL* (20:131–201).
34. Vā. Sī. Bendre, "Śekh Mahaṃmadbābā Śrigondkar," in *Tukārām Mahārāj Yāñce Santsāṅgātī* (Mumbaī: Mauj Prakāśan, 1957), 57–61.
35. Hugh van Skyhawk, *Bhakti Und Bhakta: Religionsgeschichtliche Untersuchungen Zum Heilsbegriff Und Zur Religiösen Umwelt Des Śrī Sant Ekanāth* (Stuttgart: Franz Steiner Verlag, 1990), 53–71.
36. Dusan Deak, "Maharashtra Saints and the Sufi Tradition: Eknath, Chand Bodhle and the Datta Sampradaya," *Deccan Studies* 3, no. 2 (2005): 22–47.
37. Whoever Cānd Bodhle may have been historically, his reputation grew after his death. A large *dargāh* with his name rests in a repurposed stone structure in Daulatābād.
38. Literally, seven fan-palm trees tall, which is a Marathi idiom to express extreme height.
39. Hugh van Skyhawk suggests that knowledge transfer through prechewed food resembles stories in some *ṣūfī* lineages. Skyhawk, *Bhakti Und Bhakta*, 63–67. In the 13th-century *Līḷācaritra*, a story depicts the Mahānubhāv founder Cakradhar giving *pān* that he had chewed to the wife of the Yādava minister Hemādri. See Novetzke, *The Quotidian Revolution*, 203.
40. In Chapter 5:3–56, Eknāth and Janārdana travel to Pañcāvatī, near what is now Nāsik, to meet a learned brahman named Candramābhaṭ. They share a meal and encourage Eknāth to write a commentary on Candramābhaṭ's favorite section of the *BhP*. But Candramābhaṭ is never said to be Janārdana's guru. Keśavsvāmī concludes this episode by commenting that later in his life, Candramābhaṭ became known as Cānd Bodhlā, and he achieved a profound spiritual state in which he transcended duality and eventually took *samādhi*. He decided to have the shrine constructed in a Muslim style, to reflect that he had taught both brahmans and *yavana*s and to "break with Hindu-Muslim conflict" (*vād sampūrṇa khaṇḍilā*). Keśavsvāmī explains that this shrine is still a place of miracles and is widely respected in Devgiri (Daulatābād) today. This story seems to be ironing out some cognitive dissonances.
41. Śirgāvkar, "Bhaktalīlāmṛt," 73.

42. Kṛṣṇadās Jagadānanda-nandan and Jon Keune, "Eknāth's Ancestral Feast," in *Sources of Indian History*, ed. Rachel McDermott, Vidya Dehejia, and Indira Peterson (New York: Columbia University Press, forthcoming).
43. *brāhmaṇ teci janārdana*. The *PC*'s Marathi spelling is often imprecise and inconsistent, so I am cautious about how to translate *brāhmaṇ* in this case. I think Kṛṣṇadās means that brāhmaṇ men are the same as Janārdana and the ancestors. In a nondualist view, of course, all distinctions would dissolve in Brahman anyway.
44. The context of the passage makes it clear that "Brahman" here refers to ultimate reality, not the god Brahmā.
45. *sarvāṃbhūtīṃ janārdana | bhoktā ekaci jāṇ | kalpī bhinna to mūrkha.*
46. Cf. Eknāth and Nānāmahārāj Sākhre, #4005. This composition appears at the very end of Sākhre's and others' editions of the *Gāthā*, which makes me wonder if the poem was acquired from Keśavsvāmī's text rather than *kīrtankārs*' notebooks.
47. The lack of nominal declensions in this sentence allows it to be rendered grammatically in multiple ways.
48. Since the sentence does not articulate a subject, it is unclear who says "Come" (*āṅgat*). Since Eknāth is visibly surprised by this turn of events, while Kṛṣṇa knows what is happening, it would seem that Kṛṣṇa is speaking here.
49. Literally, "Lord Kṛṣṇa being my mother-father" (*māybāp astāṃ kṛṣṇanāth*).
50. Molesworth lists two definitions for *anasūṭ*. I follow the first, that it is a corruption of *anucchiṣṭa* (food that has not yet been touched and rendered stale). The other definition may also apply: the oblations of a male descendent to the manes on the day preceding the *śrāddha*. J. T. Molesworth, *Molesworth's Marathi-English Dictionary* (Pune: Shubhada-Saraswat Prakashan, 1857 [2005]), 18.
51. R. Krishnamurthy, *The Saints of the Cauvery Delta* (New Delhi: Concept, 1979), 45–46. My thanks to Anand Venkatkrishnan for calling this story to my attention.
52. Raghavan and Jackson, *The Power of the Sacred Name*, 119–21.
53. Davesh Soneji, "The Powers of Polyglossia: Marathi *Kīrtan*, Multilingualism, and the Making of a South Indian Devotional Tradition," *International Journal of Hindu Studies* 17, no. 3 (2013): 1–31.
54. Keune, "The Challenge of the Swappable Other."
55. *yācemṃ anāmikpaṇācemṃ jñān maja tava na dise oḷkhaṇ. disto ātma[t]vemṃ paripūrṇa sarvasamān sārikhā.* Intriguingly, this verse was omitted from a modern edition of the *EC* that was otherwise relatively free of printing errors. Keśavsvāmī and Madhukar Gosāvī, *Śrīkeśavkṛt Ovībaddha Śrīeknāth Caritra* (Paiṭhaṇ: Madhukarbuvā Gosāvī, 1997), 154, 17:25.
56. Keśavsvāmī's reference to "six *guṇas*" here does not correspond with any common convention in modern Marathi. For a range of possible interpretations, see Śrīdhar Śāmrāv Haṇamant, *Saṅket-Koś* (Puṇe: Ānand Mudraṇālaya, 1964), 158.
57. Since Rāṇyā's second invitation does not reference the first invitation and even repeats it somewhat, this may be a seam in the narrative where two formerly independent episodes were merged.

58. Eknāth also cited this verse in his Marathi commentary on the 11th skandha of the *BhP*. Eknāth and Jñāneśvar Tāndaḷe, *Sārtha Śrīeknāthī Bhāgavat* (Puṇe: Sarasvatī Pablikeśans, 1999), 14.292.
59. Mahīpati may be mocking the brahmans by showing that they do not realize that the *BhP* is not a Veda, or this passage may represent a vernacular view that the *BhP* did in fact hold vedic authority.
60. *kiṃcit anvaya bolilom̥.* I think that Abbott's translation "I spoke a little line" wrongly implies that Eknāth minimized the significance of his action.
61. Khaṇḍerāya, "Eknāth-Caritra," in *Laghukāvyamālā, Bhāg Pahilā*, ed. Vāman Dājī Ok (Mumbaī: Nirṇaysāgar, 1895), 185–61.
62. Khānolkar, *Marāṭhī Vāṅmaykoś*, 53.
63. Feldhaus and Tulpule's *Dictionary of Old Marathi* shows that the affix *-nāk* was an honorific title based on the Sanskrit *nāyak* (leader) and was not uncommon in older Marathi literature. Molesworth states that *-nāk* is an affix of "courtesy" specifically for the names of Mahārs. Zelliot states that until the beginning of the 20th century all Mahār names ended in *-nāk*. Zelliot, "Chokhamela and Eknath," 146. Vā. Dā. Ok claims that the affix applies to Mahār names in the Konkan "and other" regions. Khaṇḍerāya, "Eknāth-Caritra," 185–61.
64. I presume that *gītā* refers to a physical copy of the *BhG*, but I do not know what its significance here might be.
65. Eknāth or his interpretations could have designated caste rigidity as just such an emergency, but this would have required a wholesale re-envisioning of *āpad-dharma*, which is traditionally framed in terms of caste.

Chapter 6

1. I follow narratology as method rather than as theory. Jan-Noël Thon, *Transmedial Narratology and Contemporary Media Culture*, Frontiers of Narrative Series (Lincoln: University of Nebraska Press, 2016), 4–5.
2. Marie-Laure Ryan, "Story/Worlds/Media: Tuning the Instruments of a Media-Conscious Narratology," in *Storyworlds across Media: Toward a Media-Conscious Narratology*, ed. Marie-Laure Ryan and Jan-Noël Thon (Lincoln: University of Nebraska Press, 2014), 29–30.
3. Ibid., 11–13.
4. Thon, *Transmedial Narratology and Contemporary Media Culture*, 19.
5. Novetzke, *Religion and Public Memory*, 99–131.
6. The anonymous author of these introductions might have been Rāvjī Śāstrī Goḍboḷe, who edited *Navnīt* after his father Pārśurāmpant died. Parśurām Ballāḷ Goḍbole and Rāvjī Śāstrī Goḍbole, eds., *Navnīt Athvā Marāṭhī Vakitāṃce Veṃce*, 6th rev. ed. (Mumbaī: Vāsudev Gaṇeś Jośī, 1882 [1910]).
7. Ibid.

8. Dhoṇḍo Bāḷkṛṣṇa Sahasrabuddhe, *Paiṭhaṇ Yethīl Prasiddha Sādhu, Kavi Va Tatvavette Śrī Eknāth Mahārāj Yāñceṃ Caritra* (Mumbaī: Nirṇayasāgara Pres, 1883), 29.
9. Ibid., 84–85.
10. Bhāgvat, "Eknāthāñce Caritra," 76.
11. Ibid., 87.
12. Ibid., 88.
13. Ibid., 89. Bhāgvat describes Eknāth serving the *śrāddha* meal to Dalits and to the *trimūrti*/Muslims as if they were two separate events rather than variant renditions of the same story.
14. Ibid., 91. *Jar mī brāhmaṇāṃbarobarac viśvarūpāt hoto, tar brāhmaṇ malā va mājhyā jātīlā itke aspṛśya kā samajtāt?*
15. Ibid., 92.
16. Pāṅgārkar, *Eknāth Caritra*, 63–64.
17. Ibid., 102.
18. Ibid., 103.
19. Ibid.
20. Jagannāth Raghunāth Ājgāvkar, *Mahārāṣṭra Kavi Caritra: Śrī Eknāth Mahārāj Yāñceṃ Caritra*, vol. 7 (Mumbaī: Keśav Bhikājī Ḍhevaḷe, 1925), 26.
21. Ibid., 27.
22. Hanumān-svāmī, *Srīhanumānsvāmīñcī Bakhar* (Puṇe: Yaśvant Prakāśan, 1984), 120.
23. An exceptional English book published anonymously in Madras paid a great deal of attention to caste. *Shri Ekanath*. Nearly two decades earlier, this press had printed a book about Dalit bhakti poets. K. V. Ramaswami, *India's Untouchable Saints* (Madras: G. A. Natesan, 1900).
24. Rachel Dwyer, *Filming the Gods: Religion and Indian Cinema* (London: Routledge, 2006), 3.
25. Meera Kosambi, *Gender, Culture and Performance: Marathi Theatre and Cinema before Independence* (New Delhi: Routledge, 2015), 318–19.
26. For the most extensive published scholarship on *Dharmātmā*, see Hugh van Skyhawk, "Saint, Cinéma et *Dharma*: Ekanāth et les Intouchables au Temps de V. Śāntārām," in *Construction Hagiographiques dans le Monde Indien*, ed. Françoise Mallison (Paris: Librairie Honoré Champion, 2001), 36–42; "The Social Expression of the Unity with the Divine: The Saint's Conduct as a Component of Hindu Ethics," in *In the Company of Gods: Essays in Memory of Günther-Dietz Sontheimer*, ed. Aditya Malik, Anne Feldhaus, and Heidrun Brückner (Delhi: Manohar, 2005).
27. Kosambi, *Gender, Culture and Performance*, 9–60.
28. I am grateful to Rachel Ball-Phillips for helpful conversations about this transition.
29. Rā. Śrī. Jog, ed., *Marāṭhī Vāṅmayācā Itihās (1875 Te 1920)*, vol. 5, pt. 2 (Puṇe: Mahārāṣṭra Sāhitya Pariṣad, 1973 [1999]), 22. *Rāṇā Bhīmdev* was adapted by Śirvaḷkar into Marathi from Richard Brinsley Sheridan's English play *Pizarro* (1799), which in turn was based on August von Kotzebue's German play, *Spanier in Peru* (1796). Cf. Julie A. Carlson, "Trying Sheridan's Pizarro," *Texas Studies in Literature and Language* 38, no. 3/4 (1996): 359–78.

30. Kulkarṇī, *Marāṭhī Vāṅmaykoś*, 155; Daḍkar et al., *Saṅkṣipta Marāṭhī Vāṅmaykoś*, 569; Jog, *Marāṭhī Vāṅmayācā Itihās* 5.2, 28.
31. Kosambi, *Gender, Culture and Performance*, 178–80.
32. Daḍkar et al., *Saṅkṣipta Marāṭhī Vāṅmaykoś*, 569.
33. Vāsudev Raṅganāth Śirvaḷkar, *Śrī Eknāth (Bhaktirasapar Va Aitihāsik Nāṭak)* (Puṇe: Āryabhūṣaṇ Chāpkhānā, 1903).
34. Ibid., 9.
35. "Śrīeknāth," *Kesarī*, May 12, 1903.
36. *BhL* 24:27–93, Justin E. Abbott, Narhar R. Godbole, and Mahīpati, *The Life of Eknāth* (Delhi: Motilal Banarsidass, 1927 [1997]), 227–33.
37. Śirvaḷkar, *Śrī Eknāth*, 98.
38. Ibid., 34.
39. Ibid., 65.
40. Ibid., 64–65.
41. Ibid., 73.
42. Ibid., 74. *parameśvarācyā gharīṃ āpaṇ ubhayatāṃ ekac āhoṃ.*
43. Ibid., 84.
44. Cf. Abbott and Godbole, *Stories of Indian Saints*, 23:64.
45. Śirvaḷkar, *Śrī Eknāth*, 88.
46. Ibid., 89.
47. Ibid. The full text of this composition can be found in the most commonly available edition of Eknāth's Gāthā. Eknāth and Nānāmahārāj Sākhre, #3910. Anne Feldhaus has suggested that this *bhārūḍ* is the song of a *poṭrāj*, an itinerant goddess worshipper.
48. Ḍhere does not assume that Eknāth was implying that Muslims are the enemy, but he does see Eknāth invoking the goddess (through the mouth of a goddess worshipper) to overthrow wicked powers. Rāmcandra Cintāmaṇ Ḍhere, "Bayā Dār Ughaḍ," in *Vividhā* (Puṇe: Nīlakaṇṭh Prakāśan, 1966 [1967]), 67. A Marathi work of historical fiction published in the same year imbued the *bhārūḍ* with a stronger sense of Hindu-Muslim antagonism. Gopāl Nīlakaṇṭha Dāṇḍekar, *Bayā Dār Ughaḍ* (Mumbaī: Majeṣṭik Buk Sṭal, 1966).
49. Śirvaḷkar, *Śrī Eknāth*, 90; Eknāth and Nānāmahārāj Sākhre, *Śrī Eknāth Gāthā . . .*, #3911. For more on *bhārūḍs* about Mahārs and other marginalized figures, see Keune, "Pedagogical Otherness."
50. Śirvaḷkar, *Śrī Eknāth*, 91.
51. Ibid., 93.
52. Ibid.; Eknāth and Sākhre Mahārāj, *Śrī Eknāth Gāthā . . .*, #3894.
53. K. S. Thackeray is commonly called *Prabodhankar* or "Awakener," due to the sociopolitical activist serial that he edited, *Prabodhan*. Jog, *Marāṭhī Vāṅmayācā Itihās* 5.2, 123; Thomas Blom Hansen, *Wages of Violence: Naming and Identity in Postcolonial Bombay* (Princeton: Princeton University Press, 2001), 41.
54. Stewart Gordon, *The Marathas: 1600–1818* (Cambridge: Cambridge University Press, 1993), 145. O'Hanlon, "Caste and Its Histories in Colonial India." For another historical example of such conflict, see N. K. Wagle, "Ritual and Change in Early Nineteenth Century Society in Maharashtra: Vedokta Disputes in Baroda, Pune and Satara,

1824–1838," in *Religion and Society in Maharashtra*, ed. Milton Israel and N. K. Wagle (Toronto: University of Toronto Press, 1987), 145–77.

55. "Vartamānsār: Sabhā-Saṃmelaneṃ," *Kesarī*, July 14 1933, 11. In a poignant coincidence, the other major statement by the orthodox Hindu group mentioned in the article was their condemnation of a recent inter-caste marriage. "Kharā Brāhmaṇ Sudhārlā," *Kesarī*, August 15, 1933, 12.
56. The Home Department of the Bombay Presidency maintained an entire folder of newspaper clippings and summaries related to complaints again this play. File No. 131, Maharashtra State Archives, Home Department (Political), 1933, 37–38. I am grateful to Rachel Ball-Phillips for calling this file to my attention.
57. Ṭhākre, "Kharā Brāmhaṇ," 279.
58. Thackeray's choice of a Rāma temple is strategic; Rāma is not widely worshipped in Maharashtra, but he is central to Hindu nationalist ideology.
59. Here Bhāgavat Dharma is used in its older Marathi sense as another term for the Vārkarī *sampradāy*, not necessarily in its sense of the Prārthanā Samāj's reformist idea of Bhāgavat Dharma. Keśav Sītārām Ṭhākre, *Kharā Brāmhaṇ* (Mumbaī: Rāmkṛṣṇa Prakāśan, 1953), 1–4.
60. Ibid., 14–15.
61. Ibid., 15.
62. Ibid., 29. The use of the word *uddhar* appeared often in hagiographical literature to name Eknāth's salvific activity. In the 20th century, it took on the sense of improving the social and material situations of Dalits. Thackeray is obviously concerned with the modern sense of *uddhar*.
63. My interpretation is that Thackeray intended the Dalits' strike to be one of (selfish?) protest, whereas Eknāth was moved to work for everyone's well-being. The Dalit characters are moved by Eknāth's example and change their perspective on removing carcasses. I am not aware of Dalit groups in the early 20th century refusing to remove carcasses as an act of protest, but some Dalit communities followed the Arya Samāj's program of distancing themselves from "unclean" customs and occupations as a way of self-improvement. Ambedkar refers to such a case of Mahārs in Sholapur District doing this in 1927, which led to harassment by caste Hindus. Ambedkar, *Dr. Babasaheb Ambedkar*, 2:281.
64. Ṭhākre, *Kharā Brāmhaṇ*, 55.
65. That the *svāmī* is first interested in Eknāth's Marathi composition accords with a hagiographical story in which the *paṇḍit*s in Varanasi challenge Eknāth. Thackeray has brought the skeptical *paṇḍit* community to Paiṭhaṇ in the form of the *svāmī*. In the hagiographical story, the *paṇḍit*s show care only about Eknāth writing in Marathi.
66. Ṭhākre, *Kharā Brāmhaṇ*, 69.
67. Ibid., 72.
68. Ibid.
69. Ibid., 75.
70. Ibid., 76.
71. Several insightful conversations with Meera Kosambi helped me think about this material. She expanded on these ideas in her book *Gender, Culture and Performance*.

72. Dwyer, *Filming the Gods*, 31.
73. Ibid., 33.
74. The script apparently was published in a special issue of the Marathi serial *Nirbhīḍ* in 1936 that was devoted exclusively to the film. Pramod Kale (son of K. N. Kāḷe), Personal communication, May 27, 2010. Nearly fifty years later, the play was reprinted with an introduction and appendices. Ke. Nārāyaṇ Kāḷe, Pramod Kāḷe, and Rāmdās Bhaṭkaḷ, *Dharmātmā: Citrakathā* (Mumbaī: Pāpyular Prakāśan, 1982).
75. Ibid., *āṭh*.
76. Ibid., *dahā-akrā*. One reviewer found the scene superfluous and surmised that it had been inserted "for Punjab." Śāmrāv Niḷkaṇṭh Ok, "Pariśiṣṭa 1 (Reprinted Review of Dharmātmā)," in *Dharmātmā: Citrakathā*, ed. Ke. Nārāyaṇ Kāḷe, Pramod Kāḷe, and Rāmdās Bhaṭkaḷ (Mumbaī: Pāpyular Prakāśan, 1982), 65–69.
77. Bāpū Vāṭve, *Ek Hotī Prabhātnagarī* (Puṇe: Anant Vi. Dāmle, 1993), 100.
78. "Film News," *Kiran Weekly*, May 4, 1935, 4.
79. Dwyer, *Filming the Gods*, 63, 72.
80. Ibid., 69."The Case of the Missing Mahatma: Gandhi and the Hindi Cinema," *Public Culture* 23, no. 2 (2011): 349–76.
81. *Filming the Gods*, 70.
82. V. Shantaram, "The Eternal Conflict," *Filmfare*, January 6, 1956, 32–33. Cited in Dwyer, *Filming the Gods*, 75.
83. Ibid., 75; Skyhawk, "The Social Expression of the Unity with the Divine," 216.
84. Miriam Sharma, "Censoring India: Cinema and the Tentacles of Empire in the Early Years," *South Asia Research* 29, no. 1 (2009): 46–47.
85. Christian Lee Novetzke, "The Brahmin Double: The Brahminical Construction of Anti-Brahminism and Anti-Caste Sentiment in Religious Cultures of Precolonial Maharashtra," *South Asian History and Culture* 2, no. 2 (2011): 247.
86. "The Bombay Governmental Gazette: Register of Films Examined by the Bombay Board of Film Censors—October 1935" (Bombay: Secretary, Board of Film Censors, 1935), 2146.
87. Kāḷe, Kāḷe, and Bhaṭkaḷ, *Dharmātmā: Citrakathā*, 62–63.
88. Śāntārām Āṭhavaḷe, "Prabhātcā Dharmātmā," in *Śrīeknāth Darśan*, ed. Aravind Doḍe (Mumbaī: Sudarśan Prakāśan, 2006), 107.
89. "Film News," *Kiran Weekly*, November 2, 1935, 9.
90. Kāḷe, Kāḷe, and Bhaṭkaḷ, *Dharmātmā: Citrakathā*, 1. The English subtitles in the commonly available DVD version of the film gloss over many Marathi expressions and largely fail to convey the social tensions and nuances in the original script. Through the currently available subtitles, one can follow the gist of the film, but much is lost—and unnecessarily so—in translation. V. Shantaram, "Dharmatma" (Mumbai: Eros Multimedia Pvt. Ltd., 1935 [2009]).
91. Kāḷe, Kāḷe, and Bhaṭkaḷ, *Dharmātmā: Citrakathā*, 2.
92. Marathi *bhāva* is difficult to render in English; "faith" here should not be understood in a Protestant Christian sense but rather as an emotional state of ecstatic love and divine absorption.

93. Kāḷe, Kāḷe, and Bhaṭkaḷ, *Dharmātmā: Citrakathā*, 3. This *abhaṅga* appears in some editions of Eknāth's collected poems. Cf. Eknāth, *Śrīeknāth Mahārājāñcyā Abhaṅgāñcī Gāthā*, ed. Rā. Ra. Tukārām Tātyā (Mumbaī: Tattvavivecak Chāpkhānā, 1903), #965; *Śrī Eknāthsvāmīkṛt Abhaṅgācī Gāthā* (Mumbaī: Induprakāś Pres, 1906), 175.
94. Kāḷe, Kāḷe, and Bhaṭkaḷ, *Dharmātmā: Citrakathā*, 4.
95. Ibid., 7, *jayā mhaṇtī nīcavarṇa strīśūdrādi hīna jana | sarvāṃbhūtīṃ dev vase nīcā ṭhāyī kāy nase*; Eknāth, *Śrī Eknāth Gāthā, Śrī Bhānudās, Śrī Janārdana Yāñcyā Abhaṅgāsaha*, #2504.
96. I am not aware of this teaching anywhere in Eknāth's writings. Since it had not occurred earlier in the film, I wonder if Kāḷe invented it to respond to the censor board without disrupting the original film too much.
97. Kāḷe, Kāḷe, and Bhaṭkaḷ, *Dharmātmā: Citrakathā*, 21.
98. Ibid., 30.
99. This scene occurs at 1:07:10–48 in the film.
100. "Pariśiṣṭa 2 (Official Letter from Prabhat Studios to Secretary of Bombay Board of Film Censors)," in *Dharmātmā: Citrakathā*, ed. Ke. Nārāyaṇ Kāḷe, Pramod Kāḷe, and Rāmdās Bhaṭkaḷ (Mumbaī: Pāpyular Prakāśan, 1982), 62–63.
101. Kāḷe, Kāḷe, and Bhaṭkaḷ, *Dharmātmā: Citrakathā*, 32.
102. Ibid., 53. This sounds very similar to what Keśavsvāmī says about Eknāth in his *Eknāthcaritra*. "The superiority of compassion [*dayā*] is to be established at the head of all *dharma*—this was the mark of Śrī Nāth's own nature" (21:40).
103. Kāḷe, Kāḷe, and Bhaṭkaḷ, *Dharmātmā: Citrakathā*, 53–54.
104. According to Pramod Kale (Personal communication, May 27, 2010), Eknāth's descendants in Paiṭhaṇ sued Prabhāt Films and Kāḷe for misrepresenting the *sant*, but I have not yet seen corroborating evidence of this.
105. "Dharmātmyāce Guṇadharma," *Kesarī*, December 20, 1935, 10; Ok, "Pariśiṣṭa 1 (Reprinted Review of Dharmātmā)," 59; Āṭhavaḷe, "Prabhātcā Dharmātmā," 232.
106. Rachel Dwyer provides excerpts from four reviews. Dwyer, *Filming the Gods*, 75–76.
107. Kosambi, *Gender, Culture and Performance*, 335.
108. "Film News," 21.
109. Ok, "Pariśiṣṭa 1 (Reprinted Review of Dharmātmā)," 60.
110. Āṭhavaḷe, "Prabhātcā Dharmātmā," 228–40. The original source of this article was *Prabhātkāla* (Puṇe: Vhīṇas Prakāśan, 1965).
111. Ibid., 233.
112. Vāṭve, *Ek Hotī Prabhātnagarī*, 104.
113. Āṭhavaḷe, "Prabhātcā Dharmātmā," 235.
114. Ibid.
115. These advertisements can be found in December 1935 issues of *Kiran Weekly* and almost certainly in other film-related publications and newspapers at the time.
116. Vāṭve, *Ek Hotī Prabhātnagarī*, 105.
117. I am immensely grateful to Śaśikalā and Rajaṇī Śirgopīkar for sharing with me their memories of Gopāḷ Govind Śirgopīkar, their father and husband, respectively. They provided me with a printed copy of the play and rich information about the

inter-caste, inter-religious troupe that performed it. I am also grateful to Manohar Kulkarṇī and the staff at the Bhārat Nāṭya Saṃśodhan Mandir in Pune for introducing me to the Śirgopīkars.

118. Anant Hari Limaye, *Sahyādricī Śikhare*, vol. 2 (Puṇe: Ināmdār Bandhu Prakāśan, 1963), 53.
119. Ibid., 63. According to the troupe's meticulous records, in 1934 alone the troupe performed *Gokuḷcā Cor* 130 times and earned 65,000 rupees.
120. Ibid., 55.
121. The Śirgopīkars' discipline in keeping business records was apparently held in very high regard. A long newspaper article published in 1964 recommends this approach in detail to other drama organizations. (This article was given to me by Śaśikalā Śirgopīkar, without noting a page number.) Vā. Ya. Gāḍgīḷ, "Jamākharcācā Tol Sāmbhāḷlā Mhaṇje Nāṭyasaṃsthā Jagte—Śirgopīkar," *Maharashtra Times*, November 22 1964.
122. Limaye, *Sahyādricī Śikhare*, 2.
123. Gāḍgīḷ, "Jamākharcācā Tol Sāmbhāḷlā Mhaṇje Nāṭyasaṃsthā Jagte—Śirgopīkar."
124. Śaśikalā fondly described her father as a very open-minded man who welcomed people from diverse backgrounds into the troupe and their home. By living so closely with the troupe for so long, they felt like a family to her. Rajaṇī agreed that the atmosphere was quite creative and friendly, but she noted that so many people living in the house also created an immense amount of work (cooking and cleaning) for the women at that time. Śaśikalā and Rajaṇī Śirgopīkar, personal communication, February 16, 2010.
125. Gāḍgīḷ, "Jamākharcācā Tol Sāmbhāḷlā Mhaṇje Nāṭyasaṃsthā Jagte—Śirgopīkar."
126. Śaśikalā and Rajaṇī Śirgopīkar, personal communication, February 16, 2010.
127. Śaśikalā and Rajaṇī Śirgopīkar, personal communication, February 16, 2010.
128. Gopāḷ Govind Śirgopīkar, *Bhāva Toci Dev* (Puṇe: Vi. Ra. Paracure, 1964), 3.
129. Ibid., 21.
130. The Gaṅgā, Yamunā, and Sarasvatī are regarded as the *triveṇī* ("three rivers") whose confluence is said to purify anyone who touches it. The Gaṅgā and Yamunā are both physical rivers in northern India. The Sarasvatī is understood to be an invisible, spiritual river that may have existed during Vedic times.
131. Śirgopīkar, *Bhāva Toci Dev*, 24.
132. Ibid., 31.
133. Ibid., 49.
134. Ibid.
135. "Bhāva Toci Dev: Ek Sundar Nāṭyā—Ānand Saṅgīt Maṇḍaḷīcā Kharokhar Gaurav Viṣay," unknown newspaper, 1966. This review was given to me by Śaśikalā Śirgopīkar but without full bibliographic details.
136. Rājā Kārḷe, "Camatkārāśivāy . . . Namaskār Nāhīṃ!," *Loksatta*, n.d. This citation also was given to me with incomplete bibliographic details.
137. "Bhav Toci Dev: An Excellent Drama," *Nagpur Times*, November 9, 1966. The reporter also mentioned that the "discerning critic" G. D. Madgulkar was quite impressed.

138. Śirgopīkar, *Bhāva Toci Dev*, 49.
139. Rājū Phulkar, "Sant Eknāth Mahārāj: Marāṭhī Video Compact Disc" (Puṇe: Sumeet, 2004).
140. Rājeś Limkar, "Sant Eknāth" (Pune: Fountain Music Company, 2005).
141. Ibid., Disc 2, Part 2, 19:00.
142. Mahīpati, *Bhaktalīlāmṛt*, ed. Vi. Ke. Phaḍke (Puṇe: Yaśvant Prakāśan, 1988), 19:19–53.
143. Limkar, "Sant Eknāth," Disc 3, Part 2, 26:00.
144. Abbott and Godbole, *Stories of Indian Saints*, 17:99–126.
145. This story comes from the tale of Ciruttoṇṭar in the 12th-century compendium of Tamil Śaiva saints, the *Periyapurāṇamu* by Cekkiḻār.
146. Anne E. Monius, "Love, Violence, and the Aesthetics of Disgust: Śaivas and Jains in Medieval South India," *Journal of Indian Philosophy* 32, no. 2–3 (2004): 113–72; D. Dennis Hudson, "Violent and Fanatical Devotion among the Nāyanārs: A Study in the Periya Purānam of Cēkkilār," in *Criminal Gods and Demon Devotees: Essays on the Guardians of Popular Hinduism*, ed. Alf Hiltebeitel (Albany: State University of New York Press, 1989).
147. Muhammad Hedayetullah, *Kabir: The Apostle of Hindu-Muslim Unity* (Delhi: Motilal Banarsidass, 1977). For a thoughtfully critical reflection, see John Stratton Hawley, "Kabir: The Apostle of Hindu-Muslim Unity. By Muhammad Hedayetullah," *The Journal of Asian Studies* 39, no. 2 (1980): 385–86.
148. On two examples of depictions of caste conflict without antagonism in a film about Nāmdev, see Novetzke, *Religion and Public Memory*, 232–33.

Chapter 7

1. Jon Keune, "God Eats with Mahars: Untouchables, Brahmans, and Intertextuality in the Vārkarī Canon," in *Bhakti and the Self*, ed. Martin Fuchs (Forthcoming).
2. For more on definitions of "Vārkarī" in practice, see Jon Keune and Christian Lee Novetzke, "Vārkarī Sampradāy," in *Brill Encyclopedia of Hinduism*, ed. Knut Axel Jacobsen (Leiden: Brill, 2011), 617.
3. Aditya Behl, "Presence and Absence in Bhakti: An Afterword," *International Journal of Hindu Studies* 11, no. 3 (2007): 321.
4. Peter G. Friedlander, "The Struggle for Salvation in the Hagiographies of Ravidās," in *Myth and Mythmaking: Continuous Evolution in Indian Tradition*, ed. Julia Leslie (Surrey: Curzon, 1996), 119–20.
5. Novetzke, *Religion and Public Memory*, 66–67.
6. *Bhaktalīlāmṛta* 11.11–54, Abbott, Godbole, and Mahīpati, *The Life of Eknāth*, 151–55.
7. Stith Thompson, *Motif-Index of Folk-Literature* (Bloomington: Indiana University Press, 1989); Alan Dundes, "The Motif-Index and the Tale Type Index: A Critique," *Journal of Folklore Research* 34, no. 3 (1997): 195–202.

8. George Steiner, "The Uncommon Reader," in *No Passion Spent: Essays 1978–1996* (London: Faber, 1996), 14.
9. Eleanor Zelliot and Rohini Mokashi-Punekar, *Untouchable Saints: An Indian Phenomenon* (New Delhi: Manohar, 2005), 127.
10. Ra. Rā. Gosāvī, ed. *Śrī Eknāth Gāthā* (Puṇe: Sārthī Prakāśan, 2000), 690–92, #3680–87. The quoted verse is #3685.
11. Novetzke, *The Quotidian Revolution*, 10.
12. Precedents of such caste inclusivity can be seen in the Kannada and Tamil Śaiva traditions and the *Mānasollāsa*'s conscious efforts to include multiple regional languages. Pollock, *The Language of the Gods in the World of Men*, 301–02. I am grateful to Jack Hawley for pointing out this thematic connection.
13. James W. Laine, "Out of Character: Marginal Voices and Role-Transcendence in the Mahābhārata's Book of the Forest," *Journal of Indian Philosophy* 19, no. 3 (1991): 274.
14. Lorenzen, "The Lives of *Nirguṇi* Saints"; David N. Lorenzen, "Traditions of Non-Caste Hinduism: The Kabir Panth," *Contributions to Indian Sociology* 21, no. 2 (1987): 263–83; John S. Hawley, "The *Nirguṇ/Saguṇ* Distinction in Early Manuscript Anthologies of Hindu Devotion," in *Bhakti Religion in North India: Community Identity and Political Action*, ed. David N. Lorenzen (Albany: State University of New York Press, 1995). Hawley points out that, historically, *nirguṇa* and *saguṇa* were more complex and mixed in practice than later taxonomy makes it appear.
15. On *sādhāraṇa dharma*, see Pandurang Vaman Kane, *History of Dharmaśāstra*, vol. 2, pt. 1 (Poona: Bhandarkar Oriental Research Institute, 1941), 5–11.
16. Olivelle, *Dharmasūtras*, 90–91.
17. Kane, *History of Dharmaśāstra*, vol. 2, pt. 1, 643–44.
18. Personal communication with Don Davis, January 26, 2019.
19. Hawley discusses this ethical conundrum under the category of "bhakti virtues." Hawley, "Morality Beyond Morality," 63–64.
20. Novetzke, *The Quotidian Revolution*, 137.
21. Hawley and Juergensmeyer, *Songs of the Saints in India*, 41.
22. Keune, "Pedagogical Otherness," 736–41.
23. Mitchell, "Paṇḍharpūr," 151–52.
24. Claude Lévi-Strauss, "The Structural Study of Myth," *The Journal of American Folklore* 68, no. 270 (1955): 443.
25. Catherine M. Bell, *Ritual Theory, Ritual Practice* (New York: Oxford University Press, 1992), 109.
26. Ibid., 184.
27. Schultz, *Singing a Hindu Nation*, 14.
28. I take for granted an expansive view of authorship in much bhakti literature, as outlined by Hawley, "Three Bhakti Voices"; Novetzke, "Divining an Author."
29. Yigal Bronner, *Extreme Poetry: The South Asian Movement of Simultaneous Narration* (New York: Columbia University Press, 2010).
30. Parry, "Egalitarian Values in a Hierarchical Society," 117.
31. Burchett, "Bhakti Rhetoric in the Hagiography of 'Untouchable' Saints."

32. Michel de Certeau, *The Practice of Everyday Life*, trans. Steven Rendall (Berkeley: University of California Press, 1984), 29–30.
33. Novetzke, *The Quotidian Revolution*, 265.
34. Ibid., 216.
35. Jon Keune, "Review: The Quotidian Vernacular: Vernacularization, Religion, and the Premodern Public Sphere in India (Columbia University Press, 2016)," *Reading Religion* (2018).
36. Piliavsky, "Egalitarian Fantasy and Politics in the Real World."
37. Thomas J. Green, *Religion for a Secular Age: Max Müller, Swami Vivekananda and Vedanta* (New York: Ashgate, 2016), 128–31.
38. Kane, *History of Dharmaśāstra*, vol. 2, pt. 1, 7.
39. Ibid., 8.
40. Andrew O. Fort, *Jīvanmukti in Transformation: Embodied Liberation in Advaita and Neo-Vedanta* (Albany: State University of New York Press, 1998), 180.
41. Andrew Nicholson, "Vivekananda's Non-Dual Ethics in the History of Vedanta," in *Swami Vivekananda: New Reflections on His Life, Legacy, and Influence*, ed. Rita D. Sherma and James McHugh (Dordrecht, the Netherlands: Springer, forthcoming), 4.
42. Hacker also directed his polemics against the Lutheran tradition, from which he had converted to Catholicism. Paul Hacker, *Das Ich im Glauben bei Martin Luther* (Köln: Styria, 1966).
43. Wilhelm Halbfass, *Tradition and Reflection: Explorations in Indian Thought* (Albany: State University of New York Press, 1991), 385.
44. Jonathan Z. Smith, "A Matter of Class: Taxonomies of Religion," *The Harvard Theological Review* 89, no. 4 (1996): 396.
45. Paul Hacker, "Westöstliche Mystik," in *Kleine Schriften* (Wiesbaden: Franz Steiner Verlag, 1978), 821; Hamid Reza Yousefi and Ina Braun, *Gustav Mensching—Leben Und Werk: Ein Forschungsbericht Zur Toleranzkonzeption* (Würzburg: Königshausen & Neumann, 2004), 225n837; Horst F. Rupp and Klaas Huizing, *Religion Im Plural* (Würzburg: Königshausen & Neumann, 2011), 150n63.
46. Nicholson, "Vivekananda's Non-Dual Ethics in the History of Vedanta," 24.
47. James Madaio, "Rethinking Neo-Vedānta: Swami Vivekananda and the Selective Historiography of Advaita Vedānta," *Religions* 8, no. 6 (2017): 6–7.
48. Hugh van Skyhawk, "Perceptions of Hindu Ethics in German Indology," *Annals of the Bhandarkar Oriental Research Institute* 74, Amṛtamahotsava Supplementary Volume (1994): 87–89.
49. Paul Hacker and Wilhelm Halbfass, *Philology and Confrontation: Paul Hacker on Traditional and Modern Vedanta* (Albany: State University of New York Press, 1995), 171.
50. Anantanand Rambachan, *The Advaita Worldview: God, World, and Humanity* (Albany: State University of New York Press, 2006), 28.
51. Ibid., 111.
52. Anantanand Rambachan, *A Hindu Theology of Liberation: Not-Two Is Not One* (Albany: State University of New York Press, 2015).

53. https://twitter.com/SadhanaHindus/status/936699311110402048. Accessed July 27, 2020.
54. "Dismantling Caste: A Hindu Apology for Caste and Untouchability," https://www.sadhana.org/dismantling-caste, accessed July 27, 2020.
55. Ambedkar, *Annihilation of Caste*, 25:4–6.
56. Scott R. Stroud, "Pragmatism, Persuasion, and Force in Bhimrao Ambedkar's Reconstruction of Buddhism," *The Journal of Religion* 97, no. 2 (2017): 214–43. See also Rohini Shukla, "B. R. Ambedkar and the Study of Religion at Columbia: Castes in India, Gender, and Primitivity." https://www.borderlines-cssaame.org/posts/2020/1/31/b-r-ambedkar-and-the-study-of-religion-at-columbia-university, accessed July 27, 2020.
57. Philip C. Almond, *The British Discovery of Buddhism* (New York: Cambridge University Press, 1988), 71–74; Gregory Schopen, "Archaeology and Protestant Presuppositions in the Study of Indian Buddhism," *History of Religions* 31, no. 1 (1991): 1–23.
58. For an excellent start on this project, see Douglas Fairchild Ober, "Reinventing Buddhism: Conversations and Encounters in Modern India, 1839–1956," PhD dissertation, University of British Columbia, 2016.
59. Guha, *Beyond Caste*, 12.
60. Viswanath, *The Pariah Problem*; P. Sanal Mohan, "Narrativizing Oppression and Suffering: Theorizing Slavery," *South Asia Research* 26, no. 1 (2006): 5–40.
61. Tulpule, "The Development of Mystical Thought in Maharashtra," 208.
62. Keune, "God Eats with Mahars."
63. Hawley, "Introduction," xiii.
64. Hudson, "Violent and Fanatical Devotion among the Nāyanārs," 376–86.
65. Bynum, *Holy Feast and Holy Fast*, 7.
66. Priyoḷkar, *Paramahaṃsa Sabhā Va Tīce Adhyakṣa Rāmcandra Bāḷkṛṣṇa*, 10.
67. I retain the older English transliteration of this site, which is named after five water tanks (*haud*).
68. Aravind Ganachari, *Gopal Ganesh Agarkar: The Secular Rationalist Reformer* (Mumbai: Popular Prakashan, 2005), 162.
69. "The Panch Howd Tea Episode (1892–3): An Index of Social Tension in Maharashtra," in *Nationalism and Social Reform in the Colonial Situation* (Delhi: Kalpaz Publications, 2005).
70. Ganachari, *Gopal Ganesh Agarkar*, 166.
71. Charles H. Heimsath, *Indian Nationalism and Hindu Social Reform* (Princeton: Princeton University Press, 1964), 185.
72. Sanjay Paswan and Pramanshi Jaideva, *Encyclopaedia of Dalits in India* (Delhi: Kalpaz Publications, 2002), 13:123.
73. Keer, *Dr. Ambedkar*, 93.
74. Paswan and Jaideva, *Encyclopaedia of Dalits in India*.
75. Keune, "Vārkarīs in Rural Western India," 159.
76. Bargu, "The Politics of Commensality," 41.

77. A recent Marathi documentary, *Ajaat* (Casteless), attempts to recover what is known about Babhutkar's life and legacy. The filmmaker comes to widely shared conclusion of disappointment at unrealized potential. https://scroll.in/reel/838972/documentary-ajaat-is-a-rich-history-of-ganpati-maharajs-efforts-to-set-up-a-caste-free-society, accessed July 1, 2019.
78. Pragya Singh, "Politics of Lunch Diplomacy: What Does the Dine-with-Downtrodden Drive Say?," *Outlook*, August 2, 2017.
79. Bargu, "The Politics of Commensality," 36.
80. Piliavsky, "Egalitarian Fantasy and Politics in the Real World."
81. C. J. Fuller, *The Camphor Flame: Popular Hinduism and Society in India* (Princeton: Princeton University Press, 1992), 212–13.
82. The Aṅgulimāla story, in the Majjhima Nikāya of the Pāli Canon, is traditionally understood as an extreme illustration of the Buddha's power to reform wicked people. Before encountering the Buddha, Aṅgulimāla attained fame as a serial killer who added a finger from each victim to a string around his neck, earning him the name "Finger-garland." This poem is translated from Marathi. Tryambak Sapkale, "Angulimala," in *The Norton Anthology of World Religions: Hinduism*, ed. Wendy Doniger (New York City: W. W. Norton & Co., 2015), 615–16.
83. Bansoḍe, *Phiryād*, 149–51.
84. Gabrielle M. Spiegel, "The Future of the Past: History, Memory and the Ethical Imperatives of Writing History," *Journal of the Philosophy of History* 8, no. 2 (2014): 177.
85. Jan Assmann, *Moses the Egyptian: The Memory of Egypt in Western Monotheism* (Cambridge: Harvard University Press, 1997), 9.

Bibliography

Abbott, Justin E., and Narhar R. Godbole. *Stories of Indian Saints: A Translation of Mahipati's Marathi Bhaktavijaya*. Delhi: Motilal Banarsidass, 1933 [1988].

Abbott, Justin E., Narhar R. Godbole, and Mahīpati. *The Life of Eknāth*. Delhi: Motilal Banarsidass, 1927 [1997].

Āgarkar, Gopāḷ Gaṇeś. *Āgarkar Vāṅmay*. 3 vols. Mumbaī: Mahārāṣṭra Rājya Sāhitya āṇi Saṃskṛti Maṇḍaḷ, 1974 [1999].

Ājgāvkar, Jagannāth Raghunāth. *Mahārāṣṭra Kavi Caritra: Śrī Eknāth Mahārāj Yāñceṃ Caritra*. Vol. 7. Mumbaī: Keśav Bhikājī Ḍhevaḷe, 1925.

Ājrekar, Rāmcandra Pāṇḍuraṅg. *Śrī Viṣṇubābā Brahmacārī Yāñce Caritra*. Mumbaī: Ātmārām Kaṇhobā, 1872.

Aklujkar, Vidyut. "Sharing the Divine Feast: Evolution of Food Metaphor in Marathi Sant Poetry." In *The Eternal Food: Gastronomic Ideas and Experiences of Hindus and Buddhists*, edited by R. S. Khare, 95–115. Albany: State University of New York Press, 1992.

Aktor, Mikael. "Untouchability in Brahminical Law Books: Ritual and Economic Control." In *From Stigma to Assertion: Untouchability, Identity and Politics in Early and Modern India*, edited by Mikael Aktor and Robert Deliège, 30–63. Copenhagen: Museum Tusculanum Press, University of Copenhagen, 2010.

Almond, Philip C. *The British Discovery of Buddhism*. New York: Cambridge University Press, 1988.

Ambedkar, B. R. *Annihilation of Caste*. Annotated critical ed., edited by S. Anand. London: Verso, 2014.

———. "A Reply to the Mahatma." In *Annihilation of Caste*, Annotated critical ed., edited by S. Anand, 332–56. London: Verso, 2014.

———. *Dr. Babasaheb Ambedkar: Writings and Speeches*. New Delhi: Dr. Ambedkar Foundation, 1979 [2014].

———. *Ranade, Gandhi, and Jinnah*. Bombay: Thackeray and Co. Ltd., 1943.

Apffel-Marglin, Frédérique. "Types of Opposition in Hindu Culture." In *Purity and Auspiciousness in Indian Society*, edited by John Braisted Carman and Frédérique Apffel-Marglin, 65–83. Leiden: Brill, 1985.

Appadurai, Arjun. "Gastro-Politics in Hindu South Asia." *American Ethnologist* 8, no. 3 (1981): 494–511.

Apte, Mahadev L. "Lokahitavadi and V. K. Chiplunkar: Spokesmen of Change in Nineteenth-Century Maharashtra." *Modern Asian Studies* 7, no. 2 (1973): 193–208.

Apte, Vaman Shivaram, P. K. Gode, Cintāmaṇa Gaṇeśa Karve, and Kashinath Vasudev Abhyankar. *Practical Sanskrit-English Dictionary*. Revised and enlarged ed. Poona: Prasad Prakashan, 1957.

Armitage, David. *The Declaration of Independence: A Global History*. Cambridge: Harvard University Press, 2007.

Arokiasamy, Soosai. "Dharma, Hindu and Christian according to Roberto De Nobili: Analysis of Its Meaning and Its Use in Hinduism and Christianity." PhD dissertation, Pontifical Gregorian University, 1986.

Arthur, John. *Race, Equality, and the Burdens of History*. Cambridge: Cambridge University Press, 2007.

Assmann, Jan. *Moses the Egyptian: The Memory of Egypt in Western Monotheism*. Cambridge, MA: Harvard University Press, 1997.

Āṭhavaḷe, Śāntārām. "Prabhātcā Dharmātmā." In *Śrīeknāth Darśan*, edited by Aravind Doḍe, 228–40. Mumbaī: Sudarśan Prakāśan, 2006.

———. *Prabhātkāla*. Puṇe: Vhīṇas Prakāśan, 1965.

Āvaṭe, Tryambak Hari, ed. *Gāthā Pañcak*. 5 vols. Puṇe: Indirā Chāpkhāna, 1908.

Bahiraṭ, Bhā. Paṃ., and Pa. Jñā. Bhālerāv. *Vārkarī Sampradāy: Uday va Vikās*. Puṇe: Vhīnas Prakāśan, 1972 [1988].

Bahirat, Bhalchandra Pandharinath. *The Philosophy of Jñānadeva*. Delhi: Motilal Banarsidass, 1956.

Bansoḍe, Hirā. *Phiryād*. Puṇe: Samāj Prabodhan Saṃsthā Prakāśan, 1984.

Bargu, Banu. "The Politics of Commensality." In *The Anarchist Turn*, 35–58. London: Pluto Books, 2013.

Barnett, Steve, Lina Fruzzetti, and Akos Ostor. "Hierarchy Purified: Notes on Dumont and His Critics." *The Journal of Asian Studies* 35, no. 4 (1976): 627–46.

Bayly, Christopher A. *Recovering Liberties: Indian Thought in the Age of Liberalism and Empire: The Wiles Lectures Given at the Queen's University of Belfast, 2007*. Cambridge: Cambridge University Press, 2012.

Bayly, Susan. *Saints, Goddesses and Kings: Muslims and Christians in South Indian Society 1700–1900*. Cambridge: Cambridge University Press, 1989.

Behl, Aditya. "Presence and Absence in Bhakti: An Afterword." *International Journal of Hindu Studies* 11, no. 3 (2007): 319–24.

Bell, Catherine M. *Ritual Theory, Ritual Practice*. New York: Oxford University Press, 1992.

Bellah, Robert N. *Religion in Human Evolution: From the Paleolithic to the Axial Age*. Cambridge, MA: Belknap Press of Harvard University Press, 2011.

Ben-Herut, Gil. *Śiva's Saints: The Origins of Devotion in Kannada according to Harihara's Ragaḷegaḷu*. New York: Oxford University Press, 2017.

Ben-Herut, Gil, Jon Keune, and Anne E. Monius, eds. *Regional Communities of Devotion in South Asia: Insiders, Outsiders and Interlopers*. New York: Routledge, 2019.

Bendre, Vā. Sī. "Śekh Mahaṃmadbābā Śrigondkar." In *Tukārām Mahārāj Yāñce Santsāṅgātī*, 50–82. Mumbaī: Mauj Prakāśan, 1957.

Benke, Theodore. "The Śūdrācāraśiromaṇi of Kṛṣṇa Śeṣa: A 16th Century Manual of Dharma for Śūdras." PhD dissertation, University of Pennsylvania, 2010.

The Bhāgavata Purāṇa (Skandha X). Pt. IV. Translated by G. V. Tagare. Delhi: Motilal Banarsidass, 1978 [2002].

Bhāgvat, Rājārām Rāmkṛṣṇa. *Rājārāmśāstrī Bhāgvat Yāñce Nivaḍak Sāhitya*. Edited by Durgā Bhāgvat. 6 vols. Puṇe: Varadā Buks, 1979.

———. *Eknāthāce Caritra*. Mumbaī: Phyāmilī Pres, 1890.

"Bhav Toci Dev: An Excellent Drama." *Nagpur Times*, November 9, 1966.

"Bhāva Toci Dev: Ek Sundar Nāṭyā—Ānand Saṅgīt Maṇḍaḷīcā Kharokhar Gaurav Viṣay." Unknown newspaper, 1966.

Bloch, Maurice. "Commensality and Poisoning." *Social Research* 66, no. 1 (1999): 133–49.

Bodewitz, H. W. *Jaiminīya Brāhmaṇa I, 1–65 Translation and Commentary with a Study Agnihotra and Prāṇāgnihotra*. Leiden: Brill, 1973.

Boer, Roland. "E. P. Thompson and the Psychic Terror of Methodism." *Thesis Eleven* 110, no. 1 (2012): 54–67.

"The Bombay Governmental Gazette: Register of Films Examined by the Bombay Board of Film Censors—October 1935." Bombay: Secretary, Board of Film Censors, 1935.

Bourdieu, Pierre. *An Invitation to Reflexive Sociology*. Translated by Loïc J. D. Wacquant. Chicago: University of Chicago Press, 1992.

Breckenridge, Carol Appadurai, and Peter van der Veer. *Orientalism and the Postcolonial Predicament: Perspectives on South Asia*. Philadelphia: University of Pennsylvania Press, 1993.

Bronner, Yigal. *Extreme Poetry: The South Asian Movement of Simultaneous Narration*. New York: Columbia University Press, 2010.

Brubaker, Rogers, and Frederick Cooper. "Beyond 'Identity.'" *Theory and Society* 29, no. 1 (2000): 1–47.

Buechler, Steven M. *Understanding Social Movements: Theories from the Classic Era to the Present*. Boulder: Paradigm Publishers, 2011.

Buell, Denise Kimber, and Caroline Johnson Hodge. "The Politics of Interpretation: The Rhetoric of Race and Ethnicity in Paul." *Journal of Biblical Literature* 123, no. 2 (2004): 235–51.

Burchett, Patton. "Bhakti Rhetoric in the Hagiography of 'Untouchable' Saints: Discerning Bhakti's Ambivalence on Caste and Brahminhood." *International Journal of Hindu Studies* 13, no. 2 (2009): 115–41.

———. *A Genealogy of Devotion: Bhakti, Tantra, Yoga, and Sufism in North India*. New York: Columbia University Press, 2019.

Bynum, Caroline Walker. *Holy Feast and Holy Fast: The Religious Significance of Food to Medieval Women*. Berkeley: University of California Press, 1987.

Carlson, Julie A. "Trying Sheridan's Pizarro." *Texas Studies in Literature and Language* 38, no. 3–4 (1996): 359–78.

Certeau, Michel de. *The Practice of Everyday Life*. Translated by Steven Rendall. Berkeley: University of California Press, 1984.

Cháirez-Garza, Jesús Francisco. "Touching Space: Ambedkar on the Spatial Features of Untouchability." *Contemporary South Asia* 22, no. 1 (2014): 37–50.

Chakrabarty, Dipesh. *Provincializing Europe: Postcolonial Thought and Historical Difference*. Princeton: Princeton University Press, 2000.

Chakravarti, Ananya. "Between Bhakti and Pietà: Untangling Emotion in Marāṭhī Christian Poetry." *History of Religions* 56, no. 4 (2017): 365–87.

Champakalakshmi, R. "From Devotion and Dissent to Dominance: The Bhakti of the Tamil Alvars and Nayanars." In *Religious Movements in South Asia, 600–1800*, edited by David N. Lorenzen, 47–80. New Delhi: Oxford University Press, 2005.

Chandra Shobhi, Prithvi Datta. "Pre-Modern Communities and Modern Histories: Narrating Virasaiva and Lingayat Selves." PhD dissertation, University of Chicago, 2005.

Charsley, Simon. "'Untouchable': What Is in a Name?" *Journal of the Royal Anthropological Institute* 2, no. 1 (1996): 1–23.

Conlon, Frank F. "The Polemic Process in Nineteenth Century Maharashtra: Vishnubawa Brahmachari and Hindu Revival." In *Religious Controversy in British India: Dialogues in*

South Asian Languages, edited by Kenneth W. Jones, 5–26. Albany: State University of New York Press, 1982.

Constable, Philip. "Early Dalit Literature and Culture in Late Nineteenth- and Early Twentieth-Century Western India." *Modern Asian Studies* 31, no. 2 (1997): 317–38.

Cort, John E. "Bhakti in the Early Jain Tradition: Understanding Devotional Religion in South Asia." *History of Religions* 42, no. 1 (2002): 59–86.

Daḍkar, Jayā, Prabhā Gaṇorkar, Vasant Ābāji Ḍahāke, and Sadānand Bhaṭkaḷ. *Saṅkṣipta Marāṭhī Vāṅmaykoś*. Mumbaī: Jī. Ār. Bhaṭkaḷ Phāuṇḍeśan, 2003.

Dalmia, Vasudha. *The Nationalization of Hindu Traditions*. Delhi: Oxford University Press, 1997.

Dandekar, G. N. "The Last *Kīrtan* of Gadge Baba." In *The Experience of Hinduism: Essays on Religion in Maharashtra*, edited by Eleanor Zelliot and Maxine Berntsen, 223–50. Albany: State University of New York Press, 1988.

Dāṇḍekar, Gopāl Nīlakaṇṭha. *Bayā Dār Ughaḍ*. Mumbaī: Majeṣṭik Buk Sṭal, 1966.

Dāṇḍekar, Śaṅkar Vaman (Sonopant). *Vārkarī Pantācā Itihās*. 3rd ed. Āḷandī: Prā. Dāṇḍekar Dhārmik Vāṅmay Prakāśan, 1927 [1966].

Dann, Otto. "Gleichheit." In *Geschichliche Grundbegriffe*, edited by Otto Brunner, Werner Conze and Reinhart Koselleck, 997–1046. Stuttgart: Ernst Klett Verlag, 1975.

Das, Bhagwan, and S. Anand. *In Pursuit of Ambedkar*. New Delhi: Navayana Pub., 2009.

Daukes, Jacqueline. "Female Voices in the Vārkarī Sampradāya: Gender Constructions in a Bhakti Tradition." PhD dissertation, SOAS, University of London, 2014.

Deak, Dusan. "Maharashtra Saints and the Sufi Tradition: Eknath, Chand Bodhle and the Datta Sampradaya." *Deccan Studies* 3, no. 2 (July–December 2005): 22–47.

Deliège, Robert. "Replication and Consensus: Untouchability, Caste and Ideology in India." *Royal Anthropological Institute of Great Britain and Ireland* 27, no. 1 (1992): 155–73.

Deming, Wilbur S. *Rāmdās and the Rāmdāsīs*. London: Oxford University Press, 1928.

Deshpande, Prachi. "Caste as Maratha: Social Categories, Colonial Policy and Early Twentieth-Century Maharashtra." *Indian Economic Social History Review* 41, no. 1 (2004): 7–32.

———. *Creative Pasts: Historical Memory and Identity in Western India, 1700–1960*. New York: Columbia University Press, 2007.

Desjardins, Michel. "Religious Studies That Really Schmecks: Introducing Food to the Academic Study of Religion." In *Failure and Nerve in the Academic Study of Religion*, edited by Russell T. McCutcheon, Willi Braun, and William Arnal, 147–56. Sheffield: Equinox, 2012.

Desjardins, Michel, and Ellen Desjardins. "Food That Builds Community: The Sikh Langar in Canada." *Cuizine* 1, no. 2 (2009). https://id.erudit.org/iderudit/037851ar.

Devare, Aparna. "Historicity Meets Its Limits: M.G. Ranade and a Faith-Based Private/Public Sphere." *Postcolonial Studies* 12, no. 1 (2009): 47–67.

———. *History and the Making of a Modern Hindu Self*. New Delhi: Routledge, 2011.

"Dharmātmyāce Guṇadharma." *Kesarī*, December 20, 1935, 10.

Ḍhere, Rāmcandra Cintāmaṇ. "Bayā Dār Ughaḍ." In *Vividhā*, 65–71. Puṇe: Nīlakaṇṭh Prakāśan, 1966 [1967].

Dirks, Nicholas B. *Castes of Mind: Colonialism and the Making of Modern India*. Princeton: Princeton University Press, 2001.

Dirks, Robert, and Gina Hunter. "The Anthropology of Food." In *Routledge International Handbook of Food Studies*, edited by Ken Albala, 3–13. London: Routledge, 2013.

"Dismantling Caste: A Hindu Apology for Caste and Untouchability." https://www.sadhana.org/dismantling-caste.

Dobe, Timothy S. "Dayānanda Sarasvatī as Irascible Ṛṣi: The Personal and Performed Authority of a Text." *The Journal of Hindu Studies* 4, no. 1 (2011): 79–100.

Doniger, Wendy. *The Hindus: An Alternative History*. Oxford: Oxford University Press, 2010.

Donnelly, Mark, and Claire Norton. *Doing History*. London: Routledge, 2011.

Douglas, Mary. *Natural Symbols: Explorations in Cosmology*. New York: Routledge, 2003.

———. "Standard Social Uses of Food." In *Food in the Social Order*, edited by Mary Douglas, 1–39. New York: Russell Sage Foundation, 1984.

Dube, Saurabh. *Untouchable Pasts: Religion, Identity, and Power among a Central Indian Community, 1780–1950*. Albany: State University of New York Press, 1998.

Dumont, Louis. *Homo Hierarchicus: The Caste System and Its Implications*. Translated by Mark Sainsbury, Louis Dumont, and Basia Gulati. Revised ed. Delhi: Oxford University Press, 1966 [1980].

———. *Homo Hierarchicus: The Caste System and Its Implications*. Chicago: University of Chicago Press, 1980.

Dundes, Alan. "The Motif-Index and the Tale Type Index: A Critique." *Journal of Folklore Research* 34, no. 3 (1997): 195–202.

Dvivedī, Hajārīprasād. *Hajārīprasād Dvivedī Granthāvalī*. 11 vols. Nayī Dillī: Rājakamala, 1981.

Dwyer, Rachel. "The Case of the Missing Mahatma: Gandhi and the Hindi Cinema." *Public Culture* 23, no. 2 (2011): 349–76.

———. *Filming the Gods: Religion and Indian Cinema*. London: Routledge, 2006.

Ebeling, Sascha. "Another Tomorrow for Nantaṉār: The Continuation and Re-Invention of a Medieval South-Indian Untouchable Saint." In *Geschichten Und Geschichte: Historiographie Und Hagiographie in Der Asiatischen Religionsgeschichte*, edited by Peter Schalk, 433–516. Uppsala: Uppsala University, 2010.

Eknāth. *Śrī Eknāthsvāmīkṛt Abhaṅgācī Gāthā*. Mumbaī: Induprakāś Pres, 1906.

———. *Śrīeknāth Mahārājāñcyā Abhaṅgāñcī Gāthā*. Edited by Rā. Ra. Tukārām Tātyā. Mumbaī: Tattvavivecak Chāpkhānā, 1903.

Eknāth and Nānāmahārāj Sākhre. *Śrī Eknāth Gāthā, Śrī Bhānudās-Mahārāj Āṇi Śrī Janārdana-Mahārāj Yāñcyā Abhaṅgāsahit*. Puṇe: Varadā Buks, 1990 [2002].

Eknāth and Jñāneśvar Tāndaḷe. *Sārtha Śrīeknāthī Bhāgavat*. Puṇe: Sarasvatī Pablikeśans, 1999.

Eknāth Darśan Khaṇḍa 1-Lā. Auraṅgābād: Eknāth Saṃśodhan Mandir, 1952.

Eliot, Charles N. E. "Hinduism in Assam." *Journal of the Royal Asiatic Society of Great Britain and Ireland* 42, no. 4 (1910): 1155–86.

Engels, Friedrich. *The German Revolutions: The Peasant War in Germany, and Germany: Revolution and Counter-Revolution*. Translated by Leonard Krieger. Chicago: University of Chicago Press, 1967.

Falcao, Nelson. *Kristapurāṇa: A Christian-Hindu Encounter*. Anand: Gujarat Sahitya Prakash, 2003.

Fárek, Martin. "Were Shramana and Bhakti Movements against the Caste System?" In *Western Foundations of the Caste System*, edited by Martin Fárek, Dunkin Jalki, Sufiya Pathan, and Prakash Shah, 127–72. Cham, Switzerland: Palgrave Macmillan, 2017.

Fenech, Louis E., and W. H. McLeod. *Historical Dictionary of Sikhism*. 3rd ed. Lanham: Rowman & Littlefield, 2014.

"Film News." *Kiran Weekly*, May 4, 1935, 4.
"Film News." *Kiran Weekly*, November 2, 1935, 9.
"Film News." *Kiran Weekly*, December 28, 1935, 21.
Fischler, Claude. "Commensality, Society and Culture." *Social Science Information* 50, no. 3–4 (2011): 528–48.
Fitzgerald, John. "Equality, Modernity, and Gender in Chinese Nationalism." In *Performing "Nation": Gender Politics in Literature, Theater, and the Visual Arts of China and Japan, 1880–1940*, edited by Doris Croissant, Catherine Vance Yeh, and Joshua S. Mostow, 19–54. Leiden: Brill, 2008.
Fort, Andrew O. *Jīvanmukti in Transformation: Embodied Liberation in Advaita and Neo-Vedanta*. Albany: State University of New York Press, 1998.
Fourie, Carina, Fabian Schuppert, and Ivo Wallimann-Helmer, eds. *Social Equality: On What It Means to Be Equals*. Oxford: Oxford University Press, 2015.
Freiberger, Oliver. "Elements of a Comparative Methodology in the Study of Religion." *Religions* 9, no. 2 (2018): 38. https://doi.org/10.3390/rel9020038.
Friedlander, Peter G. "The Struggle for Salvation in the Hagiographies of Ravidās." In *Myth and Mythmaking: Continuous Evolution in Indian Tradition*, edited by Julia Leslie, 106–23. Surrey: Curzon, 1996.
Freeman, Rich. "Untouchable Bodies of Knowledge in the Spirit Possession of Malabar." *Paragrana* 18, no. 1 (2009): 135–64.
Fuchs, Martin, and Antje Linkenbach. "Social Movements." In *Oxford India Companion to Sociology and Social Anthropology*, edited by Veena Das, Andre Beteille, and T. N. Madan, 1524–63. Delhi: Oxford University Press, 2003.
Fuller, C. J. *The Camphor Flame: Popular Hinduism and Society in India*. Princeton: Princeton University Press, 1992.
Gāḍgīḷ, Vā. Ya. "Jamākharcācā Tol Sāmbhāḷlā Mhaṇje Nāṭyasaṃsthā Jagte—Śirgopīkar." *Maharashtra Times*, November 22, 1964.
Gadkari, Jayant. *Society and Religion: From Rugveda to Puranas*. Bombay: Popular Prakashan, 1996.
Galanter, Marc. *Competing Equalities: Law and the Backward Classes in India*. Berkeley: University of California Press, 1984.
Ganachari, Aravind. *Gopal Ganesh Agarkar: The Secular Rationalist Reformer*. Mumbai: Popular Prakashan, 2005.
———. "The Panch Howd Tea Episode (1892–3): An Index of Social Tension in Maharashtra." In *Nationalism and Social Reform in the Colonial Situation*, 225–32. Delhi: Kalpaz Publications, 2005.
Gilhus, Ingvild Sœlid. "Ritual Meals and Polemics in Antiquity." In *Commensality: From Everyday Food to Feast*, edited by Susanne Kerner, Cynthia Chou, and Morten Warmind, 203–16. London: Bloomsbury Academic, 2015.
Gnanasambandan, A. S., and Gomati Narayanan. "An Excerpt from 'Kamban—Putiya Parvai': An Ideal Monarch." *Indian Literature* 29, no. 5 (1986): 225–28.
Goḍbole, Parśurām Ballāḷ, and Rāvjī Śāstrī Goḍbole, eds., *Navnīt Athvā Marāṭhī Vakitāṃce Veṃce*. 6th rev. ed. Mumbaī: Vāsudev Gaṇeś Jośī, 1882 [1910].
Goldstone, Jack A. *Revolution and Rebellion in the Early Modern World*. Berkeley: University of California Press, 1991.
Gondhaḷekar, Rāvjī Śrīdhar, ed. *Śrī Eknāthācī Gāthā*. Puṇe: Jagaddhitecchu Press, 1895.
———, ed. *Śrī Nāmdevācī Gāthā*. Puṇe: Jagaddhitecchu Press, 1892.

Gondhaḷekar, Rāvjī Śrīdhar, Pāṇḍuraṅg Ābājī Moghe, and Vāman Eknāthśāstrī Kemkar. *Kīrtantaraṅgiṇī Bhāg Dusrā*. Puṇe: Keśav Rāvjī Gondhaḷekar, 1915.

Goodwillie, Christian, and Glendyne R. Wergland. *Shaker Autobiographies, Biographies and Testimonies, 1806–1907*. London: Pickering & Chatto, 2014.

Goody, Jack. *Cooking, Cuisine and Class: A Study in Comparative Sociology*. Cambridge: Cambridge University Press, 1982.

Gordon, Stewart. *The Marathas: 1600–1818*. New Cambridge History of India. Cambridge: Cambridge University Press, 1993.

Gosāvī, Ra. Rā., ed. *Śrī Eknāth Gāthā*. Puṇe: Sārthī Prakāśan, 2000.

———, ed. *Śrī Sakal Santa Gāthā*. Puṇe: Sārthī Prakāśan, 2000.

Goudriaan, Teun, and Sanjukta Gupta. *Hindu Tantric and Śākta Literature*. A History of Indian Literature. Wiesbaden: Harrassowitz, 1981.

Green, Thomas J. *Religion for a Secular Age: Max Müller, Swami Vivekananda and Vedanta*. New York: Ashgate, 2016.

Grierson, George A. "Bhakti-Marga." In *Encyclopedia of Religion and Ethics*, edited by J. Hastings, 539–51. Edinburgh: T&T Clark, 1909.

Grierson, George Abraham, and Lionel David Barnett. *Lallā-Vākyāni: Or, the Wise Sayings of Lal Dĕd, a Mystic Poetess of Ancient Kashmīr*. London: Royal Asiatic Society, 1920.

Griffith, R. Marie. "Body Salvation: New Thought, Father Divine, and the Feast of Material Pleasures." *Religion and American Culture: A Journal of Interpretation* 11, no. 2 (2001): 119–53.

Grignon, Claude. "Commensality and Social Morphology: An Essay of Typology." In *Food, Drink and Identity: Cooking, Eating and Drinking in Europe since the Middle Ages*, edited by Peter Scholliers, 23–33. New York: Berg, 2001.

Guha, Ranajit. *Dominance without Hegemony: History and Power in Colonial India*. Cambridge, MA: Harvard University Press, 1997.

Guha, Sumit. *Beyond Caste: Identity and Power in South Asia, Past and Present*. Leiden: Brill, 2013.

———. "Speaking Historically: The Changing Voices of Historical Narration in Western India, 1400–1900." *American Historical Review* 109, no. 4 (2004): 1084–103.

———. "Wrongs and Rights in the Maratha Country: Antiquity, Custom and Power in Eighteenth-Century India." In *Changing Concepts of Rights and Justice in South Asia*, edited by M. R. Anderson and Sumit Guha, 14–29. New Delhi: Oxford University Press, 2000.

Gupta, Ravi M., and Kenneth Russell Valpey. *The Bhāgavata Purāṇa: Sacred Text and Living Tradition*. New York: Columbia University Press, 2013.

Gurney, John. "Gerrard Winstanley and the Left." *Past & Present* 235, no. 1 (2017): 179–206.

Hacker, Paul. *Das Ich im Glauben bei Martin Luther*. Köln: Styria, 1966.

———. "Westöstliche Mystik." In *Kleine Schriften*, 818–22. Wiesbaden: Franz Steiner Verlag, 1978.

Hacker, Paul, and Wilhelm Halbfass. *Philology and Confrontation: Paul Hacker on Traditional and Modern Vedanta*. Albany: State University of New York Press, 1995.

Halbfass, Wilhelm. *Tradition and Reflection: Explorations in Indian Thought*. Albany: State University of New York Press, 1991.

———. "Traditional Indian Xenology." In *India and Europe: An Essay in Understanding*, 172–96. Albany: State University of New York Press, 1988.

Haṇamant, Śrīdhar Śāmrāv. *Saṅket-Koś*. Puṇe: Ānand Mudraṇālaya, 1964.

Hangloo, Rattan Lal. "Kashmiriyat: The Voice of the Past Misconstrued." In *The Parchment of Kashmir: History, Society, and Polity*, edited by Nyla Ali Khan, 37–68. New York: Palgrave Macmillan, 2012.

Hans, Rajkumar. "Making Sense of Dalit Sikh History." In *Dalit Studies*, edited by Ramnarayan S. Rawat and K. Satyanarayana, 131–51. Durham: Duke University Press, 2016.

Hansen, Thomas Blom. *Wages of Violence: Naming and Identity in Postcolonial Bombay*. Princeton: Princeton University Press, 2001.

Hanumān-svāmī. *Srīhanumānsvāmīñcī Bakhar*. Puṇe: Yaśvant Prakāśan, 1984.

Hardiman, David. *The Coming of the Devi: Adivasi Assertion in Western India*. Oxford, UK: Oxford University Press, 1987.

Hardy, Friedhelm. *Viraha-Bhakti: The Early History of Kṛṣṇa Devotion in South India*. Delhi: Oxford University Press, 1983.

Hawley, John S., and Mark Juergensmeyer. *Songs of the Saints in India*. New Delhi: Oxford University Press, 1988 [2004].

Hawley, John Stratton. "Author and Authority." In *Three Bhakti Voices: Mirabai, Surdas, and Kabir in Their Time and Ours*, 21–47. New Delhi: Oxford University Press, 2005.

———. "Bhakti." In *Encyclopedia of Asian History*, edited by Ainslee T. Embree, 154–57. New York: Charles Scribner's Sons, 1988.

———. "Bhakti, Democracy, and the Study of Religion." In *Three Bhakti Voices*, 318–36. New Delhi: Oxford University Press, 2005.

———. "The Four Churches of the Reformation." *Modern Asian Studies* 52, no. 5 (2018): 1457–85.

———. "Introduction." In *Saints and Virtues*, x–xxiv. Berkeley: University of California Press, 1987.

———. "Kabir: The Apostle of Hindu-Muslim Unity. By Muhammad Hedayetullah." *The Journal of Asian Studies* 39, no. 2 (1980): 385–86.

———. "Morality beyond Morality." In *Three Bhakti Voices*, 48–69. New Delhi: Oxford University Press, 2005.

———. "The *Nirgun/Sagun* Distinction in Early Manuscript Anthologies of Hindu Devotion." In *Bhakti Religion in North India: Community Identity and Political Action*, edited by David N. Lorenzen, 160–80. Albany: State University of New York Press, 1995.

———, ed. *Saints and Virtues*. Berkeley: University of California Press, 1987.

———. *A Storm of Songs: India and the Idea of the Bhakti Movement*. Cambridge, MA: Harvard University Press, 2015.

Hayter, Mary. *The New Eve in Christ: The Use and Abuse of the Bible in the Debate about Women in the Church*. Grand Rapids: W.B. Eerdmans, 1987.

Hedayetullah, Muhammad. *Kabir: The Apostle of Hindu-Muslim Unity*. Delhi: Motilal Banarsidass, 1977.

Heesterman, J. C. *The Broken World of Sacrifice: An Essay in Ancient Indian Ritual*. Chicago: University of Chicago Press, 1993.

Heimsath, Charles H. *Indian Nationalism and Hindu Social Reform*. Princeton: Princeton University Press, 1964.

Henn, Alexander. *Hindu-Catholic Encounters in Goa: Religion, Colonialism, and Modernity*. Bloomington: Indiana University Press, 2014.

Hess, Linda. *Bodies of Song: Kabir Oral Traditions and Performative Worlds in North India*. New York: Oxford University Press, 2015.

Hessayon, Ariel. "Fabricating Radical Traditions." *Cromohs Virtual Seminars. Recent Historiographical Trends of the British Studies* (2006–2007): 1–6. http://www.fupress.net/public/journals/49/Seminar/hessayon2_radical.html.

Hickel, Jason. *Democracy as Death: The Moral Order of Anti-Liberal Politics in South Africa*. Berkeley: University of California Press, 2015.

Hill, Christopher. "The English Civil War Interpreted by Marx and Engels." *Science & Society* 12, no. 1 (1948): 130–56.

Holdrege, Barbara A. *Bhakti and Embodiment: Fashioning Divine Bodies and Devotional Bodies in KṛṢṆa Bhakti*. New York: Routledge, 2015.

———. "The Gauḍīya Discourse of Embodiment: Re-Visioning Jñāna and Yoga in the Embodied Aesthetics of Kṛṣṇa Bhakti." *The Journal of Hindu Studies* 6, no. 2 (August 1, 2013): 154–97.

Hoole, Elijah. *Madras, Mysore, and the South of India: Or, a Personal Narrative of a Mission to Those Countries from 1820 to 1828*. 2nd ed. London: Longman, Brown, Green and Longmans, 1844.

Howard, Thomas Albert. "A 'Religious Turn' in Modern European Historiography?" *Historically Speaking* 4, no. 5 (2003): 24–26.

Hudson, D. Dennis. "Violent and Fanatical Devotion among the Nāyanārs: A Study in the Periya Purānam of Cēkkilār." In *Criminal Gods and Demon Devotees: Essays on the Guardians of Popular Hinduism*, edited by Alf Hiltebeitel, 373–404. Albany: State University of New York Press, 1989.

Israel, Hephzibah. *Religious Transactions in Colonial South India: Language, Translation, and the Making of Protestant Identity*. New York: Palgrave Macmillan, 2011.

Jaffrelot, Christoph. "Dr. Ambedkar's Strategies against Untouchability and the Caste System." *Institute of Dalit Studies Working Paper Series* 3, no. 4 (2009): 1–23. http://dalitstudies.org.in/wp/0904.pdf.

Jagadānanda-nandan, Kṛṣṇadās. *Pratiṣṭhān-Caritra*. Edited by Raghunāth Hamaṇpanth Koṭnīs. Mumbaī: Trinity Publicity Society, 1948.

Jagadānanda-nandan, Kṛṣṇadās, and Jon Keune. "Eknāth's Ancestral Feast." In *Sources of Indian History*, edited by Rachel McDermott, Vidya Dehejia, and Indira Peterson. New York: Columbia University Press, forthcoming.

Jambhekar, Ganesh Gangadhar, ed. *Memoirs and Writings of Acharya Bal Gangadhar Shastri Jambhekar*. 3 vols. Poona: Ganesh Gangadhar Jambhekar, 1950.

Jamison, Stephanie W., and Joel P. Brereton. *The Rigveda: The Earliest Religious Poetry of India*. Vol. 1. New York: Oxford University Press, 2014.

Jha, D. N. *The Myth of the Holy Cow*. London: Verso, 2002.

Jñāndev. *Śrījñāneśvarī*. Mumbaī: Mahārāṣṭra Śāsan, Śikṣaṇ Vibhāg, 1977 [1991].

Jog, Rā. Śrī., ed. *Marāṭhī Vāṅmayācā Itihās (1875 Te 1920)*. Vol. 5, Pt. 2. Puṇe: Mahārāṣṭra Sāhitya Pariṣad, 1973 [1999].

Jones, Charles B. "Buddhism and Marxism in Taiwan: Lin Qiuwu's Religious Socialism and Its Legacy in Modern Times." *Journal of Global Buddhism* 1 (2000): 82–111.

Jones, Kenneth W. *Socio-Religious Reform Movements in British India*. New Cambridge History of India. Cambridge: Cambridge University Press, 1989.

Joshi, P. L. *Political Ideas and Leadership in Vidarbha*. Nagpur: Dept. of Political Science & Public Administration, Nagpur University, 1980.

Jośī, Pra. Na. "Svāgat." In *Śrī Sakal Santa Gāthā*, edited by Ra. Rā. Gosāvī. *sahā-sāt*, vi–vii. Puṇe: Sārthī Prakāśan, 2000.

Julier, Alice P. *Eating Together: Food, Friendship, and Inequality*. Urbana: University of Illinois Press, 2013.

Justice, Steven. "Religious Dissent, Social Revolt and 'Ideology.'" *Past & Present* 195, Supplement 2 (2007): 205–16.

Kadam, S. B. *Śrī Sant Cokhāmeḷā Mahārāj Yāñce Caritra Va Abhaṅga Gāthā*. Mumbaī: Mandākinī S. Kadam, 1967.

Kāḷe, Ke. Nārāyaṇ, Pramod Kāḷe, and Rāmdās Bhaṭkaḷ. *Dharmātmā: Citrakathā*. Mumbaī: Pāpyular Prakāśan, 1982.

Kane, Pandurang Vaman. *History of Dharmaśāstra*. Vol. 2, Pt. 1. Poona: Bhandarkar Oriental Research Institute, 1941.

———. *History of Dharmaśāstra*. Vol. 2, Pt. 2. Poona: Bhandarkar Oriental Research Institute, 1941.

Kapferer, Bruce. "In the Event: Toward an Anthropology of Generic Moments." *Social Analysis* 54, no. 3 (2010): 1–27.

Karanth, G. K. "Made Snana: Indignity in the Name of Tradition?" *Economic and Political Weekly* 47, no. 13 (2012): 27–29.

Kārḷe, Rājā. "Camatkārāśivāy . . . Namaskār Nāhīṃ!" *Loksatta*, n.d.

Karve, Irawati. "On the Road." *Journal of Asian Studies* 22, no. 1 (1962): 13–29.

———. "'On the Road': A Maharashtrian Pilgrimage." In *The Experience of Hinduism: Essays on Religion in Maharashtra*, edited by Eleanor Zelliot and Maxine Berntsen, 143–73. Albany: State University of New York Press, 1988.

Karve, Irāvatī. *Paripūrtī*. Puṇe: Deśmukh āṇi Kampanī, 1951.

Kavibhāratī, Rāmacandra, and Haraprasād Śāstrī. "Bhakti Śataka: One Hundred Slokas on Reverence and Love." *The Buddhist Text Society of India* 1, no. 2 (1893): 21–29.

Keer, Dhananjay. *Dr. Ambedkar: Life and Mission*. 2nd ed. Bombay: Popular Prakashan, 1962.

Kennedy, Vans. *Dictionary of the Maratha Language*. Bombay: Courier Press, 1824.

Kerner, Susanne, and Cynthia Chou. "Introduction." In *Commensality: From Everyday Food to Feast*, edited by Susanne Kerner, Cynthia Chou, and Morten Warmind, 1–12. London: Bloomsbury Academic, 2015.

Keśavsvāmī and Madhukar Gosāvī. *Śrīkeśavkṛt Ovībaddha Śrīeknāth Caritra*. Paiṭhaṇ: Madhukarbuvā Gosāvī, 1997.

Keune, Jon. "The Challenge of the Swappable Other: A Framework for Interpreting Otherness in Bhakti Texts." In *Regional Communities of Devotion in South Asia*, edited by Gil Ben-Herut, Jon Keune, and Anne E. Monius, 101–21. New York: Routledge, 2019.

———. "Eknāth in Context: The Literary, Social, and Political Milieus of an Early Modern Saint-Poet." *South Asian History and Culture* 6, no. 1 (2015): 70–86.

———. "Eknāth Remembered and Reformed: Bhakti, Brahmans, and Untouchables in Marathi Historiography." PhD dissertation, Columbia University, 2011.

———. "Gathering the Bhaktas in Marāṭhī." *Journal of Vaishnava Studies* 15, no. 2 (Spring 2007): 169–87.

———. "God Eats with Mahars: Untouchables, Brahmans, and Intertextuality in the Vārkarī Canon." In *Bhakti and Self*, edited by Martin Fuchs. New Delhi: Oxford University Press, forthcoming.

———. "Pedagogical Otherness: The Use of Muslims and Untouchables in Some Hindu Devotional Literature." *Journal of the American Academy of Religion* 84, no. 3 (2016): 727–49.

———. "Review: The Quotidian Vernacular: Vernacularization, Religion, and the Premodern Public Sphere in India (Columbia University Press, 2016)." *Reading Religion* (2018). http://readingreligion.org/books/quotidian-revolution.

———. "Vārkarīs in Rural Western India." In *Contemporary Hinduism*, edited by P. Pratap Kumar, 148–61. Durham: Acumen Publishing, 2013.

Keune, Jon, and Christian Lee Novetzke. "Vārkarī Sampradāy." In *Brill Encyclopedia of Hinduism*, edited by Knut Axel Jacobsen, 617–26. Leiden: Brill, 2011.

Khan, Mohammad Ishaq. "The Rishi Movement as Social Force in Medieval Kashmir." In *Religious Movements in South Asia, 600–1800*, edited by David N. Lorenzen, 128–49. New York: Oxford University Press, 2004.

Khaṇḍerāya. "Eknāth-Caritra." In *Laghukāvyamālā, Bhāg Pahilā*, edited by Vāman Dājī Ok, 158–61. Mumbaī: Nirṇaysāgar, 1895.

Khānolkar, Gaṃ. De., ed. *Marāṭhī Vāṅmaykoś (Khaṇḍa Pahilā—Marāṭhī Granthakār, I.S. 1070–1866)*. Mumbaī: Mahārāṣṭra Rājya Sāhitya Saṃskṛti Maṇḍaḷ, 1977.

"Kharā Brāhmaṇ Sudhārlā." *Kesarī*, August 15, 1933, 12.

Kharāt, Śaṅkarrāv. *Cokhobācā Vidroha*. Puṇe: Sugāva Prakāśan, 2002.

Khare, R. S. "Anna." In *The Hindu World*, edited by Sushil Mittal and Gene R. Thursby, 407–28. New York: Routledge, 2004.

———. *Caste, Hierarchy, and Individualism: Indian Critiques of Louis Dumont's Contributions*. New Delhi: Oxford University Press, 2006.

———. *Culture and Reality: Essays on the Hindu System of Managing Foods*. Simla: Indian Institute of Advanced Study, 1976.

———. *The Eternal Food: Gastronomic Ideas and Experiences of Hindus and Buddhists*. Albany: State University of New York Press, 1992.

———. "Food with the Saints: An Aspect of Hindu Gastrosemantics." In *The Eternal Food: Gastronomic Ideas and Experiences of Hindus and Buddhists*, edited by R. S. Khare, 27–52. Albany: State University of New York Press, 1992.

———. *The Hindu Hearth and Home*. New Delhi: Vikas, 1976.

———. "A Paradoxical Gift of Memory: The Pain, Pride, and History of an Untouchable 'Kitchen Poetess.'" *Anthropology and Humanism* 21, no. 1 (1996): 19–30.

———. *The Untouchable as Himself: Ideology, Identity, and Pragmatism among the Lucknow Chamars*. Cambridge: Cambridge University Press, 1984.

Khare, R. S., and M. S. A. Rao, eds. *Food, Society and Culture: Aspects in South Asian Food Systems*. Durham: Carolina Academic Press, 1986.

King, Richard. *Orientalism and Religion: Postcolonial Theory, India and "the Mystic East."* London: Routledge, 1999.

Kippenberg, Hans G. *Discovering Religious History in the Modern Age*. Princeton: Princeton University Press, 2002.

Kleen, Michael. "Feasting at God's Table." https://michaelkleen.com/2016/11/24/feasting-at-gods-table/.

Knipe, David. "Sapindikarana: The Hindu Rite of Entry into Heaven." In *Religious Encounters with Death: Insights from the History and Anthropology of Religions*, edited by Frank E. Reynolds and Earle H. Waugh, 111–24. University Park: Penn State University Press, 1977.

Kolb, Robert. "Luther on Peasants and Princes." *Lutheran Quarterly* 23, no. 2 (Summer 2009): 125–46.

Kolte, Viṣṇu Bhikājī, ed. *Mhāiṃbhaṭ Saṅkalit Śrīcakradhar Līḷācaritra*. 2nd ed. Mumbaī: Mahārāshṭra Rājya Sāhitya Saṃskṛti Maṇḍaḷ, 1982.

Korsmeyer, Carolyn. *Making Sense of Taste: Food and Philosophy*. Ithaca: Cornell University Press, 1999.

Kosambi, D. D. *Myth and Reality*. Bombay: Popular Prakashan, 1962.

Kosambi, Meera. *Gender, Culture and Performance: Marathi Theatre and Cinema before Independence*. New Delhi: Routledge, 2015.

Krishnamurthy, R. *The Saints of the Cauvery Delta*. New Delhi: Concept, 1979.

Kulkarṇī, Go. Ma. *Marāṭhī Vāṅmaykoś (Khaṇḍa Dusrā, Bhāg Ek)*. Mumbaī: Mahārāṣṭra Rājya Sāhitya āṇi Saṃskṛtī Maṇḍaḷ, 2003.

Kumar, Aishwary. *Radical Equality: Ambedkar, Gandhi, and the Risk of Democracy*. Cultural Memory in the Past. Stanford: Stanford University Press, 2015.

Laine, James W. "Out of Character: Marginal Voices and Role-Transcendence in the Mahābhārata's Book of the Forest." *Journal of Indian Philosophy* 19, no. 3 (1991): 273–96.

———. *Shivaji: Hindu King in Islamic India*. Oxford: Oxford University Press, 2003.

Latour, Bruno. *Reassembling the Social: An Introduction to Actor-Network-Theory*. Oxford: Oxford University Press, 2005.

Lederle, Matthew. *Philosophical Trends in Modern Maharāṣṭra*. Bombay: Popular Prakashan, 1976.

Lee, Joel. "In Memoriam: Doyenne of Dalit Studies—Eleanor Zelliot (1926–2016)." *Biblio: Review of Books* 21 (September–October 2016): 17–18.

Lele, Jayant. "Community, Discourse and Critique in Jnanesvar." *Journal of Asian and African Studies* 15, no. 1–2 (1980): 104–12.

———. "From Reformism to Interest Group Pluralism: The Relevance of the Non-Brahman Movement for an Understanding of Contemporary Maharashtra." In *Writers, Editors and Reformers: Social and Political Transformations in Maharashtra*, edited by N. K. Wagle, 13–22. Delhi: Manohar Publishers, 1999.

———. "Vārkarī Sampradāyātīl Krāntikārak Āśay." *Samāj Prabodhan Patrikā* (October–December 1991): 183–86.

Lele, Jayant K., and R. Singh. "Language and Literature of *Dalits* and *Sants*: Some Missed Opportunities." In *Language and Society: Steps toward an Integrated Theory*, edited by J. K. Lele and R. Singh, 121–41. Leiden: E. J. Brill, 1989.

Leopold, David. "'Socialist Turnips': The Young Friedrich Engels and the Feasibility of Communism." *Political Theory* 40, no. 3 (2012): 347–78.

Leslie, Julia. "Some Traditional Indian Views on Menstruation and Female Sexuality." In *Sexual Knowledge, Sexual Science: The History of Attitudes to Sexuality*, edited by Roy Porter and Mikuláš Teich, 63–81. Cambridge: Cambridge University Press, 1994.

Lévi-Strauss, Claude. *The Raw and the Cooked*. Translated by John Weightman and Doreen Weightman. New York: Harper & Row, 1969.

———. "The Structural Study of Myth." *The Journal of American Folklore* 68, no. 270 (1955): 428–44.

Limaye, Anant Hari. *Sahyādricī Śikhare*. Vol. 2. Puṇe: Ināmdār Bandhu Prakāśan, 1963.

Limkar, Rājeś. "Sant Eknāth." Pune: Fountain Music Company, 2005.

Lindberg, Carter. *The European Reformations*. 2nd ed. Malden: Wiley-Blackwell, 2010.

Linderman, Michael Christian. "Charity's Venue: Representing Indian Kingship in the Monumental Pilgrim Rest Houses of the Maratha Rajas of Tanjavur, 1761–1832." PhD dissertation, University of Pennsylvania, 2009.

Lochtefeld, James G. *The Illustrated Encyclopedia of Hinduism*. 1st ed. 2 vols. New York: Rosen, 2002.

Lokahitavādī. *Lokahitavādī: Samagra Vāṅmay*. 2 vols. Mumbaī: Mahārāṣṭra Rājya Sāhitya Saṃskr̥tī Maṇḍaḷa, 1988.

Lorenzen, David N. "Bhakti." In *The Hindu World*, edited by Sushil Mittal and Gene Thursby, 185–209. New York: Routledge, 2004.

———, ed. *Bhakti Religion in North India: Community Identity and Political Action*. Albany: State University of New York Press, 1995.

———. "The Historical Vicissitudes of Bhakti Religion." In *Bhakti Religion in North India: Community Identity and Political Action*, edited by David N. Lorenzen, 1–34. Albany: State University of New York Press, 1995.

———. *Kabir Legends and Ananta-Das's Kabir Parachai*. Albany: State University of New York Press, 1991.

———. "The Lives of *Nirguṇi* Saints." In *Bhakti Religion in North India: Community Identity and Political Action*, edited by David N. Lorenzen, 181–211. Albany: State University of New York Press, 1995.

———. "The Social Ideologies of Hagiography: Sankara, Tukaram and Kabir." In *Who Invented Hinduism? Essays on Religion in History*, edited by David N. Lorenzen, 120–43. New Delhi: Yoda Press, 2006.

———. "Traditions of Non-Caste Hinduism: The Kabir Panth." *Contributions to Indian Sociology* 21, no. 2 (July 1, 1987): 263–83.

Lutgendorf, Philip. "Dining out at Lake Pampa: The Shabari Episode in Multiple Ramayanas." In *Questioning Ramayanas: A South Asian Tradition*, edited by Paula Richman, 119–36. Berkeley: University of California Press, 2001.

———. *The Life of a Text: Performing the Rāmcaritmānas of Tulsīdās*. Berkeley: University of California Press, 1991.

MacRaild, Donald M., and Avram Taylor. *Social Theory and Social History*. New York: Palgrave Macmillan, 2004.

Madaio, James. "Rethinking Neo-Vedānta: Swami Vivekananda and the Selective Historiography of Advaita Vedānta." *Religions* 8, no. 6 (2017): 101.

Madhava-vidyaranya. *Sankara-Dig-Vijaya: The Traditional Life of Sri Sankaracharya*. Translated by Swami Tapasyananda. Madras: Sri Ramakrishna Math, 1986.

Mahārāṣṭra Śabdakoś. Edited by Yaśvant Rāmkr̥ṣna Dāte and Cintamaṇ Gaṇeś Karve. 8 vols. Puṇe: Varadā Buks, 1932 [1995].

Mahīpati. *Bhaktalīlāmr̥t*. Edited by Vi. Ke. Phaḍke. Puṇe: Yaśvant Prakāśan, 1988.

Maier, Pauline. "The Strange Case of All Men Are Created Equal." *Washington and Lee Review* 56, no. 3 (1999): 873–90.

Malamoud, Charles. *Cooking the World: Ritual and Thought in Ancient India*. New York: Oxford University Press, 1996.

Mandair, Arvind-Pal. *Religion and the Specter of the West: Sikhism, India, Postcoloniality, and the Politics of Translation*. New York: Columbia University Press, 2009.

Māṇikkavācakar. *The Tiruvāçagam*. Translated by G. U. Pope. Oxford: Clarendon Press, 1900.

Mantena, Rama Sundari. *The Origins of Modern Historiography in India: Antiquarianism and Philology, 1780–1880*. 1st ed. New York: Palgrave Macmillan, 2012.

Marlow, Louise. *Hierarchy and Egalitarianism in Islamic Thought*. New York: Cambridge University Press, 1997.

Marra, Claudia. "Fucha Ryori: The Monastic Cuisine of the Obaku-Zen School." *The Journal of Nagasaki University of Foreign Studies in History* 15 (2011): 215–32.

Marriott, McKim. "Hindu Transactions: Diversity without Dualism." In *Transaction and Meaning: Directions in the Anthropology of Exchange and Symbolic Behavior*, edited by Bruce Kapferer, 109–42. Philadelphia: Institute for the Study of Human Issues, 1976.

Marx, Karl, Friedrich Engels, and Robert C. Tucker. *The Marx-Engels Reader*. 2nd ed. New York: W.W. Norton, 1978.

Mauss, Marcel. *The Gift: The Form and Reason for Exchange in Archaic Societies*. London: Routledge Classics, 1990 [2002].

Mazumdar, Shampa, and Sanjoy Mazumdar. "'Women's Significant Spaces': Religion, Space, and Community." *Journal of Environmental Psychology* 19, no. 2 (1999): 159–70.

McCrea, Lawrence. "Freed by the Weight of History: Polemic and Doxography in Sixteenth Century Vedānta." *South Asian History & Culture* 6, no. 1 (2015): 87–101.

McIntire, C. T. "Transcending Dichotomies in History and Religion." *History and Theory* 45, no. 4 (2006): 80–92.

Mehta, Uday Singh. *Liberalism and Empire: A Study in Nineteenth-Century British Liberal Thought*. Chicago: University of Chicago Press, 1999.

Meśrām, Satyavān. *Sant Gāḍge Mahārāj: Kāl āṇi Kartṛtva*. Mumbaī: Mahārāṣṭra Rājya āṇi Saṃskṛtī Maṇḍaḷ, 1998.

Meyer-Rochow, Victor Benno. "Food Taboos: Their Origins and Purposes." *Journal of Ethnobiology and Ethnomedicine* 5, no. 1 (2009): 1–10.

Mines, Diane P. *Caste in India*. Ann Arbor: Association for Asian Studies, 2009.

Mintz, Sidney W. *Sweetness and Power: The Place of Sugar in Modern History*. New York: Penguin, 1986.

Mitchell, J. Murray. *The Great Religions of India*. Edinburgh: Oliphant, 1905.

———. *Hinduism Past and Present*. 2nd ed. London: Religious Tract Society, 1897.

———. "Paṇdharpūr." *Indian Antiquary* 11 (June 1882): 149–56.

———. "The Story of Tukaráma. From the Marathí-Prákrit." *Journal of the Bombay Branch of the Royal Asiatic Society* 3, no. 1 (1849): 1–28.

Mitchell, John Murray, and William Muir. *Two Old Faiths: Essays on the Religions of the Hindus and the Mohammedans*. New York: Chautauqua Press, 1891.

Mohan, P. Sanal. "Narrativizing Oppression and Suffering: Theorizing Slavery." *South Asia Research* 26, no. 1 (2006): 5–40.

Mokashi, D. B. *Palkhi: An Indian Pilgrimage*. Translated by Philip Engblom. Albany: State University of New York Press, 1964 [1987].

Molesworth, J. T. *Molesworth's Marathi-English Dictionary*. Pune: Shubhada-Saraswat Prakashan, 1857 [2005].

Monier-Williams, Monier. *Religious Thought and Life in India: An Account of the Religions of the Indian Peoples, Based on a Life's Study of Their Literature and on Personal Investigations in Their Own Country*. London: John Murray, 1883.

———. *A Sanskrit-English Dictionary*. Oxford: Clarendon Press, 1956.

Monius, Anne E. "Love, Violence, and the Aesthetics of Disgust: Śaivas and Jains in Medieval South India." *Journal of Indian Philosophy* 32, no. 2–3 (2004): 113–72.

Morje, Gaṅgādhar. *Jñānoday Lekhan-Sār-Sūcī: Khaṇḍa Pahilā Bhāg Pahilā, Jun 1842 Te Dec 1850*. Mumbaī: Mahārāṣṭra Rājya Sāhitya āṇi Saṃskṛtī Maṇḍaḷ, 1986.

Morse, Jeremy G. "Devotion according to the Rules: Guru-Bhakti in the Texts and Practices of the Datta Sampradāya." PhD dissertation, University of Chicago, 2017.

Moss, Jeremy. *Reassessing Egalitarianism*. Basingstoke: Palgrave Macmillan, 2014.

Moyn, Samuel. *The Last Utopia: Human Rights in History*. Cambridge: Belknap Press of Harvard University Press, 2010.

Nabhādās. *Śrī Bhaktāmāla Compiled by Śrī Nābhā Goswāmī with Commentary by Śrī Priyādāsa*. Translated by Bhumipati Dāsa. Vrindaban: Rasbihari Lal & Sons, 2017.

Nagaraj, D. R. "Critical Tensions in the History of Kannada Literary Culture." In *Literary Cultures in History: Reconstructions from South Asia*, edited by Sheldon Pollock, 323–83. Berkeley: University of California Press, 2003.

Naik, J. V. "D. G. Vaidya and the Prarthana Samaj." In *Region, Nationality and Religion*, edited by A. R. Kulkarni and N. K. Wagle, 185–202. Mumbai: Popular Prakashan, 1999.

———. "'Dharmavivechan': An Early 19th Century Rationalistic Reform Manifesto in Western India." In *Social Reform Movements in India: A Historical Perspective*, edited by G. T. Kulkarni, M. R. Kantak, and V. D. Divekar, 62–72. Pune: Bharat Itihas Samshodhak Mandal: Popular Prakashan, 1991.

———. "Social Composition of the Prarthana Samaj: A Statistical Analysis." *Proceedings of the Indian History Congress* 48 (1987): 502–11.

Narain, A. K. "Dr. Ambedkar, Buddhism, and Social Change: A Reappraisal." In *Dr. Ambedkar, Buddhism, and Social Change*, edited by A. K. Narain and D. C. Ahir, 77–98. Delhi: B. R. Publishing Corporation, 1994.

Nārāyaṇa, Bhaṭṭa, and Richard Salomon. *The Bridge to the Three Holy Cities = the Sāmānya-Praghaṭṭaka of Nārāyaṇa Bhaṭṭa's Tristhalīsetu*. Delhi: Motilal Banarsidass, 1985.

Narayana Rao, Velcheru. "Purāṇa as Brahminic Ideology." In *Purāṇa Perennis: Reciprocity and Transformation in Hindu and Jaina Texts*, edited by Wendy Doniger, 85–100. Delhi: Sri Satguru Publications, 1993.

Narayanan, M. G. S., and Kesavan Veluthat. "Bhakti Movement in South India." In *The Feudal Order: State, Society, and Ideology in Early Medieval India*, edited by D. N. Jha, 385–410. New Delhi: Manohar, 2000.

Narayanan, Vasudha. "Diglossic Hinduism: Liberation and Lentils." *Journal of the American Academy of Religion* 68, no. 4 (2000): 761–79.

Naregal, Veena. *Language Politics, Elites, and the Public Sphere: Western India under Colonialism*. London: Anthem Press, 2002.

Nicholson, Andrew. "Vivekananda's Non-Dual Ethics in the History of Vedanta." In *Swami Vivekananda: New Reflections on His Life, Legacy, and Influence*, edited by Rita D. Sherma and James McHugh, 45–64. York: Lexington, 2020.

Norman, Corrie E. "Food and Religion." In *The Oxford Handbook of Food History*, edited by Jeffrey M. Pilcher, 409–27. Oxford: Oxford University Press, 2012.

Novetzke, Christian Lee. "Bhakti and Its Public." *International Journal of Hindu Studies* 11, no. 3 (2007): 255–72.

———. "The Brahmin Double: The Brahminical Construction of Anti-Brahminism and Anti-Caste Sentiment in Religious Cultures of Precolonial Maharashtra." *South Asian History and Culture* 2, no. 2 (2011): 232–52.

———. "Divining an Author: The Idea of Authorship in an Indian Religious Tradition." *History of Religions* 42, no. 3 (2003): 213–42.

———. "A Family Affair: Krishna Comes to Pandharpur and Makes Himself at Home." In *Alternative Krishnas: Regional and Vernacular Variations on a Hindu Deity*, edited by Guy Beck, 113–38. Albany: State University of New York Press, 2005.

———. *The Quotidian Revolution: Vernacularization, Religion, and the Premodern Public Sphere in India*. New York: Columbia University Press, 2016.

———. *Religion and Public Memory: A Cultural History of Saint Namdev in India*. New York: Columbia University Press, 2008.

———. "Religion and the Public Sphere in Premodern India." *Asiatische Studien—Études Asiatiques* 72, no. 1 (2018): 147–76.

———. "The Subaltern Numen: Making History in the Name of God." *History of Religions* 46, no. 2 (2006): 99–126.

———. "The Theographic and the Historiographic in an Indian Sacred Life Story." *Sikh Formations* 3, no. 2 (2007): 169–84.

Novetzke, Christian Lee, John Stratton Hawley, and Swapna Sharma, eds. *Bhakti and Power: Social Location and Religious Affect in India's Religion of the Heart.* Seattle: University of Washington Press, 2019.

Ober, Douglas Fairchild. "Reinventing Buddhism: Conversations and Encounters in Modern India, 1839–1956." PhD dissertation, University of British Columbia, 2016.

Oddie, Geoffrey A. *Imagined Hinduism: British Protestant Missionary Constructions of Hinduism, 1793–1900.* Thousand Oaks, CA: Sage, 2006.

O'Hanlon, Rosalind. "Caste and Its Histories in Colonial India: A Reappraisal." *Modern Asian Studies* 51, no. 2 (2017): 432–61.

———. *Caste, Conflict and Ideology: Mahatma Jotirao Phule and Low Caste Protest in Nineteenth-Century Western India.* Cambridge: University of Cambridge Press, 1985 [2002].

———. "Narratives of Penance and Purification in Western India, c. 1650–1850." *Journal of Hindu Studies* 2, no. 1 (2009): 48–75.

Ok, Śāmrāv Niḷkaṇṭh. "Pariśiṣṭa 1 (Reprinted Review of Dharmātmā)." In *Dharmātmā: Citrakathā*, edited by Ke. Nārāyaṇ Kāḷe, Pramod Kāḷe, and Rāmdās Bhaṭkaḷ, 57–61. Mumbaī: Pāpyular Prakāśan, 1982.

Olivelle, Patrick. *Dharmasūtras: The Law Codes of Āpastamba, Gautama, Baudhāyana, and Vasiṣṭha.* Oxford: Oxford University Press, 1999.

———, ed. *The Early Upaniṣads: Annotated Text and Translation.* New York: Oxford University Press, 1998.

Olivelle, Patrick, and Donald R. Davis. *Hindu Law: A New History of Dharmaśāstra.* Oxford: Oxford University Press, 2018.

Omvedt, Gail, and Bhārat Pāṭaṅkar. *The Songs of Tukoba.* New Delhi: Manohar Publishers & Distributors, 2012.

Orr, Leslie C. "The Sacred Landscape of Tamil Śaivism: Plotting Place in the Realm of Devotion." In *Mapping the Chronology of Bhakti: Milestones, Stepping Stones, and Stumbling Stones*, edited by Valérie Gillet, 189–219. Pondicherry: Institut Français de Pondichéry, 2014.

Orsini, Francesca, and Stefano Pellò. "Bhakti in Persian." Unpublished Paper. Presented at *21st European Conference on Modern South Asian Studies.* Bonn, 2010.

Osterhammel, Jürgen. *Die Entzauberung Asiens: Europa Und Die Asiatischen Reiche Im 18. Jahrhundert.* München: C. H. Beck, 1998 [2010].

Pāḷande, Bhāskar Dāmodar. *Ratnamālā: Hī Parameśvar Prārthanecī Kavitā Sarva Jñātīñcyā Lokāṅkaritāṃ.* 3rd ed. Puṇe: Dī-Brāñc Buddhiprakāśa Chā. Chā., 1847 [1895].

Pāṅgārkar, Lakṣmaṇ Rāmcandra. *Eknāth Caritra: Caritra Āṇi Vāṅmay Darśan.* 9th ed. Puṇe: Varadā Buks, 1910 [2003].

"Pariśiṣṭa 2 (Official Letter from Prabhat Studios to Secretary of Bombay Board of Film Censors)." In *Dharmātmā: Citrakathā*, edited by Ke. Nārāyaṇ Kāḷe, Pramod Kāḷe, and Rāmdās Bhaṭkaḷ, 62–63. Mumbaī: Pāpyular Prakāśan, 1982.

Parry, Jonathan. "Egalitarian Values in a Hierarchical Society." *South Asian Review* 7, no. 2 (1974): 95–122.

Parvate, Tryambak Visnu. *Mahadev Govind Ranade. A Biography*. Bombay: Asia Publishing House, 1963.

Paswan, Sanjay, and Pramanshi Jaideva. *Encyclopaedia of Dalits in India*. Delhi: Kalpaz Publications, 2002.

Patwardhan, W. B. (Vasudev Balwant). "Wilson Philological Lectures, 1917, Lecture 5: Ekanath and His Circle." *Fergusson College Magazine* 9, no. 3 (1918): 93–101.

———. "Wilson Philological Lectures, 1917, Lecture 7: What Did the Bhakti School Do for Marathi Literature?" *Fergusson College Magazine* 10, no. 1 (1919): 30–37.

Pawar, G. M. *The Life and Works of Maharshi Vitthal Ramji Shindé (1873–1944)*. Translated by Sudharkar Marathe. New Delhi: Sahitya Akademi, 2013.

Peacock, Vita. "The Negation of Hierarchy and Its Consequences." *Anthropological Theory* 15, no. 1 (2015): 3–21.

Pechilis, Karen. *The Embodiment of Bhakti*. New York: Oxford University Press, 1999.

Pennington, Brian K. *Was Hinduism Invented?: Britons, Indians, and Colonial Construction of Religion*. New York: Oxford University Press, 2005.

Peterson, Indira V. "Singing of a Place: Pilgrimage as Metaphor and Motif in the Tevaram Songs of the Tamil Śaivite Saints." *Journal of the American Oriental Society* 102, no. 1 (1982): 69–90.

———. "Lives of the Wandering Singers: Pilgrimage and Poetry in Tamil Śaivite Hagiography." *History of Religions* 22, no. 4 (1983): 338–60.

Phule, Jotirāv Govindrāv. *Mahātmā Phule: Samagra Vāṅmay*. Edited by Ya. Di. Phaḍke. 6th ed. Mumbāi: Mahārāṣtra Rājya Sāhitya āṇi Saṃskṛtī Maṇḍaḷ, 2006.—
—. *Collected Works of Mahatma Jotirao Phule*. Translated by P. G. Patil. 1st ed. Vol. 2. Bombay: Education Dept., Govt. of Maharashtra, 1991.

Phule, Jotīrāv Govindarāv, and G. P. Deshpande. *Selected Writings of Jotirao Phule*. New Delhi: Leftword, 2002.

Phulkar, Rāju. "Sant Eknāth Mahārāj: Marāṭhī Video Compact Disc." Puṇe: Sumeet, 2004.

Piliavsky, Anastasia. "Egalitarian Fantasy and Politics in the Real World." *Anthropology of This Century* (2018). http://aotcpress.com/articles/egalitarian-fantasy/.

Pinch, Vijay. "Bhakti and the British Empire." *Past & Present* 179, no. 1 (2003): 159–96.

Pinch, William R. *Warrior Ascetics and Indian Empires*. Cambridge Studies in Indian History and Society. New York: Cambridge University Press, 2006.

Pinkney, Andrea Marion. "Prasāda, the Gracious Gift, in Contemporary and Classical South Asia." *Journal of the American Academy of Religion* 81, no. 3 (2013): 734–56.

Pollock, Sheldon. *The Language of the Gods in the World of Men*. Berkeley: University of California Press, 2006.

———. "Literary History, Indian History, World History." *Social Scientist* 23, no. 10–12 (1995): 112–42.

Priolkar, Anant Kakba. *The Printing Press in India, Its Beginnings and Early Development, Being a Quatercentenary Commemoration Study of the Advent of Printing in India, in 1556*. Bombay: Marathi Samshodhana Mandala, 1958.

Priyoḷkar, Anant Kākbā. *Paramahaṃsa Sabhā va tīce Adhyakṣa Rāmcandra Bāḷkṛṣṇa*. Mumbaī: Mumbaī Marāṭhī Grantha Saṅgrahālaya, 1966.

Priyoḷkar, Anant Kākbā, and Parśurām Ballāḷ Goḍbole, eds. *Navnīt athvā Marāṭhī Kavitāṃce Veṃce*. Puṇe: Śubhadā-Sārasvat Prakāśan, 1990.

Punday, Daniel. *Narrative Bodies: Toward a Corporeal Narratology*. New York: Palgrave Macmillan, 2003.

Puri, Harish K. "Scheduled Castes in Sikh Community: A Historical Perspective." *Economic and Political Weekly* 38, no. 26 (2003): 2693–701.

Quack, Johannes. *Disenchanting India: Organized Rationalism and Criticism of Religion in India*. New York: Oxford University Press, 2012.

Raghavan, V. *The Great Integrators: The Saint-Singers of India*. Patel Memorial Lectures, 1964. Delhi: Publications Division, Ministry of Information and Broadcasting, 1966.

Raghavan, V., and William J. Jackson. *The Power of the Sacred Name: V. Raghavan's Studies in Nāmasiddhānta and Indian Culture*. Delhi: Sri Satguru Publications, 1994.

Rājvāḍe, Vi. Kā. "Dāmājipant Va Viṭhyā Mahār." In *Caturtha Sammelan Vṛtta*, edited by Kanderāv Cintāman Mehendale, 53–67. Puṇe: Bhārat Itihās Saṃśodhak Maṇḍaḷ, 1917.

Ram, Ronki. "Social Exclusion, Resistance and Deras: Exploring the Myth of Casteless Sikh Society in Punjab." *Economic and Political Weekly* 42, no. 40 (2007): 4066–74.

Ramanujachary, N. C. "Tookaram Tatya." *The Theosophist* 130, no. 10 (2009): 389–93.

Ramaswami, K. V. *India's Untouchable Saints*. Madras: G.A. Natesan, 1900.

Ramaswamie, Cavelly Venkat. *Biographical Sketches of Dekkan Poets, Being Memoirs of Several . . . Bards Both Ancient and Modern Who Have Flourished in . . . the Indian Peninsula; Compiled from Authentic Documents*. Calcutta: [publisher not identified], 1829.

Rambachan, Anantanand. *The Advaita Worldview: God, World, and Humanity*. Albany: State University of New York Press, 2006.

———. *A Hindu Theology of Liberation: Not-Two Is Not One*. Albany: State University of New York Press, 2015.

Rambelli, Fabio. *Zen Anarchism: The Egalitarian Dharma of Uchiyama Gudo*. Berkeley, CA: Institute of Buddhist Studies and BDK America, 2013.

Rāmcandrajī, Janārdana. *Kavicaritra, Mhaṇje Hindusthānātīl Prācīn va Arvācīn Kavi āṇi Granthakāra yāñce Itihāsa*. Mumbaī: Gaṇpat Kṛṣṇājī Chāpkhānā, 1860.

Ranade, Mahadev Govind. *The Miscellaneous Writings of . . . Mr Justice M.G. Ranade*. Poona: Ramabai Ranade, 1915.

———. *Religious and Social Reform: A Collection of Essays and Speeches*. Bombay: Gopal Narayen and Co., 1902.

———. *Rise of the Maratha Power*. Delhi: Ministry of Information and Broadcasting, 1900 [1961].

Rānaḍe, Mahādev Govind, and Rāmābāī Rānaḍe. *Nyā. Mū. Mahādev Govind Rānaḍe Hyāñcīṃ Dharmapar Vyākhyānem*. 4th ed. Mumbaī: Karnāṭak Press, 1940.

Ranade, Ramcandra Dattatreya. *Mysticism in Maharashtra*. Delhi: Motilal Banarsidass, 1933 [1982].

———. *Pathway to God in Marathi Literature*. Bombay: Bharatiya Vidya Bhavan, 1961.

Ranjan, Purnendu. *History of Kabirpanth: A Regional Process*. New Delhi: Anamika, 2008.

Rao, Anupama. *The Caste Question: Dalits and the Politics of Modern India*. Berkeley: University of California Press, 2009.

Rawat, Ramnarayan. *Reconsidering Untouchability: Chamars and Dalit History in North India*. Bloomington: Indiana University Press, 2011.

Rhodes, Peter J. "Isonomia." In *Brill's New Pauly (Antiquity)*, 984. Leiden: Brill, 2006.

Richards, Audrey Isabel. *Hunger and Work in a Savage Tribe*. London: G. Routledge & Sons, 1932.

Riches, John Kenneth. *Galatians through the Centuries*. Oxford: Wiley-Blackwell, 2013.

Ricœur, Paul. "From Interpretation to Translation." In *Thinking Biblically: Exegetical and Hermeneutical Studies*, edited by André Lacocque and Paul Ricœur, 331–61. Chicago: University of Chicago Press, 1998.

Rigopoulos, Antonio. *Dattātreya: The Immortal Guru, Yogin, and Avatāra*. Albany: State University of New York Press, 1998.

Roberts, Nathaniel. *To Be Cared For: The Power of Conversion and Foreignness of Belonging in an Indian Slum*. Berkeley: University of California Press, 2016.

Rocher, Ludo. *The Purāṇas*. A History of Indian Literature. Vol. 2—Epics and Sanskrit Religious Literature. Wiesbaden: Harrassowitz, 1986.

Rodrigues, Valerian. "Kabir as Ambedkar's Guru: Complex Mediations." Unpublished Paper. Presented at *Dalits and Religion Conference*. Erfurt, 2017.

Roncaglia, Sara. *Feeding the City: Work and Food Culture of the Mumbai Dabbawalas*. Translated by Angela Armone. Cambridge: Open Book Publishers, 2013.

Rondolino, Massimo A. *Cross-Cultural Perspectives on Hagiographical Strategies: A Comparative Study of the Standard Lives of St. Francis and Milarepa*. New York: Routledge, 2017.

Rotman, Andy. *Thus Have I Seen: Visualizing Faith in Early Indian Buddhism*. New York: Oxford University Press, 2009.

Rupp, Horst F., and Klaas Huizing. *Religion Im Plural*. Würzburg: Königshausen & Neumann, 2011.

Ryan, Marie-Laure. "Story/Worlds/Media: Tuning the Instruments of a Media-Conscious Narratology." In *Storyworlds across Media: Toward a Media-Conscious Narratology*, edited by Marie-Laure Ryan and Jan-Noël Thon, 25–49. Lincoln: University of Nebraska Press, 2014.

Sahasrabuddhe, Dhoṇḍo Bāḷkṛṣṇa. *Paiṭhaṇ Yethīl Prasiddha Sādhu, Kavi Va Tatvavette Śrī Eknāth Mahārāj Yāñceṃ Caritra*. Mumbaī: Nirṇayasāgara Press, 1883.

Sāḷuṅkhe, Ā. Ha. *Vidrohī Tukārām*. Sātārā: Rākeś Ā. Sāḷuṅkhe, 1997 [2008].

San Chirico, Kerry P. C., Rachel J. Smith, and Rico G. Monge, eds. *Hagiography and Religious Truth: Case Studies in the Abrahamic and Dharmic Traditions*. London: Bloomsbury Academic, 2016.

Sanal Mohan, P. *Modernity of Slavery: Struggles against Caste Inequality in Colonial Kerala*. Oxford: Oxford University Press, 2015.

Sand, Erik Reenberg. "The *Gopālakālā* as Reflected in the *Pāṇḍuraṅgamāhātmya* of Pralhāda Mahārāj and the *Abhaṅgas* of Tukārām." In *Studies in South Asian Devotional Literature, 1888–1991*, edited by Alan W. Entwistle and Francoise Mallison, 121–34. Delhi: Manohar, 1994.

———. "Gopālpūr-*Kālā*: Some Aspects of the History of the Sacred Places South of Pandharpur." In *Folk Culture, Folk Religion, and Oral Traditions as a Component in Maharashtrian Culture*, edited by Günther-Dietz Sontheimer, 107–25. New Delhi: Manohar, 1995.

Śaṅkara. "Manīṣā Pañcakam." In *The Works of Sri Sankaracharya*. Vol. 2—Miscellaneous Prakaranas, 53–56. Srirangam: Vani Vilas Press, 1910.

Śaṅkarācārya. *The Vishnu Sahasranama with the Bhasya of Sri Sankaracharya*. Madras: Theosophical Publishing House, 1927.

Sapkale, Tryambak. "Angulimala." Translated by Jayant Karve and Eleanor Zelliot. In *The Norton Anthology of World Religions: Hinduism*, edited by Wendy Doniger, 615–16. New York City: W. W. Norton & Co., 2015.

Sardār, Gaṅgādhar Bāḷkṛṣṇa. *Sant Vāṅmayācī Sāmājik Phalaśrutī*. 7th ed. Mumbaī: Lokvāṅmay Gṛha, 1950 [2006].

Sayers, Matthew R. *Feeding the Dead: Ancestor Worship in Ancient India*. New York: Oxford University Press, 2013.

Schmidt, Leigh Eric. "The Making of Modern 'Mysticism.'" *Journal of the American Academy of Religion* 71, no. 2 (2003): 273–302.

Scholliers, Peter. *Food, Drink and Identity: Cooking, Eating and Drinking in Europe since the Middle Ages*. Oxford: Berg, 2001.

Schopen, Gregory. "Archaeology and Protestant Presuppositions in the Study of Indian Buddhism." *History of Religions* 31, no. 1 (1991): 1–23.

Schultz, Anna. "From Sants to Court Singers: Style and Patronage in Marathi Kirtan." *Journal of Vaishnava Studies* 17, no. 2 (2009): 127–46.

———. *Singing a Hindu Nation: Marathi Devotional Performance and Nationalism*. New York: Oxford University Press, 2013.

Scott, J. Barton. "Luther in the Tropics: Karsandas Mulji and the Colonial 'Reformation' of Hinduism." *Journal of the American Academy of Religion* 83, no. 1 (2015): 181–209.

Sedgwick, Leonard John. "Bhakti." *Journal of the Bombay Branch of the Royal Asiatic Society* 23 (1914): 109–34.

Shantaram, V. *Dharmatma*. Mumbai: Eros Multimedia Pvt. Ltd., 1935 [2009].

———. "The Eternal Conflict." *Filmfare*, January 6, 1956, 32–33.

Sharma, Krishna. *Bhakti and the Bhakti Movement: A New Perspective*. New Delhi: Munshiram Manoharlal Publishers, 1987.

Sharma, Miriam. "Censoring India: Cinema and the Tentacles of Empire in the Early Years." *South Asia Research* 29, no. 1 (2009): 41–73.

Shields, James Mark. *Against Harmony: Progressive and Radical Buddhism in Modern Japan*. New York: Oxford University Press, 2017.

Shih, Vincent Yu-Chung. *The Taiping Ideology*. Tokyo: University of Tokyo Press, 1967.

Shri Ekanath: A Sketch of His Life and Teachings. Madras: G. A. Natesan & Co., 1918 [1935].

Simmel, Georg. "Sociology of the Meal." In *Simmel on Culture: Selected Writings*, edited by David Frisby and Mike Featherstone, 130–36. Thousand Oaks: Sage Publications, 1997.

Śinde, Viṭṭhal Rāmjī. *Mājhyā Āṭhavaṇni va Anubhava*. Puṇe: Vātsala Sāhitya Prakāśan, 1940.

Singh, Hulas. *Rise of Reason: Intellectual History of 19th-Century Maharashtra*. 1st South Asia ed. Abingdon: Routledge, 2016.

Singh, Pragya. "Politics of Lunch Diplomacy: What Does the Dine-with-Downtrodden Drive Say?" *Outlook*, August 2, 2017.

Singh, Sherry-Ann. "The Ramayana in Trinidad: A Socio-Historical Perspective." *The Journal of Caribbean History* 44, no. 2 (2010): 201–23.

Śirgāvkar, Bhīmasvāmī. "Bhaktalīlāmṛt." In *Rāmdās Āṇi Rāmdāsī: Bhāg Dusrā—Śrīsamarthāñcī Don Junīṃ Caritreṃ*, 1–170. Dhuḷe: Satkāryottejak Sabhā, 1906.

Śirgopīkar, Gopāḷ Govind. *Bhāva Toci Dev*. Puṇe: Vi. Ra. Paracure, 1964.

Śirvaḷkar, Vāsudev Raṅganāth. *Śrī Eknāth (Bhaktirasapar Va Aitihāsik Nāṭak)*. Puṇe: Āryabhūṣaṇ Chāpkhānā, 1903.

Skinner, Quentin. *Visions of Politics: Regarding Method*. New York: Cambridge University Press, 2002.

Skinner, Quentin, and James Tully. *Meaning and Context: Quentin Skinner and His Critics*. Cambridge: Polity, 1988.

Skyhawk, Hugh van. *Bhakti Und Bhakta: Religionsgeschichtliche Untersuchungen Zum Heilsbegriff Und Zur Religiösen Umwelt Des Śrī Sant Ekanāth*. Stuttgart: Franz Steiner Verlag, 1990.

———. "Perceptions of Hindu Ethics in German Indology." *Annals of the Bhandarkar Oriental Research Institute* 74, Amṛtamahotsava Supplementary Volume (1994): 86–99.

———. "Saint, Cinéma et *Dharma*: Ekanāth et les Intouchables au Temps de V. Śāntārām." In *Construction Hagiographiques dans le Monde Indien*, edited by Françoise Mallison, 325–36. Paris: Librairie Honoré Champion, 2001.

———. "The Social Expression of the Unity with the Divine: The Saint's Conduct as a Component of Hindu Ethics." In *In the Company of Gods: Essays in Memory of Günther-Dietz Sontheimer*, edited by Aditya Malik, Anne Feldhaus, and Heidrun Brückner, 211–22. Delhi: Manohar, 2005.

Smith, Brian K. "Eaters, Food, and Social Hierarchy in Ancient India: A Dietary Guide to a Revolution of Values." *Journal of the American Academy of Religion* 58, no. 2 (1990): 177–205.

Smith, Jonathan Z. "A Matter of Class: Taxonomies of Religion." *The Harvard Theological Review* 89, no. 4 (1996): 387–403.

———. "Religion, Religions, Religious." In *Critical Terms for Religious Studies*, edited by Mark C. Taylor, 269–84. Chicago: University of Chicago Press, 1998.

Smith, Travis L. "Tantras." In *Brill Encyclopedia of Hinduism*, edited by Knut Axel Jacobsen, 168–81. Leiden: Brill, 2010.

Soneji, Davesh. "The Powers of Polyglossia: Marathi Kīrtan, Multilingualism, and the Making of a South Indian Devotional Tradition." *International Journal of Hindu Studies* 17, no. 3 (2013): 1–31.

Spencer, George W. "The Sacred Geography of the Tamil Shaivite Hymns." *Numen* 17, no. 3 (1970): 232–44.

Spiegel, Gabrielle M. "The Future of the Past: History, Memory and the Ethical Imperatives of Writing History." *Journal of the Philosophy of History* 8, no. 2 (2014): 149–79.

"Śrīeknāth." *Kesarī*, May 12, 1903, 5.

Srinivas, M. N. "Caste in Modern India." In *The Oxford India Srinivas*, 251–76. New Delhi: Oxford University Press, 2009.

State of the Global Islamic Economy Report 2016/17. Thomson Reuters in collaboration with DinarStandard, 2016. http://13.251.163.42/wp-content/uploads/2019/02/ThomsonReuters-stateoftheGlobalIslamicEconomyReport201617.pdf. Accessed February 5, 2021.

Steiner, George. "The Uncommon Reader." In *No Passion Spent: Essays, 1978–1996*, 1–19. London: Faber, 1996.

Stephens, Thomas, and Nelson Falcao. *Phādar Thomas Sṭīphanskṛt Khristapurāṇa*. Beṅgaluru: Khristu Jyotī Pablikeśans, 2010.

Stephenson [Stevenson], John. "On the Ante-Brahmanical Worship of the Hindus (from P.195 V.5 No.1)." *Journal of the Royal Asiatic Society of Great Britain and Ireland* 5, no. 2 (1839): 264–67.

———. "On the Ante-Brahmanical Worship of the Hindus in the Dekhan (Continued from P.267, V.5)." *Journal of the Royal Asiatic Society of Great Britain and Ireland* 6, no. 2 (1841): 239–41.

Stevenson, John, and John Wilson. "On the Ante-Brahmanical Worship of the Hindus in the Dekhan." *Journal of the Royal Asiatic Society of Great Britain and Ireland* 5, no. 1 (1839): 189–97.

Stroud, Scott R. "Pragmatism, Persuasion, and Force in Bhimrao Ambedkar's Reconstruction of Buddhism." *The Journal of Religion* 97, no. 2 (2017): 214–43.

Suṇṭhaṇkar, Bāḷkṛṣṇa Raṅgarāv. *Mahārāṣṭrīya Sant-Maṇḍaḷāce Aitihāsik Kārya*. Mumbaī: Lokvāṅmay Gṛha, 1948 [2008].

Sviatoslav, Dmitriev. "Herodotus, Isonomia, and the Origins of Greek Democracy." *Athenaeum* 103, no. 1 (2015): 53–83.

Tambs-Lyche, Harald. "Caste." In *Brill Encyclopedia of Hinduism*, edited by Knut Axel Jacobsen. Vol. 3, 1–14. Leiden: Brill, 2011.

Taylor, Charles. "Modern Social Imaginaries." *Public Culture* 14, no. 1 (2002): 91–124.

———. "Modes of Secularism." In *Secularism and Its Critics*, edited by Rajeev Bhargava, 31–53. Delhi: Oxford University Press, 2004.

———. *A Secular Age*. Cambridge, MA: Belknap Press of Harvard University Press, 2007.

Tayob, Shaheed. "'O You Who Believe, Eat of the Tayyibāt (Pure and Wholesome Food) That We Have Provided You': Producing Risk, Expertise and Certified Halal Consumption in South Africa." *Journal of Religion in Africa* 46 (2016): 67–91.

Teltumbde, Anand. *Dalits: Past, Present and Future*. New York: Routledge, 2017.

———. *The Persistence of Caste: The Khairlanji Murders and India's Hidden Apartheid*. New Delhi: Navayana, 2010.

Ṭhākre, Keśav Sītārām. *Kharā Brāmhaṇ*. Mumbaī: Rāmkṛṣṇa Prakāśan, 1953.

———. "Kharā Brāmhaṇ." In *Pabodhankār Ṭhākre Samagra Vāṅmay*, 278–346. Mumbaī: Mahārāṣṭra Rājya Sāhitya āṇi Saṃskṛtī Maṇḍaḷ, 1999.

Thapar, Romila. "Society and Historical Consciousness: The Itihasa-Purana Tradition." In *Interpreting Early India*, 137–73. New Delhi: Oxford University Press, 2001.

Thomas, Keith. *Religion and the Decline of Magic: Studies in Popular Beliefs in Sixteenth and Seventeenth Century England*. New York: Oxford University Press, 1971 [1997].

Thompson, E. P. *The Making of the English Working Class*. New York: Pantheon Books, 1964.

Thompson, Stith. *Motif-Index of Folk-Literature*. Bloomington: Indiana University Press, 1989.

Thon, Jan-Noël. *Transmedial Narratology and Contemporary Media Culture*. Frontiers of Narrative. Lincoln: University of Nebraska Press, 2016.

Tierney, R. Kenji, and Emiko Ohnuki-Tierney. "Anthropology of Food." In *The Oxford Handbook of Food History*, edited by Jeffrey M. Pilcher, 117–33. Oxford: Oxford University Press, 2012.

Toomey, Paul Michael. *Food from the Mouth of Krishna: Feasts and Festivals in a North Indian Pilgrimage Centre*. Studies in Sociology and Social Anthropology. Delhi: Hindustan Pub. Corp., 1994.

———. "Krishna's Consuming Passions: Food as Metaphor and Metonym for Emotion at Mount Govardhan." In *Religion and Emotion: Approaches and Interpretations*, edited by John Corrigan, 223–48. Oxford: Oxford University Press, 2004.

———. "Mountain of Food, Mountain of Love: Ritual Inversion in the Annakuta Feast at Mount Govardhan." In *The Eternal Food: Gastronomic Ideas and Experiences of Hindus and Buddhists*, edited by R. S. Khare, 117–46. Albany: State University of New York Press, 1992.

Toshkani, S. S., ed. *Lal Ded: The Great Kashmiri Saint-Poetess*. New Delhi: A.P.H. Publishing Corporation, 2000.

Townsend, Robert B. "A New Found Religion? The Field Surges among AHA Members." https://www.historians.org/publications-and-directories/perspectives-on-history/december-2009/a-new-found-religion-the-field-surges-among-aha-members.

Tukārām. *The Songs of Tukoba*. Translated by Gail Omvedt and Bhārat Pāṭaṇkar. New Delhi: Manohar Publishers & Distributors, 2012.

Tulpule, Shankar Gopal. *Classical Marāṭhī Literature: From the Beginning to A.D. 1818*. History of Indian Literature. Wiesbaden: Harrassowitz, 1979.

———. "The Development of Mystical Thought in Maharashtra." In *Region, Nationality and Religion*, edited by A. R. Kulkarni and N. K. Wagle, 203–09. Mumbai: Popular Prakashan, 1999.

———. *Gurudev Rā. Da. Rānaḍe: Caritra āṇi Tatvajñān*. Nimbāḷ, Dt. Bijāpūr: Śrī Gurudev Rānaḍe Samādhī Trust, 2002.

———. *Mysticism in Medieval India*. Wiesbaden: Harrassowitz, 1984.

Tulpule, S. G., and Anne Feldhaus. *A Dictionary of Old Marathi*. Oxford: Oxford University Press, 2000.

Tweed, Thomas A. *Crossing and Dwelling: A Theory of Religion*. Cambridge: Harvard University Press, 2006.

Urban, Hugh. "Elitism and Esotericism: Strategies of Secrecy and Power in South Indian Tantra and French Freemasonry." *Numen* 44, no. 1 (1997): 1–38.

Urban, Hugh B. *The Power of Tantra: Religion, Sexuality, and the Politics of South Asian Studies*. New York: I.B. Tauris, 2010.

———. *Songs of Ecstasy: Tantric and Devotional Songs from Colonial Bengal*. New York: Oxford University Press, 2001.

Vaca, Daniel. "'Great Religions' as Peacemaker: What Unitarian Infighting Did for Comparative Religion." *History of Religions* 53, no. 2 (2013): 115–50.

Vaidya, Dvārkānāth Govind. *Prārthanāsamājācā Itihās*. Mumbaī: Prārthanā Samāj, 1927.

Vaitheespara, Ravi (aka V. Ravindran). "Discourses of Empowerment: Missionary Orientalism in the Development of Dravidian Nationalism." In *Nation Work: Asian Elites and National Identities*, edited by Timothy Brook and Andre Schmid, 51–82. Ann Arbor: University of Michigan Press, 2000.

"Vartamānsār: Sabhā-Saṃmelanem." *Kesarī*, July 14, 1933, 11.

Vāṭve, Bāpū. *Ek Hotī Prabhātnagarī*. Puṇe: Anant Vi. Dāmle, 1993.

Vendell, Dominic. "Jotirao Phule's Satyashodh and the Problem of Subaltern Consciousness." *Comparative Studies of South Asia, Africa and the Middle East* 34, no. 1 (2014): 52–66.

Venkatkrishnan, Anand. "Philosophy from the Bottom Up: Eknāth's Vernacular Advaita." *Journal of Indian Philosophy* 48, no. 1 (2020): 9–21.

Viswanath, Rupa. *The Pariah Problem: Caste, Religion, and the Social in Modern India*. New York: Columbia University Press, 2014.

Wagle, N. K. "Ritual and Change in Early Nineteenth Century Society in Maharashtra: Vedokta Disputes in Baroda, Pune and Satara, 1824–1838." In *Religion and Society in Maharashtra*, edited by Milton Israel and N. K. Wagle, 145–77. Toronto: University of Toronto Press, 1987.

Wakankar, Milind. *Subalternity and Religion: The Prehistory of Dalit Empowerment in South Asia*. London: Routledge, 2010.

———. "System and History in Rajwade's 'Grammar' for the Dnyaneswari (1909)." In *Subalternity and Religion: The Prehistory of Dalit Empowerment in South Asia*, 93–124. New York: Routledge, 2010.

Ward, William. *A View of the History, Literature, and Mythology of the Hindoos: Including a Minute Description of Their Manners and Customs, and Translations from Their Principal Works*. Vol. 2. Serampore: Printed at the Mission Press, 1818.

Weber, Max. *The Religion of India: The Sociology of Hinduism and Buddhism*. Translated by Hans Heinrich Gerth and Don Martindale. Glencoe: Free Press, 1958.

Weisenfeld, Judith. *New World A-coming: Black Religion and Racial Identity during the Great Migration*. New York: New York University Press, 2016.

Werner, Karel. "Love and Devotion in Buddhism." In *Love Divine: Studies in Bhakti and Devotional Mysticism*, edited by Karel Werner, 37–52. Richmond: Curzon Press, 1993.

White, David Gordon. *Kiss of the Yoginī: "Tantric Sex" in Its South Asian Contexts*. Chicago: University of Chicago Press, 2003.

———. *Myths of the Dog-Man*. Chicago: University of Chicago Press, 1991.

Williams, Raymond. *Keywords: A Vocabulary of Culture and Society*. Oxford: Oxford University Press, 2015.

Wilson, H. H. *Sketch of the Religious Sects of the Hindus*. London: Christian Literature Society, 1846 [1904].

Wolf, Werner. "Intermediality." In *Routledge Encyclopedia of Narrative Theory*, edited by David Herman, Manfred Jahn, and Marie-Laure Ryan, 252–56. London: Routledge, 2005.

———. "The Relevance of 'Mediality' and 'Intermediality' to Academic Studies of English Literature." In *Mediality/Intermediality*, edited by Martin Heusser, Andreas Fischer, and Andreas H. Jucker, 15–43. Tübingen: Gunter Narr Verlag, 2008.

X, Malcolm. *The Autobiography of Malcolm X as Told to Alex Haley*. New York: Ballentine Books, 2015.

Yousefi, Hamid Reza, and Ina Braun. *Gustav Mensching—Leben Und Werk: Ein Forschungsbericht Zur Toleranzkonzeption*. Würzburg: Königshausen & Neumann, 2004.

Yusufji, Salim. *Ambedkar: The Attendant Details*. New Delhi: Navayana, 2017.

Zelliot, Eleanor. "Caste in Contemporary India." In *Contemporary Hinduism: Ritual, Culture and Practice*, edited by Robin Rinehart, 243–71. Santa Barbara: ABC-CLIO, 2004.

———. "Chokhamela and Eknath: Two 'Bhakti' Modes of Legitimacy for Modern Change." *Journal of Asian and African Studies* 15, no. 1–2 (1980): 136–56.

———. "Chokhamela: Piety and Protest." In *Bhakti Religion in North India: Community Identity and Political Action*, edited by David N. Lorenzen, 212–20. Albany: State University of New York Press, 1995.

———. "Dalit—New Cultural Context for an Old Marathi Word." In *From Untouchable to Dalit: Essays on the Ambedkar Movement*, 267–333. New Delhi: Manohar, 1992.

———. "The Early Voices of Untouchables: The Bhakti Saints." In *From Stigma to Assertion: Untouchability, Identity and Politics in Early and Modern India*, edited by Mikael Aktor and Robert Deliège, 64–96. Copenhagen: Museum Tusculanum Press, 2010.

———. "Eknath's Bharude: The Sant as a Link between Cultures." In *The Sants*, edited by Karine Schomer and W. H. McLeod, 91–110. Delhi: Motilal Banarsidass, 1987.

———. "Four Radical Saints in Maharashtra." In *Religion and Society in Maharashtra*, edited by Milton Israel and N. K. Wagle, 130–44. Toronto: University of Toronto Press, 1987.

———. *From Untouchable to Dalit: Essays on the Ambedkar Movement*. New Delhi: Manohar Publications, 1992.

———. "The Indian Rediscovery of Buddhism, 1855–1956." In *Studies in Pali and Buddhism*, edited by A. K. Narain, 389–406. New Delhi: D. K. Publishers' Distributors, 1978.

———. "The Medieval Bhakti Movement in History." In *Hinduism: New Essays in the History of Religions*, edited by Bardwell L. Smith, 143–68. Leiden: E. J. Brill, 1976.

———. "Sant Sahitya and Its Effect on Dalit Movements." In *Intersections: Socio-Cultural Trends in Maharashtra*, edited by Meera Kosambi, 187–93. New Delhi: Orient Longman Limited, 2000.

Zelliot, Eleanor, and Mulk Raj Anand, eds. *An Anthology of Dalit Literature*. New Delhi: Gyan, 1992.

Zelliot, Eleanor, and Vā. La. Manjūḷ, eds. *Sant Cokhāmeḷā Vividh Darśan*. Puṇe: Sugāvā Prakāśan, 2002.

Zelliot, Eleanor, and Rohini Mokashi-Punekar. *Untouchable Saints: An Indian Phenomenon*. New Delhi: Manohar, 2005.

Ziegenbalg, Bartholomaeus, Will Sweetman, R. Ilakkuvan, Institut français de Pondichéry, and École française d'Extrême-Orient. *Bibliotheca Malabarica: Bartholomäus Ziegenbalg's Tamil Library*. Collection Indologie. Pondicherry: Institut Français de Pondichéry: École Française D'extrême-Orient, 2012.

Index

For the benefit of digital users, indexed terms that span two pages (e.g., 52–53) may, on occasion, appear on only one of those pages.

Tables and figures are indicated by *t* and *f* following the page number